STUDY AND LISTENING GUIDE

FOR

A History of Western Music

Seventh Edition

by J. Peter Burkholder, Donald Jay Grout, and Claude V. Palisca

AND

Norton Anthology of Western Music

Fifth Edition

by J. Peter Burkholder and Claude V. Palisca

J. PETER BURKHOLDER

JENNIFER L. KING

W. W. NORTON & COMPANY   NEW YORK   LONDON

ISBN 0-393-97992-X (pbk.)

W. W. Norton & Company, Inc., 500 Fifth Avenue, New York, N.Y. 10110
    www.wwnorton.com

W. W. Norton & Company Ltd., Castle House, 75/76 Wells Street, London W1T 3QT

1 2 3 4 5 6 7 8 9 0

Study and Listening Guide

FOR

A History of Western Music
Seventh Edition

AND

Norton Anthology of Western Music
Fifth Edition

CONTENTS

READ THIS SECTION FIRST

The purpose of this *Study and Listening Guide* is to help you learn the material in *A History of Western Music,* Seventh Edition (HWM), by J. Peter Burkholder, Donald Jay Grout, and Claude V. Palisca, and acquaint yourself with the music in the *Norton Anthology of Western Music,* Fifth Edition (NAWM), by J. Peter Burkholder and Claude V. Palisca. Each chapter of the *Study and Listening Guide* is coordinated with a chapter of HWM and several pieces in NAWM.

There is much to know about the history of Western music and much to discover in the music itself. The best way to learn it is to follow some simple rules of successful learning.

1. Know your goals. It is easier to learn and to chart your progress if you know what you are trying to accomplish.
2. Proceed from what you know to what is new or less familiar. We learn best when what we are learning relates to what we already know. Thus it is usually easiest to start with the big picture and proceed from the general to the specific, from the main points to the details; this helps us see quickly how each element relates to the others, and what is most important. But it is also helpful to get to know a single example and discover broader principles by looking at it closely; indeed, broad statements may not be meaningful or clear until we have a concrete example.
3. Do not try to do everything at once. Trying to do too much, too fast, makes learning difficult and frustrating. Divide the task into units small enough to grasp at one sitting. Do not cram for tests; study every day.
4. Write down what you learn. You will retain information and concepts much more readily if you write them down for yourself rather than merely read them or hear them or highlight them in a book. The mental act of putting ideas into your own words and the physical act of writing out names, terms, dates, and other information create multiple pathways in your brain for recalling what you have learned.
5. Apply what you know. You learn and retain the skills and knowledge that you use.
6. Review what you know. We learn through repetition.
7. Have fun. You learn better and remember more when you are having fun. This means allowing yourself to enjoy the process of learning, mastering, and applying concepts and skills, whether riding a bike or discovering music history.

This *Study and Listening Guide* is designed to help you do all of these, through the following features.

Chapter Objectives

Each chapter begins with an outline of what you should learn from reading the texts and studying the music. These are the central issues addressed in the chapter. When you read the objectives before studying the material, they will pinpoint what you are trying to achieve. When you reread them after you have read the chapter, studied the music, and worked through the study questions, they can help you to evaluate your achievement. They direct you to the big picture, so you do not miss the forest for the trees.

Chapter Outline

The chapter outline shows how the corresponding chapter in HWM is divided into sections, summarizes the main points in each section, introduces important terms and names (highlighted in *italics*), and indicates which selections in NAWM relate to each topic. If you read the outline *first,* before reading the chapter in HWM, you begin with an overview of the subject. Then, as you read the chapter itself, the details presented there will flesh out the general concepts in the outline. Since you have already read the main ideas in the outline, as you read the text you are beginning to review and reinforce what you have learned, while increasing the depth of your knowledge. When you have finished a section or chapter, reread the outline to make sure you grasp the main points. The outline will also be useful as you review.

Study Questions

The readings are full of information, and it may sometimes be difficult to figure out what is more and less significant. The study questions are designed to help you focus on the most important issues and concepts addressed in each section of each chapter and apply those concepts to the music in NAWM. Material related to any of the questions may be found in a single place in HWM or scattered throughout the section. Relevant material may also be found in the analytical discussions of individual pieces in NAWM.

Questions are grouped by topic, and each question focuses on a single issue. This divides each chapter into units of manageable size and allows you to proceed step by step. The questions vary in kind, from fill-in-the-blank questions to short essays that ask you to synthesize material and apply it to the music, and even exercises that ask you to sing or play through the music. Tackling the material in small units and doing a variety of things in each section can help to make your work more fun.

Write down your answers. Space is provided to answer the study questions in this book. Writing down what you learn, rather than merely reading or highlighting the text, will help you retain it better. This is particularly helpful for recalling terms, names, and titles in foreign languages, since spelling them out for yourself will make them more familiar. If you have trouble remembering how to spell a foreign or unfamiliar word or name, writing it several times will help you recall it.

The study questions are not review questions, to be filled in after you have finished reading and have closed the book. They are guides to the reading and to the music. After you have read a section of the text, or even while you are reading it, work through the relevant study questions, rereading the text for answers as needed. Always respond to the questions in your own words, rather than copying directly from the text; this will help you to master each concept, making it your own by phrasing it in your own way. If there is anything you do not understand, return to the reading (in HWM, NAWM, or the outline in this *Study and Listening Guide*) to find the missing information, or ask for help from your instructor.

Some study questions ask you to define or to use terms that are introduced in the text. There is rote learning in every subject, and in music much of it is of terminology. Each musical repertory has its own specialized vocabulary, often borrowed from Italian, Latin, French, or German. You cannot communicate with others about this music without mastering these terms.

Many questions ask you to apply to the pieces in NAWM concepts and terms that are presented in the text. In this way you will to get to know the music better and will reinforce your grasp of the concepts and terms by applying what you know to the music itself. These study questions on the music are set off in groups headlined *Music to Study*. Each of these subsections begins with a list of the pieces in NAWM under consideration, indicating the CD number and tracks for each piece on the recordings that accompany NAWM.

You should listen to each piece in NAWM several times, including at least once before reading about it and at least once afterward. The heart of music history is the music itself, and a major part of your study should be listening to and becoming familiar with the music.

Terms and Names to Know

Near the end of each chapter is a list of important terms and names that appear in the texts and are highlighted in italics in the chapter outline. Most of these are covered in the study questions. They are listed separately here to help you review and to test your retention of what you have learned. In addition to these names, you should know the composers and titles of the pieces you studied. Use the lists in reviewing at the end of each chapter and in reviewing for examinations.

Review Questions

Each chapter ends with review questions that ask you to reflect more generally on the material you have learned. Most of them are like essay questions that you might encounter on a test. These may be used as springboards for discussion in class or with your study group, or as essay questions to use for practice as you study for examinations. Others are exercises that ask you to pull together information from several places in the chapter.

How to Proceed

The following procedure is recommended, but any procedure that helps you learn the most effectively and efficiently is the right one for you. You might vary your approach until you find the one that works best.

1. As you start each chapter, **read the chapter objectives** first to see what is expected of you.

2. **Read through the chapter outline.** Notice the topics that are covered, the main points that are made, and the terms that are introduced. Important new terms and names are given in italics.

3. Now work through the chapter section by section, as marked by roman numerals in the chapter outline and section headings in HWM.

4. Start each section by **listening to the pieces in NAWM** that are listed in this section of the outline. Read through the text and translation before listening to vocal pieces, and listen to every piece with the score. (If you have time, you might first listen to each piece without the score, and you might also sing or play through the piece yourself, which will help you learn it better.) This lets you encounter the music first, just as music. Later, you will come back to it and apply the principles you learn in reading the text.

5. Next, **read the section in HWM,** using the chapter outline as a guide. As the text refers you to pieces in NAWM, look again at the music and read the analytical discussion of each piece.

6. **Work through the study questions** for this section. Refer again to the music when the questions direct you to do so, and study the music or review HWM and the analytical discussions in NAWM to find the information you need to answer the questions. (Instead of reading first and then working through the study questions, you may find it more convenient to answer the study questions as you read through the text.)

7. When you have answered the study questions, **review the chapter outline** for this section and look over your answers to the questions. If there is anything you do not understand, refer back to the text, or make a note of it in the margin and ask your instructor for help.

8. **Listen to the music again,** and check your answers to the relevant study questions. Then congratulate yourself for finishing this section of the chapter. You may move on to the next section, or save it for another day.

9. At the end of the chapter, review by checking your knowledge of the **terms and names to know,** rereading the chapter outline, and reviewing your answers to the study questions. **Read the objectives again** to make sure you have accomplished them. Read the review questions and write brief answers in outline form, or use them as practice essay questions before examinations.

NOTE TO THE INSTRUCTOR

This *Study and Listening Guide* is designed to walk the student through the material in HWM and NAWM step by step. Not every instructor will want to include all the content covered in the texts, and each is likely to emphasize different aspects of the music and its history. Each instructor is encouraged to tailor this study guide to the needs of the individual course.

The study questions are designed to be used as guides for the student, as the basis for work in discussion sessions, or as problem sets to be handed in. There are many questions, so that each significant topic can be covered. The instructor is encouraged to select which of the questions students should do on their own, which they may omit, and which should be handed in, if any. The review questions can also be used in several ways: as guides for individual review, as model test questions, or as short writing assignments in or out of class. For courses in which this *Study and Listening Guide* is a required text, permission is granted to use any of the questions on examinations.

ACKNOWLEDGMENTS

We are grateful to the many instructors and students who have used previous editions of this *Study and Listening Guide* and have shown us how it is helpful and what can be improved. Thanks to Margaret Murata for detailed feedback and suggestions on the prior edition. The staff at W. W. Norton were wonderful. Kathy Talalay edited the entire manuscript and cheerfully solved problems as they came up. JoAnn Simony contributed the handsome design and layout and spent many late nights steering the book through production. We are especially grateful to them. Thanks finally to Andy King and Doug McKinney for their support and encouragement.

Study and Listening Guide

FOR

A History of Western Music
Seventh Edition

AND

Norton Anthology of Western Music
Fifth Edition

Chapter 1   Music in Antiquity

CHAPTER OBJECTIVES

After you complete the reading, study of the music, and study questions for this chapter, you should be able to

1. explain how we can learn about music of the past, using prehistoric cultures, ancient Mesopotamia, and ancient Greece and Rome as examples;

2. identify several elements of Western music and music theory that derive from the music of ancient Mesopotamia, Greece, or Rome;

3. describe in general terms ancient Greek music and ideas about music and the musical life of ancient Greece and Rome;

4. explain why the ancient Greeks linked music to numbers, astronomy, and poetry, and how they thought it affected a person's character and behavior; and

5. identify some basic terms of Greek music theory and some ancient writers on music.

CHAPTER OUTLINE

I. Introduction (HWM 4–5)

Western culture has roots in the ancient Near East, Greece, and Rome. Although little ancient m usic survived, ancient writings about music, particularly music theory, had a strong influence on later centuries.

A. Types of evidence

We can learn about music of the past by using four main types of evidence:

• Physical remains, including musical instruments;

• Images of musicians and instruments;

• Writings about music and musicians; and

• Music itself in notation, oral tradition, or (after 1890) recordings.

1

II. The Earliest Music (HWM 5–6)

The earliest traces of music are instruments and images from prehistoric cultures. Our knowledge of their music is limited by the lack of a written record.

III. Music in Ancient Mesopotamia (HWM 6–10)

A. Mesopotamian Civilizations

Sumerians developed the first civilization and one of the first known forms of writing in Mesopotamia over five thousand years ago.

1. Instruments and images

Several Sumerian instruments survive, including *lyres, harps,* and *bull lyres,* and pictures show how and in what situations they were played.

2. Written records

The written records of Mesopotamian cultures tell us about their uses of music, their *genres,* and other aspects of musical life. The earliest composer known by name was *Enheduanna* (fl. ca. 2300 B.C.E.), a priestess who wrote *hymns.*

3. Babylonian writings on music

Babylonian musicians began to write down their knowledge around 1800 B.C.E., describing aspects of music that are still familiar today.

4. Diatonic scales

Among those writings are instructions for tuning instruments in *diatonic* scales, later used by the Greeks and still used today.

5. The earliest notated music

The Babylonians used interval names to devise the earliest known *notation* for music, but most music was played by memory or improvised.

B. Other Civilizations

Instruments, images, and writings survive from other ancient civilizations, including India, China, Egypt, and Israel, but not their music.

IV. Music in Ancient Greek Life and Thought (HWM 10–21, NAWM 1–2)

Ancient Greece is the earliest civilization that offers enough evidence to construct a well-rounded view of musical life, including instruments, images, writings about music and its effects, and music itself.

A. Instruments and Their Uses

There were three main instruments: *aulos, lyre,* and *kithara.*

1. Aulos

The aulos was a reed instrument linked with *Dionysus,* god of fertility and wine, and used in Greek drama.

2. Lyre

The lyre was a seven-string instrument strummed with a plectrum and associated with *Apollo.* It was played alone or to accompany dancing, singing, or recitation.

3. Kithara
   The kithara was a large lyre used in religious ceremonies and the theater.

4. Memory and improvisation
   Pictures and writings show that the Greeks generally performed from memory or improvised, rather than reading from notation.

5. Competitions and professional musicians
   Music festivals and contests were an important part of Greek musical life after the fifth century B.C.E., and they encouraged increasing virtuosity and complexity in music. Some performers won wealth and fame, but most professional musicians had low status.

B. Greek Musical Thought
   In both philosophical and theoretical writings about music, the Greeks achieved insights and formulated principles that have survived to this day.

1. Music, religion, and society
   Music was linked to the gods and pervaded all aspects of life. The Greeks considered it both an art and a science.

2. Music, poetry, and dance
   Greek music was *monophonic* but was often performed in *heterophony.* Music was closely tied to poetry, which was usually sung. The Greek term for music as a performing art, *melos,* could denote *melody* alone, melody with text, or melody, text, and dance movement as a whole.

3. Music and number
   Greek theory associated music with numbers. *Pythagoras* (ca. 500 B.C.E.) discovered that the consonant intervals are produced by simple number ratios of 2:1 for the octave, 3:2 for the fifth, and 4:3 for the fourth.

4. Harmonia
   Because musical sounds and rhythms were ordered by numbers, they were thought to exemplify *harmonia,* the union of parts in an orderly whole.

5. Music and astronomy
   Through number and *harmonia,* music was linked to astronomy, as in the "music of the spheres" described by *Plato* (ca. 429–347 B.C.E.).

C. Music and *Ethos*
   The Greeks held that music could directly affect behavior and character, or *ethos* (related to the English word "ethics").

1. The doctrine of imitation
   According to *Aristotle* (384–322 B.C.E.), music affected behavior by imitating a certain ethos and thus arousing the same ethos in the listener.

2. Music in education
   Because of this power, both Plato and Aristotle gave music a central role in education but argued that only certain kinds of music were desirable: while the right kind of music disciplines the mind and fosters virtue, music that stimulates undesirable attitudes should be avoided.

D. Greek Music Theory

Greek theorists defined concepts we still use today, as well as ones specific to ancient Greek music.

1. Rhythm

Rhythm in music was closely aligned with poetic rhythm. Each duration was a multiple of a basic unit of time.

2. Note and interval

Theorists distinguished *diastematic* motion between discrete pitches from the continuous motions of the voice in speech. They defined the concepts of *note, interval,* and *scale,* establishing a basis for all later music theory.

3. Tetrachord and genus

Greek scales were constructed from *tetrachords,* groups of four notes spanning a perfect fourth. There were three *genera* (plural of *genus,* meaning type or class) of tetrachords: *diatonic, chromatic,* and *enharmonic.*

4. The Greater Perfect System

To cover larger ranges, tetrachords were combined, either overlapping by one note (*conjunct*) or separated by a whole tone (*disjunct*). The *Greater Perfect System* was an arrangement of four tetrachords over two octaves.

5. Species of consonances

The theorist Cleonides noted that in the diatonic genus the perfect fourth, fifth, and octave could be divided into whole tones and semitones in only a limited number of ways, which he called *species.* He named seven species of octave, like the scales that can be played on the white keys of the modern piano starting on the seven different white notes.

6. Tonoi

The *tonoi* were scales within a specific range, equivalent to transposing the system of tones up or down by some number of semitones.

E. Ancient Greek Music

About forty-five pieces or fragments of ancient Greek music survive in notation, most from relatively late periods. They conform very closely to the precepts of the theorists, including ethos, the three genera, and the tonoi.

1. *Epitaph of Seikilos*

The *Epitaph of Seikilos* uses the diatonic genus and a moderate tonos, suiting the ethos of its text, and has clear rhythmic notation. **Music: NAWM 1**

2. Euripides' *Orestes*

A chorus from the play *Orestes* by *Euripides* (ca. 485–406 B.C.E.) projects grief and agitation through its rhythm, changes of register, and use of the chromatic or enharmonic genus along with the diatonic. **Music: NAWM 2**

V. Music in Ancient Rome (HWM 22–23)

We have instruments, images, and written descriptions of music in ancient Rome, but no music. The Romans adopted many aspects of Greek musical culture, including religious and ceremonial music, music in private entertainment, and public festivals and competitions.

VI. The Greek Heritage (HWM 23)

The ancient Greeks developed ideas about music theory, performance, ethos, and the relationship between text and music that continue to influence Western musical traditions.

STUDY QUESTIONS

Introduction (HWM 4–5)

1. Artists and writers of the Middle Ages and later periods imitated the art and literature of ancient Greece and Rome. Why did musicians find it difficult to imitate ancient music? What aspects of ancient music did they draw on?

The Earliest Music (HWM 5–6)

2. What is the earliest evidence we have of music-making? What types of evidence exist from the era before civilization, and what types are missing?

Music in Ancient Mesopotamia (HWM 6–10)

3. How do we know about Mesopotamian instruments? What is the difference between a *lyre* and a *harp*? How are they played?

4. At what types of events and in what circumstances was music performed in Mesopotamian cultures?

5. What is a *genre*?

6. Who is the earliest composer known by name, and what sorts of pieces did this composer write?

7. Why do we know more about Babylonian music after 1800 B.C.E.? What are some elements Babylonian music shared with later European music?

Music in Ancient Greek Life and Thought (HWM 10–21, NAWM 1–2)

8. What were the three main instruments used by the ancient Greeks? How was each played, and on what occasions was it used? Which instrument was associated with Apollo, and which with Dionysus?

     a. _____

     b. _____

     c. _____

9. What was the social status of professional musicians in ancient Greece?

10. What issues did ancient Greeks address in their writings about music?

11. Who was Pythagoras, and when did he live? What is he credited with discovering?

12. What is the ancient Greek concept of *harmonia,* and how does it relate to music?

13. In the Greek conception, what were the links between music, numbers, and astronomy?

14. According to Plato and Aristotle, how could music affect a person's character and behavior? Why should certain kinds of music be promoted and other kinds suppressed? What is the relevance of this debate for our own time?

15. What is a *tetrachord*?

16. What are the three *genera* of tetrachord? What intervals appear in each, in order from top to bottom?

    1. _____   _____

    2. _____   _____

    3. _____   _____

17. How are tetrachords combined in the *Greater Perfect System*?

18. What are *species of fourth, species of fifth,* and *species of octave*? How are they defined, and how many of each are there?

Music to Study

NAWM 1: *Epitaph of Seikilos,* song (ca. first century C.E.)   CD 1|1   CD 1|1

NAWM 2: Euripides (ca. 485–ca. 406 B.C.E.), *Orestes,* tragedy,   CD 1|2
excerpt: *Stasimon* chorus (408 B.C.E.; the music may be later)

19. How do the *Epitaph of Seikilos* (NAWM 1) and the *stasimon* chorus from Euripides' *Orestes* (NAWM 2) exemplify the characteristics typical of Greek music as described in HWM, pp. 14–21 and the summary on p. 23?

20. Of the three genera you identified in question 8 above, which are used in the *Epitaph of Seikilos*? How can you tell? How does the music reflect the text?

Which genera are used in the chorus from *Orestes*? How does the music reflect the text?

Music in Ancient Rome (HWM 22–23)

21. In what ways did musical life in Rome resemble that of ancient Greece?

TERMS TO KNOW

Terms Related to Ancient Mesopotamian Music

lyre
harp
bull lyre
genre

hymn
diatonic
notation

Terms Related to Ancient Greek Music

aulos
lyre
kithara
melody
monophony, heterophony
harmonia
ethos
diastematic
note

interval
scale
tetrachord
genus (pl. genera): diatonic,
   chromatic, enharmonic
conjunct, disjunct
Greater Perfect System
species (of consonance)
tonos (pl. tonoi)

NAMES TO KNOW

Enheduanna
Pythagoras
Plato

Aristotle
Euripides

REVIEW QUESTIONS

1. What types of evidence exist for music of the distant past? From the surviving evidence, what can we learn about music in the Stone Age, in ancient Mesopotamia, and in ancient Greece, and what limitations are there on what we can know?
2. What are some basic characteristics of ancient Greek music? Which of these are shared with other ancient musical traditions?
3. What are some similarities between Greek music and ours? What are some similarities between Greek music theory and common-practice music theory?
4. The modern piano has white and black keys, and we use scales that span an octave and include a perfect fourth and fifth degree. How do these phenomena relate to ancient Greek music theory?
5. What are some Greek ideas about the power of music and its role in society that are still relevant today?
6. How has the social status of the professional musician changed or remained the same since ancient Greek times?

Chapter 2 The Christian Church in the First Millennium

CHAPTER OBJECTIVES

After you complete the reading, study of the music, and study questions for this chapter, you should be able to

1. name some aspects of the liturgy and music of the western Christian church that parallel or derive from Jewish and Byzantine practices;
2. explain how Gregorian chant came to be the standard repertory of liturgical song for the western Church;
3. describe the development of chant notation;
4. read a melody in Solesmes chant notation;
5. characterize the eight church modes by their final, tenor, and range and identify the mode of a given chant or song; and
6. summarize early Christian attitudes toward music, including the role of music in the church, the place of music among the liberal arts, and the relation of audible music to the mathematical proportions that govern nature and humans, and explain how these views relate to ancient Greek views of music.

CHAPTER OUTLINE

I. Introduction (HWM 24)

The church was the dominant social institution in the Middle Ages. Many aspects of Western music first developed within church music.

II. The Diffusion of Christianity (HWM 24–25)

Despite persecution, Christianity spread throughout the Roman world.

1. Legalization and establishment
Christianity was legalized in 313 by *Emperor Constantine*. By 600, almost the entire area of the former Roman Empire was Christian.

III. The Judaic Heritage (HWM 25–27)

Some elements of Christian observance, such as chanting Scripture and singing *psalms,* come from Jewish traditions.

1. Temple sacrifice
   Jewish Temple observances centered around a sacrifice and included the singing of psalms accompanied by instruments.

2. Synagogues
   Public readings from Scripture at the synagogue were probably chanted, employing *cantillation.*

3. Christian parallels
   The Christian Mass focuses on a symbolic sacrifice, like Temple services, yet also resembles Jewish Passover meals accompanied by psalm singing. Christian psalm singing may have been influenced by Jewish melodies.

IV. Music in the Early Church (HWM 27–29)

The history of singing psalms and hymns in Christian worship extends from the time of Jesus to the present day.

1. Rejection of music for pleasure
   Many leaders in the early Christian church opposed cultivating music for pleasure and believed that music in worship should inspire devotion.

2. Exclusion of instruments and pagan associations
   Instruments were not allowed in Christian worship. Music in the early church consisted of unaccompanied singing.

V. Divisions in the Church and Dialects of Chant (HWM 29–34)

A. Divisions in the Christian Church
   After the division of the Roman Empire, the Christian church divided into eastern and western churches. The eastern church used Greek and was centered in Constantinople. The western church used Latin, was centered in Rome, and was led by the pope.

1. Rite, calendar, liturgy, and music
   Each branch of Christianity created its own rite, consisting of a *church calendar,* a *liturgy,* and a repertory of *plainchant,* or *chant.* Different regions had different *chant dialects.* Those most important to the study of Western music are *Gregorian, Byzantine, Ambrosian,* and *Old Roman chant.*

B. Byzantine Chant
   Byzantine chant was classed into eight modes or *echoi,* which served as a model for the eight modes of the western church. Hymns were the most characteristic Byzantine chant.

1. Centonization
   Many Byzantine chant melodies were created from melodic formulas in a process called *centonization.*

C. Western Dialects

Western Europe was divided among several peoples who converted to Christianity. Many regions developed their own rites, liturgy, and chant repertories.

1. Ambrosian chant

Outside Rome, the most important church center was Milan. The chant there was called *Ambrosian chant,* named after St. Ambrose.

2. The dominance of Rome

From the eighth century on, chant was standardized, and local dialects were absorbed into a single practice emanating from Rome.

D. The Creation of Gregorian Chant

This standardization led to the repertory known as *Gregorian chant.*

1. Dissemination of Roman chant to the Franks

Due to political ties with the Roman popes and a desire for uniformity, the Frankish kings imposed the Roman liturgy and chant in their domain, which under *Charlemagne* comprised much of western Europe.

2. Frankish contributions

Roman chant provided the original source for Gregorian chant, but additions and changes were made to the repertory by the Franks.

3. The legend of St. Gregory

Although chant was likely codified in the eighth century, Gregorian chant was named after *Pope Gregory I* (r. 590–604). A legend arose that the Holy Spirit had dictated the chants to Gregory directly. Aided by the legend and political support, Gregorian chant spread across western Europe.

4. Old Roman chant

Old Roman chant is a body of chant that survived in Rome.

VI. The Development of Notation (HWM 34–41, NAWM 3d)

A. Oral Transmission

Words for the Roman liturgy were written down by the early eighth century, but the music was learned through oral transmission. Many chants share common melodic figures, suggesting that they were improvised by singers using a set of conventions and melodic formulas.

B. Stages of Notation

Notation was developed in a series of innovations to standardize chant mel-odies and promote uniformity.   **Music: NAWM 3d**

1. Neumes

The earliest notations used *neumes,* signs above the words that served as reminders of the correct melodic shape of music learned by ear.

2. Diastematic notation

In the tenth and eleventh centuries, scribes used *heighted* or *diastematic neumes* to indicate the relative size of intervals.

3. Lines, clefs, staff
   Other scribes included lines labeled with letters to further specify heighted neumes. These letters evolved into clefs. *Guido of Arezzo* (ca. 991–after 1033) suggested colored lines that evolved into a four-line staff.

4. Reading music
   Notation allowed scribes to indicate precise pitches, and singers could learn to read the notation and sing melodies they had never heard before.

5. Rhythm
   Staff notation conveyed pitch but not durations. Chant was probably sung in relatively free rhythm.

C. Solesmes Chant Notation
   Monks at the *Abbey of Solesmes* in France developed a modernized chant notation in the late nineteenth and early twentieth centuries featuring a four-line staff, two clefs (C and F), and neumes of various shapes.

Music in Context: In the Monastic *Scriptorium*
   Monasteries preserved music in manuscripts. A group of monks engaged in producing manuscripts was called a scriptorium. They copied text and music, decorated and illustrated the pages, and bound them in books. The entire process was laborious and very expensive.

VII. Music Theory and Practice (HWM 41–48)

A. The Transmission of Greek Music Theory
   Church musicians looked to music theory and philosophy from ancient Greece to understand the chant repertory.

1. Martianus Capella
   Martianus Capella (early fifth century) helped to codify the seven liberal arts: three verbal arts called the trivium (grammar, dialectic, and rhetoric) and four mathematical disciplines called the quadrivium (geometry, arithmetic, astronomy, and harmonics, or music).

2. Boethius
   Boethius (ca. 480–ca. 524) treated music as a science of numbers in *De institutione musica* (The Fundamentals of Music). He described three types of music: *musica mundana* (music of the universe), the numerical relations that control the natural world; *musica humana* (human music), which controls the human body and soul; and *musica instrumentalis,* audible music produced by voices or instruments. He believed in music education for the young, not as a practical activity but rather as an object of knowledge.

B. Practical theory
   Many treatises from the ninth century on focused on practical concerns.

1. *Musica enchiriadis* and *Micrologus*
   Musica enchiriadis (Music Handbook, ninth century) covers chant notation, eight modes, sight-reading, and consonances. In his *Micrologus* (ca. 1025–28), Guido of Arezzo offered a practical guide to singers.

C. The Church Modes

By the eleventh century, the system of *modes* encompassed eight modes identified by number and distinguished by *final, range,* and *tenor.*

1. Final

   The *final* is the main note in the mode, usually the last note in a melody.

2. Authentic and plagal modes

   Modes that have the same final differ in range. Odd-numbered modes are called *authentic* and have a range roughly from a step below the final to an octave above it. Even-numbered modes are called *plagal* and have a range from a fourth or fifth below the final to a fifth or sixth above it.

3. Use of B-flat

   B♭ often appears in place of B in chants in which F is prominent.

4. Species of fifth and fourth

   Some theorists applied to the modes the species of fifth and fourth described by Cleonides.

5. Tenor or reciting tone

   The *tenor* or *reciting tone* is often the most prominent note in a chant. In most authentic modes it is a fifth above the final, and in plagal modes it is a third lower; if it would fall on B by this rule, it is raised to C.

6. Modal theory and chant

   Modes are used to classify chants. Some chants fit the theory well. Others existed before the theory and may not fit easily into any mode.

7. Application of Greek names

   In the tenth century, some writers applied names of Greek scales to the church modes in an attempt to link their music to ancient Greek theory.

D. Solmization

Guido of Arezzo introduced *solmization* syllables to help singers locate whole tones and semitones.

E. The Hexachord System

Guido's musicians developed a system of *hexachords* (natural, hard, and soft). The signs indicating whether B was sung in the hard or soft hexachord evolved into our natural, sharp, and flat signs.

1. Mutation

   Mutation is the process of changing from one hexachord to another to cover a wider range and account for both B♭ and B♮.

2. Guidonian hand

   The "Guidonian hand" assigned a pitch to each joint of the left hand as a visual tool to teach notes and intervals.

VIII. Echoes of History (HWM 48–49)

Early Christians borrowed the practice of singing psalms and chanting Scripture from ancient Jewish customs and also drew on Greek views of music. Popes and kings unified their realms by standardizing liturgy and music. The western church adopted a system of eight modes to classify chant. To preserve the repertory and teach it more quickly, musicians developed notation and solmization, which are still part of musical life. The invention of notation was fundamental to later Western music. The preservation and dissemination of chant made it the basis for much of the music from the ninth through the sixteenth centuries.

STUDY QUESTIONS

The Diffusion of Christianity (HWM 24–25)

1. Why are the history of the Christian church and its diffusion across western Europe important to the study of a history of Western music?

The Judaic Heritage (HWM 25–27)

2. What similarities do you notice between Jewish religious practices and the liturgy and music of early Christian worship? In particular, what are *psalms,* and how were they used in each tradition?

Music in the Early Church (HWM 27–29)

3. What attitudes toward music were held by the leaders of the early Christian Church? How do these views compare to the views of Plato and Aristotle?

Divisions in the Church and Dialects of Chant (HWM 29–34)

4. What is a *rite*? What is a *church calendar*? What is a *liturgy*?

5. What is *plainchant,* or *chant*?

6. What is a *chant dialect*? Why did different chant dialects emerge?

7. What is *centonization*?

8. What role did Frankish kings, especially Charlemagne, play in relation to liturgy and chant? What is Gregorian chant? What were the sources for Gregorian chant, and what did it replace?

The Development of Notation (HWM 34–41, NAWM 3d)

9. When did chant melodies begin to be written down? _____

10. How were chant melodies transmitted before notation was developed? Why was notation useful?

11. Describe the circumstances in which manuscripts of chant were prepared

12. How did chant notation evolve? What stages did it go through? What is one of its limitations?

13. Example 2.2 in HWM (p. 38) is in Solesmes chant notation. This same chant is transcribed in modern notation in Example 2.3 on the facing page. The Solesmes chant notation uses a four-line staff. As in the modern five-line staff, each line stands for a pitch a third lower than the line above it, and the spaces stand for the pitches in between. The first symbol in each line is a clef; here it is a C clef on the second line from the top, indicating middle C. What pitch does each of the following lines and spaces stand for?

    the top line   _____   the bottom line   _____

    the space below it _____   the space below it   _____

In Solesmes chant notation, what does a dot after a note signify? What do vertical lines signify? What does the asterisk (*) signify? What do *ij* and *iij* signify? (Note: These are signs added by modern editors and do not appear in medieval manuscripts.)

Musical exercise in reading chant notation (HWM 38–41)

You do not have to know the names of the different noteshapes, or *neumes*. But with a little practice you should be able to read the chant notation. Refer to HWM, pp. 38–41 and p. 8 in NAWM. Practice the following:

Reading the modern notation in Example 2.3, sing or play on an instrument the first phrase of the chant (the top line of the example). You may omit the words if it is easier for you to do so.

Then sing (or play) the same phrase, using the plainchant notation. Go back and forth between the two ways to notate the phrase until you understand how the plainchant notation indicates the same pitches as the modern notation. Go through the same process for each phrase in turn.

When you have finished, sing (or play) through the whole chant from the plainchant notation. If you get stuck, refer to the modern transcription.

Music Theory and Practice (HWM 41–48)

14. How does music fit into the seven liberal arts? Why is music (or harmonics) grouped with the mathematical arts, rather than with the verbal arts?

15. Who was Boethius? Why was he important for music in the Middle Ages?

16. In Boethius's view, what was *musica instrumentalis,* and how did it relate to *musica mundana* and *musica humana*? How does this view compare to ancient Greek ideas about music?

17. How do *Musica enchiriadis* (ninth century) and *Micrologus* (ca. 1025–28) differ from Boethius' *De institutione musica*? What types of musical issues do these later treatises address?

18. The eight church modes are labeled by number and name. Each is defined by (1) its *final,* (2) its *tenor* or *reciting note,* and (3) its *range.* For each of the modes, give the name, final, tenor, typical range of chants in that mode, and octave range as given by some later theorists (see Example 2.4 in HWM, p. 44 for the difference).

Number	Name	Final	Tenor	Range	Octave
1	_____	___	___	_____	_____
2	_____	___	___	_____	_____
3	_____	___	___	_____	_____
4	_____	___	___	_____	_____
5	_____	___	___	_____	_____
6	_____	___	___	_____	_____
7	_____	___	___	_____	_____
8	_____	___	___	_____	_____

19. Which modes are *authentic* (indicate by number)? _____

   Which are *plagal*? _____

   What does a plagal mode share with its corresponding authentic mode?

   How does it differ?

20. Using the criteria of final and range, identify (by number) the mode of each of the following chants:

   Christe Redemptor omnium (NAWM 4b)   _____

   Quem queritis in presepe (NAWM 6)   _____

   Conditor alme siderum (NAWM 35, verse 1) _____

21. What is *solmization*? Why was it useful? When was it invented, and by whom? How is modern solmization similar to medieval practice? How does it differ?

22. What are the *natural, hard,* and *soft hexachords*? Why was it necessary to have all three? What is *mutation,* and how is it useful in singing?

23. What is the "Guidonian hand," what was it used for, and how was it used?

Echoes of History (HWM 48–49)

24. Describe the impact of Gregorian chant and its notation on the history of Western music.

TERMS TO KNOW

Terms Related to Judeo-Christian Music

psalms

cantillation

rite

church calendar

liturgy

plainchant, chant

chant dialects: Gregorian, Byzantine, Ambrosian, Old Roman

echos (pl. *echoi*)

centonization

Terms Related to Notation

neumes

heighted or diastematic neumes

Terms Related to Music Theory and Practice

musica mundana, musica humana, music instrumentalis

mode: the eight church modes

final

range

tenor, reciting tone

authentic modes

plagal modes

solmization

hard, soft, natural hexachords

mutation (of hexachords)

NAMES TO KNOW

Constantine

Charlemagne

Pope Gregory I

Guido of Arezzo

Abbey of Solesmes

Boethius

De institutione musica

Musica enchiriadis

Micrologus

REVIEW QUESTIONS

1. What are some of the sources of Gregorian chant, the repertory of melodies used in the western church? What were the contributions of the Judaic tradition, Syria, Byzantium, and Europe? How did Gregorian chant come to be standardized?
2. How did early Christian writers, including St. Augustine and Boethius, view music? How do their attitudes compare to those of the ancient Greeks, including Plato and Aristotle?
3. Why was notation devised, and how was it useful? How would your life as a musician be different if there was no notation?
4. What practical contributions to the theory and performance of monophonic music were made between the seventh and the twelfth centuries?

Chapter 3   Roman Liturgy and Chant

CHAPTER OBJECTIVES

After you complete the reading, study of the music, and study questions for this chapter, you should be able to

1. describe in general terms the liturgical context for chant in the Roman church, including the main outline of the Mass and names of the Offices;
2. explain how the shape and manner of performance of each chant relate to its liturgical function; and
3. describe the new chants and types of chant that were added to the authorized liturgical chant.

CHAPTER OUTLINE

I. Introduction (HWM 50)

Gregorian chant is shaped by its role in the liturgy, its text, and its manner of performance. New chants and types of chant were added to the body of liturgical music authorized by the church.

II. The Roman Liturgy (HWM 50–56, NAWM 3)

Gregorian chant is music for religious observances, and to understand this music we must also understand the services in which it is used.

A. Purpose of the Liturgy

The liturgy reinforced the main beliefs of Christianity through spoken and/or sung texts and rituals performed during each service.

B. Church Calendar

The *church calendar* is organized by feast days, commemorating saints or important events in the life of Jesus.

C. Mass

The *Mass* is the most important service in the Roman church and is composed of prayers, Bible readings, and psalm-singing. **Music: NAWM 3**

1. Proper and Ordinary

   The texts for the *Proper* change from day to day. The texts of the *Ordinary* are the same at every Mass, although the melodies may vary. (For this reason, the Proper chants are called by their function, while the Ordinary chants are named by their first words.)

2. Evolution of the Mass

   The form of the Mass evolved over the years into an Introductory section, the Liturgy of the Word, and the Liturgy of the Eucharist.

Music in Context: The Experience of the Mass

The Mass was instructional and inspirational for medieval believers, many of whom were illiterate. Music was used to engage the worshippers and to carry words throughout large, resonant worship spaces. It was sung by the priest, choir, and soloists. The Mass begins with an Introductory that includes the *Introit,* the *Kyrie,* and the *Gloria.* This is followed by the Liturgy of the Word, which includes the *Gradual,* the *Alleluia* or *Tract,* sometimes a *sequence,* and the *Credo.* The Liturgy of the Eucharist includes the *Offertory,* the *Sanctus,* the *Agnus Dei,* and the *Communion.*

D. The Office

The *Office* was a series of services celebrated at specific times throughout the day. These services included psalms with *antiphons,* lessons (Bible readings) with *responsories,* hymns, *canticles,* and prayers. Monasteries and convents followed the liturgy described in the Rule of St. Benedict (ca. 530).

E. Liturgical Books

Important books for the Mass are the Missal (containing texts) and *Gradual* (containing chants). Important books for the Office are the Breviary (containing texts) and the *Antiphoner* (containing chants).

1. Solesmes editions

   The Abbey of Solesmes prepared modern editions of chant and issued the *Liber usualis,* a book containing chants used most often for the Mass and the Office.

III. Characteristics of Chant (HWM 56–57)

Gregorian chants feature a variety of styles and of approaches to performance, treatment of text, and melodic character.

1. Manner of performance

   There are three manners for singing chant: *responsorial* (alternating solo and group), *antiphonal* (alternating groups), and *direct* (without alteration).

2. Text setting

   There are also three styles of setting texts: *syllabic* (mainly one note per syllable), *neumatic* (one to six notes per syllable), and *melismatic* (with *melismas,* long melodies on a single syllable).

3. Recitation formulas and independent melodies
Some parts of the Mass and Office are chanted to *recitation formulas,* and some are sung to fully formed melodies.

A. Melody and Declamation
Chant melodies reflect the inflection and rhythm of the words. Each melody divides into phrases and periods, following divisions in the text. Phrases tend to be archlike—rising, sustaining, then falling.

IV. Genres and Forms of Chant (HWM 57–65, NAWM 3–4)

Each genre of chant has a distinctive form and particular way to perform it.

A. Recitation Formulas
The simplest chants are *recitation formulas* for reciting prayers and Bible readings.

B. Psalm Tones
Psalm tones are formulas for singing the psalms in the Office. There is one psalm tone for each of the eight church modes, plus one "wandering tone." Each psalm tone follows the two-part form of the psalm text and consists of an *intonation,* a recitation on the tenor or reciting note, the *mediant,* further recitation, and a *termination.* The *Lesser Doxology,* praising the Trinity, is sung at the end of each psalm, using the same psalm tone. **Music: NAWM 4a**

C. Office Antiphons
An Office psalm or canticle is preceded and followed by an antiphon. The mode of the antiphon determines the mode of the psalm. **Music: NAWM 4a**

1. Performance
In medieval monastic practice, monks or nuns were divided into two choirs, singing the two halves of the psalm verses antiphonally. In modern performances, the *cantor* (choir leader) sings the opening words of both antiphon and psalm.

2. Style
Most Office antiphons are relatively simple and syllabic. Antiphon and psalm tone combine to create a piece composed of free melody (emphasizing the final) and recitation (emphasizing the tenor).

D. Office Hymns
Hymns are *strophic* and are sung by the choir in every Office service. The shapely rising and falling melodic contour seen in chant hymns has been typical of western European melodies since the Middle Ages. **Music: NAWM 4b**

E. Antiphonal Psalmody in the Mass
Antiphonal *psalmody* was also part of the Mass. The Introit and Communion were once full psalms with antiphons sung antiphonally by the choir. The Introit now has only one psalm verse (plus Doxology), and the

Communion is a single antiphon. The antiphons for the Introit and Communion are usually neumatic in style.   **Music: NAWM 3a and 3j**

F. Responsorial Psalmody in Office and Mass

Office responsories and the Gradual, Alleluia, and Offertory from the Mass are sung responsorially. These chants are typically melismatic, because of their historical association with solo singing. A choral *respond* precedes (and sometimes follows) a single psalm verse.

1. Office responsories
An Office responsory always includes a respond, a verse, and a full or partial repetition of the respond.

2. Gradual
Graduals are melismatic chants with a respond followed by a single psalm verse. The cantor begins the respond, which is completed by the choir. A soloist (or solo group) sings the verse, and the choir joins in the last phrase.   **Music: NAWM 3d**

3. Alleluia
Alleluias are melismatic chants and include a respond on the word "alleluia," a psalm verse, and a repetition of the respond, usually closing with a long melisma called a *jubilus*.   **Music: NAWM 3e**

4. Offertory
The Offertory is comprised of the respond only. It lost its verses when the ceremony it accompanied was shortened.   **Music: NAWM 3g**

5. Tract
Tracts are long, melismatic, and formulaic and evolved from direct solo psalmody. They are sung only at Advent and Lent.

G. Chants of the Mass Ordinary

Originally, the chants of the Ordinary were simple syllabic melodies sung by the congregation. Later they became more elaborate and were sung by the choir. Ordinary chants often reflect the shape of their texts.

1. Gloria and Credo
The Credo was always set in syllabic style, but most Gloria settings are neumatic. Both often use recurring melodic motives.   **Music: NAWM 3c and 3f**

2. Sanctus and Agnus Dei
The Sanctus and Agnus Dei are typically neumatic. Because their texts include repetitions, the melodies usually do as well.   **Music: NAWM 3h and 3i**

3. Kyrie
The Kyrie is melismatic, is usually performed antiphonally, and also includes text repetitions with repetitions in the music.   **Music: NAWM 3b**

4. Cycles of Ordinary chants
Beginning in the thirteenth century, Ordinary chants (excepting the Credo) were grouped in *cycles*.

H. Style, Use, and History

The style of a chant reflects its role in the liturgy, and when that role was revised, musicians changed the form or style of the chant. The styles and uses of chant in Christian worship have their roots in ancient traditions.

V. Additions to the Authorized Chants (HWM 65–68, NAWM 5-6)

After chant repertory was standardized, church musicians developed three new types of chant: tropes, sequences, and liturgical drama.

A. Trope

Tropes are newly composed additions to existing chants. There were three types: adding both text and music; adding music only; and adding text to existing melismas. Typically sung by soloists and set neumatically, tropes flourished in the tenth and eleventh centuries, then fell out of fashion. Most were banned by the *Council of Trent* (1545–63). **Music: NAWM 6**

B. Sequence

Sequences (late ninth through twelfth centuries) are set syllabically and usually sung after the Alleluia at Mass. Most melodies were newly composed, but some composers drew on material from the Alleluia. *Notker Balbulus* (ca. 840–912) was among the first composers of sequences.

1. Form

Most sequences consist of a series of paired sentences framed by single sentences. Each pair or single sentence has a distinctive musical phrase, resulting in the musical form A BB CC . . . N. **Music: NAWM 5**

C. Liturgical Drama

Liturgical dramas were short dialogues set to chant and linked to the liturgy. **Music: NAWM 6**

VI. Hildegard of Bingen (HWM 68–70, NAWM 7)

In convents, women held leadership positions, sang and composed music, and participated in a thriving intellectual life not available to lay women. *Hildegard of Bingen* (1098–1179) wrote in a variety of styles and forms, and her melodies are striking in their individuality.

1. Ordo virtutum

Ordo virtutum (The Virtues, ca. 1151) is a sacred music drama by Hildegard. She uses music (and the absence of it) to reflect relationships between characters. **Music: NAWM 7**

2. Reputation

In her own time, Hildegard was known more for her visions than her music, which was rediscovered only recently. Today, she is the most recorded and best-known composer of sacred monophony.

Biography: Hildegard of Bingen

Hildegard entered the monastery at age fourteen and in 1150 founded her own convent. She corresponded with many powerful men who were interested in her prophesies, and she set her own religious poetry to music.

Her *Ordo virtutum* is the earliest surviving music drama not attached to the liturgy.

VII. The Continuing Presence of Chant (HWM 70)

Gregorian chant was used in Catholic services from the Middle Ages until the 1960s. Today, chant is sung primarily in monasteries and convents, and only rarely in public Catholic services. Chant formed the foundation for most polyphonic music from the ninth through the thirteenth centuries and was a source for much later music as well. Because it was part of the musical world of most Europeans for over a thousand years, it also established expectations for how melodies should be shaped and how music should sound.

STUDY QUESTIONS

The Roman Liturgy (HWM 50–56, NAWM 3)

1. What events make up the church calendar?

2. What does the *Mass* commemorate?

3. What is the *Ordinary* of the Mass? What is the *Proper*?

   Which of the following chants are from the Mass Ordinary, and which are from the Proper?

Introit	_____	Credo	_____
Kyrie	_____	Offertory	_____
Gloria	_____	Sanctus	_____
Gradual	_____	Agnus Dei	_____
Alleluia	_____	Communion	_____
Tract	_____	Ite, missa est	_____

   What is the Office? Who participates in it? What is its purpose?

4. Fill in the names of the Offices celebrated at the following times of day. Circle the ones that are most important for music.

before sunrise	_____	about noon	_____
sunrise	_____	about 3 P.M.	_____
about 6 A.M.	_____	sunset	_____
about 9 A.M.	_____	just after sunset	_____

Characteristics of Chant (HWM 56–57)

5. List the three manners of performance for chant and describe each one.

6. Describe the three styles of setting chant texts.

Genres and Forms of Chant (HWM 57–65, NAWM 3–4)

Music to Study

NAWM 3: Mass for Christmas Day, Gregorian chant Mass

3a: Introit: *Puer natus est nobis*	CD 1|4
3b: Kyrie	CD 1|8 CD 1|2
3c: Gloria	CD 1|12
3d: Gradual: *Viderunt omnes*	CD 1|13
3e: *Alleluia Dies sanctificatus*	CD 1|15
3f: Credo	CD 1|18
3g: Offertory: *Tui sunt caeli*	CD 1|19
3h: Sanctus	CD 1|20
3i: Agnus Dei	CD 1|21 CD 1|6
3j: Communion: *Viderunt omnes*	CD 1|22
3k: Ite, missa est	CD 1|23

NAWM 4: Chants from Vespers for Christmas Day, Gregorian chant Office

4a: Antiphon: *Tecum principium*, with psalm *Dixit Dominus*	CD 1|24 CD 1|7
4b: Hymn: *Christe Redemptor omnium*	CD 1|28

7. Of the chants in the Ordinary of the Mass in NAWM 3, which ones are generally syllabic, which tend to be neumatic, and which are melismatic? For those that use musical repetition, show the pattern of repetition.

8. Of the chants in the Proper of the Mass in NAWM 3, which ones are generally syllabic, which tend to be neumatic, and which are melismatic?

9. What are some of the ways that the music of chant reflects the accentuation and phrasing of the text? For each way you mention, find an example among the chants of the Mass or Office in NAWM 3 and 4.

10. What are *psalm tones*? Where and how are they used?

11. How are psalm tones shaped, and how do they adjust to suit the many different texts they are used with? Give an example from NAWM.

12. How is the melodic contour of Proper chants similar to the melodic contour of psalm tones? How is it different? Give an example from NAWM.

13. What is the *Lesser Doxology*? What does the abbreviation *E u o u a e* indicate (as in NAWM 3a and NAWM 4a)?

14. What is an antiphon? Diagram the way an antiphon and psalm would be performed in the Vespers in NAWM 4a, using A for Antiphon, V for each psalm verse, and D for the Lesser Doxology.

15. What is a *respond*?

16. The Gradual and Alleluia are responsorial chants. What is the structure of each now? (Use the same symbols as in question 14 above, plus R for Respond.)

   Gradual _____   Alleluia _____

17. The Introit and Communion were once antiphons with psalms. What is the structure of each now? Diagram each, using the same symbols as in question 14 above.

   Introit _____   Communion _____

Addition to the Authorized Chants (HWM 65-68, NAWM 5-6)

18. What is a *trope*? What are the three types of trope? When were most tropes created? Why are they not part of the modern liturgy?

19. What is a *sequence*? Where does it occur in the liturgy? When were most sequences composed? Why are there so few sequences in the modern liturgy?

Music to Study

NAWM 5: Ascribed to Wipo of Burgundy, *Victimae paschali laudes,* sequence (first half of the eleventh century)

CD 1|29   CD 1|11

NAWM 6: Tropes on *Quem queritis in presepe and melisma,* texted trope (liturgical drama), and untexted trope (late tenth century)

CD 1|30

20. Diagram the form of the sequence *Victimae paschali laudes* (NAWM 5). Use a new letter for each new melodic segment (A for the first line of text, B for the second, and so on), and repeat that letter when a segment of melody repeats with a new text.

21. In what sense is *Quem queritis in presepe* (NAWM 6) a trope? Where does it fit in the Mass to which it is attached?

22. What makes *Quem queritis in presepe* a *liturgical drama*? (In what sense is it liturgical? In what sense is it a drama?) Why is *Ordo virtutum* not a liturgical drama?

23. How is the music of *Quem queritis in presepe* unified through melodic repetition?

Hildegard of Bingen (HWM 68–70, NAWM 7)

24. Briefly summarize Hildegard of Bingen's career. How was her work in the Church affected by her gender?

Music to Study

NAWM 7: Hildegard of Bingen, *In principio omnes,*
from *Ordo virtutum,* sacred music drama (ca. 1151)

[CD 1|33] [CD 1|12]

25. How is melodic repetition used in Hildegard of Bingen's *In principio omnes* (NAWM 7)? How does this song differ from liturgical chant in function and in style?

The Continuing Presence of Chant (HWM 70)

26. What is the significance of Gregorian chant in the history of Western music? Where might you hear chant performed today?

TERMS TO KNOW

Terms Related to Liturgy

church calendar

Mass

Proper of the Mass: Introit, Gradual,
Alleluia or Tract, Offertory,
Communion

Ordinary of the Mass: Kyrie,
Gloria, Credo, Sanctus, Agnus
Dei, Ite, missa est

Office

antiphon

responsory

canticle

Terms Related to Chant

antiphonal, responsorial, or
direct performance

syllabic, neumatic, melismatic

melisma

recitation formula

psalm tone

intonation, mediant, termination

Lesser Doxology

cantor

strophic

psalmody

respond

jubilus

cycle (of Ordinary chants)

Terms Related to Additions to the Authorized Chants

trope

sequence

liturgical drama

NAMES TO KNOW

Council of Trent

Notker Balbulus

Hildegard of Bingen

Ordo Virtutum

REVIEW QUESTIONS

1. Make a timeline from 800 to 1300 and locate on it the pieces in NAWM 5–7, their composers, and the following: Charlemagne, Notker Balbulus, and Guido of Arezzo. (The chants in NAWM 3–4 come from many centuries and most cannot be dated accurately, so they cannot be fixed on your timeline.)

2. How has the music of chant been shaped by its role in the ceremonies and liturgy of the Roman church, by the texts, and by the manner in which it has been performed? Use as examples at least two individual chants of varying types, and show in what ways the musical characteristics of each are appropriate for its liturgical role, its text, and its manner of performance.

3. Write a chant melody to the text of the Kyrie, Sanctus, or Agnus Dei from the Mass in NAWM 3. Use the original chant as a model for the form, including repetition of words and of music. Use any of the eight church modes *except* the mode of the original chant or its corresponding plagal or authentic mode. (For instance, since the Kyrie is in mode 1, do not use mode 1 or mode 2 to write your Kyrie.)

Try to follow the style of chant as you have come to know it, including melodic contour, phrasing, and accentuation. You may use either modern or chant notation.

4. If you were composing new monophony to a nonliturgical text, what decisions would you need to make about text, form, modes, melodic contour, phrasing, and accentuation?

5. Create your own trope to a chant from NAWM 3 as if you were a composer in the early eleventh century. Does it matter which chant you choose? What types of changes can you make to that chant? Would you be allowed to add new words to it? New music? Why or why not?

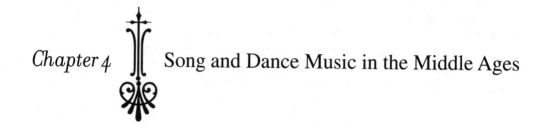

Chapter 4 — Song and Dance Music in the Middle Ages

CHAPTER OBJECTIVES

After you complete the reading, study of the music, and study questions for this chapter, you should be able to

1. name several kinds of secular musicians active during the Middle Ages and the regions and social classes from which they came;

2. describe some examples of medieval secular song by troubadours, trouvères, and *Minnesinger*;

3. describe the *estampie,* the oldest surviving form of instrumental music;

4. name and briefly describe some of the instruments played during the Middle Ages; and

5. name and briefly identify a few of the people who contributed to the repertory of medieval monophonic secular music.

CHAPTER OUTLINE

I. Introduction (HWM 71)

Songs, poems, dance tunes, descriptions and pictures of music-making, and instruments from the Middle Ages can tell us about music in medieval society.

II. European Society, 800–1300 (HWM 71–74)

1. Three successors to Rome
    European culture owes much to the three principal successors to the Roman Empire: the Byzantine Empire, the Arab world, and western Europe.

2. The changing map of Europe
    The modern nations of France and England emerged during the Middle Ages, but Germany, Italy, and Spain remained divided. Rulers in courts

and cities competed for prestige and fueled the development of music by hiring the best poets, performers, and composers.

3. Economic growth and social classes
Europe grew in population and economic strength between 1000 and 1300. By the twelfth century, a new middle class was formed (comprising artisans, doctors, merchants, and lawyers).

4. Learning and the arts
Cathedral schools and schools for laymen fostered a rise in literacy, translations of ancient writings into Latin, and poetry independent from ancient models.

III. Latin and Vernacular Song (HWM 74–76)

A. Latin Song

1. Versus and conductus
The *versus* and *conductus* had sacred functions originally and used newly composed melodies not based on chant.

2. Latin secular songs
Latin secular songs were performed outside religious contexts.

3. Goliard songs
Goliard songs had secular Latin texts on a variety of topics, including love, morality, and earthly pleasures.

B. Vernacular Song
We know very little about vernacular songs because they were rarely written down or written about.

1. Epics
The *chanson de geste* is one type of epic narrative poem in the vernacular sung to simple melodic formulas. An example is *Song of Roland* (ca. 1100).

C. Minstrels and Other Professional Musicians
Bards (poet-singers), *jongleurs,* and *minstrels* were professional musicians in the Middle Ages.

IV. Troubadour and Trouvère Song (HWM 76–81, NAWM 8–10)

Troubadours (feminine: *trobairitz*) were poet-composers active in southern France who wrote in Occitan. Among the most widely known was Bernart de Ventadorn (?ca. 1130–ca. 1200). Their counterparts in northern France, called *trouvères,* wrote in Old French. Both types of musicians were supported by aristocrats at court and in cities. Their songs were preserved in *chansonniers.*

A. Poetry
Most troubadour and trouvère poetry is strophic, and love is the most common topic. Dance songs often include a *refrain.*

1. Fin'amors and fine amour
The most common theme is *fin'amors*, or *fine amour* (also called *courtly love*), an idealized love in which a discreet, unattainable woman was

adored from a distance. Women poets such as the Countess of Dia (*Comtessa de Dia*) adapted similar language.   **Music: NAWM 8–9**

B. Melodies

Troubadour and trouvère melodies are strophic and mostly syllabic with a narrow range.

1. Rhythm

Usually the notation of these songs does not indicate rhythm.

C. Musical Plays

Jeu de Robin et de Marion (ca. 1284) is the most famous musical play and is by the trouvère *Adam de la Halle* (ca. 1240–?1288). Among the song forms he uses is the *rondeau*.   **Music: NAWM 10**

D. Dissemination

By the late twelfth century, the troubadour tradition from southern France spread to the trouvères in northern France and to countries beyond.

V. Song in Other Lands (HWM 81–83, NAWM 11–12)

The troubadour and trouvère tradition inspired lyric song in other languages.

A. English Song

English royalty used French and supported French poet-composers; therefore, few melodies for medieval English poems survive.

B. Minnesinger

The *Minnesinger* were knightly poet-composers active in German-speaking lands from the twelfth through the fourteenth centuries. One of the best known was Walther von der Vogelweide (?ca. 1170–?ca. 1230). They sang *Minnelieder* (love songs) about a spiritual, idealized love (*Minne*). Their strophic melodies are in *bar form*: AAB, with the melody for the B section (*Abgesang*) often ending with some or all of the A section (*Stollen*).   **Music: NAWM 11**

C. Laude

Laude (nonliturgical, Italian monophonic songs) were sung in processions.

D. Cantigas

Cantigas were Spanish monophonic songs. The most famous collection, *Cantigas de Santa Maria,* includes over four hundred cantigas in honor of the Virgin Mary.   **Music: NAWM 12**

VI. Medieval Instruments (HWM 83–85)

Although medieval monophonic songs were notated as single melodic lines, some may have been accompanied by instruments.

1. String instruments

Medieval instruments included bowed strings such as the *vielle*; plucked strings such as the *psaltery*; and the *hurdy-gurdy,* a mechanical string instrument.

2. Wind and percussion instruments

Medieval wind and percussion instruments included the *transverse flute, shawm,* and *pipe and tabor.*

3. Bagpipes, bells, and organs
   There were large organs in some monasteries and cathedrals, and smaller organs (such as the *portative organ* and *positive organ*) for smaller spaces.

VII. Dance Music (HWM 85–86, NAWM 13)

Dancing in the Middle Ages was accompanied by songs or instrumental music, but only about fifty melodies survive. A popular dance in France was the *carole*.

1. Instrumental dances
   Medieval instrumental dance music had a steady beat, clear meter, repeated sections, and predictable phrasing.

2. Estampie
   The most common medieval French dance form was the *estampie,* in which each section was played twice, first with an *open* cadence and then with a *closed* one.   **Music: NAWM 13**

VII. The Lover's Complaint (HWM 86)

Lyric songs by troubadours and their successors have much in common with lyric songs by composers from subsequent generations. Their strophic, diatonic, and mostly syllabic musical style and poetic topics of unattainable love resurface in songs of later generations.

STUDY QUESTIONS

European Society, 800–1300 (HWM 71–74)

1. What were some of the general changes in European society in the Middle Ages, and what effect did they have on music and the other arts?

Latin and Vernacular Song (HWM 74–76)

2. Describe the different types of Latin song in the Middle Ages. Where would each type have been performed? Why were they performed?

3. Who were the *Goliards*? Who were the *jongleurs, bards,* and *minstrels*? What kinds of music did each perform, and when and where did they perform it?

Troubadour and Trouvère Song (HWM 76–81, NAWM 8–10)

4. What is a *troubadour*? a *trobairitz*? a *trouvère*? When were they active, and what languages did they use? From what social classes did they come?

5. What is *fin'amors,* or *fine amour* (also called *courtly love*)?

| *Music to Study*

NAWM 8: Bernart de Ventadorn, *Can vei la lauzeta mover,* ⟨ CD 1|36 ⟩ ⟨ CD 1|15 ⟩
  troubadour song (ca. 1170–80)

NAWM 9: Comtessa de Dia, *A chantar,* canso or troubadour song ⟨ CD 1|37 ⟩
  (second half of twelfth century)

NAWM 10: Adam de la Halle, *Robins m'aime,* rondeau or trouvère ⟨ CD 1|38 ⟩
  song, from *Jeu de Robin et de Marion* (ca. 1284)

6. Describe the melodic characteristics of troubadour songs, using Bernart de Ventadorn's *Can vei* (NAWM 8) and Comtessa de Dia's *A chantar* (NAWM 9) as examples.

   How many notes are set to each syllable? _____

   How large a range does the melody typically cover? _____

   Does the notation indicate the rhythm? _____

   How else would you characterize the melodic style?

7. How is the trouvère song *Robins m'aime* (NAWM 10) by Adam de la Halle different in style from the troubadour songs (NAWM 8–9)? How is it similar?

8. How do *Can vei, A chantar,* and *Robins m'aime* use melodic repetition? Chart the form of each. (For the first two, chart the form of a single strophe; for the third, use capital letters for repetitions of music *and* text, and lowercase letters for repetitions of music with new words.)

     Can vei   _____

     A chantar   _____

     Robins m'aime   _____

9. What is the mode of each of these songs? (Use the mode number.)

     Can vei   _____

     A chantar   _____

     Robins m'aime   _____

Song in Other Lands (HWM 81–83, NAWM 11–12)

10. Who were the *Minnesinger*? When and where were they active?

Music to Study

NAWM 11: Walter von der Vogelweide, *Palästinalied* (*Nu alrest lebe ich mir werde*), Minnelied (?ca. 1228)   [CD 1|39]

11. How is the Minnelied by von der Vogelweide like the troubadour and trouvère songs in NAWM 8–10, and how does it differ?

12. What is *bar form*? How is it used in NAWM 11? Does the *Abgesang* repeat material from the *Stollen*?

13. What is a *lauda,* and where is it from?

Music to Study

NAWM 12: Cantiga 159, *Non sofre Santa Maria* from *Cantigas de Santa Maria* (ca. 1270–90)

CD 1|40   CD 1|16

14. What is a cantiga and where is it from?

15. How is *Non sofre Santa Maria* (NAWM 12) musically and textually similar to the other monophonic songs we have studied (NAWM 8–11), and how does it differ?

Medieval Instruments (HWM 83–85)

16. For each of the following medieval instruments, briefly describe it, explain how each was played, and name one or more modern instruments of which it is an ancestor.

    vielle

    psaltery

    shawm

    portative organ

    positive organ

17. What other instruments were used in the Middle Ages?

Dance Music (HWM 85–86, NAWM 13)

Music to Study

NAWM 13: *La quarte estampie royal* from *Le manuscrit du roi*,   ⏹CD 1|40   ⏹CD 1|16
estampie (late-thirteenth century)

18. What is an *estampie*? Which of its sections were repeated? How do the "open" and "closed" cadences work in the *La quarte estampie royal* (NAWM 12)? (Note: This may be easier to follow while listening to the music.)

TERMS TO KNOW

Terms Related to Latin and Vernacular Song

versus
conductus
goliard song
chanson de geste

bard
jongleur
minstrel

Terms Related to Troubadour and Trouvère Song

troubadour, trobairitz
trouvère
chansonnier

refrain
fin'amors, fine amour, courtly love
rondeau

Terms Related to Song in Other Lands

Minnesinger
Minnelieder
bar form: Stollen, Abgesang

lauda (pl. laude)
cantiga

Terms Related to Medieval Instruments and Dance Music

vielle
hurdy-gurdy
psaltery
transverse flute
shawm

pipe and tabor
portative organ, positive organ
carole
estampie
open and closed cadences

NAMES TO KNOW

Song of Roland
Bernart de Ventadorn
Comtessa de Dia

Adam de la Halle
Walther von der Vogelweide
Cantigas de Santa María

REVIEW QUESTIONS

1. Continue your timeline from 800 to 1300 and locate on it the pieces in NAWM 8–13 and their composers.
2. Trace the history of monophonic secular song. For each group of poet-composers, note their region, language, place in society, and time of activity, and briefly describe their music.
3. What do the secular songs in NAWM 8–12 have in common with Gregorian chant (NAWM 3–4)? How do they differ from it?
4. In what ways are instrumental music and the use of instruments in accompanying singing similar in the Middle Ages and the present time, and in what ways do they most differ?

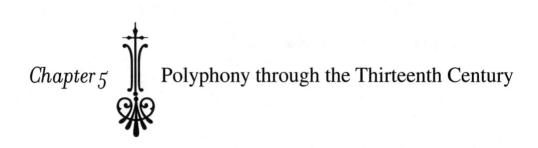

Chapter 5   Polyphony through the Thirteenth Century

CHAPTER OBJECTIVES

After you complete the reading, study of the music, and study questions for this chapter, you should be able to

1. name the new trends in music from 1050 to 1300 that became distinguishing characteristics of Western music;

2. describe the varieties of polyphony practiced between the 1050 and 1300 and trace their historical development;

3. define important terms and identify the people, works, and schools of composition that played a major role in the development of early polyphony; describe the origins and early evolution of the motet; and describe how early English polyphony differs from early polyphony on the European continent.

CHAPTER OUTLINE

I. Introduction (HWM 87–88)

From 1050 to 1300, the church enjoyed prosperity. *Polyphony,* music for two or more independent voices, heightened the grandeur of chant. Like medieval art, it was valued as decoration. Notation developed in the eleventh, twelfth, and thirteenth centuries allowed musicians to write down polyphony and develop more elaborate varieties. The rise of written polyphony signals the beginning of Western music's distinctive precepts: *counterpoint, harmony,* the centrality of notation, and *composition as distinct from performance.*

II. Early Organum (HWM 88–92, NAWM 14–15)

A. Early Types of Polyphony

Europeans performed music in multiple parts long before it was described in writing. The simplest type (though not a true form of polyphony) is accompanying a melody with a *drone.*

1. Organum

   Polyphony was first described in the ninth-century treatises *Musica enchiriadis* and *Scolica enchiriadis,* which used the term *organum* for the various styles of polyphony and for a piece that uses polyphony (pl. *organa*).

2. Parallel organum

   In *parallel organum,* an added voice (*organal voice*) appears below a chant melody (*principal voice*), moving in parallel fifths. Either or both voices may be doubled at the octave.   **Music: NAWM 14a–b**

3. Mixed parallel and oblique organum

   In *mixed parallel and oblique organum,* an organal voice either moves in parallel fourths below a principal voice or remains stationary in order to avoid sounding a tritone.   **Music: NAWM 14c**

4. From performance to composition

   The earliest sources of organum give examples of how to extemporize an organal voice below chant in performance. As the range of choices increased, some organa were written down as compositions, including those in the *Winchester Troper* (early eleventh century).

B. Free Organum

In *free organum* the added voice usually sings above the chant (although the voices may cross), moving in contrary, oblique, parallel, and similar motion to the chant and forming consonant intervals with it (unison, fourth, fifth, and octave). Instructions on how to compose or improvise organum of this type are preserved in the treatise *Ad organum faciendum* (On Making Organum, ca. 1100). Only the portions of chant that were sung by soloists were set polyphonically, so that in performance sections of polyphony alternate with sections of monophonic chant sung by the choir.   **Music: NAWM 15**

III. Aquitanian Polyphony (HWM 92–94, NAWM 16)

New types of polyphony, called *Aquitanian polyphony,* appeared early in the twelfth century in the duchy of Aquitaine in southwestern France.

1. Polyphonic versus

   Polyphonic settings of *versus* (a type of Latin poem) are the earliest known polyphony not based on chant.

2. Discant versus organum

   The two main styles of Aquitanian polyphony are *discant* (both voices move at about the same rate) and *florid organum* (the upper voice sings many notes for each note in the lower voice). In both styles the lower voice is called the *tenor* and is decorated by the upper voice.   **Music: NAWM 16**

3. Score notation and rhythm

   Score notation was used in the early twelfth century to show the alignment of the parts, but the durations were not indicated. Modern editors and performers vary in the solutions they offer.

IV. Notre Dame Polyphony (HWM 94–103, NAWM 17–19)

An even more elaborate style of composed polyphony was developed at the *Notre Dame Cathedral* in Paris in the late twelfth and early thirteenth centuries.

A. The Rhythmic Modes

The Notre Dame composers developed the first rhythmic notation since ancient Greece. They used combinations of notegroups, or *ligatures,* to indicate patterns of *longs* and *breves.* These patterns are known today as the six *rhythmic modes.* The basic unit of time (*tempus*) was always grouped in threes.

1. Variety

Composers altered the six rhythmic modes for greater rhythmic variety while maintaining the basic patterns of longs and breves.

2. Notation

Rhythmic mode was indicated with ligatures, signs denoting two-note groups or three-note groups. The pattern of two- and three-note groups indicated the rhythmic mode.

B. Léonin and the *Magnus liber organi*

Léonin (fl. 1150s–ca. 1201) and *Pérotin* (fl. late twelfth and early thirteenth centuries) composed polyphony associated with Notre Dame.

1. *Magnus liber organi*

Léonin compiled a *Magnus liber organi* ("great book of polyphony"), containing two-voice settings of the solo portions of the responsorial chants for major feasts for the church year.

2. Layers of adaptation

Many composers added to and altered *Magnus liber organi* to further decorate the chant.

Biographies: Léonin and Pérotin

Léonin and Pérotin worked at Notre Dame, and the few facts we know about them come from a treatise known as *Anonymous IV* (ca. 1275). According to the treatise, Léonin was the best composer of organa. Pérotin was the best composer of discant and wrote three- and four-voice organa and monophonic and polyphonic conductus.

C. Léonin Organum

Léonin's organum (for soloists) is in two voices and alternates sections of organum style with sections in discant style. The sections for choir are plainchant and sung in unison. **Music: NAWM 17**

1. Organum style

In organum style (like Aquitanian florid organum), the chant melody is in long notes in the tenor while the upper voice sings melismas.

2. Discant style

The sections in discant style use the rhthmic modes in both voices and tend to appear where there are melismas in the original chant.

D. Substitute Clausulae

A *clausula* is a self-contained section of an organum, setting a word or syllable from the chant and closing with a cadence. *Substitute clausulae* were new sections designed to replace the original setting of a particular segment of a chant. Typically they were in discant style. **Music: NAWM 18**

1. Repetition and structure

In discant of Pérotin's generation, the tenor typically repeats a rhythmic motive based on a rhythmic mode.

E. Pérotin Organum

1. Organum duplum, triplum, and quadruplum

A two-voice organum was called *organum duplum*; a three-voice organum was called a *triplum*; and a four-voice organum was called a *quadruplum*. *Duplum, triplum,* and *quadruplum* are also the names of the voices in ascending order above the tenor. All upper voices use rhythmic modes and move in similar ranges.

2. Pérotin's *Viderunt*

Pérotin's setting of *Viderunt* is an *organum quadruplum* that uses several of his typical traits, including repetition of phrases and *voice exchange* (where voices trade phrases). **Music: NAWM 19**

V. Polyphonic Conductus (HWM 103, NAWM 20)

The *polyphonic conductus* is a two- to four-voice setting of a rhymed, rhythmic, strophic Latin poem on a sacred or serious topic (like the earlier monophonic conductus and Aquitanian versus). The tenor is newly written, not based on chant. All voices sing the text together in a predominantly syllabic and homorhythmic texture known as "conductus style," when used in other genres. Some conductus feature long melismas called *caudae* (tails), especially at the beginning or end. Conductus with caudae are usually through-composed, but those without tend to be strophic. **Music: NAWM 20**

VI. Motet (HWM 104–111, NAWM 21–22)

Starting in the early thirteenth century, words were often added to the upper voices of a discant clausula. This produced a new genre, the *motet* (from the French word *mot,* for "word"). The duplum of a motet is called the *motetus.* New types of motets developed, including ones with French texts, secular topics, three or more voices, or rhythms increasingly free of the rhythmic modes.

A. Early Motets

1. The first motets

Motets usually have different texts in each voice and therefore are identified by the first few words of each voice from highest to lowest. In the earliest motets, the texts in the upper voices often elaborate on the words and meaning of the chant text. **Music: NAWM 21a**

2. Motet as independent genre
Because motets were sung for secular as well as sacred occasions, the tenor (chant) soon lost its exclusively liturgical function and became raw material for composition. Composers reworked existing motets in various ways: by writing a new Latin or French text for the duplum, by adding a third or fourth voice with separate texts (a *double motet* has two texts above the tenor, and a *triple motet* has three), or by deleting the original duplum and writing new voices. They also wrote motets from scratch. In most motets for three or more voices, the upper voices rarely rest with each other or the tenor.   **Music: NAWM 21b–c**

3. Performance
Sacred motets might have been performed in services, but secular motets were not. The tenor may have been played on an instrument.

4. Reception
Motets were intended for listeners who appreciated the witty interrelationships of multiple texts on related topics, borrowed material, and new elements.

B. Motets in the Later Thirteenth Century
After 1250, composers used tenor melodies from other chants and secular music. The tenor became simply a *cantus firmus*—an existing melody, usually a plainchant, on which a new polyphonic work was based. Later motets were less dependent on rhythmic modes, and their increasing rhythmic variety and complexity called for a new notational system.

1. Franconian notation
This new system was called *Franconian notation* after the theorist *Franco of Cologne* and was described in his *Ars cantus mensurabilis* (ca. 1280). In this system, relative durations were signified by noteshapes (the same principle underlying modern notation). These notehapes are the double long, long, breve, and semibreve. The basic time unit was the *tempus* (pl. *tempora*), and there were three tempora in a *perfection,* equivalent to a modern measure of three beats. A long was either perfect (three tempora) or imperfect (two), and divisions of the breve were notated by semibreves. Although this notation still emphasized three-fold divisions, it gave new freedom from the rhythmic modes.

2. Format
In a three-voice motet, the triplum and motetus were written on facing pages or in separate columns on the same page with the tenor across the bottom.

3. Franconian motet
Using Franconian notation, composers wrote motets in which the upper voices feature more rhythmic freedom and variety, and the same pattern rarely repeats from one measure to the next. The tempo is slower in order to accommodate for shorter durations, and voices rarely cadence together.   **Music: NAWM 22**

4. Petrus de Cruce

   Petrus de Cruce (fl. ca. 1270–1300) extended even greater rhythmic variety in his motets, producing a stratified texture, with the tenor as harmonic foundation and the duplum as accompaniment to the very active triplum.

5. Harmonic vocabulary

   In motets throughout the thirteenth century, perfect consonances (fifth and octave) were expected at the beginning of each perfection, and thirds were allowed. In the typical cadence, the tenor descends by a step and the upper voices rise a step to form a 1-5-8 sonority.

6. Tradition and innovation

   The motet went through many changes in the thirteenth century, from an existing piece with new text to a highly complex and individual work.

VII. English Polyphony (HWM 111–14, NAWM 21c, 23)

English composers wrote in all the Notre Dame genres, focused on sacred Latin texts, and tended to prefer the relatively homorhythmic style and regular phrasing of the conductus.

1. Distinctive features

   English composers favored harmonic thirds and sixths (imperfect consonances) in parallel motion, which seems to reflect influences from folk music. They also preferred four-voice textures and long-short rhythms. **Music: NAWM 21c**

2. Rondellus

   A *rondellus* is a three-voice song or passage in which voices in the same range exchange two or three phrases, first heard simultaneously, and then taken up in turn by each voice.

3. Rota

   The *rota* is a round at the unison. The most famous is *Sumer is icumen in.* **Music: NAWM 23**

VIII. A Polyphonic Tradition (HWM 114)

The development of polyphony through the thirteenth century reflected the medieval preference for decoration, adding layers of elaboration (new texts and new music) to existing compositions. It also was a major turning point in Western music. Composers developed systems of notation where voices are aligned vertically to coordinate parts and where different noteshapes indicate relative duration. Since the late nineteenth century, composers have looked back to early polyphony and incorporated elements of it into their modern compositions.

STUDY QUESTIONS

Introduction (HWM 87–88)

1. What important new developments in European music were under way in the eleventh century? Which of the trends that were new then are still typical of Western music today?

Early Organum (HWM 88–92, NAWM 14–15)

2. In what treatise was polyphony first described? _____

   Name the textbook that accompanied this treatise. _____

   When were they written? _____

   What three styles of organum do they describe?

Music to Study

NAWM 14a–c: *Organum from Musica enchiriadis* (ca. 850–900)

 14a: *Tu patris sempiternus,* parallel organum at the fifth below   CD 1|48

 14b: *Sit gloria domini,* parallel organum with octave doublings   CD 1|49

 14c: *Rex caeli,* mixed parallel and oblique organum   CD 1|50

3. Which voice sings the original chant in *Tu patris sempiternus* (NAWM 14a) and *Sit gloria domini* (NAWM 14b)? In each case, state the rules that govern the derivation of the other voice(s).

4. In *Rex caeli domine* (NAWM 14c), why can the chant (the upper line) *not* be accompanied throughout by a parallel fourth in the lower voice? What adjustments have been made to solve this problem?

5. Describe the new style of organum common in the late eleventh century.

 What is this style called? _____

 Name a source in which this style is described. _____

Music to Study

NAWM 15: *Alleluia Justus ut palma,* free organum,
    from *Ad organum faciendum* (ca. 1100)

⟮ CD 1|51 ⟯ ⟮ CD 1|17 ⟯

6. In the eleventh-century organum *Alleluia Justus ut palma* (NAWM 15), some sections are not set in polyphony. Why not?

   In the sections in two-voice polyphony, which part is the original chant and which is the added voice? Which of the two is more disjunct (fewer steps, more skips)? Why?

7. What are the main harmonic intervals in NAWM 15? Why were these intervals considered consonant while others were considered dissonant?

8. Using *Alleluia Justus ut palma* as a model, add an organal voice in eleventh-century style (note-against-note organum) to the first two verses of *Victimae paschali laudes,* given below. Here the organal voice will be above the chant, rather than below it (although it may cross below on occasion). Start the first phrase on a unison D with the chant, and end each verse on an octave D–D. Each vertical sonority should be a unison, a perfect fourth, a perfect fifth, an octave, or (rarely) a perfect eleventh, with a third or sixth permissible just before a unison or octave cadence. Use contrary motion most often and parallel and oblique motion for variety, but avoid parallel octaves and unisons. Make the organal voice as smooth as possible, and avoid leaps larger than a fifth. Do not go higher than the A above the staff. Do not use any accidental other than B♭, and avoid using both B♮ and B♭ in close proximity. Have fun with this, and try to write something you like while following all these rules.

Aquitanian Polyphony (HWM 92–94, NAWM 16)

9. In Aquitanian polyphony, which voice has the chant? _____

   What is this voice called? _____

   Why did it receive this name?

   Describe the relationship between the parts in florid organum. What are the characteristics of each voice?

10. What is a polyphonic *versus*? How does it differ from organum in respect to the derivation of its text and its music?

Music to Study

NAWM 16: *Jubilemus, exultemus,* versus in Aquitanian polyphony ⎡ CD 1|53 ⎤
   (early twelfth century)

11. How does *Jubilemus, exultemus* (NAWM 16) differ from the eleventh-century organum *Alleluia Justus ut palma* (NAWM 15)? How are they similar?

12. Where in *Jubilemus, exultemus* is organum style used? Where is discant style used?

Notre Dame Polyphony (HWM 94–103, NAWM 17–19)

13. Show the rhythmic pattern for each of the six rhythmic modes:

    Mode I   _____

    Mode II   _____

    Mode III   _____

    Mode IV   _____

    Mode V   _____

    Mode VI   _____

14. For which chants of the Mass and Office did Léonin write organa?

    Of these chants, which portions did he set in polyphony?

    What was his collection of organa called?   _____

15. According to the treatise called Anonymous IV, what was Léonin best at?

    What was Pérotin noted for?

16. What is a *clausula*?

    What is a *substitute clausula*? What does it substitute for?

Music to Study

NAWM 17: Léonin, *Viderunt omnes,* organum duplum
 (second half of the twelfth century)

CD 1|57

NAWM 18: Clausulae on *Dominus,* from *Viderunt omnes*
 (late twelfth or early thirteenth century)

  18a. *Dominus,* clausula No. 26

CD 1|66

  18b. *Dominus,* clausula No. 29

CD 1|67

17. Léonin's setting of *Viderunt omnes* in NAWM 17 includes sections in both organum duplum and discant style. What are the main features of each style?

 organum duplum

 discant style

18. Which sections of Léonin's *Viderunt omnes* use organum style?

 Which sections use discant style? Why is discant used in these passages?

19. Which sections of NAWM 17 use no polyphony? Why are these sections not sung polyphonically?

20. In the substitute clausula No. 26 on *Dominus* (NAWM 18a), which rhythmic mode predominates in the upper voice? in the lower voice?

    upper voice _____   lower voice _____

    In substitute clausula No. 29 on *Dominus* (NAWM 18b), what rhythmic mode predominates in the upper voice? in the lower voice?

    upper voice _____   lower voice _____

21. In the two clausulae on *Dominus,* where do cadences occur? What vertical sonorities appear on the cadential note?

    How many times does each of these vertical sonorities appear on a downbeat?

    octave _____   perfect fifth _____   third _____   unison _____   other _____

22. Describe how the substitute clausulae (NAWM 18a and 18b) would be performed with Léonin's organum duplum on *Viderunt omnes* (NAWM 17).

23. What are the names for the various voices in an organum?

    bottom voice   _____

    second voice from the bottom   _____

    third voice from the bottom (if any)   _____

    fourth voice from the bottom (if any)   _____

    Which voice carries the chant?   _____

Music to Study

NAWM 19: Pérotin, *Viderunt omnes,* organum quadruplum
(late twelfth or early thirteenth century)

CD 2|1   CD 1|19

24. Compare the organum duplum on *Viderunt omnes* of Léonin in NAWM 17 with the organum quadruplum on the same chant by Pérotin in NAWM 19. How is Pérotin's style like Léonin's, and how is it different?

25. Why does Pérotin use rhythmic modes in the upper voices?

26. What vertical sonority is used most often at the cadences in *Viderunt omnes*?

27. Compare the upper voices of Pérotin's *Viderunt omnes* at longs 8–19. How are they related?

   What is this technique called?

Polyphonic Conductus (HWM 103, NAWM 20)

28. How is a polyphonic conductus like a monophonic conductus?

Music to Study

NAWM 20: *Ave virgo virginum,* conductus   CD 2|13
    (late twelfth or early thirteenth century)

29. In what ways is *Ave virgo virginum* (NAWM 20) typical of the polyphonic conductus, as described in HWM, p. 103?

How is it different from organum and from discant? How is it similar?

Motet (HWM 104–11, NAWM 21–22)

30. How did the motet originate, and how did it acquire its name?

31. What does the title of a motet indicate?

Music to Study

NAWM 21a: *Factum est salutare/Dominus,* motet
(thirteenth century)

[CD 2|14]

NAWM 21b: *Fole acostumance/Dominus,* motet
(thirteenth century)

[CD 2|15] [CD 1|23]

NAWM 21c: *Super te/Sed fulsit/Primus Tenor/Dominus,* motet
(thirteenth century)

[CD 2|17]

32. How are the motets in NAWM 21a, 21b, and 21c related to the discant clausulae in NAWM 18a and 18b? What has been added, deleted, or changed in creating these new works? What has stayed the same?

33. Describe the relationship between the text of the upper voice in *Factum est salutare/Dominus* (NAWM 21a) and the chant *Viderunt omnes* (NAWM 3d), on which the tenor is based. How do the words and sounds of the motet text relate to the chant text? How does the meaning of the motet text relate to the meaning of the original chant text? How does the motet text relate to the occasion (Mass for Christmas Day) on which this chant was originally sung?

34. How does *Fole acostumance/Dominus* (NAWM 21b) relate to *Factum est salutare/Dominus* and to the chant *Viderunt omnes,* musically and textually?

35. How does *Super te/Sed fulsit/Primus Tenor/Dominus* (NAWM 21c) compare to the other two motets in regard the form of its text, the way it was composed, and its musical characteristics?

36. What new notational system was devised to indicate rhythm in motets? How was it different from the notation for the rhythmic modes? Why was this change necessary, and what results did it have?

37. In what treatise was this notational system codified? Who wrote it, and when?

Music to Study

NAWM 22: Adam de la Halle, *De ma dame vient/* ⟨ CD 2|18 ⟩
Dieus, comment porroie/Omnes, motet in Franconian style
(ca. 1260s–80s)

38. What makes *De ma dame vient/Dieus, comment porroie/Omnes* (NAWM 22) a
Franconian motet, and how does it differ from earlier motets?

39. Describe the organization of the tenor in this motet.

40. Describe the relationship between the voices in this motet, including harmony,
counterpoint, and rhythm. How are cadences formed? How is the rhythmic interest
maintained? How do the rhythms used compare to the rhythmic modes?

English Polyphony (HWM 111–14, NAWM 21c, 23)

41. What are some distinctive characteristics of early English polyphony that set it
apart from early polyphony on the European continent?

42. What is a *rondellus,* and how does it work?

43. What is a *rota*?

Music to Study

NAWM 23: *Sumer is icumen in,* rota (ca. 1250)   (CD 2|21)   [CD 1|25]

44. *Sumer is icumen in* (NAWM 23) has traits of the *rondellus* and the *rota*. Which voices create the rondellus? the rota?

45. How is *Sumer is icumen in* different harmonically from Adam de la Halle's motet (NAWM 22)?

46. What other English traits does *Sumer is icumen in* exemplify?

A Polyphonic Tradition (HWM 114)

47. Summarize the most significant developments in music during the period between about 1050 and 1300 and their relevance to music today.

TERMS TO KNOW

Terms Related to Early Polphony

polyphony

counterpoint

harmony

composition

drone

organum

parallel organum

principal voice, organal voice

mixed parallel and oblique organum

free organum

Aquitanian polyphony

polyphonic versus

discant

florid organum

tenor (in florid organum, discant, and motet)

score notation

Terms Related to Notre Dame Polyphony

Notre Dame polyphony

ligatures

longs, breves

rhythmic modes

tempus (pl. *tempora*)

clausula (pl. *clausulae*)

substitute clausula

organum duplum

organum triplum

organum quadruplum

duplum, triplum, quadruplum

voice exchange

polyphonic conductus

cauda (pl. *caudae*)

Terms Related to the Thirteenth-Century Motet

motet

motetus

double motet, triple motet

cantus firmus

Franconian notation

perfection

Terms Related to English Polyphony

rondellus

rota

NAMES TO KNOW

Musica enchiriadis

Scolica enchiriadis

Winchester Troper

Ad organum faciendum

Notre Dame, Cathedral of Paris

Léonin

Pérotin

Magnus liber organi

Anonymous IV

Franco of Cologne

Ars cantus mensurabilis

Petrus de Cruce

Sumer is icumen in

REVIEW QUESTIONS

1. Make a timeline for the pieces discussed in this chapter, their composers (when known), Franco of Cologne, and the treatises *Musica enchiriadis, Scolica enchiriadis, Ad organum faciendum,* and *Ars cantus mensurabilis.*

2. What different forms of polyphony can be found between 1050 and 1300? Describe an example of each type.

3. Describe the music of Notre Dame polyphony. Include in your discussion the major composers, the genres they cultivated, the rhythmic and harmonic style of their music, and the way new pieces used, embellished, or substituted for existing music.

4. Write a passage in Notre Dame organum, following the model of Léonin's setting of the opening word "Viderunt" from *Viderunt omnes* (NAWM 17). For a tenor, use the opening "Alleluia" (just the first ten notes, up to the asterisk) from the *Alleluia Dies sanctificatus* (NAWM 3e) from the Mass for Christmas Day.

5. Write a passage in discant style, following the model of the two-voice discant clausulae on *Dominus* in NAWM 17, 18a, and 18b. For a tenor, use the seventeen notes to the word "Dies" in *Alleluia Dies sanctificatus* (NAWM 3e), laid out in a repeating rhythmic pattern derived from mode 5, as in NAWM 18a. In the duplum, use rhythmic patterns derived from mode 1 and 5 (*or* 2 and 5).

6. Trace the development of the motet from its origins through the end of the thirteenth century, using NAWM 21a, 21b, 21c, and 22 as examples of four stages in that development.

7. How did changing musical styles and changing notational practices for polyphonic music interrelate during the period 1050–1300?

8. Looking back over chapters 2 to 5, what developments during the period 1050–1300 were most significant for the later evolution of music? What styles, practices, techniques, attitudes, or approaches that were new in this time have continued to affect Western music in the last 700 years? In your opinion, which of these traits have made the music of the western European tradition different from music of other cultures?

Chapter 6 French and Italian Music
in the Fourteenth Century

CHAPTER OBJECTIVES

After you complete the reading, study of the music, and study questions for this chapter, you should be able to

1. explain the increased prominence of secular literature and music in the fourteenth century;

2. describe the notational innovations found in Ars Nova music;

3. describe some of the rhythmic and other stylistic features that characterize the music of the Ars Nova, Trecento, and Ars Subtilior;

4. describe isorhythm and its use in fourteenth-century motets and mass movements;

5. name and describe the forms of secular polyphonic song practiced in France and Italy during the fourteenth century; and

6. identify some of the major figures, works, and terms associated with music in the fourteenth century.

CHAPTER OUTLINE

I. Introduction (HWM 116)

In the fourteenth century, composers explored creative approaches to structure (including *isorhythm*), melody, harmony, rhythm, and meter.

II. European Society in the Fourteenth Century (HWM 116–20)

The fourteenth century saw economic troubles, famines, plague, and war. Composers responded to the disorder and discontent in society by emphasizing structure and pleasure in their music.

1. The Church in crisis
The authority of the Church was questioned and criticized, undermined by the move of the pope to Avignon (1305–77) and a schism between rival popes (1378–1417).

2. Science and secularism
   In the fourteenth century, people separated science from religion, reason and experience from faith.

3. The arts
   Through their works, writers and artists reflected daily life and people of all social classes more realistically than before.

4. Sacred and secular in music
   Composers in the fourteenth century focused on secular music, although the composition of sacred music remained strong.

5. *Roman de Fauvel*
   Typical of the period is the *Roman de Fauvel,* a satirical poem with interpolated music, including 34 motets, many with texts referring to contemporary events.

III. The Ars Nova in France (HWM 120–26, NAWM 24)

The music and teaching of *Philippe de Vitry* (1291–1361) introduced a new French style called the *Ars Nova* (1310s–1370s), named after the treatise *Ars nova* (New Art).

A. Ars Nova Notation
   The principal innovations of the Ars Nova are the use of duple as well as triple divisions of note values, smaller note values (*minims*), new meters, syncopation, and *mensuration signs.*

1. Arguments against the *Ars Nova*
   A written debate arose between opponents and supporters of the new art and reflected differences in what is valued in music.

Innovations: Writing Rhythm
   With Ars Nova notation, composers could write down rhythms that could not be notated in the thirteenth century. The long, breve, and semibreve could each be divided into either two or three of the next smaller note value. These divisions were called *mode, time,* and *prolation,* respectively; triple divisions were *perfect* and duple *imperfect* (for prolation, *major* and *minor,* respectively). The *minim* was a new note value, smaller than a semibreve. The four possible combinations of time and prolation produced four different meters, each indicated with a different *mensuration sign.* About 1425, noteheads began to be left open ("white notation") instead of being filled in. The resulting noteshapes evolved into modern notation (whole note, half note, and so on).

B. Isorhythm
   Philippe de Vitry used the device of *isorhythm* in his motets.

1. Talea and color
   The tenor of an isorhythmic motet is composed of a recurring rhythmic pattern, called the *talea,* and a recurring melodic pattern, called the *color.* The talea and color are not always the same length and can be combined in various ways. **Music: NAWM 24**

2. Isorhythm in upper voices

Upper voices may also be isorhythmic in whole or in part, to emphasize repeating rhythmic patterns in the tenor and give further unity and form to long compositions.

3. Audience

Isorhythmic motets were sung by and for people who understood and appreciated their structure.

C. Hocket

The technique *hocket,* in which voices rapidly alternate, each resting while the other sings, was often used in fourteenth-century isorhythmic works.

D. Harmonic practice

Imperfect consonances were used more often in Ars Nova style than in thirteenth-century music, but they still resolved to perfect consonances, and parallel fifths and octaves were still permitted.

IV. Guillaume de Machaut (HWM 126–32, NAWM 25–26)

Guillaume de Machaut (ca. 1300–1377) was the leading composer and poet of the French Ars Nova.

Biography: Guillaume de Machaut

Machaut spent most of his career working for royalty, including kings of Bohemia, Navarre, and France. We know about him because of his poetry; he wrote about himself, his patrons, and significant events. Machaut made a special effort to organize his works and preserve them for future generations. He was the first composer to do so. With the help of patrons, he prepared several illuminated manuscripts of his works, an expensive and time-consuming undertaking.

A. Motets

Machaut composed isorhythmic motets that are more structurally complex than Vitry's.

B. Mass

Machaut's *La Messe de Nostre Dame* (The Mass of Our Lady) is probably the first polyphonic setting of the Mass Ordinary to be written by a single composer and conceived as a unit.

1. Polyphonic settings of the Ordinary

Fourteenth-century composers set Ordinary texts as individual movements. Machaut, however, linked the six movements by similarities in compositional style and approach. His mass is set for four voices: triplum, duplum, tenor, and *contratenor*.

2. Isorhythmic movements

The Kyrie, Sanctus, Agnus Dei, and Ite, missa est are isorhythmic. The tenor carries a cantus firmus and, with the contratenor, forms the harmonic foundation. Both the tenor and contratenor are isorhythmic. **Music: NAWM 25**

3. Discant-style movements

The Gloria and Credo are in the style of discant: mostly syllabic, with the four voices declaiming the long text together.

C. Monophonic Songs

Machaut's monophonic French songs continued the trouvère tradition.

1. Virelais

The *virelai,* one of the *formes fixes* (fixed forms), is usually in the form A bba A bba A bba. All the *formes fixes* have patterns of repetition, including a refrain.

D. Polyphonic Songs

Unlike the motet, in which the tenor provides structure and was written first, in polyphonic *chansons* (songs) the *cantus* or *treble* (the top part) is the principal line and was written first. This is called *treble-dominated style.*

1. *Formes fixes*

The virelai, *ballade,* and *rondeau* are *formes fixes.* Although the *formes fixes* were traditionally associated with dancing, Machaut's polyphonic chansons in *formes fixes* genres were not.

2. Ballades

Ballades consist of three stanzas, each sung to the same music (in the form aab) and each ending with a refrain.

3. Rondeaux

The rondeau has the form ABaAabAB, with a refrain in two sections (A and B), the first repeating in the middle of the stanza. The stanza uses the same two sections of music as the refrain, a and b, but with different words. **Music: NAWM 26**

E. Reputation

Machaut was influential on composers and poets during and after his life, but a lack of sources for music of his time leaves his true place in history unclear.

V. The Ars Subtilior (HWM 132–35, NAWM 27)

In the later fourteenth century at courts in southern France and northern Italy, composers developed the Ars Nova style to a height of complexity and intricacy. Music historians call this music *Ars Subtilior.*

1. Rhythmic complexity

Composers tested the limits of Ars Nova notation with syncopations, different meters in different voices, and rhythmic disjunction. **Music: NAWM 27**

2. A limited and brief fashion

Ars Subtilior music was intended for professional performers and cultivated listeners. A simpler and more influential style flourished at the same time in northern France.

VI. Italian Trecento Music (HWM135–41, NAWM 28–30)

1. Social roles for Italian music
   In the *Trecento* (Italian for the 1300s), music accompanied almost every aspect of Italian social life, but most music was not written down.

2. Italian secular polyphony
   The largest surviving repertory of Italian music from the Trecento is secular polyphonic songs for elite audiences in northern Italian cities.

3. Italian notation
   In Italian Trecento music, the breve can be divided into variety of equal or unequal groupings, resulting in florid melodic lines.

4. Squarcialupi Codex
   The richly decorated *Squarcialupi Codex* contains 354 pieces for two or three voices from the 1300s and early 1400s and was probably copied about 1410–15.

A. The Fourteenth-Century Madrigal
   The fourteenth-century *madrigal* (not to be confused with the sixteenth-century form) is for two or three voices without instruments. It has two or more three-line stanzas, all set to the same music, with a closing pair of lines called the *ritornello,* set to new music in a different meter. **Music: NAWM 28**

B. The Caccia
   The *caccia* (in fashion about 1345–70) features two voices in canon at the unison. The texts are often about hunting or other animated scenes. **Music: NAWM 29**

C. The Ballata
   The *ballata* (from *ballare,* "to dance") evolved from monophonic dance songs with choral refrains. The form of the polyphonic ballata of the late fourteenth century is AbbaA, resembling a single stanza of the French virelai.

D. Francesco Landini
   Francesco Landini (ca. 1325–1397) was the leading Italian composer of the fourteenth century. He is best known for his 140 ballate for two or three voices. Most lines of the poem are set with melismas on the first and next-to-last syllables. Many cadences use the "under-third" cadence, also known as the "Landini cadence."   **Music: NAWM 30**

Biography: Francesco Landini
   Landini was from northern Italy and was a brilliant performer on the portative organ who first learned his art after being blinded by disease at a young age. Written accounts attest to his great skill. He worked at a monastery and then a church, yet no sacred music by him survives, and he is known for his secular songs.

E. French Influence
   Italian composers began to absorb aspects of the French style in the fourteenth century, and in the fifteenth century, northern composers and musicians began to settle in Italy and an international style developed.

VI. Fourteenth-Century Music in Performance (HWM 141–44)

A. Voices and Instruments

In the fourteenth and early fifteenth centuries, polyphonic music could be performed by a small group of voices or instruments or a combination of the two.

B. Instruments

1. *Haut* and *bas*

Instruments were classified as loud (*haut* or "high") or soft (*bas* or "low"). Low instruments include the harp, vielle, lute, psaltery, portative organ, transverse flute, and recorder. High instruments include shawms, *cornetts,* and trumpets. Percussion was used with instruments of both kinds.

2. Keyboard instruments

Portative organs, positive organs, and larger organs (with pedal keyboards and *stops*) were used more widely beginning in the fourteenth century.

C. Instrumental Music

Little purely instrumental music survives from the fourteenth century. What does survive includes keyboard arrangements of vocal works and some dances.

D. Musica Ficta

Performers often altered notes chromatically, a practice known as *musica ficta* ("feigned music," notes lying outside the standard gamut). The alterations were made to avoid tritones or to create smoother lines.

1. Cadences

At cadences, a sixth expanding to an octave should be major and a third contracting to a unison should be minor. A three-voice cadence in which the upper voices are raised is called a *double leading-tone cadence.* In a *Phrygian cadence,* the lowest voice descends a half-step; no chromatic alterations are needed, since the intervals are already the right size.

2. Omission of accidentals in notation

Composers and scribes tended not to write in accidentals, leaving it up to the performers to judge where they were needed. Modern editors suggest where changes should be made by indicating accidentals above notes.

VI. Echoes of the New Art (HWM 145)

The fourteenth century is characterized by an increased interest in the individual, growing emphasis on secular music, greater diversity in rhythm, more use of imperfect consonances, musica ficta, and treble-dominated style, all of which continued in the music of the Renaissance. Music from the Ars Nova fell out of favor in the fifteenth century but in recent decades has been revived and performed regularly.

STUDY QUESTIONS

European Society in the Fourteenth Century (HWM 116–20)

1. What currents in religion, philosophy, politics, and literature helped to make the fourteenth century a secular age?

2. What is the *Roman de Fauvel*? When was it written? What music does it contain?

The Ars Nova in France (HWM 120–26, NAWM 24)

3. What does the Latin phrase *ars nova* mean? _____

   How do we use the term now?

4. Briefly describe fourteenth-century French notation. What are the divisions of the long, breve, and semibreve called? What are the four prolations, and how do they correspond to modern meters?

5. How is the tenor of an isorhythmic motet constructed? What are the names of the elements that repeat?

Music to Study

NAWM 24: Philippe de Vitry, *In arboris/Tuba sacre fidei/*   ⌈ CD 2|22 ⌉
Virgo sum, motet (ca. 1320)

6. What is Vitry's motet *In arboris/Tuba sacre fide/Virgo sum* (NAWM 24) about? What does each text say, and how do the texts relate to each other?

7. How does this motet illustrate the innovations of Ars Nova notation?

8. Write out the color of this motet as a series of note names (C G A, and so forth).

How many notes does the color contain? _____

How many times is the color stated in the motet? _____

9. Write out the talea of this motet as a series of durations. Include the rests. To make it easier to follow the rhythm, reduce the value of each note or rest to a third of its value, so that a dotted whole note becomes a half note, a dotted half note becomes a quarter note, and so on. In this notation, the first note would be a whole note, the second a half note, and so on.

   How many notes does the talea contain? _____

   How many times is the talea stated in the motet? _____

   How is the talea altered after the midpoint of the motet?

   In this motet, how are the talea and color coordinated? How does this give form to the motet?

10. How does the tenor of this piece compare in its structure with those of the motets in NAWM 21a–c and 22? In what ways is it structured according to similar ideas, and in what ways is it more complex?

11. What is *hocket*? Where (in which measures) is it used in this motet? Aside from the use of hocket, what do these passages have in common?

12. Where in this Vitry motet (in which measures) can you find parallel octaves between the voices?

Where can you find parallel fifths between the voices?

Where can you find a double leading-tone cadence (defined and illustrated on HWM, p. 144)?

13. Describe the context in which this motet was most likely performed. How is it different from or similar to likely performance contexts for NAWM 21a–c?

Guillaume de Machaut (HWM 126–32, NAWM 25–26)

14. Briefly describe Guillaume de Machaut's career. Where did he live, whom did he serve, and what did he do?

Music to Study

NAWM 25: Guillaume de Machaut, *La Messe de Nostre Dame* ⸢ CD 2|28 ⸣ ⸢ CD 1|26 ⸣
(Mass of Our Lady, ca. 1364), excerpt: Kyrie

15. What is *La Messe de Nostre Dame*? What is so special about it? How does it differ
from cycles of Ordinary chants (see HWM, p. 64)?

Which movements are isorhythmic?

What other style is used, and in what movements? Why is it appropriate for these
movements?

16. The tenor in Machaut's Kyrie is the second line from the bottom and is the plainchant *Kyrie Cunctipotens Genitor* (NAWM 3b). Note how the mass tenor follows
the pitches of the original chant.

Where do repetitions occur in the chant melody (NAWM 3b)?

How does the form of Machaut's Kyrie (NAWM 25) as performed on the recording follow the form of the chant melody? (Hint: This is more apparent in performance than in notation.)

17. Write out the talea for the Kyrie I (include rests). _____

How many measures long (in this modern transcription) is this talea? _____

How many times is it stated? _____

To what extent are the other three voices isorhythmic? For each voice, indicate in what measures exact or near-exact isorhythm occurs.

contratenor

duplum

triplum

Write out the talea for the Christe (include rests). _____

How many measures long (in this modern transcription) is this talea? _____

How many times is it stated? _____

To what extent are the other three voices isorhythmic? For each voice, in what measures exact or nearly exact rhythmic repetition occurs.

contratenor

duplum

triplum

18. Diagram the form of the three *formes fixes,* using letters to indicate musical repetitions and capital letters to show the refrains.

virelai _____   ballade _____   rondeau _____

19. How does the fourteenth-century rondeau resemble *Robins m'aime* (NAWM 10) by the thirteenth-century trouvère Adam de la Halle?

Music to Study

NAWM 26: Guillaume de Machaut, *Rose, liz, printemps, verdure,* [CD 2|35] [CD 1|33]
rondeau (mid-fourteenth century)

20. Note the rondeau form in your answer to question 19. Which measures in the music of *Rose, liz, printemps, verdure* (NAWM 26) correspond to each letter of your diagram?

How do the rhymes in the poetry coordinate with this form?

How do the cadences help to delineate the form?

21. In this rondeau, what relation does the music in mm. 32–37 have to music heard previously? How does this help to delineate the form?

22. Describe the melodic and rhythmic style of the two upper parts of this rondeau—the triplum and the cantus. How do these compare to the upper parts of Adam de la Halle's motet in NAWM 22 and to Adam's monophonic rondeau in NAWM 10? Describe what is distinctive about Marchaut's style, as compared with melodies of the late thirteenth century.

23. How does Machaut's Kyrie compare to his rondeau *Rose, liz, printemps, verdure* (NAWM 26)? How do the upper two voices of each piece compare in melodic and rhythmic style?

The Ars Subtilior (HWM 132–35, NAWM 27)

24. What are the special traits of the late-fourteenth-century Ars Subtilior, particularly in the realm of rhythm?

Music to Study

NAWM 27: Johannes Ciconia, *Sus une fontayne,* virelai (ca. 1400) 〔 CD 2|39 〕

25. How does Johannes Ciconia's virelai *Sus une fontayne* (NAWM 27) resemble Machaut's rondeau (NAWM 26), and how is it different in style? What aspects of the Ciconia link it to the Ars Subtilior?

26. Which measures in the music of *Sus une fontayne* (NAWM 27) correspond to each letter of your virelai form diagram from question 18? How do cadences help to delineate the form?

Italian Trecento Music (HWM 135–41, NAWM 28–30)

27. How is Italian Trecento notation different from Ars Nova notation?

Music to Study

NAWM 28: Jacopo da Bologna, *Fenice fù,* madrigal (ca. 1360) [CD 2|42]

NAWM 29: Gherardello da Firenze, *Tosto che l'alba,* caccia [CD 2|44]
(mid-fourteenth century)

NAWM 30: Francesco Landini, *Non avrà ma' pietà,* ballata [CD 2|46] [CD 1|37]
(second half of fourteenth century)

28. What is a fourteenth-century madrigal? Describe the type of poetry used, the poetic form, the form of the piece, and the melodic style, and show how Jacopo da Bologna's *Fenice fù* (NAWM 28) exemplifies these traits.

29. How does the melodic style of *Fenice fù* differ from that of Machaut's rondeau (NAWM 26)?

30. What is a caccia? Describe its melodic style and the type of poetry used. Show how Gherardello da Firenze's *Tosto che l'alba* (NAWM 29) exemplifies these traits.

31. Compare the poetic and musical forms of the fourteenth-century madrigal (NAWM 28) and the caccia (NAWM 29). How are they similar? How are they different? How do they differ from the rondeau and the virelai?

32. In a ballata, what is the *ripresa*? What measures of Landini's *Non avrà ma' pietà* (NAWM 30) correspond to this part of the form?

    What are the *piedi* and *volta*? Where do these appear in Landini's ballata?

    How is the form of a ballata similar to that of a virelai? How is it different?

33. What is an under-third cadence? Where do cadences of this type appear in Landini's ballata?

34. Compare the melodic, rhythmic, and harmonic style of Landini's ballata to that of Machaut's rondeau (NAWM 26). Where do melismas occur in each piece, and how is the composers' practice similar or different in this respect? What other similarities and differences do you observe?

35. What are *partial signatures*? Which pieces studied in this chapter use them?

Fourteenth-Century Music in Performance (HWM 141–44)

36. What combinations of voices and instruments were possible in performing secular polyphonic songs in the fourteenth century?

37. What types of instruments were in use in the 1300s? What are *haut* ("high") and *bas* ("low") instruments?

38. What is *musica ficta*? Under what circumstances is it used, and why? Why were accidentals not written down?

39. The editor has suggested where musica ficta should be applied in Jacopo da Bologna's *Fenice fù* (NAWM 28) by placing accidentals above certain notes. Using the rules given by Prosdocimo de' Beldomandi (see HWM, p. 143) and summarized in HWM, pp. 142–44, explain why the editor has suggested each of these alterations.

m. 15, third beat _____

m. 15, fourth beat _____

m. 17 _____

Echoes of the New Art (HWM 145)

40. What characteristics distinguish fourteenth-century music from music of earlier periods? What traits continued in music of the Renaissance or later periods?

TERMS TO KNOW

Terms Related to Ars Nova Music

Ars Nova

mode, time, prolation

perfect (major), imperfect (minor)

minim

mensuration sign

isorhythm

color (pl. colores)

talea (pl. taleae)

hocket

contratenor

formes fixes

virelai

rondeau (pl. rondeaux)

ballade

chansons

cantus, treble

treble-dominated style

Terms Related to Ars Subtilior Music and Trecento Music

Ars Subtilior

Trecento

madrigal (fourteenth-century)

ritornello

caccia

ballata

Terms Related to Performance and Instruments

haut and bas instruments

cornett

stops (on organ)

musica ficta

double leading-tone cadence

Phrygian cadence

NAMES TO KNOW

Roman de Fauvel

Philippe de Vitry

Ars nova

Guillaume de Machaut

La Messe de Nostre Dame

Squarcialupi Codex

Francesco Landini

REVIEW QUESTIONS

1. Make a timeline for the pieces, composers, and treatises discussed in this chapter.

2. What is new about the Ars Nova? How does it compare to thirteenth-century music? How does late-fourteenth-century French music (the Ars Subtilior) extend the ideas of the Ars Nova?

3. Describe isorhythm as practiced in Vitry's motets and Machaut's mass.

4. Write a short textless isorhythmic piece in three voices, in 6/8, modeled on the style and procedures of Vitry's *In arboris/Tuba sacre fidei/Virgo sum* (NAWM 24) and the Kyrie from Machaut's Mass (NAWM 25). Follow these steps:

   a. For the color in the tenor, use the fourteen notes on "hodie" in the *Alleluia Dies sanctificatus* (NAWM 3e) from the Mass for Christmas Day. Devise a talea of seven notes and one to four rests, using only notes and rests that are one or two longs (dotted half notes) in length; the 6/8 measures should be laid out in groups of two. Using this color and talea, write out the tenor.

    b. Write a duplum above the tenor, using only quarter, eighth, dotted quarter, and dotted half notes (and rests). Write it as a series of phrases separated by rests, making sure that all sonorities on downbeats are constant and that the beginnings and ends of phrases form perfect consonances with the tenor. Do not cross below the tenor. Avoid resting during rests in the tenor.

    c. Add a triplum in the same style as the duplum or slightly more florid. It can cross below the duplum but not below the tenor. Avoid resting during rests in the other voices. Make sure that all sonorities on downbeats are consonant and that phrases end on perfect consonances.

5. Name and describe the forms of secular song practiced in France and Italy during the fourteenth century. How are French and Italian music similar? How do they differ?

6. Describe the melodic, rhythmic, and harmonic style of Machaut. How do the works of Vitry, Ciconia, Jacopo da Bologna, Ghirardello da Firenze, and Landini resemble or differ from those of Machaut in melodic, rhythmic, and harmonic style? What features do they all share?

Chapter 7 The Age of the Renaissance

CHAPTER OBJECTIVES

After you complete the reading, study of the music, and study questions for this chapter, you should be able to

1. describe some aspects of the influence of humanism on the culture and music of the fifteenth and sixteenth centuries;
2. name some of the most significant theorists and treatises of the time and explain their importance;
3. describe the beginnings and early development of music printing and its effects on musical life; and
4. describe the characteristics that distinguish Renaissance music from music of earlier periods.

CHAPTER OUTLINE

I. Introduction (HWM 148–49)

The *Renaissance* ("rebirth") was a time of great change as well as a strengthening of practices from the Middle Ages. Some musical developments from this period include an international style, two principal textures (imitative counterpoint and homophony), new focus on correct declamation of text and on reflecting its meaning and emotion, music printing, amateur music-making, and reformation of the Church.

II. The Renaissance in Culture and Art (HWM 149–54)

In this history of Western music, we will define the span of the Renaissance as fifteenth and sixteenth centuries, while realizing that some of its characteristics were developing much earlier.

A. Europe in the Renaissance
    During the Renaissance, Europe became a world power by establishing trade with and colonies in other lands.

1. Economy and society
Economic growth brought increasing prosperity to rulers, cities, and citizens of differing social classes, all of whom were important in supporting music.

B. Humanism
Ancient Greek and Roman writings were rediscovered and translated in the Renaissance. *Humanism* emphasized the study of these works and the development of the individual's mind.

C. Renaissance Art and Architecture

1. Classical models, beauty, and naturalism
Renaissance artists and architects imitated classical models, the ideal of beauty, and naturalism. They also developed techniques for realistic representation.

2. Perspective and chiaroscuro
Painters developed techniques for realistic representations of three-dimensional scenes through perspective and chiaroscuro (treatment of light and shade)

3. Clarity and classical models in architecture
Renaissance architecture emphasized clarity, symmetry, and structure, imitating ancient architecture.

4. Interest in individuals
During the Renaissance, patrons were increasingly interested in being memorialized in artwork, and artists sought to capture the individual personality of each subject.

5. Musical parallels
Composers also emphasized contrast and clarity in their music, and increasingly they developed individuality in style.

III. The Musical Renaissance (HWM 155–63)

Some aspects of music in the Renaissance were influenced by intellectual and artistic trends, yet others were newly created in reinterpreting ancient ideals.

A. Patronage and Cosmopolitan Musicians
New musical institutions and enhanced support for musicians led to a flowering of music.

1. Court chapels
Court *chapels* were groups of salaried musicians and clerics who were associated with an individual rather than an institution.

2. Training musicians
Most Renaissance composers were trained at choir schools and usually had other jobs outside of music.

3. Patronage for music
In the Renaissance, Italy provided many patrons, including royalty, ruling families, and religious figures.

4. Cosmopolitan musicians
Because many composers served patrons in a variety of geographical lo-
cations, they were exposed to a variety of musical styles.

5. International style, new national styles
In the fifteenth century, an international musical style developed, and in
the sixteenth century, new national song styles emerged.

B. The New Counterpoint
The fifteenth-century international style was based on a new counterpoint in which thirds and sixths were consonant, and strict control of dissonance was essential.

1. Johannes Tinctoris
Johannes Tinctoris (1435–1511) explained rules for using dissonance in
his treatise *Liber de arte contrapuncti* (A Book on the Art of Counterpoint, 1477). Dissonances were limited to passing and neighbor tones on
unstressed beats and suspensions at cadences, and parallel octaves and
fifths were forbidden. These rules were further refined by *Gioseffo
Zarlino* (1577–1590) in *Le istitutioni harmoniche* (The Harmonic Foun-
dations, 1558).

C. New Compositional Methods and Textures
Musical styles and textures changed during the Renaissance.

1. Equality of voices
During the second half of the fifteenth century, composers moved away
from counterpoint of lines around a structural voice (tenor or cantus) and
toward greater equality of voices.

2. Imitation and homophony
In *imitative counterpoint,* voices *imitate* a motive or phrase in another
voice. In *homophony,* all voices move together in essentially the same
rhythm.

D. Tuning and Temperament
Theorists had to develop new theories and tuning systems for dealing
with thirds and sixths, which were now treated as consonances in music.

1. Pythagorean intonation
In *Pythagorean intontation,* fourths and fifths were perfectly tuned, but
thirds and sixths were out of tune.

2. Just intonation
In *just intonation,* most thirds and sixths in a diatonic scale were perfectly tuned.

3. Temperaments
Temperaments adjusted pitches so all intervals were usable. Two examples are *mean-tone temperament* and *equal temperament.* The new tuning systems reflected the humanist insistence on pleasing the ear.

E. Reawakened interest in Greek theory
The Renaissance brought the discovery and translation of Greek writings
on music.

1. Franchino Gaffurio
   Franchino Gaffurio (1451–1522) incorporated Greek ideals and theory into his very influential treatises on music theory.
2. Heinrich Glareanus
   Heinrich Glareanus (1488–1563) added four new modes (authentic and plagal modes on A and C) to the eight earlier modes in his book *Dodeka-chordon* (The Twelve-String Lyre, 1547).

F. New Applications of Greek Ideas
   People in the Renaissance applied Greek ideas about music to music of their own time.

1. Music as social accomplishment
   Gentlemen and ladies were expected to know the basics of making music for the purpose of entertaining one another.
2. Words and music
   Renaissance composers were concerned with reflecting in their music the syntax, punctuation, and natural accentuation of the texts they set.
3. Emotion and expression
   By the late fifteenth century, composers used particular intervals, sonorities, melodic shapes, and other techniques to dramatize the content and convey the feelings of the text.
4. Power of the modes
   In the Renaissance, each of the modes was thought to convey certain emotions.
5. Chromaticism
   In the mid-sixteenth century, composers began to use direct chromatic motion, inspired by the Greek chromatic genus.

G. Music Printing and Distribution
   Music printing allowed for wider dissemination of written music to a broader public, encouraging the growth of musical literacy.

1. Effects of music printing
   Innovation in music printing allowed for uniformity of multiple copies, lower prices, growing numbers of amateur musicians, high demand for new music, and growth in popular styles.

Innovations: Music Printing
   Printing allowed wider distribution of music at a lower cost with greater accuracy and less time spent recopying by hand, creating the first true market for music as a commodity. Johann Gutenberg perfected the art of printing words from movable type in 1450, and by the 1470s books of chant were being printed the same way. *Ottaviano Petrucci* (1466–1539) of Venice was the first to print polyphonic music from movable type in 1501, using a triple-impression process (for the staff lines, for the notes, and for the text) to create beautiful, clear collections of music. Petrucci obtained a "privilege" that gave him exclusive rights to printing music in Venice for twenty years. The single-impression process used by *Pierre*

Attaingnant (ca. 1494–1551/52) was less expensive but also less elegant. Most ensemble music was published as *partbooks,* with a separate bound volume for each voice or instrumental part.

IV. Music as a Renaissance Art (HWM 163–66)

The musical language of the Renaissance lasted for generations and provided the foundation for the treatment of dissonance, consonance, voice leading, and text setting in most later styles. This time period also continues to shape expectations of listeners who believe that music should convey emotion or appeal to a broad audience.

STUDY QUESTIONS

The Renaissance in Culture and Art (HWM 149–54)

1. Renaissance means "rebirth" in French. What ideas were reborn during the Renaissance and where did they originate? How did people in the Renaissance learn about these ideas?

2. How did political stability and economic growth in Europe affect developments in music?

3. What is *humanism*? What was its role in Renaissance intellectual life? What aspects of music did it influence, and how was its influence manifested?

The Musical Renaissance (HWM 155–63)

4. How was patronage in the Renaissance similar to and different from patronage in the Middle Ages?

5. How were professional musicians educated in the Renaissance? What circumstances limited musical training and careers for women?

6. Why did Italy provide an ideal ground for Renaissance humanism as a movement?

7. What circumstances fostered the development of the international musical style of the late fifteenth and sixteenth centuries?

8. What new elements of harmony, counterpoint, and texture distinguish music of the Renaissance from medieval music?

9. Why did Pietro Aaron consider it important to compare all the parts at once (see Source Reading, HWM, p. 159)? How does this practice differ from that of fourteenth-century composers such as Machaut?

10. Why was the traditional Pythagorean tuning no longer ideal for Renaissance music? What other tuning options were developed?

11. Who were four of the most important theorists of the late fifteenth and sixteenth centuries, and what were their contributions?

12. What ancient Greek ideas about music were revived in the Renaissance, and what were the effects on Renaissance music and musical life?

13. What were the new approaches to text-setting in music of the Renaissance? How do these approaches embody ideals of humanism?

14. When did printing of polyphonic music from movable type begin? _____

    Who was the first printer to use this technique, and where was he active?

    _____   _____

    What was the name of his first publication? _____

    What kind of music did it contain? _____

    Describe the usual format for printing ensemble music in the sixteenth century.

    What impact did printing have on the dissemination of musical works?

Music as a Renaissance Art (HWM 163–66)

15. What elements of musical style, music theory, and musical thought from the Renaissance continue to influence music today?

TERMS TO KNOW

Renaissance

humanism

court chapels

imitative counterpoint

imitate

homophony

Pythagorean intonation

just intonation

temperaments

mean-tone temperament

equal temperament

partbooks

NAMES TO KNOW

Johannes Tinctoris

Gioseffo Zarlino,

    Le istitutioni harmoniche

Franchino Gaffurio

Heinrich Glareanus, *Dodekachordon*

Ottaviano Petrucci

Pierre Attaingnant

REVIEW QUESTIONS

1. Make a timeline for the fifteenth and sixteenth centuries and place on it the people and treatises discussed in this chapter. Leave plenty of space for additions in later chapters.
2. Define humanism as a movement in the Renaissance, and explain how it was reflected in the culture, arts, and music of the time.
3. What elements of Renaissance music and musical life reflect the influence of ancient Greek ideas, directly or indirectly?
4. Describe the differences between sixteenth-century music and fourteenth-century music in respect to counterpoint, compositional methods, tuning, and setting of texts.
5. Trace the early history of music printing, describing the variety of printing methods, the important publishers, and the effects music printing had on musical life.

Chapter 8   England and Burgundy in
the Fifteenth Century

CHAPTER OBJECTIVES

After you complete the reading, study of the music, and study questions for this chapter, you should be able to

1. describe genres practiced in England during the fifteenth century;

2. explain how English music influenced music on the Continent during the fifteenth century;

3. explain how an international musical style developed in the mid-fifteenth century and the historical and cultural circumstances that placed Burgundian composers at the center of these developments;

4. describe the music of Burgundian composers, particularly Binchois and Du Fay, and explain the differences between their musical practices and those of the fourteenth century; and

5. describe techniques used by fifteenth-century composers to unify the polyphonic mass cycle.

CHAPTER OUTLINE

I. Introduction (HWM 167)

In the fifteenth century, English music influenced Continental composers in the development of an international musical style and the polyphonic mass cycle. John Dunstable, Guillaume Du Fay, and Binchois were important composers from this time.

II. English Music (HWM 167–75, NAWM 31–32)

Throughout the Middle Ages, England had political and artistic ties with France.

1. The contenance angloise

   Continental composers noticed that English music sounded different from their own, with frequent harmonic thirds and sixths, often in parallel motion, resulting in pervasive consonance. Poet Martin le Franc called this English quality the *contenance angloise.*

A. Polyphony on Latin Texts

   To embellish chant, English composers would add a voice a fourth above the chant and one a third below, producing parallel § sonorities. The lower voice opens to a fifth at cadences and other points for variety, but parallel fifths are avoided.

   1. Faburden

      Faburden was an English practice of improvised polyphony that produced parallel § sonorities, resolving to octaves and fifths at cadences.

   2. Cantilena, motet, and Mass Ordinary

      The English preference for thirds and sixths was also evident in the genres *cantilena,* motet, and settings of Mass Ordinary texts.

B. The Carol

   The fifteenth-century carol is a setting of a religious poem in English or Latin (or a mixture of both), often about the Christmas season, with a recurring *burden,* or refrain, and a series of stanzas.   **Music: NAWM 31**

C. John Dunstable

   John Dunstable (ca. 1390–1453) was one of the leading English composers of the first half of the fifteenth century. He wrote in all the prevailing types of polyphony.

   1. Three-voice sacred works

      Dunstable is best known for his three-voice sacred works. They use a variety of techniques. Some have a cantus firmus in the tenor. Others *paraphrase* a chant in the top voice, ornamenting the chant with rhythm and added notes. Dunstable also composed sacred works not based on chant. **Music: NAWM 32**

Biography: John Dunstable [Dunstaple]

   Dunstable was a mathematician, astronomer, and musician. He served several noble and royal patrons in England and probably France. He is noted as the English composer who most influenced Continental composers, and his music is found chiefly in Continental manuscripts.

D. Redefining the Motet

   In the fifteenth century, the isorhythmic motet waned in popularity. The term *motet* was eventually applied to a polyphonic setting of a Latin text other than the Mass Ordinary.

E. The English Influence

   Continental composers incorporated traits of English music into their own, including homorhythmic textures, third and sixth sonorities, and greater equality of voices.

III. Music in the Burgundian Lands (HWM 175–80, NAWM 33)

In the fifteenth century, musicians connected to Burgundian courts helped to develop an international musical style.

A. The Duchy of Burgundy

Most of the leading composers of the late fifteenth century came from lands controlled by the duke of *Burgundy*, mainly from modern-day Belgium and northeastern France.

1. Burgundian chapel and minstrels

The dukes of Burgundy maintained one of the largest chapels, comprising about two dozen singers. They also hired minstrels.

Music in Context: The Feast of the Oath of the Pheasant

Burgundian duke Philip the Good assembled hundreds of nobles for a banquet called The Feast of the Oath of the Pheasant in Lille on June 17, 1454. It was a lavish affair with religious meaning, showcasing food, music, dance, and characters in costume, all meant to show support for the eastern Church after the fall of Constantinople.

B. Cosmopolitan Style

An increased trade across the Continent and the movement of musicians from court to court fostered a common musical style.

C. Genres and Texture

The main polyphonic genres in the mid-fifteenth century were secular chansons with French texts, motets, Magnificats, and settings of the Mass Ordinary. Most pieces were for three voices, with the main melody usually in the cantus, and with larger ranges for each voice than in the previous century.

D. Binchois and the Burgundian Chanson

In the fifteenth century, chanson was the term for any polyphonic setting of a French secular poem. Most chansons were in the form of the rondeau.

1. Binchois's chansons

Binchois (c. 1400–1460) served the Burgundian court chapel for most of his career. He was best known for his chansons. **Music: NAWM 33**

2. Meter and rhythm

Triple meter and compound meters were more common than duple meter at this time. Binchois varied the rhythm from measure to measure and sometimes used *hemiola*.

3. Music and text

Burgundian chansons are mostly syllabic with melismas on only the most important cadences.

4. Melody and counterpoint

The main melody is conjunct and in the cantus, while the tenor line is slower and the contratenor uses skips and leaps.

5. Cadences

The traditional sixth-to-octave cadence between tenor and cantus was sometimes harmonized with a contratenor that leapt up an octave from a fifth below the tenor to a fifth above the tenor's note of resolution, creating a sound similar to a modern dominant-tonic cadence.

Biography: Binchois [Gilles de Bins]

Binchois worked in the chapel of Philip the Good and was one of its key musical figures. He had direct contact with English musicians, and his music incorporates English influences.

IV. Guillaume Du Fay (HWM 180–84, NAWM 34–36a)

Guillaume Du Fay (ca. 1397–1474) was the most famous composer of his time, and his music represents well the international style of the mid-fifteenth century.

Biography: Guillaume Du Fay [Dufay]

Du Fay was born near Brussels and studied at the Cambrai cathedral school. He served powerful and rich patrons in major cities in Italy and Savoy in the 1420s and 1430s, went back to Cambrai, returned to Savoy in the 1450s, and finished his career at Cambrai, making him a truly international composer. He maintained continuous employment even during heated political and religious crises. His music was still being imitated one hundred years after his death.

A. Chansons and the International Style

Du Fay's ballade *Resvellies vous* (1423) blends French and Italian characteristics. A later chanson, *Se la face ay pale* (1430s), illustrates the international style, blending the tuneful consonances, brief phrases, and mostly syllabic text-setting of English music with the melismas, syncopation, and varied rhythms of French style and the melodic lyricism of Italian style. **Music: NAWM 34 and 36a**

B. Motets and Chant Settings

Motets in this period were often written in the style of the chanson, with the main melody (often paraphrased from chant) in the treble, supported by the tenor and contratenor.

1. Fauxbourdon

Fauxbourdon is a technique (probably inspired by faburden) in which two notated voices move mostly in parallel sixths, resolving to an octave at cadences, while a third unwritten part is sung a fourth below the cantus, producing parallel $\frac{6}{3}$ sonorities. **Music: NAWM 35**

2. Isorhythmic motets

Du Fay and his contemporaries still wrote isorhythmic motets for ceremonial events.

V. The Polyphonic Mass (HWM 184–89, NAWM 36b)

In the fifteenth century, it became standard practice for composers to set the Mass Ordinary texts as a coherent whole, thus creating a *mass* (or polyphonic mass cycle).

A. Mass Cycles
Composers in the fifteenth century used a variety of means to link the separate sections of a mass to each other.

1. Stylistic coherence
One technique was to use the same general style for all five movements.

2. Plainsong mass
A composer could write a *plainsong mass* by basing each movement on an existing chant for that text.

3. Motto mass
A *motto mass* uses a *head-motive* to begin each of the mass movements.

B. Cantus-Firmus Mass
Another way to link movements was to write a *cantus-firmus mass,* or *tenor mass.* In the cantus-firmus mass, the cantus firmus was usually placed in the tenor in long notes and treated in isorhythmic fashion. The cantus firmus could be taken from a chant, a secular song, or the tenor of a polyphonic chanson. One secular tune frequently used as a tenor was *L'homme armé.* Some composers borrowed material from more than one voice of the polyphonic chanson, creating a *cantus firmus/imitation mass.*

1. Four-voice texture
Four-voice texture became standard in cantus-firmus masses. Below the borrowed tenor was a *contratenor bassus* (low contratenor) or *bassus* (*bass*) to provide a harmonic foundation; above it was the *contratenor altus,* or *altus* (*alto*). The top part was called the *cantus,* or *superius,* from which comes the term *soprano.*

2. Du Fay's *Missa Se la face ay pale*
Du Fay's *Missa Se la face ay pale* is a cantus-firmus mass, whose tenor is taken from his own ballade *Se la face ay pale.* Other voices from the ballade are borrowed from in this mass as well. Each voice of the mass has a distinctive function and character. **Music: NAWM 36b**

3. Why the cantus-firmus mass?
Composers were commissioned to write masses for specific occasions, and the cantus firmus could refer to an institution, saint, or individual connected to that event. A cantus-firmus mass served a functional purpose and was also designed for connoisseurs. The mass became the most prestigious genre of the time.

VI. The Musical Language of the Renaissance (HWM 189)

The cosmopolitan musical language of the fifteenth century became fundamental to the musical language of the Renaissance. Performances of music by Du Fay and his contemporaries were rare by the early sixteenth century, but musicologists in the twentieth century produced editions for performance, and fifteenth-century music is regularly performed and recorded.

STUDY QUESTIONS

English Music (HWM 167–75, NAWM 31–32)

1. What historical circumstances may have led to the spread on the Continent of English music and musical style? What characteristics of English music did Continental composers recognize as the *contenance angloise*?

2. Describe *faburden*. How does it work?

3. Following the rules for faburden, write a faburden on the first verse of the sequence *Victimae paschali laudes*:

Vic - ti - mae   pa - scha - li   lau - des   im - mo - lent   Chri - sti - a - ni.

Music to Study

NAWM 31: *Alleuia: A newë work,* carol (first half of the fifteenth century)   [CD 2|49]

4. What is a *carol*? How does *Alleuia: A newë work* (NAWM 31) conform to the description of a fifteenth-century carol in HWM?

5. Describe the elements of *Alleuia: A newë work* that create the *contenance angloise* described in question 1. Give measure numbers where those elements occur.

6. Why is John Dunstable significant to the history of Western music?

7. What genres of music did Dunstable compose? What compositional techniques appear in his music?

8. Describe the relationship between the Dunstable melody and the plainchant melody it paraphrases in Example 8.3 in HWM, p. 173. How does Dunstable embellish the chant?

Music to Study

NAWM 32: John Dunstable, *Quam pulchra es,* motet or cantilena ⟮CD 2|52⟯ ⟮CD 1|40⟯
(first half of the fifteenth century)

9. In what sense is Dunstable's *Quam pulchra es* (NAWM 32) a motet? Which part, if any, has the chant? How are the parts related to each other? How had the definition of "motet" changed by the early fifteenth century to include a piece such as this?

10. How does Dunstable shape the music of *Quam pulchra es* to reflect the divisions of the text and the rhythms of the words? Describe specific examples and provide measure numbers.

11. Where are there passages in *Quam pulchra es* that feature parallel thirds, sixths, or tenths? (Note that the middle voice is performed an octave lower than written, so that all three parts begin on middle C.)

12. How often in *Quam pulchra es* do harmonic dissonances appear? How often do parallel unisons, fifths, or octaves occur? How does this compare with the thirteenth-century conductus *Ave virgo virginum* (NAWM 20) and with Machaut's fourteenth-century Kyrie (NAWM 25)?

13. Compare the melodic style of the top voice and treatment of the text in Dunstable's motet to that of the vocal lines in Machaut's *Rose, liz, printemps, verdure* (NAWM 26) and Landini's *Non avrà ma' pietà* (NAWM 30). What are the main differences between the English style of the first half of the fifteenth century and these four-teenth-century styles?

14. Now do the same for the melodic style of the tenors, and for the relationship be-tween the vocal line and the tenor.

Music in the Burgundian Lands (HWM 175–80, NAWM 33)

15. What political conditions aided the rise of Burgundian musicians to prominence in the fifteenth century? What kinds of musicians were employed by the dukes of Bur-gundy? How did the music at the Burgundian court influence music across Europe?

16. What were the principal polyphonic genres in the mid-fifteenth century?

17. Briefly summarize Binchois's career. Why is he significant to our study of Western music?

Music to Study

NAWM 33: Binchois, *De plus en plus,* rondeau (ca. 1425)   `CD 2|54`   `CD 1|42`

18. How does the musical and poetic form of Binchois's *De plus en plus* (NAWM 33) compare to that of Machaut's *Rose, liz* (NAWM 26)?

19. Compare the melodic style of the top voice and treatment of the text in Binchois's *De plus en plus* to those of the vocal line of Machaut's *Rose, liz* and of the top voice of Dunstable's *Quam pulchra es* (NAWM 32). (See question 13 above for your comparison of the latter two.) What traits does Binchois share with his English contemporary? How do these traits differ from Machaut's style?

20. How do the Machaut, Dunstable, and Binchois pieces compare in harmonic style? For each piece, what cadence formulas are characteristic? What vertical sonorities are common? Where do parallel fifths and octaves occur, if at all? Where do successions of parallel sixths and thirds appear? Again, what traits does Binchois share with Dunstable that differ from Machaut?

Guillaume Du Fay (HWM 180–84, NAWM 34–36a)

21. Briefly summarize Du Fay's career. How was it typical of musicians of his era? How did his life facilitate the creation of an international style?

Music to Study

NAWM 34: Guillaume Du Fay, *Resvellies vous,* ballade (1423)   [CD 2|56]

NAWM 36a: Guillaume Du Fay, *Se la face ay pale,* ballade (1430s) [CD 2|61]   [CD 1|44]

22. Du Fay composed *Resvellies vous* (NAWM 34) in 1423 when he was in Italy, and it shows strong influences from fourteenth-century French and Italian music. Which elements in this piece resemble Machaut's *Rose, liz* (NAWM 20)? Which suggest the late-fourteenth-century *Ars Subtilior* style? How does the melodic line in the texted portions suggest Italian rather than French influence?

23. Which elements of Du Fay's ballade *Se la face ay pale* (NAWM 36a) reflect French influence? Which elements reflect Italian influence? Which elements reflect English influence? How does this piece exemplify the new international style?

24. Diagram the form of NAWM 34.

    Diagram the form of NAWM 36a.

    Both these pieces are ballades. Why do they have different forms?

25. What is *fauxbourdon,* and how is it similar to and different from faburden?

Music to Study

NAWM 35: Guillaume Du Fay, *Conditor alme siderum,* hymn   CD 2|59
    (ca. 1430)

26. In Du Fay's polyphonic setting of the even-numbered verses of the chant hymn *Conditor alme siderum* (NAWM 28), how is the chant melody embellished? Where in the phrase do embellishments occur?

27. How does Du Fay's setting of *Conditor alme siderum* fit the description of fauxbourdon in HWM, p. 183?

28. In what church mode is the chant hymn *Conditor alme siderum*? _____

How does the polyphonic setting reinforce the mode?

The Polyphonic Mass (HWM 184–89, NAWM 36b)

29. Why did composers begin to write polyphonic settings of the Ordinary of the Mass? What different ways were used to the movements to each other, and what different types of Mass resulted?

30. What are the four voices of a fifteenth-century mass called? For each part, what is its general character?

    top part

    second part down

    third part down

    bottom part

31. What kinds of borrowed melodies were used in cantus-firmus masses?

    In which voice does the cantus firmus usually occur? _____

    What purposes did a cantus-firmus mass serve, and why did composers in the fifteenth century write so many of them?

Music to Study

NAWM 36a: Guillaume Du Fay, *Se la face ay pale,* ballade (1430s) [CD 2|61] [CD 1|44]

NAWM 36b: Guillaume Du Fay, *Missa Se la face ay pale,* cantus- [CD 2|63] [CD 1|46]
firmus mass (ca. 1450s), excerpt: Gloria

32. How does Du Fay use the tenor of his chanson *Se la face ay pale* (NAWM 36a) in the tenor of the Gloria from his *Missa Se la face ay pale* (NAWM 36b)? How is this like isorhythm? How does it provide a form for the Gloria movement? How does it affect how easy it is to hear and recognize the source melody?

33. Where in the Gloria does Du Fay borrow material from the other two voices of his chanson? What purpose might this borrowing serve?

34. How do the four voices of the Gloria differ from each other in function and style?

35. Examine the upper voices in the Gloria. How often do two successive measures have the same rhythm? How often do the top two voices move in the same rhythm simultaneously? What does this suggest about Du Fay's use of rhythm?

36. In the isorhythmic works of Vitry (NAWM 24) and Machaut (NAWM 25), we can find parallel fifths and octaves and double leading-tone cadences. Can any of these be found in Du Fay's Gloria? How would you describe the harmony?

The Musical Language of the Renaissance (HWM 189)

37. Summarize the differences in musical style between the mid-fourteenth and mid-fifteenth centuries. Refer to Machaut and Dufay (especially NAWM 25, 26, 36a, and 36b) as the basis for your comparison.

TERMS TO KNOW

contenance angloise

faburden

cantilena

carol

burden

paraphrase

motet (fifteenth-century and later)

hemiola

fauxbourdon

mass

plainsong mass

head-motive

motto mass

cantus-firmus mass or tenor mass

cantus-firmus/imitation mass

contratenor bassus, bassus

contratenor altus, altus

superius

bass, alto, soprano

NAMES TO KNOW

John Dunstable

Burgundy

Binchois

Guillaume Du Fay

L'homme armé

REVIEW QUESTIONS

1. Add to the timeline you made in chapter 7 the pieces and composers discussed in this chapter. Include dates for the poem that mentions the *contenance angloise*; dates for the end of the duchy of Burgundy and the reigns of Philip the Good and Charles the Bold; the dates and places of Du Fay's birth, death, and employment; and dates for any major historical events with which you are familiar, to help orient you to the fifteenth century.

2. What characteristics and procedures of English music set it apart from music on the Continent in the thirteenth, fourteenth, and early fifteenth centuries? How did the Continental style change as it absorbed the influence of English music in the first half of the fifteenth century?

3. What new ways of using and reworking Gregorian chant developed during the fifteenth century?

4. What special role did the duchy of Burgundy and Burgundian composers play in the development of music during the fifteenth century?

5. Using Du Fay's *Conditor alme siderum* (NAWM 35) as a model, set the first two verses of *Victimae paschali laudes* (NAWM 5) in fauxbourdon style, with the chant paraphrased in the top voice, a second voice in parallel fourths below, and a tenor moving mostly in parallel sixths with the top line, cadencing on octaves. Use triple meter as in the Du Fay, alternating long and short notes. Introduce ornamental figures in the upper voice, especially at cadences, and rhythmic variety in the tenor.

6. Describe the music of Du Fay and explain how he synthesized elements from France, Italy, and England in a cosmopolitan style.

7. Describe the varieties of polyphonic mass cycle composed in the fifteenth century, and compare Du Fay's Missa *Se la face ay pale* (a cantus-firmus mass) to Machaut's *Messe de Notre Dame* (a plainsong mass).

Chapter 9 Franco-Flemish Composers, 1450–1520

CHAPTER OBJECTIVES

After you complete the reading, study of the music, and study questions for this chapter, you should be able to

1. describe the music and briefly describe the careers of some of the major composers active at the end of the fifteenth century and the beginning of the sixteenth century;

2. describe the new trends in musical style from 1450–1520 that are distinctive from the previous generation; and

3. explain the significance of these new trends to the history of Western music.

CHAPTER OUTLINE

I. Introduction (HWM 190)

Most prominent composers in the period 1450–1520 came from France, Flanders, or the Netherlands. The generation born around 1420 combined the new international language with medieval traits, but the next generation ended the use of formes fixes, used imitation and homophony, and matched their music to the accentuation, imagery, and emotions of the texts they set.

II. Political Change and Consolidation (HWM 190–92)

Even with the consolidation of power under the Hapsburgs, Italian courts and cities continued to be among the most generous patrons of art and music and to compete with each other for the best musicians.

III. Ockeghem and Busnoys (HWM 192–98, NAWM 37)

Jean de Ockeghem (ca. 1420–1497) and *Antoine Busnoys* (ca. 1430–1492) were the best-known musicians of their generation.

Biography: Jean de Ockeghem [Johannes Okeghem]
Ockeghem was a singer, composer, and teacher. He was born in north-eastern France and worked at the French royal court for over forty years. His long service in one place encouraged the development of an individual idiom.

A. Chansons
The chansons of Ockeghem and Busnoys combine features from Du Fay's generation with new features, including more use of imitation, greater equality among the voices, longer phrases, and more use of duple meter.

1. Popularity and reworkings
Many chansons by Ockeghem and Busnoys were very popular and were reworked into instrumental works and cantus-firmus masses.

B. Masses
Ockeghem, Busnoys, and Du Fay were active at the same time, and they were influenced by each other.

1. Range
Ockeghem and Busnoys used wider vocal ranges than Du Fay's generation in their masses, giving a fuller and darker sound. They varied the texture, setting some passages for only two or three voices. **Music: NAWM 37**

2. Cantus-firmus masses
In their cantus-firmus masses, Ockeghem and Busnoys employ cantus-firmus material more freely than Du Fay's generation had.

3. Long, overlapping phrases
Ockeghem uses long phrases and elided cadences to create continuous flowing music.

4. *Missa cuiusvis toni* and *Missa prolationum*
Ockeghem's creativity and compositional virtuosity are evident in his *Missa cuiusvis toni* (Mass in any mode), which can be sung in four different modes, and *Missa prolationum,* which is notated in two voices but sung in four, using the four prolations of mensural notation.

5. Canon
Composers used canon to show off their ingenuity and skill and employed techniques like *inversion* and *retrograde. Missa prolationum* is a *mensuration canon.*

C. Medieval and Newer Features
Medieval compositional elements retained by Ockeghem and Busnoys from Du Fay's generation became less prominent, while the newer elements they employed were extended into the next generation.

IV. The Next Generation (HWM 198–202, NAWM 38)
Jacob Obrecht (1457 or 1458–1505), *Heinrich Isaac* (ca. 1450–1517), and *Josquin des Prez* (ca. 1450–1521) were the three most eminent composers of the generation after Ockeghem.

A. General Traits

Composers active around 1480–1520 shared common elements of style that gave them greater flexibility and allowed them to communicate with a wide audience. The text determined the form, all parts were nearly equal in style and importance, full triads prevailed, and phrases were clearly articulated.

B. Jacob Obrecht

Obrecht composed masses, motets, chansons, songs in Dutch, and instrumental pieces.

1. Imitation

Composers of 1480–1520 used imitation more extensively than earlier composers, often beginning a piece, section, or phrase with a *point of imitation,* a series of imitative entrances.

2. Clarity

Music from 1480–1520 has clear tonal centers and cadences, smooth counterpoint, and phrases that begin in regular rhythms and then accelerate.

C. Henricus Isaac

Isaac worked for the most important patrons of the time, was familiar with regional music styles, and composed sacred and secular music.

1. Homophonic textures

Isaac was influenced by Italian homophonic songs and adapted the same style for some of his German songs, or *Lieder*. Homophonic texture alternating with imitative texture is an important facet of sixteenth-century polyphonic music. **Music: NAWM 38**

D. Text Setting

Obrecht, Isaac, and other composers of their generation were concerned with fitting music to words and making sure the text could be understood, so they used primarily syllabic settings and specified the alignment of words and music exactly.

V. Josquin des Prez (HWM 202–8, NAWM 39–41)

Josquin des Prez was considered the greatest composer of his time, and his works were recopied and performed well after his death.

Biography: Josquin Des Prez [Josquin Lebloitte dit Desprez]

Josquin was probably born and trained in northern France. He spent much of his career in Italy, serving in Milan and in the Sistine Chapel in Rome and becoming one of the most sought-after musicians in Italy. For the last seventeen years of his life, Josquin lived and worked in Condé sur-l'Escaut.

A. Motets

Josquin wrote more than fifty motets, which exemplify the traits of the late-fifteenth century style.

1. Text depiction and expression

Josquin was renowned for reflecting the meaning of words in his music through *text depiction* (using musical gestures to suggest images in the text) and *text expression* (conveying the emotions of the text through music).

2. *Ave Maria . . . virgo serena*

Josquin's attention to text depiction and expression can be seen in his motet *Ave Maria . . . virgo serena*. Each phrase of text receives its own musical figure, which is usually treated in a point of imitation.   **Music: NAWM 39**

B. Masses

Josquin's masses are varied in approach and abound in technical ingenuity. Most are cantus-firmus masses based on secular tunes.

1. Imitation mass

One of Josquin's masses is an *imitation mass,* in which the composer borrows extensively from all voices of a polyphonic model and reworks them to create something new in each movement of the mass.

2. Paraphrase mass

Josquin's *Missa Pange lingua* is a *paraphrase mass,* in which a borrowed monophonic melody is paraphrased in all four voices in each movement. Imitation mass and paraphrase mass differ in source material, not in style.   **Music: NAWM 40**

C. Chansons

Chansons of Josquin's generation have strophic texts or poems in no particular form; four or five voices, all essentially equal; and alternation between imitative and homophonic textures.

1. *Mille regretz*

Mille regretz illustrates the chanson style of about 1520.   **Music: NAWM 41**

VI. Old and New (HWM 209)

The music of Ockeghem and Busnoys contains both old and new elements. Josquin and his generation composed works with equal lines, mixtures of imitative polyphony and homophony, and careful expression and presentation of text. This musical language and attention to expression became the standard for later generations.

STUDY QUESTIONS

Political Change and Consolidation (HWM 190–92)

1. How did Western European political consolidation in the late fifteenth century affect patronage of the arts?

Ockeghem and Busnoys (HWM 192–98, NAWM 37)

2. Summarize Ockeghem's career and reputation.

Music to Study

NAWM 37: Johannes Ockeghem, Agnus Dei, from *Missa De plus en plus* (second half of the fifteenth century) [CD 2|70]

3. In his *Missa De plus en plus* (NAWM 37), what does Ockeghem borrow from Binchois's *De plus en plus* (NAWM 33)? How does he use the borrowed material? How does he alter it?

4. How does Ockeghem's treatment of borrowed material here compare to that of Du Fay's in the Gloria from *Missa Se la face ay pale* (NAWM 36b)?

5. How do the ranges of the four voice parts in the Ockeghem mass compare to the ranges in Du Fay's mass?

6. How does Ockeghem apply changes of texture, especially in the number of simultaneous parts? How does this compare to the Du Fay mass?

7. Describe Ockeghem's harmonic practice and treatment of dissonance.

8. If you had to assign the tenor of this mass to one of the church modes, which one would you choose? Why?

9. What is the final of this mode? _____ Where do cadences occur on this note (or on a consonant sonority with this as the lowest note)?

10. What is the tenor or reciting tone of the mode? _____ Where do cadences occur on this note?

11. Where do cadences occur on notes other than the final and reciting tone, and on what notes?

12. Summarize how this polyphonic work projects its mode. (The mode of a polyphonic work is generally the mode of its tenor and superius.)

13. What is a *mensuration canon,* and how does it work in Ockeghem's *Missa prolationum?*

    What is special about Ockeghem's *Missa cuiusvis toni?*

    What was the attitude of Ockeghem and his contemporaries toward such ingenious compositional techniques?

The Next Generation (HWM 198–202, NAWM 38)

14. In terms of general musical style, what does the music of Obrecht, Isaac, and Josquin have in common?

15. How does Obrecht's approach to texture differ from Ockeghem's? Refer to the Obrecht mass in Example 9.5 on p. 200 of HWM and to Ockeghem's mass in NAWM 37.

16. Where did Isaac live and work?

Music to Study

NAWM 38: Heinrich Isaac, *Innsbruck, ich muss dich lassen*, Lied ⌐ CD 3|1 ⌐ (ca. 1500)

17. How is Isaac's setting of *Innsbruck, ich muss dich lassen* (NAWM 38) similar to and different from Obrecht's *Missa Fortuna desperata* (Example 9.5 on p. 200 of HWM)?

Josquin des Prez (HWM 202–8, NAWM 39–41)

18. Where and when did Josquin live and work? In what genres did he compose? How was he regarded by his contemporaries and by later sixteenth-century commentators?

Music to Study

NAWM 39: Josquin des Prez, *Ave Maria . . . virgo serena,* motet   (CD 3|2)   CD 1|53
(ca. 1484–85)

NAWM 40: Josquin des Prez, *Missa pange lingua,* mass (ca. 1515–20) excerpts: Kyrie and part of Credo

40a: Kyrie   (CD 3|9)   CD 1|60

40b: Credo, excerpt: *Et incarnatus est* and *Crucifixus*   (CD 3|12)

NAWM 41: Josquin des Prez (?), *Mille regretz,* chanson (ca. 1520)   (CD 3|15)

19. In Josquin's motet, where do phrases begin with a point of imitation? List each instance, including the beginning measure number, the first words of the phrase, and the number of voices that participate in the point of imitation.

20. Where do cadences occur in Josquin's motet *Ave Maria . . . virgo serena*? How does the location of cadences relate to the structure of the text? Refer to specific words and measures.

21. How does the music reflect the natural accentuation of the words elsewhere in the motet? Refer to specific words and measures.

22. How does Josquin's music depict and express the text in his motet *Ave Maria . . . virgo serena*? Refer to specific words and measures.

23. Josquin's motet is in what mode? How can you tell? How is the mode projected in the music?

24. How are the opening two phrases of the chant hymn *Pange lingua gloriosi* used and varied in the first Kyrie of Josquin's *Missa Pange lingua* (NAWM 40a)? Describe how each of the four voices treats the chant. How does this compare to the way borrowed material is used in Du Fay's *Missa Se la face ay pale* (NAWM 36b) and Ockeghem's *Missa De plus en plus* (NAWM 37)?

25. How does Josquin use the chant melody in the Christe and second Kyrie? In the *Et incarnatus est* from the Credo?

26. How does Josquin vary the texture, especially in the number of parts sounding simultaneously? How does this compare to the Ockeghem and Du Fay masses?

27. How does Josquin use imitation between the voices in the Kyrie? What different arrangements of voices does he use for his points of imitation? How does his use of imitation compare to the Ockeghem and Du Fay masses?

28. How does Josquin's music convey the images and feelings of the text in the *Et incarnatus est*?

29. How does the musical and poetic form of Josquin's *Mille regretz* (NAWM 41) compare to that of Du Fay's *Resvellies vous* (NAWM 34) and Isaac's *Innsbruck, ich muss dich lassen* (NAWM 38)?

30. Compare the texture of Josquin's *Mille regretz* to that of Du Fay's *Resvellies vous* and Isaac's *Innsbruck*. What traits does Josquin share with his contemporary that differ from Du Fay's style?

31. How do the Du Fay, Isaac, and Josquin pieces compare in harmonic style? For each piece, what cadence formulas are characteristic? What vertical sonorities are common? Again, what traits does Josquin share with Isaac that differ from Du Fay?

Old and New (HWM 209)

32. Describe the changes in musical style in Europe from 1450 to 1520. How does musical style of Josquin's generation differ from that of Du Fay's generation? What did the composers of each of those generations contribute that became a common feature of later music?

TERMS TO KNOW

canon
inversion
retrograde
mensuration canon
point of imitation

Lieder
text depiction
text expression
imitation mass
paraphrase mass

NAMES TO KNOW

Jean de Ockeghem
Antoine Busnoys
Jacob Obrecht

Heinricus Isaac
Josquin des Prez

REVIEW QUESTIONS

1. Add to the timeline you made in chapter 7 the pieces, composers, treatises, and theorists discussed in this chapter.

2. Trace the development of the motet from the fourteenth through the early sixteenth centuries, using the motets in NAWM by Vitry, Dunstable, and Josquin as examples.

3. Write a point of imitation for two voices, about eight to ten measures of cut time, in the style of Josquin. Use as models the points of imitation in his motet *Ave Maria . . . virgo serena* (NAWM 39) or his *Missa Pange lingua* (NAWM 40). Either the upper or the lower voice may enter first, but the upper must enter a fifth higher than the lower. The first few measures should be in exact imitation; the rest may be in freer counterpoint, ending with a cadence on an octave or unison. Follow the same rules of counterpoint and dissonance treatment that Josquin followed, and try to make your vocal lines as varied in rhythm as his, with no two successive measures having the same rhythm. (Your goal in this exercise is to learn about Josquin's style by imitating it.)

4. Compare the masses of Machaut, Du Fay, Ockeghem, and Josquin that are excerpted in NAWM. What type of mass is each one? What existing musical material does each borrow? How is this material used and varied in each? How do these masses compare to each other in the role of the voice, the setting of the text, melodic style, harmonic practice, use of imitation, and other general aspects of style?

5. Compare the careers and music of any two of the following composers: Machaut, Du Fay, Ockeghem, Josquin.

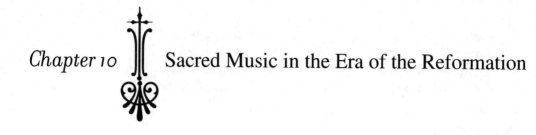

Chapter 10 Sacred Music in the Era of the Reformation

CHAPTER OBJECTIVES

After you complete the reading, study of the music, and study questions for this chapter, you should be able to

1. describe attitudes toward and uses of music in Protestant churches in the sixteenth century and the genres they used;
2. identify some of the most important composers and terms associated with these trends;
3. recount the effect of the Counter-Reformation on sixteenth-century Catholic music and identify some of the most important composers and terms associated with it;
4. describe the styles of Palestrina, Victoria, Lasso, and Byrd.

CHAPTER OUTLINE

I. Introduction (HWM 210)

The *Reformation* shattered the religious unity of central and western Europe. It brought new types of religious music, including *chorale* and chorale settings in the Lutheran church, the *metrical psalm* in Calvinist churches, and the *anthem* and *Service* in the Anglican Church, while Catholic and Jewish music held to past traditions.

II. The Reformation (HWM 210–12)

Knowing the religious and political issues behind the three principal Reformation movements helps us understand why the music for each takes the forms it does.

A. Martin Luther

Martin Luther (1483–1546) was a professor of biblical theology whose arguments that God offers salvation through faith alone and that religious authority derived from the Bible alone posed a challenge to the authority of the Church.

1. The ninety-five theses
   Luther posted a list of ninety-five arguments in 1517, and their publication eventually led to his excommunication but also won him support in German universities and among the populace. He organized the Lutheran Church, supported by German princes who wished to gain freedom from control by Rome.

III. Music in the Lutheran Church (HWM 213–18, NAWM 42)

Luther sought to give people a larger role in worship by using the vernacular as well as Latin.

1. Luther and music
   Luther gave music a central position in the Lutheran Church, and he wanted the entire congregation to participate in the services. In Germany throughout the sixteenth century, there were compromises between Roman usage and new practice. The *Deudtsche Messe* (German Mass, 1526) was Luther's German version of the Mass liturgy.

A. The Lutheran Chorale

The most important form of music in the Lutheran church was the congregational hymn or *chorale,* a metric, rhymed, strophic poem and melody in simple rhythm sung in unison, without harmonization or accompaniment. It fulfilled Luther's aim of increasing worshipers' participation.

1. Sources for chorales
   The four main sources for chorales are (1) adaptations of chant, (2) existing German devotional songs, (3) secular tunes, and (4) new melodies.

2. Adaptations of chant
   Luther's adaptations of chant changed the melody to an appealing, up-to-date style that was easier for lay worshipers to sing.   **Music: NAWM 42a–42b**

3. German devotional songs
   Religious songs in German had circulated since the ninth century, and many were used as chorales.

4. Contrafacta
   Contrafacta were created when secular tunes were given religious words.

5. New melodies
   Luther and others wrote many new tunes for chorales. The best known is Luther's *Ein' feste Burg.*   **Music: NAWM 42c**

B. Polyphonic Chorale Settings

Composers used a variety of compositional approaches to write polyphonic settings of chorales for the home, for schools, and for performance by choirs in church. *Chorale motets* borrowed techniques from the Franco-Flemish motet, such as cantus-firmus or paraphrase technique. Settings in *cantional style*—with the chorale in the top voice accompanied by block chords—became common in the late sixteenth century, and after 1600 it was customary for the organ to play all the parts while the congregation sang the tune.   **Music: NAWM 42d**

C. The Lutheran Tradition
By 1600, Lutherans had established a strong musical heritage on which later composers would build.

IV. Music in Calvinist Churches (HWM 218–21, NAWM 43)

Jean Calvin (1509–1564) led a Protestant movement in France, Switzerland, and the Low Countries that rejected papal authority and accepted predestination.

1. Calvin and music
Calvin favored congregational singing and rejected anything elaborate.

A. Metrical Psalms
Calvin insisted that only biblical texts should be sung in church, and he favored *metrical psalms*.

1. The French psalter
Metrical psalms were published in collections called *psalters*.   **Music: NAWM 43a**

2. Dutch, English, and Scottish psalters
Metrical psalms spread widely and translations were available in many countries, including New England.   **Music: NAWM 43b**

B. Polyphonic Psalm Settings
Psalm singing in churches was at first monophonic, but psalm tunes were set polyphonically for devotional use.

V. Church Music in England (HWM 221–24, NAWM 44)

A. The Church of England
The Church of England was formed for political reasons under King Henry VIII (r. 1509–47). It adopted Protestant doctrines under Edward VI (r. 1547–53), English replaced Latin in services, and the *Book of Common Prayer* was adapted in 1549. The church blended Catholic and Protestant elements under Elizabeth I (r. 1558–1603) and her successors.

1. Church music
New forms of music were created for services in English, but Latin forms continued, as well.

2. Taverner and Tallis
Two of the leading English composers of sacred music in the sixteenth century were John Taverner (ca. 1490–1545) and Thomas Tallis (ca. 1505–1585).

3. Service and anthem
The two principal forms of Anglican music were the *Service* (containing music for parts of the liturgy) and the *anthem* (the English parallel to the motet). A *full anthem* is for unaccompanied choir in contrapuntal style,

and a *verse anthem* employs chorus, one or more solo voices, and accompaniment.

B. William Byrd

William Byrd (ca. 1540–1623) was the leading English composer of the late Renaissance. He wrote secular music and both Anglican and Latin sacred music.

  1. Anglican music

Byrd composed in all the forms of Anglican music and was the first English composer to fully apply imitative techniques.   **Music: NAWM 44**

  2. Latin masses and motets

Byrd composed Latin masses and motets and compiled two books of complete polyphonic Mass Propers for the major days of the church year.

Biography: William Byrd

Byrd was probably a student of Thomas Tallis and worked under both Protestant and Catholic monarchs. He wrote in all the major genres of the time in both secular and sacred music (Catholic and Anglican), and was protected by Queen Elizabeth for his continued loyalties to the Catholic Church in Protestant England.

VI. Catholic Church Music (HWM 224–27)

Music in the Catholic Church changed during the sixteenth century primarily in matters of style rather than genre or practice.

A. The Generation of 1520–1550

Flemish composers remained prominent in the generation active between 1520 and 1550, working all over Europe.

  1. General style features

Catholic composers in this period preserved the style of the preceding generation but expanded the number of voices, used primarily duple meter, employed imitative polyphony in a new way, and used canons far less often than the previous generations.

  2. Mode in polyphony

Mode was a link between Christian tradition and the emotional effects of ancient music, so making the mode clear was important in Renaissance music.

  3. Willaert and humanism

Adrian Willaert (ca. 1490–1562) was affected by the humanist movement, and he carefully matched text to music.

B. Catholic Response to the Reformation

In response to the Protestant Reformation, the Catholic Church initiated a series of reforms called the *Counter-Reformation,* and the Society of Jesus founded schools and proselytized in an attempt to regain regions that had converted to Protestantism.

C. The Council of Trent

At the *Council of Trent* (1545–1563), Catholic Church officials reaffirmed doctrines attacked by Luther and Calvin but sought solutions for addressing abuses.

1. Effects on music

The Council eliminated tropes and all but four sequences, but had little else to say about music. Many local Italian bishops insisted that in polyphonic works, the text must always be intelligible, which led many people at the time to believe that the Council had issued statements about polyphonic music.

VII. Giovanni Pierluigi da Palestrina (HWM 227–32, NAWM 45)

Giovanni Pierluigi da Palestrina (1525/1526–1594) was the leading Italian composer of church music in the sixteenth century. A legend circulated after Palestrina's death, claiming that his *Pope Marcellus Mass* saved polyphony in the Catholic Church.   **Music: NAWM 45**

Biography: Giovanni Pierluigi da Palestrina

Palestrina spent most of his career in Rome as a church musician. He was renowned for his masses and motets but also wrote secular madrigals. After the Council of Trent, Palestrina was commissioned to revise the official chant books. He was respected during his lifetime and became an almost legendary figure after his death.

A. The Palestrina Style

Palestrina's sacred polyphony captures the essence of the Catholic response to the Reformation, yet is varied musically and sensitive to the text.

1. Masses

Palestrina wrote 104 masses, using a variety of techniques from imitation mass, cantus firmus, and paraphrase to freely composed works.

2. Melody

Palestrina's melodies are long-breathed, rhythmically varied, and easily singable, moving mostly by step in a smooth, flexible arch.   **Music: NAWM 45b**

3. Counterpoint and dissonance treatment

Palestrina's counterpoint is smooth and mostly consonant, with dissonances restricted to suspensions, passing and neighbor tones, and *cambiatas*.

4. Sonority

Although Palestrina's music seems to have a limited harmonic vocabulary, he achieves a great variety of sonorities.

5. Text declamation

Palestrina strove to accentuate the words correctly and make them understandable.   **Music: NAWM 45a**

6. Texture

Palestrina typically gave each new phrase of text to a different combination of voices, reserving the full six voices for significant moments and words.

7. Rhythm
Palestrina often uses syncopation to sustain momentum and to link phrases in both music and text.

B. Palestrina as a Model
Palestrina's style has been preserved and imitated for over four hundred years.

VIII. Spain and the New World (HWM 233–35, NAWM 46)

In Spain, the Catholic Church was identified with the monarchy, and missionaries carried the teachings of the Church as well as its music to the Americas.

A. Catholic Music in Spain
Spanish sacred polyphony was influenced by Franco-Flemish composers at court.

1. Tomás Luis de Victoria
Tomás Luis de Victoria (1548–1611) was the most famous Spanish composer of the sixteenth century, and all of his sacred music is for Catholic services. **Music: NAWM 46a**

2. Imitation mass
Victoria wrote imitation masses based on his own motets, showing how existing material can be used in new ways. **Music: NAWM 46b**

B. Music in the Spanish New World
Spanish adventurers conquered the Aztecs and Incas, and Spanish missionaries sought to convert native peoples to Christianity.

1. Aztec and Inca music
Aztec and Incan songs used a variety of styles and instruments, and much of their music was associated with dancing.

2. Catholic music
Catholic missionaries used music to spread the message of their religion to the native peoples.

IX. Germany and Eastern Europe (HWM 235–38, NAWM 47)

In the areas of central and eastern Europe that remained Catholic after the Reformation, music reflected developments in Flanders, France, and Italy.

1. Germany
German composers, like Hans Leo Hassler (1564–1612), adopted the Franco-Flemish style or blended it with local traditions.

A. Orlando di Lasso
Orlando di Lasso (ca. 1532–1594) is considered one of the great composers of sacred music in the sixteenth century.

1. Motets
Lasso wrote over seven hundred motets, each of which expresses the composer's interpretation of the text through rhetorical, pictorial, and

dramatic devices. Lasso mastered Flemish, French, Italian, and German styles, as well as every genre in sacred and secular music. **Music: NAWM 47**

Biography: Orlando di Lasso [Roland de Lassus]

Lasso was born and trained in the region of the great Franco-Flemish composers from the early Renaissance. After serving many Italian patrons, Lasso went to Munich where he served the duke for almost forty years. During these years, Lasso traveled frequently, and he kept abreast of the latest musical developments across western Europe, becoming one of the most cosmopolitan figures in music history.

IX. Jewish Music (HWM 238)

The musical tradition of the Jewish community in Europe was oral rather than written. In the sixteenth century, cantors were appointed to perform the chants. Just as early Christians borrowed music from Jewish sources, European Jews blended styles from the surrounding society with their own tradition.

X. The Legacy of Sixteenth-Century Sacred Music (HWM 238–39)

Chorales written during the Reformation for Lutheran worship were used by later composers as the basis for new compositions, giving chorales a significance for Baroque and later music equal to that of chant. Chorales, psalm tunes, anthems, and services are still used in worship today.

STUDY QUESTIONS

The Reformation (HWM 210–12)

1. What were some of Martin Luther's criticisms of the Catholic Church? What solutions did he propose?

Music in the Lutheran Church (HWM 213–18, NAWM 42)

2. In what ways was the early Lutheran service similar to the Catholic liturgy, and how was it different? What languages were used? What roles did music play?

3. What is a *chorale*? How was a chorale sung, and by whom?

4. What were the chief sources of tunes for chorales? Name an example of a chorale derived from each type of source.

5. In what ways did chorales receive polyphonic treatment in the sixteenth and early seventeenth centuries? How were these polyphonic settings performed? Include in your answer descriptions of the *chorale motet* and *cantional style*.

Music to Study

NAWM 42a: *Veni redemptor gentium,* hymn   [CD 3|16]

NAWM 42b: Martin Luther, *Nun komm, der Heiden Heiland,*   [CD 3|17]
     chorale (1524)

NAWM 42c: Martin Luther, *Ein' feste Burg,* chorale (1529)   [CD 3|18]

NAWM 42d: Johann Walter, *Ein' feste Burg,* chorale setting for   [CD 3|19]
     four voices (ca. 1551)

6. What elements of the hymn *Veni redemptor gentium* (NAWM 42a) did Luther retain in his chorale *Nun komm, der Heiden Heiland* (NAWM 42b)? What elements did he change? Why did he use a Catholic hymn as the basis for a Protestant chorale? Why did he make changes to the hymn?

7. Describe how the text, melody, and rhythm of *Ein' feste Burg* (NAWM 42c) exemplify Luther's religious ideals.

8. How does Johann Walter's polyphonic chorale setting of *Ein' feste Burg* (NAWM 42d) use the chorale melody? How does Walter's setting resemble Josquin's musical style in terms of harmony? melody? rhythm? text setting? (Refer back to chapter 9, questions 9–31.)

Music in Calvinist Churches (HWM 218–21, NAWM 43)

9. How was Jean Calvin's approach to music in the reformed church similar to Luther's? How was it different?

10. What is a *psalter,* and what does it contain?

Music to Study

NAWM 43a: Loys Bourgeois, Psalm 134 (*Or sus, serviteurs du Seigneur*), metrical psalm (ca. 1551)   CD 3|20

NAWM 43b: William Kethe, Psalm 100, *All people that on earth do dwell,* metrical psalm (ca. 1559)   CD 3|21

11. Compare Loys Bourgeois's Psalm 134 (NAWM 43a) and William Kethe's Pssalm 100 (NAWM 43b) to Luther's *Ein' feste Burg* (NAWM 42c). What do these Reformation compositions have in common? How are they different? How do they reflect musically Luther's and Calvin's approaches to reform? (See your answer for question 7.)

Church Music in England (HWM 221–24, NAWM 44)

12. Briefly relate the history of the Church of England from Henry VIII to Elizabeth I. How was the Anglican approach to music in the church similar to Luther's and Calvin's? How was it different?

13. Describe the principal forms of Anglican church music.

14. Briefly summarize William Byrd's career and the types of music he composed.

Music to Study

NAWM 44: William Byrd, Sing joyfully unto God, full anthem   (CD 3|22) (CD 1|63)
(1580s–1590s)

15. Why is Byrd's *Sing joyfully unto God* (NAWM 44) a full anthem and not a verse anthem?

16. How does Byrd illustrate the text in *Sing joyfully unto God*? How does he highlight the accentuation and phrasing of the text?

17. What compositional traits mark this as a work from the Renaissance? What compositional traits mark this as a work by Byrd?

Catholic Church Music (HWM 224–27)

18. How was the Catholic approach to music during the first thirty years of the Reformation similar to the Lutheran, Calvinist, and Anglican approaches? How was it different?

19. Describe the characteristics of the Catholic church music of Flemish composers active in the period 1520–1550, using Nicolas Gombert's *Quem dicunt homines* (Example 10.5 in HWM, p. 225) as an example.

20. What was the Council of Trent? When was it held, and what was its purpose? What matters relating to music were discussed, and what actions relating to music did the Council take?

Giovanni Pierluigi da Palestrina (HWM 227–32, NAWM 45)

21. Briefly summarize Palestrina's career. Why was his music important for later composers?

Music to Study

NAWM 45: Giovanni da Palestrina, *Pope Marcellus Mass* (ca. 1560), excerpts

    45a: Credo   CD 3|27

    45b: Agnus Dei I   CD 3|35   CD 1|68

22. Describe the legend of Palestrina's *Pope Marcellus Mass*. What aspects of its musical style led people to continue this legend for so many years? Give specific examples from the Credo and Agnus Dei I (NAWM 45a and 45b) to support your answer.

23. Describe Palestrina's style in terms of melody, counterpoint and dissonance treatment, sonority, text declamation, texture, and rhythm, using examples from the Credo and Agnus Dei I of the *Pope Marcellus Mass*.

melody

counterpoint and dissonance treatment

sonority

text declamation

texture

rhythm

Spain and the New World (HWM 233–35, NAWM 46)

24. How did the Franco-Flemish tradition and Palestrina's musical style come to influence musicians in Spain and its territories?

Music to Study

NAWM 46a: Tomás Luis de Victoria, *O magnum mysterium,* motet [CD 3|36] [CD 1|69] (ca. 1570)

NAWM 46b: Tomás Luis de Victoria, Kyrie, from *Missa O* [CD 3|40] *magnum mysterium,* mass (ca. 1580s)

25. How is each phrase of text treated in Victoria's motet *O magnum mysterium* (NAWM 46a)? How does the placement of cadences help to give shape to the piece and make clear the divisions of the text?

26. How is Victoria's treatment of text and musical style in his motet (NAWM 46a) similar to or different from Palestrina's in the Agnus Dei I from his *Pope Marcellus Mass* (NAWM 45b)?

27. Compare the Kyrie of Victoria's *Missa O magnum mysterium* (NAWM 46b) to the motet on which it is based (NAWM 46a). What has Victoria borrowed from his earlier motet, and how has he varied it?

28. What is an *imitation mass*? How does Victoria's *Missa O magnum mysterium* exemplify this kind of mass? How does this differ from or resemble a cantus-firmus mass (such as Du Fay's *Missa Se la face ay pale,* NAWM 36b) and a paraphrase Mass (such as Josquin's *Missa Pange lingua,* NAWM 40b)?

29. What was the music of the Aztecs like, when the Spanish first encountered them?

30. In what ways was the use of music by Catholic missionaries in the Spanish New World similar to or different from the use of music by Lutheran and Calvinist reformers?

Germany and Eastern Europe (HWM 235–38, NAWM 47)

31. How do Orlando di Lasso's career, music, and musical output contrast with those of Palestrina?

Music to Study

NAWM 47: Orlando di Lasso, *Tristis est anima mea,* motet (ca. 1565)

32. How does Lasso use pictorial, rhetorical, or dramatic devices to convey the meaning of the words in his motet *Tristis est anima mea* (NAWM 47)?

Jewish Music (HWM 238)

33. Describe the use of music in Jewish synagogues in the sixteenth century.

The Legacy of Sixteenth-Century Sacred Music (HWM 238–39)

34. In what ways has the sacred music of sixteenth-century Europe had a continuing presence in musical and religious life over the last five centuries?

TERMS TO KNOW

Reformation

chorale

contrafactum (pl. contrafacta)

chorale motet

cantional style

metrical psalm

psalter

Service

anthem: full anthem, verse anthem

Counter-Reformation

cambiata

NAMES TO KNOW

Martin Luther

Deudsche Messe

Jean Calvin

The Book of Common Prayer

William Byrd

Adrian Willaert

Council of Trent

Giovanni Pierluigi da Palestrina

Pope Marcellus Mass

Tomás Luis de Victoria

Orlando di Lasso

REVIEW QUESTIONS

1. Add to the timeline you made in chapter 7 the pieces, composers, and events discussed in this chapter.
2. How was music regarded, how was it used, and what musical genres were cultivated in the Lutheran church, in Calvinist churches, and in the Church of England during the sixteenth century?
3. Many chorales were adapted from Gregorian chant. Create a chorale tune based on the Gregorian hymn *Christe Redemptor omnium* (NAWM 4b). Use for your text the first four lines of the English translation ("Jesus! Redeemer of the world!"), which is rhymed and metrical. Since chorales are almost entirely syllabic, you will need to eliminate some of the extra notes in the Gregorian melody. (One strategy might be to match the eight syllables of each line of the English verse to the eight notes or neumes in the corresponding line of music, and then, for syllables with more than one note, choose the one you like best. Or you can follow the melody more flexibly.) Use any rhythm that fits the accentuation of the poetry and features only half, quarter, and eighth notes. You might create several different chorale tunes, all based on this chant.
4. Describe the musical style of Catholic sacred music before the Council of Trent. How did the Council affect music for the Catholic Church?
5. Describe Palestrina's style in his masses. Compare his style to those of Du Fay and Josquin.
6. How did composers of church music in the later sixteenth century treat the words they set? What are some of the approaches to setting or expressing a text, as exemplified by the pieces treated in this chapter?

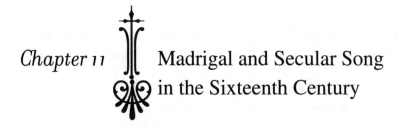

Chapter 11 Madrigal and Secular Song in the Sixteenth Century

CHAPTER OBJECTIVES

After you complete the reading, study of the music, and study questions for this chapter, you should be able to

1. describe the principal styles and genres of sixteenth-century secular vocal music;
2. describe the relation of music and words in sixteenth-century vocal music and contrast it with earlier practices of setting texts;
3. identify some of the major composers of the sixteenth century; and
4. identify the characteristics of national schools of secular vocal composition in the sixteenth century.

CHAPTER OUTLINE

I. Introduction (HWM 240)

Sixteenth-century composers cultivated national genres and styles in secular vocal music. These include the Spanish *villancico,* the Italian *frottola* and *madrigal,* new kinds of French chanson, German Lieder, and the English madrigal and *lute song.*

II. The First Market for Music (HWM 240–42)

In the sixteenth century, music was not only a service provided by musicians but was also sold as a commodity in its printed form.

1. Amateur music-making and musical literacy
Musical amateurs from the upper classes and literate urban middle classes created a demand for notated music that they could perform for their own enjoyment. The combination of this demand and music printing created the first market for music. Amateurs sought music in their own language, reinforcing the growth of national genres and styles.

III. Spain (HWM 242–43, NAWM 48)

A. The Villancico

The *villancico* was the most important form of secular polyphonic song in Renaissance Spain. Cultivated by the aristocracy, villancicos were syllabic and mostly homophonic.

1. Form and performance
The villancico always includes a refrain and one or more stanzas with the principal melody in the top voice. The other voices may have been sung or played on instruments.

2. Juan del Encina
Juan del Encina (1468–1529) was the leading composer of villancicos. **Music: NAWM 48**

IV. Italy (HWM 243–44, NAWM 49)

A. The Frottola

Like the Spanish villancico, the Italian *frottola* (pl. frottole) was a strophic, syllabic, mostly homophonic song with the melody in the upper voice.

1. Social setting
Like villancicos, frottole were mock-popular songs written for the aristocracy.

2. Performance
The top voice was sung, while the other parts were usually played on instruments.

3. Marco Cara
Marco Cara (ca. 1465–1525) was among the best-known composers of frottole.   **Music: NAWM 49**

V. The Italian Madrigal (HWM 244–55, NAWM 50–53)

A. The Madrigal

The *madrigal* was the most important Italian secular genre of the sixteenth century. Composers sought to enrich the meaning of the text through the music and developed new means of expression and drama that helped to make Italy the leader in European music for the first time.

1. Definition and form
The *madrigal* was a *through-composed* musical setting of various types of Italian poetry without refrains

2. Poetry
Poems were sentimental or erotic with pastoral references and often ended with an epigram.

3. Music
Composers used a variety of homophonic and contrapuntal textures with voices of equal importance to convey the images and emotions of the text.

4. Voices
   The earliest madrigals were for four voices, and those around midcentury were typically for five voices. Madrigals were composed for one voice per part, but instruments could also be used in performance.

5. Social roles
   Madrigals were performed chiefly for the enjoyment of the singers themselves. Madrigals were also used in plays and, after about 1570, performed by professionals.

B. Early Madrigal Composers
   Philippe Verdelot (ca. 1480/85–?1530) was the most important early madrigalist and was active in Florence and Rome, where madrigals originated in the 1520s.

1. Jacques Arcadelt
   Jacques Arcadelt (ca. 1507–1568), who also worked in Florence and Rome, blended homophony with occasional imitation and witty effects.
   Music: NAWM 50

C. The Petrarchan Movement
   The rise of the madrigal was linked to the renewed interest in the poetry and ideals of fourteenth-century Italian poet *Francesco Petrarca* or *Petrarch* (1304–1374) by scholars like *Pietro Bembo* (1470–1547), who noted the sonic values of Petrarch's poetry.

1. Adrian Willaert
   Adrian Willaert and his student Gioseffo Zarlino translated Bembo's poetic theory into musical terms by matching harsh-sounding words with major thirds and sixths and pleasing-sounding words with minor thirds and sixths.

D. Midcentury Madrigalists
   Most madrigals at midcentury were for five voices and alternated freely between homophony and imitative or free polyphony.

1. Cipriano de Rore
   Cipriano de Rore (1516–1565) was the leading madrigalist at midcentury, whose madrigals reflect his interest in humanism.

2. Rhythm and ethos
   Rore sought to revive the Greek tradition of ethos by using longer rhythms for accented syllables than for unaccented syllables. **Music: NAWM 51**

3. Texture, rests, inflection, and interval
   Rore used texture, rests, inflection, and intervals with emotional associations to express the feelings sorrow of the text.

4. Chromaticism
   Rore and other mid-sixteenth-century composers used chromaticism for expressive purposes, and theorists approved of it, citing the ancient Greeks.

5. Vicentino

Composer and theorist *Nicola Vicentino* (1511–ca. 1576) proposed reviving the chromatic and enharmonic genera of Greek music.

E. Women as Composers and Performers

Despite social limitations, several women achieved fame as poets in the sixteenth century.

1. Maddalena Casulana

Maddalena Casulana (ca. 1544–ca. 1590s) was the first woman whose music was published and the first to regard herself as a professional composer.

2. Women's vocal ensembles

Women won more renown in the sixteenth century as singers, and many took on professional status. Madrigals composed for these women were concert pieces for the pleasure of an audience.

F. Later Madrigalists

Important northern madrigalists of the later sixteenth century included Orlando di Lasso, Philippe de Monte (1521–1603), and Giaches de Wert (1535–1596).

1. Luca Marenzio

Luca Marenzio (1553–1559) was one of the leading Italian madrigalists of the time and is known for madrigals depicting contrasting feelings and visual details. Striking musical images that evoke the text almost literally have come to be called *madrigalisms*. **Music: NAWM 52**

2. Carlo Gesualdo

Unlike other madrigalists, *Carlo Gesualdo* (ca. 1561–1613) was an aristocrat. His intensified the poetry through sharp contrasts in harmony, texture, and rhythm and is known for his use of chromaticism. **Music: NAWM 53**

G. Villanella, Canzonetta, and Balletto

Italian composers also wrote lighter genres of secular song, such as the *villanella,* the *canzonetta,* and the *balletto.*

H. The Legacy of the Madrigal

Madrigals were performed for the pleasure of the singers themselves throughout the sixteenth century, but later, madrigals were also performed in private concerts. The techniques that madrigalists developed for conveying text led directly to opera and other types of dramatic music.

VI. France (HWM 255–58, NAWM 54–55)

A. The New French Chanson

During the first half of the sixteenth century, composers cultivated a new type of chanson for amateur singers that was syllabic, mostly homophonic, usually strophic, and generally light-hearted. *Pierre Attaingnant* (ca. 1494–ca. 1552) published about 1,500 of these popular chansons.

1. Claudin de Sermisy

   One of the two principal composers of this type of chanson was *Claudin de Sermisy* (ca. 1490–1562). Some of his chanson were popular for decades.   **Music: NAWM 54**

2. Clément Janequin

   Clément Janequin (ca. 1485–ca. 1560) wrote many kinds of chanson but was known especially for his descriptive chansons.

B. The Later Franco-Flemish Chanson

The homophonic chanson appeared alongside the more traditional contrapuntal chanson.

C. Musique Mesurée

French poets and composers cultivated *musique mesurée* to imitate the rhythms of Greek poetry. Jean-Antoine de Baïf wrote French in ancient Greek and Latin meters, and *Claude Le Jeune* (1528–1600) and others translated that into musical rhythm, creating freely alternating duple and triple groupings. These irregular rhythms influenced the *air de cour*. **Music: NAWM 55**

VII. Germany (HWM 258)

Sixteenth-century German secular song contains a mixture of styles. The *Meistersinger* preserved the tradition of unaccompanied solo song. German polyphonic Lieder continued, but tastes veered toward Italian madrigals by mid-sixteenth century.

VIII. England (HWM 258–62, NAWM 56–58)

A. Native Secular Traditions

English secular music from court in the first half of the sixteenth century consisted of vocal and instrumental works in three and four parts.

1. Consort song

   The *consort song* was a distinctively English genre from around midcentury for voice accompanied by a consort of viols.

B. English Madrigals

Italian culture became fashionable in the late sixteenth century, and Italian madrigals translated into English, such as those in Nicholas Yonge's *Musica transalpina* (1588), were sung in homes. Many native composers wrote new madrigals as well.

1. Thomas Morley

   Thomas Morley (1557/8–1602) wrote English madrigals, *canzonets,* and *balletts.* He also wrote a book for the amateur musician about singing, improvising, and composing.   **Music: NAWM 56**

2. The Triumphs of Oriana

   Morley published a madrigal collection called *The Triumphes of Oriana* in honor of Queen Elizabeth.

3. Thomas Weelkes

Thomas Weelkes (ca. 1575–1623) was among the best-known English madrigalists, known for his use of word-painting. **Music: NAWM 57**

4. Performance

Although English secular polyphonic songs were intended for unaccompanied solo voices, they were also performed in combination with instruments.

C. Lute Songs

The *lute song* (or *air*), a solo song with lute accompaniment, became more prominent in the early 1600s. *John Dowland* (1563–1626) was one of the leading composers of lute songs.

1. Alternate formats

Singers accompanying themselves when performing lute songs. The lute part was notated in *tablature*. Lute song composition waned in the 1620s. **Music: NAWM 58**

IX. The Madrigal and its Impact (HWM 262–63)

In the spirit of humanism, composers of the Italian madrigal and other regional secular songs explored the declamation, expression, and depiction of words, which led directly to opera around 1600. The notion that musical elements could directly communicate feelings influenced later composers of opera, ballet, tone poems, and film scores. Madrigals continued to be sung in England into the eighteenth century, and many are now performed by school or amateur groups.

STUDY QUESTIONS

The First Market for Music (HWM 240–42)

1. Describe the "first market for music." What was being sold? Who was purchasing it? What are some reasons for the development of this market?

Spain (HWM 242–43, NAWM 48)

Music to Study

NAWM 48: Juan del Encina, *Oy comamos y bebamos,* villancico CD 3|46
(late fifteenth century)

2. Who was the intended audience for *villancicos* like Encina's *Oy comamos y bebamos* (NAWM 48)? What aspects of *Oy comamos y bebamos* may have appealed to them?

3. Describe the form of *Oy comamos y bebamos*. What characteristics are typical of villancicos?

4. How would *Oy comamos e bebamos* have been performed?

Italy (HWM 243–44, NAWM 49)

5. What is a frottola? Where and when was it popular? Who was the intended audience for frottole?

Music to Study

NAWM 49: Marco Cara, *Io non compro più speranza,* frottola (ca. 1500) ⟨ CD 3|47 ⟩

6. What traits of the frottola are exemplified in Cara's *Io non compro più speranza* (NAWM 49)?

7. In what ways are the form, melody, rhythm, and texture of Cara's frottola (NAWM 49) similar to and different from Encina's villancico (NAWM 48)?

The Italian Madrigal (HWM 244–55, NAWM 50–53)

8. Describe the sixteenth-century Italian *madrigal*. How does it differ from the fourteenth-century madrigal (see NAWM 28)? How does it differ from the frottola?

9. In what circumstances were madrigals performed, and by whom?

Music to Study

NAWM 50: Jacques Arcadelt, *Il bianco e dolce cigno,* madrigal   CD 3|54   CD 2|4
(ca. 1538)

10. In what ways does Arcadelt's madrigal *Il bianco e dolce cigno* (NAWM 50) resemble a frottola, such as Cara's *Io non compro più speranza* (NAWM 49)?

In what ways is it different from a frottola?

11. In the sixteenth century, sexual climax was known as "the little death," and poets often used this image in erotic poetry. Why were madrigals that used erotic poetry so popular? Refer to question 9 above when answering this.

12. In what ways does Arcadelt reflect in his music the feelings or the imagery of the text?

13. Who was Francesco Petrarca, or Petrarch? When did he live? What was his importance for the sixteenth-century madrigal?

14. Who was Pietro Bembo? When did he live? What was his importance for the madrigal?

15. How did Adrian Willaert translate Bembo's theory into musical terms?

Music to Study

NAWM 51: Cipriano de Rore, *Da le belle contrade d'oriente,*   CD 3|56   CD 2|6
madrigal (ca. 1560–65)

16. In Rore's *Da le belle contrade d'oriente* (NAWM 51), how does the music reflect the presence of two speakers in the poem?

17. How does Rore set off the sestet from the octave in this sonnet?

18. How does the music reflect the meaning and mood of the words?

19. How does the music reflect the accentuation and rhythm of the words?

20. In light of these answers, how is Rore's madrigal similar to and different from Arcadelt's (NAWM 50) in terms of text setting?

21. Where in Rore's madrigal is there direct chromatic motion (for instance, from a B to B♭ or F to F♯ or the reverse) within a single melodic line?

    In which earlier piece(s) in NAWM does direct chromatic motion occur?

    What connections do you see between the musical culture that produced the madrigal by Rore and the musical culture(s) that produced the earlier piece or pieces?

22. What was the *concerto delle donne* (women's ensemble) at Ferrara? Who established it, when, and who took part? How did the formation of such ensembles affect the vocal techniques composers used in their madrigals?

Music to Study

NAWM 52: Luca Marenzio, *Solo e pensoso,* madrigal (1590s) [CD 3|59]

NAWM 53: Carlo Gesualdo, *"Io parto" e non più dissi,* [CD 3|65] [CD 2|9]
madrigal (ca. 1600)

23. *Solo e pensoso* (NAWM 52) is a sonnet by Petrarch. How did Marenzio set off the sestet from the octave? In what other ways does Marenzio's setting reflect the structure of the text?

24. How does Marenzio's music suggest the poetic imagery of *Solo e pensoso*? Refer to specific words and measure numbers.

25. How does the late madrigal style of Marenzio differ from the earlier madrigal styles of Arcadelt and Rore?

26. In *"Io parto" e non più dissi* (NAWM 40), how does Gesualdo suggest the two speakers?

27. How does Gesualdo use chromaticism, contrasting diatonic sections, melodic motion, and rhythm to reflect the emotional sense and imagery of the text?

28. How does the music project a single mode, despite all the chromaticism?

29. Why could Gesualdo take such bold steps with chromaticism?

30. Describe the villanella, canzonetta, and balletto. In what ways are they like frottole and in what ways are they like madrigals?

France (HWM 255–58, NAWM 54–55)

31. Describe the musical style of the most popular kind of chanson in the period 1520–50.

32. Who were the principal composers of these chansons?

Who was the major publisher of this type of chanson?

What evidence is there for the popularity of this type of chanson?

Music to Study

NAWM 54: Claudin de Sermisy, *Tant que vivray,* chanson (ca. 1530s)

〔CD 3|68〕 〔CD 2|12〕

NAWM 55: Claude Le Jeune, *Revecy venir du printans,* chanson (late sixteenth century)

〔CD 3|71〕

33. How does the new style of chanson from the period 1520–50, exemplified by Sermisy's *Tant que vivray* (NAWM 54), compare to the Italian frottola, such as Cara's *Io non compro più speranza* (NAWM 49), and the early madrigal, such as Arcadelt's *Il bianco e dolce cigno* (NAWM 50)?

34. How does this chanson compare to Josquin's *Mille regretz* (NAWM 41)?

35. What are the characteristics of *musique mesurée*? How are these qualities exemplified in Le Jeune's *Revecy venir du printans* (NAWM 55)?

Why did composers use *musique mesurée*?

36. In this strophic song with refrain, how does Le Jeune vary the verses? How does this give shape to the whole work?

Germany (HWM 258)

37. What are the types and characteristics of German secular song in the sixteenth century?

England (HWM 258–62, NAWM 56–58)

38. What was *Musica transalpina*, and when did it appear? What effect did it have on the development of the English madrigal?

Music to Study

NAWM 56: Thomas Morley, *My bonny lass she smileth,*
ballett (ca. 1595)

CD 3|79   CD 2|15

NAWM 57: Thomas Weelkes, *As Vesta was,* madrigal (ca. 1601)

CD 3|82   CD 2|18

NAWM 58: John Dowland, *Flow, my tears,* air or lute song
(ca. 1600)

CD 4|1   CD 2|23

39. What traits of the ballett are exemplified in Morley's *My bonny lass?*

40. In Weelkes's madrigal *As Vesta was* (NAWM 57), how are the images and feelings in the text conveyed in the music?

41. Comparing Weelkes's madrigal to the madrigals in NAWM 50–53, what similarities and what differences do you notice between English and Italian madrigals?

42. What are the characteristics of an English lute song ca. 1600, as exemplified by Dowland's *Flow, my tears* (NAWM 58)? How is it like a madrigal, and how is it different?

43. Why is *Flow, my tears* modal, and not tonal (following the harmonic language of the common-practice period, ca. 1670–ca. 1900)?

44. What is *tablature*? What does it convey to the performer? Explain how the lute tablature at the beginning of the second measure of *Flow, my tears* correspond to the transcription above it.

The Madrigal and its Impact (HWM 262–63)

45. What musical, poetic, and expressive aspects of the Italian madrigal were most influential on later generations?

TERMS TO KNOW

villancico

frottola

madrigal (sixteenth-century)

through-composed

madrigalisms

villanella, canzonetta, balletto

musique mesurée

air de cour

Meistersinger

consort song

canzonets, balletts

lute song, or air

tablature

NAMES TO KNOW

Juan del Encina

Marco Cara

Jacob Arcadelt

Petrarch (Francesco Petrarca)

Pietro Bembo

Cipriano de Rore

Nicola Vicentino

Maddalena Casulana

Luca Marenzio

Carlo Gesualdo

Pierre Attaingnant

Claudin de Sermisy

Claude Le Jeune

Musica transalpina

Thomas Morley

The Triumphes of Oriana

Thomas Weelkes

John Dowland

REVIEW QUESTIONS

1. Add to the timeline you made for the Renaissance in chapter 7 the pieces, composers, and events discussed in this chapter.
2. Trace the development of secular vocal music in Italy from the frottola to the madrigals of Marenzio and Gesualdo.
3. Describe the varieties of secular vocal music practiced in Spain, France, England, and Germany during the sixteenth century. Which of these forms were influenced by the Italian madrigal, and in what ways?
4. In what ways can you compare the madrigal in England (or Italy, or both) to popular music of the present or recent past? Try to come up with as many examples as you can of parallels between the madrigal, the popular music of the sixteenth century, and Top-40 pop music, rock, rap, country, or any other type of popular music current today. What are some important differences?
5. Trace the influence of humanism and the revival of ideals associated with ancient Greek music on vocal music in Italy and France during the sixteenth century, focusing on the genres most affected by these influences.
6. Describe the relation of music and words in the various forms of sixteenth-century vocal music and contrast it with earlier practices of setting texts.

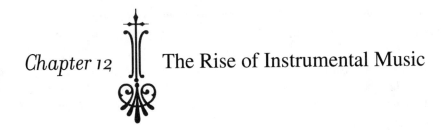

Chapter 12 The Rise of Instrumental Music

CHAPTER OBJECTIVES

After you complete the reading, study of the music, and study questions for this chapter, you should be able to

1. describe the principal instrument families from the Renaissance and how they are similar to or different from their Medieval predecessors;

2. describe the principal genres of sixteenth-century instrumental music and know which are derived from vocal music, dancing, or improvisation;

3. identify some of the composers and works associated with instrumental music in the Renaissance; and

4. explain what is distinctive about Venice and Venetian music in the late sixteenth and early seventeenth centuries.

CHAPTER OUTLINE

I. Introduction (HWM 264–65)

After 1450, churches, patrons, and musical amateurs increasingly cultivated instrumental music. It was written down more often, reflecting an increase in status and musical literacy for instrumentalists. There were new instruments, new roles for instrumental music, new styles, and new genres, such as *variations, prelude, fantasia, toccata, ricercare, canzona,* and *sonata.*

II. Instruments (HWM 265–70)

1. Books on instruments
Books about instruments were written for amateurs as well as the practicing musician. Two examples are Sebastian Virdung's *Musica getutscht* (1511) and Michael Praetorius's *Syntagma musicum* (1618). Musicians maintained the distinction between haut and bas instruments, begun during the Middle Ages.

2. Instrumental families and consorts
Instrument families provided one uniform timbre throughout the entire range from soprano to bass. In England, an instrumental ensemble was called a *consort*.

3. Wind and percussion
Wind and percussion instruments continued from the Middle Ages. Newly prominent wind instruments were the *sackbut* and *crumhorn*.

4. Plucked strings
The most popular household instrument in the sixteenth century was the *lute*, a plucked string instrument. The Spanish *vihuela* was closely related to the lute.

5. Bowed strings
The leading bowed string instrument in the sixteenth century was the *viol* or *viola da gamba*. Its distant cousin, the *violin*, became the leading bowed string instrument of the seventeenth century.

6. Keyboard
Large church organs and small positive organs were common. The *clavichord* and *harpsichord* were the two main types of keyboards. Other names for the harpsichord include *virginal* (used in England) and *clavecin* (used in France).

7. Renaissance instruments and music
Each Renaissance instrument has its own qualities particularly suited to the music performed on it.

III. Types of Instrumental Music (HWM 270–81, NAWM 59–61)

Instrumental music in the Renaissance served a variety of functions and was printed for amateurs and professionals. There were five main categories: (1) dance music; (2) arrangements of vocal pieces; (3) settings of existing melodies; (4) variations; and (5) abstract works.

A. Dance Music

Dancing was a central part of social life. Sixteenth-century composers of dance music began developing instrumental music that was distinctive from vocal music.

1. Improvisation and composition
Printed dance pieces show us that sixteenth-century performers often improvised by ornamenting a given melodic line or by adding one or more contrapuntal parts to a given melody or line.

2. Functional and stylized dance music
Published dances for ensemble were functional, but most dances for solo lute or keyboard were stylized.

3. Rhythm and form
Each dance type has a characteristic rhythm, meter, tempo, and form.

4. Basse danse and branle
The favorite courtly dance of the fifteenth and early sixteenth centuries was the *basse danse*. The *branle gay* was a dance in lively triple time.
Music: NAWM 59a–b

5. Dance pairs
   Renaissance dances were often grouped in contrasting pairs, such as the *pavane* and *galliard.*

Music in Context: Social Dance
   The best-known dance treatise from the Renaissance is *Orchésographie* by dancing master Thoinot Arbeau. Social dance was considered a pleasant and profitable activity. Not only did it help one stay physically fit, it also allowed men and women to mingle in arranged configurations and observe one another. Dancing was considered a kind of rhetoric by which persons, through movement, could make themselves understood and persuade others that they have certain desirable personality traits.

B. Arrangements of Vocal Music
   Another major source for instrumental music was vocal music, which was often played by instrumentalists.

1. Intabulations
   Lutenists and keyboard players, such as Spanish vihuelist *Luys de Narváez* (fl. 1526–49), made *intabulations* of vocal pieces, arrangements that were written in tablature and were idiomatic for the instrument. **Music: NAWM 60a**

C. Settings of Existing Melodies
   Some instrumental pieces incorporated existing melodies.

1. Chant settings and organ music
   In Catholic churches, antiphonal chants could be performed in alternation between the choir (singing chant) and the organ playing a cantus-firmus setting or paraphrase. A compilation of the organ verses for a complete Mass is an *organ mass.*

2. Organ chorales
   Polyphonic arrangements of chorales for organ (organ chorales) appeared from the 1570s on.

3. *In Nomines*
   Sixteenth- and seventeenth-century English composers wrote over two hundred *In Nomines,* pieces for consort or keyboard all based on the same cantus firmus.

D. Variations

1. Types of variations
   Variations or *variations form* was a sixteenth-century invention in which a given *theme* was followed by a series of variations on that theme. Some musicians also wrote and improvised variations on repeated bass lines, called *ostinatos,* or on standard airs for singing verses, such as *Guárdame las vacas* and the romanesca. **Music: NAWM 60b**

2. English virginalists
   English virginalists of the late sixteenth and early seventeenth centuries, such as William Byrd, cultivated the variation, primarily using dances or familiar songs as their themes. **Music: NAWM 61**

E. Abstract Instrumental Works

Beginning in the late fifteenth and sixteenth centuries, instrumentalists cultivated music that was truly independent of dance rhythms or borrowed tunes.

1. Introductory and improvisatory pieces

Improvisatory pieces like the *prelude, fantasia,* and *ricercare* were used to introduce a song, fill time during church services, establish the mode of a subsequent song, test tuning, and entertain.

2. Toccata

The *toccata* was the chief form of keyboard music in improvisatory style during the second half of the sixteenth century.

3. Ricercare

The *ricercare* or *ricercar* evolved from an early improvisatory form into a work based on a series of imitative sections, much like a motet.

4. Canzona

The *canzona* or *canzon* originated as a work in the style of a French chanson, with a typical opening figure (long-short-short), but by the late sixteenth century was a light, fast-moving, and strongly rhythmic genre of instrumental music that featured several themes, most treated in imitation, resulting in a series of contrasting sections.

IV. Music in Venice (HWM 281–84, NAWM 62)

Instrumental performers and composition in Venice reached a high level in the late sixteenth and early seventeenth centuries, and their music exemplifies traits of the late Renaissance and early Baroque period.

A. Venice

Venice, a wealthy city of traders, was the second most important Italian city after Rome.

1. Patronage of the arts

The Venetian government used lavish spectacles, music, and art as cultural propaganda.

B. Church of St. Mark

The center of Venetian musical culture was the *Church of St. Mark,* and its choirmaster position was the most coveted musical post in all of Italy. A permanent instrumental ensemble was established in 1568.

C. Giovanni Gabrieli

Giovanni Gabrieli (ca. 1555–1612) served St. Mark's for almost thirty years, and his compositions used all the available musical resources.

1. Polychoral motets

Gabrieli wrote *polychoral motets,* works for two or more choirs. Composers in the Venetian region often wrote music for divided choirs.

2. Ensemble canzonas

Gabrieli also applied the concept of divided choirs to instruments in his canzonas. **Music: NAWM 62**

3. Sonatas

   Like the canzona, the Venetian *sonata* consisted of a series of sections each based on a different subject or on variants of a single subject. Gabrieli's *Sonata pian' e forte* was among the first works to mark dynamics and designate a particular instrument for each part.

Biography: Giovanni Gabrieli

   In his early career, Gabrieli served Duke Albrecht V in Munich and studied with Orlando di Lasso. In 1585, he moved to Venice, serving at St. Mark's as organist, a position which required the supervision of instrumentalists as well. He also served the Scuola Grande in San Rocco. Both of these major Venetian institutions offered the opportunity to compose lavish ceremonial music for voices and instruments.

V. Instrumental Music Gains Independence (HWM 284–85)

Instrumental music continued to gain independence, until by the nineteenth century it reached a level of prestige higher than most vocal music. Renaissance instrumental music has been revived in recent decades, and Gabrieli's canzonas and sonatas are well known.

STUDY QUESTIONS

Introduction (HWM 264–65)

1. Why do we have so little instrumental music from before 1450? How and why did this change after about 1450? What evidence is there for a rising interest in instrumental music during the Renaissance?

Instruments (HWM 265–70)

2. What are *Musica getutscht* and *Syntagma musicum*? Who wrote them, and when? Why are they important?

3. What is an *instrument family*? Why is it significant that instruments were built in families?

4. What were the principal instruments in the sixteenth century? How do they relate to their medieval ancestors, and how do they relate to their modern relatives?

Types of Instrumental Music (HWM 270–81, NAWM 59–61)

5. What are the main categories of instrumental music in the sixteenth century?

6. What were the roles of dancing in Renaissance society?

7. What are some of the main characteristics of Renaissance dance music? Describe the difference between functional and stylized dance music.

8. How were Renaissance dances grouped? What combinations were popular?

Music to Study

NAWM 59: Pierre Attaingnant (publisher), Dances from *Danseries a 4 parties, second livre* (ca. 1547), excerpts

    59a: Basse danse   CD 4|4   CD 2|26

    59b: Branle gay, *Que je chatoulle ta fossette*   CD 4|6   CD 2|28

9. How do the Basse danse and Branle gay from Attaingnant's *Danseries a 4 parties, second book* (NAWM 59), exemplify the characteristics of Renaissance dance music?

10. What types of sixteenth-century instrumental music were derived from vocal music? How do these types differ from those written originally for instruments?

| *Music to Study* |

NAWM 60: Luis de Narváez, from *Los seys libros del Delphin* (ca. 1538)

    60a: *Cancion Mille regres,* intabluation of Josquin's *Mille regretz*   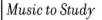 CD 4|7

    60b: *Cuatro diferencias sobre "Guárdame las vacas"*   CD 4|8
    (Four Variations on "Guárdame las vacas"), variations

NAWM 61: William Byrd, *Pavana Lachrymae,* pavane variations   CD 4|9   CD 2|29
(ca. 1600)

11. Compare Luis de Narváez's *Cancion Mille regres* (NAWM 60a) with Josquin's *Mille regretz* (NAWM 41). What does Narváez retain from the vocal model? What does he change? Why did he make those changes?

What can modern-day vocalists learn about music ficta from this instrumental piece?

12. What types of variations were written in the sixteenth century?

13. What is varied in Narváez's Four Variations on *Guárdame las vacas* (NAWM 60b)? Where does it come from? How does Narváez make each variation distinctive?

14. What is varied in Byrd's *Pavana Lachyrmae* (NAWM 61)? How does Byrd use figuration to vary the music?

15. How is this instrumental composition similar to and different from Narváez's *Cancion Mille regres* (NAWM 60a)? What accounts for those similarities and differences?

16. What role did improvisation play in sixteenth-century musical performance and education? What forms and genres relate to improvisation?

17. What is a *toccata*? On which instruments was it performed? What are its main musical characteristics, and how are they exemplified in the toccata by Claudio Merulo excerpted in Example 12.4 in HWM, p. 279?

18. What is a *ricercare* (or *ricercar*) in the sixteenth century? What are its main characteristics? What vocal genre does the late-sixteenth-century ricercare resemble?

19. What is a *canzona*? What vocal form was it related to, and what did it develop into? Describe the characteristics of a sixteenth-century canzona.

Music in Venice (HWM 281–84, NAWM 62)

20. How was Venice different from other Italian city-states? How did this affect the patronage of the arts?

Who were these patrons? What kinds of music did they support?

21. Summarize Giovanni Gabrieli's career and reputation. Where did he work, and what types of music did he write?

Music to Study

NAWM 62: Giovanni Gabrieli, *Canzon septimi toni a 8,* from *Sacrae symphoniae,* ensemble canzona (ca. 1597)

22. How does Gabrieli's *Canzon septimi toni a 8* (NAWM 62) exemplify the characteristics of the Renaissance canzona? How does it exemplify characteristics of Venetian church music?

23. How does Gabrieli structure the form of NAWM 62? How does that compare to the forms of NAWM 60a, 60b, and 61?

---

24. What was a *sonata* in the sixteenth century?

25. What is special about Giovanni Gabrieli's *Sonata pian' e forte*?

Instrumental Music Gains Independence (HWM 284–85)

26. What changes during the sixteenth century had an impact on instrumental music of the time and in later centuries? How has Renaissance instrumental music been received, in its time and over the subsequent centuries?

TERMS TO KNOW

instrumental families
consort
sackbut
crumhorn
lute
vihuela
viol, viola da gamba
violin
clavichord
harpsichord
virginal
clavecin
basse danse
branle gay

pavane and galliard
intabulation
organ mass
variations, variation form
theme
ostinatos
prelude
fantasia
toccata
ricercare, ricercar
canzona, canzon
polychoral motets
sonata (sixteenth-century)

NAMES TO KNOW

Sebastian Virdung, *Musica Getutscht*
Michael Praetorius, *Syntagma
   musicum*
Luys de Narváez

Church of St. Mark
Giovanni Gabrieli
Sonata pian' e forte

REVIEW QUESTIONS

1. Add to the timeline you made for the Renaissance in chapter 7 the pieces, composers, and events discussed in this chapter.
2. Name and describe the various types of instruments in the sixteenth century.
3. Name and describe the various types of notated instrumental music in the sixteenth century. Which ones were related to vocal models, to dancing, or to improvisation, and how?
4. What types of notated instrumental music originating in the Renaissance (see question 3 above) are still prominent today, and how is the style of today's examples similar to or different from the examples from the Renaissance?
5. In general, how is Renaissance instrumental music different from medieval instrumental music? What were some causes for these changes? Why were these changes important?

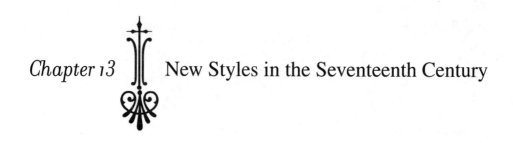

Chapter 13 | New Styles in the Seventeenth Century

CHAPTER OBJECTIVES

After you complete the reading, study of the music, and study questions for this chapter, you should be able to

1. relate music of the Baroque period to the culture and art of the time; and
2. describe the characteristics that distinguish Baroque music from music of earlier periods.

CHAPTER OUTLINE

I. Introduction (HWM 288)

Around 1600, Italian musicians created new musical idioms, styles, and genres, beginning a new period that was later named *"Baroque."* While music from this period has some common conventions, it also is quite diverse in genre and style.

II. Europe in the Seventeenth Century (HWM 289–92)

New developments in science, politics, and economics affected musicians.
1. The scientific revolution
    Mathematics, observation, and practical experiments replaced received opinion and tradition as scientific methods.
2. Politics, religion, and war
    Political and religious conflicts during the seventeenth century directly affected musicians.
3. Colonies
    Colonists brought their European musical traditions to faraway locations.
4. Capitalism
    Capitalism created a rise in public opera and concerts and increased demand for published music, instruments, and music lessons.

5. Patronage
   Music patronage came from the court, church, city, and private academies. Italy remained the dominant influence on European music, while
   French music was imitated widely and German musicians blended Italian and French styles.

III. From Renaissance to Baroque (HWM 292–99, NAWM 63)

A. The Baroque as Term and Period
   The word "baroque" was used in the mid-eighteenth century to describe
   music or art regarded as bizarre or exaggerated. Later it was used in a
   positive way to describe seventeenth- and early-eighteenth-century art
   and architecture. Music historians now use it for the period of about
   1600 to 1750. The *Baroque period* embraced a variety of musical styles
   that share some general conventions and ideals, including the belief that
   music should move the affections.

B. The Dramatic Baroque
   Seventeenth-century literature, art, and music had highly dramatic qualities.

   1. Baroque art
   The theatricality of Baroque art can be seen in Gian Lorenzo Bernini's
   dynamic *David* and rapturous *The Ecstasy of St. Teresa.*

   2. Baroque architecture
   In his design for the front of St. Peter's Basilica at the Vatican, Bernini
   used ancient and Renaissance elements in new, dramatic ways. Just as in
   architecture, the central impulse of Baroque music is dramatization.

C. The Affections
   Baroque composers sought to write music that was expressive of the *af-*
   fections, or states of the soul. These are not the composer's own emotions but generalized states of feeling.

D. The Second Practice
   To convey a poetic text, *Claudio Monteverdi* (1567–1643) used striking
   dissonances and deliberately broke the rules of counterpoint in order to
   dramatize the words. When he was criticized by *Giovanni Maria Artusi,*
   Monteverdi defended himself by distinguishing between the *prima prat-*
   ica, or *first practice,* of sixteenth-century counterpoint and the *seconda*
   pratica, or *second practice,* in which the music is the servant of the
   words rather than the dominant partner.   **Music: NAWM 63**

Biography: Claudio Monteverdi
   Monteverdi wrote only vocal and dramatic works. Born and trained in
   Cremona, he was hired by the duke of Mantua and later promoted to
   master of music in the ducal chapel. His first five books of madrigals
   shift in style from late Renaissance to seconda practica. His first operas
   were *L'Orfeo* and *L'Arianna,* both written for Mantua. Dissatisfied with
   his position, Monteverdi became maestro di capella at St. Mark's in
   Venice, where he remained until his death. In Venice, he continued to
   write both sacred and secular vocal music, including opera.

IV. General Characteristics of Baroque Music (HWM 300–6)

Music of the Baroque era shares several traits that distinguish it from music of other periods.

A. Treble-Bass Polarity

Seventeenth-century music typically emphasizes homophony with prominent bass and treble lines.

B. The Basso Continuo

In the notational system called *basso continuo* or *thoroughbass,* a melody (or melodies) and a bass line were written out, but the harmony was filled in by performers playing one or more *continuo instruments,* like the *theorbo.* Composers indicated the appropriate harmonies with *figured bass.*

1. Realization

The *realization* of a bass varied according to the type of piece and skill and taste of the player.

C. The Concertato Medium

Seventeenth-century composers frequently used the *concertato medium,* combining voices with instruments, to create a musical *concerto,* such as the *concerted madrigal* and the *sacred concerto.*

D. Mean-Tone and Equal Temperaments

Joining instruments and voices required compromises between just intonation, used by singers and string players; mean-tone temperament, used for keyboards; and more equal temperaments, used by lutes and viols. As composers explored a wider range of chords, more nearly equal temperaments became more accepted.

E. Chords, Dissonance, and Chromaticism

Musicians came to think of vertical sonorities as chords, and of dissonances as nonchord tones. Chromaticism was used especially to express intense emotions.

F. Harmonically Driven Counterpoint

A new kind of counterpoint evolved in which the lines had to fit the chords of the basso continuo so that the counterpoint was governed by harmony.

G. Regular and Flexible Rhythm

Two types of rhythm, very flexible and very metric, were often used in succession to provide contrast. By midcentury, barlines were used to mark off *measures.*

H. Idiomatic Styles

The growing importance of soloists led seventeenth-century musicians to develop distinctive idiomatic styles for voice and each instrument family.

I. Embellishments and Improvisation in Performance

Baroque musicians regarded pieces as occasions for performance, not unalterable texts, and performers were expected to fill out or embellish what the composer had written.

1. Ornamentation

   Ornamentation was a means of moving the affections, and it was done by using *ornaments* (brief formulas) or more extended embellishments in a process called *division, diminution,* or *figuration.*

2. Alterations

   Performers could also change the score in other ways, including omitting and substituting sections, or adding *cadenzas.*

J. From Modal to Tonal Music

By the last third of the seventeenth century, composers were writing *tonal* music, after a gradual evolution from modality to *tonality.*

V. Enduring Innovations (HWM 306)

Many innovations of the Baroque era, including dramatic effects, expressivity, chordal harmony, and tonality, endured into the eighteenth and nineteenth centuries, while others, such as basso continuo and mean-tone temperament, gradually passed out of fashion.

STUDY QUESTIONS

Europe in the Seventeenth Century (HWM 289–92)

1. What new developments in science, politics, and economics arose during the seventeenth century? How did they influence music?

2. How was music supported financially in the seventeenth and eighteenth centuries, and by whom? How did the situation differ in various countries, and how did this affect music?

From Renaissance to Baroque (HWM 292–99, NAWM 63)

3. What did the term "baroque" mean in the eighteenth century?

   How was it later used in writing on art history?

   How is it used now in music history? Why is it more helpful to refer to "the Baroque period" than to "Baroque style"?

4. In what ways was the literature, art, and architecture of the seventeenth century theatrical or dramatic? How does this compare to music of the time?

5. What are the *affections*? How does the representation of affections in music differ from the later idea of expressing an individual artist's feelings?

Music to Study

NAWM 63: Claudio Monteverdi, *Cruda Amarilli,* madrigal   (late 1590s)

6. How does Monteverdi use dissonances, and particularly unprepared dissonances, to convey the meaning of the text in *Cruda Amarilli* (NAWM 63)?

7. To what did Giovanni Maria Artusi object in *Cruda Amarilli*? Why did he object so strongly? What was he defending?

8. Monteverdi claimed that he was following a "second practice" (*seconda pratica*). What was the basis for this second practice? With what other practice does Monteverdi contrast it, and how do the two practices differ?

9. Summarize Monteverdi's career and reputation.

General Characteristics of Baroque Music (HWM 300–6)

10. How does the typical musical texture in the Baroque period differ from that of the Renaissance?

11. Define the following terms, and explain the significance of each concept.

basso continuo or thoroughbass

continuo instruments

figured bass

realization

12. What is the *concertato medium*? What did *concerto* mean in the early seventeenth century?

13. Compare the opening of Giulio Caccini's *Vedrò 'l mio sol* as it appears in NAWM 64 with the original publication, shown in HWM, p. 301. (In the latter, note that the vocal line is notated in soprano clef.) What notes are present in the NAWM edition that are not present in the original publication?

How are these notes differentiated from the others on the page?

Why are they present in the NAWM edition? Why are they absent in the original publication?

14. How did the emphasis on the bass and the use of basso continuo change how counterpoint was conceived and written and how dissonance was defined?

15. What is new about rhythm in seventeenth-century music, in contrast to earlier music?

16. How did the Renaissance ideal of writing music that could be performed by any combination of voices and instruments change in the seventeenth century? What was the effect on composition?

17. In what ways did performers in the Baroque era alter the written music? Why did they do this? What does this tell us about the roles of composer, performer, and notation?

18. What is *tonality*? When and how did it evolve? Why was figured bass important in its development?

Enduring Innovations (HWM 306)

19. What elements of seventeenth century music are still with us?

TERMS TO KNOW

Baroque period
affections
prima pratica, first practice
seconda pratica, second practice
basso continuo, thoroughbass
continuo instruments
theorbo
figured bass
realization
concertato medium

concerto (seventeenth century)
concerted madrigal
sacred concerto
measure
ornamentation
ornament
division, diminution, figuration
cadenza
tonal, tonality

NAMES TO KNOW

Claudio Monteverdi

Giovanni Maria Artusi

REVIEW QUESTIONS

1. Make a timeline for the seventeenth century and place on it the important people, writings, and events discussed in this chapter. Leave enough space to add more items as you work through the next four chapters.
2. What are the principal characteristics that distinguish music of the Baroque period from music of the Renaissance?
3. What new concepts or procedures were developed in the period 1600–1650 as composers sought to find ways to capture human emotions in music?

Chapter 14 The Invention of Opera

CHAPTER OBJECTIVES

After you complete the reading, study of the music, and study questions for this chapter, you should be able to

1. describe the forerunners of opera, identify the composers involved, and explain what they contributed to opera;

2. trace the development of Italian opera from its forerunners through the middle of the seventeenth century; and

3. identify some of the major composers of early opera and describe their significance to its history.

CHAPTER OUTLINE

I. Introduction (HWM 307)

Opera is the union of text (the *libretto*), drama, and music. Opera was inspired by ancient Greek tragedy and was influenced by existing musical genres.

II. Forerunners of Opera (HWM 307–12, NAWM 64)

The association of music and drama goes back to ancient times.

A. Renaissance Antecedents

1. Pastoral drama
The subject, style, mythological characters, and use of music and dance in the *pastoral drama* were adopted by the earliest opera composers.

2. Madrigal and madrigal style
Madrigal composers had experience in expressing emotions and dramatizing text, and sometimes they linked madrigals together to create the *madrigal comedy* or *madrigal cycle*.

3. Intermedio

The *intermedio,* a musical interlude between acts of a play, was perhaps the most direct source for opera, containing dialogue, various types of vocal and instrumental music, dances, costumes, scenery, and stage effects.

4. The 1589 intermedi

Several artists who worked on the intermedi for *La pellegrina* in 1589 were later involved in the earliest operas.

B. Greek Tragedy as a Model

The creators of opera sought to recreate the emotional power of ancient Greek tragedies.

1. Music in Greek tragedy

Some Renaissance scholars believed that only choruses were sung in ancient tragedy.

2. Girolamo Mei

Girolamo Mei (1519–1594) believed that the entire text of Greek tragedy was sung and that the Greeks achieved powerful emotional effects through melody that followed the natural inflections and rhythms of expressive speech.

C. The Florentine Camerata

The *Camerata* met at the home of *Giovanni de' Bardi* (1534–1612) in Florence and discussed a variety of topics, including Mei's ideas about Greek music.

1. Vincenzo Galilei

In his *Dialogo della musica antica et della moderna* (Dialogue of Ancient and Modern Music, 1581), *Vincenzo Galilei* (ca. 1520s–1591) used Mei's ideas to suggest that solo melody could express poetry better than polyphony.

D. Monody, Aria, and Solo Madrigal

1. Monody

Galilei advocated *monody,* accompanied solo singing.

2. Caccini's *Le nuove musiche*

Giulio Caccini (ca. 1550–1618) wrote two types of monody in *Le nuove musiche* (The New Music, 1602): *arias* (strophic songs) and *solo madrigals* (through-composed songs). Caccini wrote into the music the embellishments singers usually added in performance.   **Music: NAWM 64**

III. The First Operas (HWM 312–16, NAWM 65)

1. Peri and Rinuccini's *Dafne*

In 1598, poet *Ottaviano Rinuccini* (1562–1621) and composer *Jacopo Peri* (1561–1633) produced *Dafne,* the first opera, modeled on Greek plays.

2. Cavalieri

Emilio de' Cavalieri (ca. 1550–1602) produced in Rome in 1600 *Rappresentatione di Anima et di Corpo* (Representation of the Soul and the Body, 1600), which was the longest entirely musical stage work at the time.

A. *L'Euridice*

The first surviving opera is Peri and Rinuccini's *L'Euridice,* produced in Florence in 1600. Peri devised a vocal style that imitated speech and varied his approach to match the dramatic situation.

1. The recitative style
Recitative style imitated speech by supporting sustained or stressed syllables with consonant harmonies and freely using consonances and dissonances for syllables that were unstressed or passed over quickly in speech.

2. Varied styles of monody
Peri employed several types of monody in *L'Euridice,* including strophic aria with a *ritornello,* a song framed by a *sinfonia,* and recitative, using dissonance and other effects for expressivity. He also borrowed from traditions of madrigal, aria, pastoral drama, and intermedio. **Music: NAWM 65**

B. The Impact of Monody

Various styles of monody were used by both sacred and secular music. Monody made musical theater possible.

IV. Claudio Monteverdi (HWM 316–19, NAWM 66–67)

Monteverdi was the first to show the full potential of opera.

A. *L'Orfeo*

Monteverdi's *L'Orfeo* (Mantua, 1607), to a libretto by Alessandro Striggio, is in five acts, mixes musical styles, and uses a larger and more varied group of instruments than Peri's opera used.

1. Monody
Like Peri, Monteverdi employed several kinds of monody, including arias that use *strophic variation.*

2. Ensembles
Monteverdi also used many duets, dances, and ballettos and ensemble madrigals to reflect the varying emotions of the drama. Act I is an arch, centering on a recitative by Orfeo, with repeating choruses and ritornellos creating large-scale forms.

3. Act II
The structure of Act II pushes forward the momentum of the drama, from the unbroken string of arias and ensembles expressing Orfeo's happiness to the Messenger's news of Euridice's death to Orfeo's lament. **Music: NAWM 66**

B. Later Dramatic Works

1. *L'Arianna*
Although only a fragment of *L'Arianna* (Monteverdi's second opera) survives, it was just as successful as *L'Orfeo.*

2. *Combattimento*
In *Combattimento di Tancredi e Clorinda* (The Combat of Tancred and Clorinda, 1624), Monteverdi devised the *stile concitato* to convey anger and warlike actions.

3. Venetian operas
Monteverdi wrote three operas for Venice, of which two survive: *Il ritorno d'Ulisse* (The Return of Ulysses, 1640) and *L'incoronazione di Poppea* (The Coronation of Poppea, 1643). For *Poppea,* Monteverdi changed styles frequently to reflect the characters and their feelings, using recitative, aria styles, and *recitative arioso,* or *arioso.* **Music: NAWM 67**

V. The Spread of Italian Opera (HWM 319–27, NAWM 68)

As opera spread from courts to cities, it changed from entertainment based on humanist ideals to a theatrical spectacle centered on singers.

A. Florence: Francesca Caccini
Only a few more operas were staged in Florence through the 1620s. The court preferred ballets and intermedi, such as *La liberazione di Ruggiero* (1625), an opera-like blend of ballet and intermedio by *Francesca Caccini* (1587–ca. 1645). She was a singer, a teacher, and one of the most prolific composers of dramatic music at the time.

B. Rome
In the 1620s, the center for new developments in opera was Rome where plot subjects were expanded to include religious and comic topics.

1. Music
Roman opera included clearly defined recitative and aria for solo singing, vocal ensembles, extended finales for each act, choral singing, dancing, and an opening sinfonia.

2. Castrati
Castrati sang the female roles in Roman opera because women were not allowed to sing on stage. Elsewhere they mostly sang male roles.

C. Venice
Teatro San Cassiano, the first public opera house, opened to a paying public in Venice in 1637.

1. Audience
Venice was ideal for public opera, with many visitors in Carnival season, wealthy backers, and a steady audience.

2. Librettos and music
Plots were drawn from mythology, epics, and Roman history and featured dramatic conflicts and striking stage effects. The separation of recitative and aria became conventional in Venice, and the number of arias increased.

3. Cavalli and Cesti
The leading Venetian opera composers were Francesco Cavalli (1602–1676) and *Antonio Cesti* (1623–1669), both of whom wrote arias in a lyric style.

4. Singers
Singers attracted the paying public, and the best women and castrati were paid high fees.

Innovations: Singer-Power and Singer-Worship—The Diva

Opera was a commercial venture, and to turn a profit, it required successful management by the *impresario,* collaboration between librettist and composer, backstage workers, and star power. The *diva* was the female face of opera, winning the favor of audiences and patrons, and even demanding alterations to a role to suit her voice. *Anna Renzi* rose to prominence because of her talent as well as her image, and she set the standard for the *prima donna*. Star singers influenced the development of opera by guiding the audience's tastes.

D. Italian Opera Abroad

Touring companies took Italian opera from Venice to other Italian cities and then to other lands, including England, Austria, France, and Germany.

E. Italian Opera at Midcentury

1. Cesti's *Orontea*

Cesti's *Orontea,* written for Innsbruck in Austria, was one of the most successful operas in the seventeenth century, combining different scene and character types into an entertaining whole.

2. Recitative style

Most of the action in *Orontea* unfolds in simple recitative common to most midcentury opera.   **Music: NAWM 68a**

3. Aria style

By the middle of the seventeenth century, Italian opera focused on solo singing, the separation of recitative and aria, and the use of varied styles as illustrated in Cesti's *Orontea*. Unlike their Florentine predecessors, Venetian opera composers and their imitators gave music a place of prominence above poetry and drama.   **Music: NAWM 68b**

VI. Opera as Drama and as Theater (HWM 327)

Opera has always combined dramatic ideals with theatrical spectacle. At different points in history, the tension between drama, spectacle, and vocal display has sparked many debates and reforms. Most seventeenth-century operas lasted only a single season, and those that received new productions were usually revised to fit new singers' voices. Styles cultivated in opera can be found in vocal and instrumental music for the church and the chamber.

STUDY QUESTIONS

Forerunners of Opera (HWM 307, NAWM 64)

1. What forms of theater before 1600 used music? In what ways did they resemble opera?

2. What is a *pastoral drama*? What is the importance of pastoral subjects and poetry in the development of opera? In what sense is *L'Euridice* (excerpted in NAWM 65) a pastoral?

3. What was the function of an *intermedio* (pl. *intermedi*)? How was it like and unlike an opera?

   What is the significance of the 1589 intermedi for the play *La pellegrina* in the development of opera?

4. In what sense was ancient Greek tragedy a model for opera? Who were Girolamo Mei, Giovanni Bardi, and Vincenzo Galilei, and what did each one do to promote the revival of Greek ideals that ultimately led to opera?

5. What was the Florentine *Camerata,* and what is its significance?

6. What were the roles of Ottavio Rinuccini, Jacopo Peri, and Giulio Caccini in the creation of the first musical dramas (what we now call operas)? What was their relationship to the Camerata?

7. What does the term *monody* mean? What different types of monody did Caccini use in his vocal music?

Music to Study

NAWM 64: Giulio Caccini, *Vedrò 'l mio sol,* solo madrigal (ca. 1590)

CD 4|26   CD 2|38

8. How does *Vedrò 'l mio sol* differ from other madrigals we have seen?

   What traits does it share with other sixteenth-century Italian madrigals? Why is it a madrigal, and not an aria?

9. What kinds of ornaments does Caccini use in the vocal line of *Vedrò 'l mio sol,* and where do they appear? What other ornaments might have been performed by the singer?

10. Why is *Le nuove musiche* a useful book for singers today?

The First Operas (HWM 312–16, NAWM 65)

Music to Study

NAWM 65: Jacopo Peri, *Le musiche sopra l'Euridice* (The Music for *The Euridice*), opera (1600), excerpts

65a: Prologue, *Io, che d'alti sospir,* strophic aria   [CD 4|28]

65b: *Nel pur ardor,* aria   [CD 4|29]

65c: *Per quel vago boschetto,* dialogue in recitative   [CD 4|30]

11. What is the *recitative style*? How does Peri describe it in the preface to *L'Euridice* (excerpted in HWM, p. 314)? How does the dialogue from his setting of *L'Euridice* (NAWM 65c) reflect his conception?

12. How does Peri use harmony, dissonance, and rhythm in Orfeo's response to the death of *Euridice* (mm. 63–87) to convey the meaning of the words and the feelings they reflect?

13. What other styles of monody does Peri use in the other excerpts from *Euridice* (NAWM 65a and 65b)? How do these excerpts differ from recitative style?

14. How did monody make musical theater possible?

Claudio Monteverdi (HWM 316–19, NAWM 66–67)

Music to Study

NAWM 66: Claudio Monteverdi, *L'Orfeo,* opera (1607), excerpt from Act II

66a: *Vi ricorda o boschi ombrosi,* aria (canzonetta)   [CD 4|34]   [CD 2|40]

66b: *Mira, deh mira Orfeo,* song   [CD 4|35]

66c: *Ahi, caso acerbo,* dialogue in recitative   [CD 4|36]   [CD 2|41]

66d: *Tu se' morta,* recitative   [CD 4|40]   [CD 2|45]

66e: *Ahi, caso acerbo,* choral madrigal   [CD 4|41]   [CD 2|46]

15. Compare and contrast Monteverdi's aria *Vi ricordi* (NAWM 66a) from *L'Orfeo* with Peri's aria *Nel pur ardor* (NAWM 65b) from *L'Euridice.* In what ways is Monteverdi's similar and different?

16. In what ways is Monteverdi's recitative style in the Messenger's scene (NAWM 66c) similar to or different from Peri's at the parallel place in *L'Euridice* (NAWM 65c)?

17. How does Monteverdi use dissonance, rhythm, melodic contour, and other elements to convey the meaning of the text and the feelings it reflects in Orfeo's recitative *Tu se' morta* (NAWM 66d)?

18. How is Monteverdi's approach to this scene similar to or different from Orfeo's lament in Peri's *L'Euridice* (NAWM 65c)?

19. In *Orfeo,* Monteverdi uses particular musical forms and styles to convey the changing dramatic situation and the feelings of the characters. What characteristics make each of the following forms and styles appropriate in building and expressing the drama of this scene?

    66a: Orfeo, canzonetta

    66c: Messenger, Shepherds, and Orfeo, recitative

    66d: Orfeo, recitative

    66e: Chorus, choral madrigal

20. In what ways was Monteverdi's *L'Orfeo* suitable for its intended audience? (Be sure to mention the opera's plot, structure, instrumentation, and musical style.)

21. What is the *stile concitato*? Who first used it? When, and in what piece? What does it represent, and how does it achieve its effects?

Music to Study

NAWM 67: Claudio Monteverdi, *L'incoronazione di Poppea,* opera (1642), Act I, scene 3 $\boxed{\text{CD 4|42}}$ $\boxed{\text{CD 2|47}}$

22. Compare and contrast the scene from Monteverdi's *L'incoronazione di Poppea* in NAWM 67 with the scene from *Orfeo* in NAWM 66. What devices, forms, and vocal styles does Monteverdi use in each case to depict the text and portray the dramatic situation?

23. In this scene from *L'incoronazione di Poppea,* the music shifts back and forth often between recitative and aria styles. Why does Monteverdi set Poppea's "Deh non dir di partir" (mm. 30–37) as recitative, and her words "Vanne, vanne ben mio" (mm. 53–58) as a brief aria? (Hint: Do not be fooled by the notation of the latter; it is in a fast triple time.)

How does this approach to writing dialogue differ from Peri's in *L'Euridice* (NAWM 65c) or Monteverdi's in *L'Orfeo* (NAWM 66c)?

The Spread of Italian Opera (HWM 319–27, NAWM 68)

24. Who was Francesca Caccini, when and where did she live and work, and for what was she renowned? How did her family background contribute to her success?

25. How was opera supported and financed in Rome in the period 1620–50?

    How was Roman opera of this period different from earlier opera in Florence and Mantua?

26. When and where was opera first made available to the paying public?

    What made this city ideal for public opera?

27. Compare the performance context of Venetian opera to that of *L'Euridice* and *L'Orfeo*. What effects did the shift in audience and performing context have on the development of opera?

28. Who was Antonio Cesti? When and where did he live and work, and what were his musical contributions?

29. What role did the *impresario* play in opera productions?

30. What did the terms *diva* and *prima donna* mean in seventeenth-century opera? What was their significance?

31. Name an important diva and describe her career.

Music to Study

NAWM 68: Antonio Cesti, *Orontea*, opera (1656), excerpt from Act II

    68a: Scene 16: *E che si fa?*, recitative   CD 4|48

    68b: Scene 17, opening aria: *Intorno all' idol mio*   CD 4|49

32. In what ways is the style of recitative used in Cesti's *Orontea*, Act II, scene 16 (NAWM 68a), similar to and different from the style of recitative used by Peri (NAWM 65) and Monteverdi (NAWM 66–67)?

33. Contrast the aria from Cesti's *Orontea* (ca. 1656) in NAWM 68b with the arias from Peri's *Euridice* (1600) in NAWM 65a and 65b. How did the style of operatic song change from the beginning to the middle of the seventeenth century?

34. What important characteristics of opera took shape in Italy by the middle of the seventeenth century? How did opera in Rome and Venice at midcentury differ from Florentine operas of about 1600?

Opera as Drama and as Theater (HWM 327)

35. Describe the relationship between opera as drama and opera as theater. How is this evident in early opera? (We will return to this question in later chapters.)

TERMS TO KNOW

opera
libretto
pastoral drama
madrigal comedy, madrigal cycle
intermedio (p. intermedi)
monody
aria
solo madrigal
recitative style

ritornello
sinfonia
strophic variation
stile concitato
recitativo arioso, arioso
castrati
impresario
diva
prima donna

NAMES TO KNOW

Girolamo Mei
Camerata
Giovanni de' Bardi
Vincenzo Galilei
*Dialogo della musica antica
    et della moderna*
Giulio Caccini
Le nuove musiche
Ottavio Rinuccini

Jacopo Peri
Emilio de' Cavalieri
L'Euridice
L'Orfeo
L'incoronazione di Poppea
Francesca Caccini
Antonio Cesti
Anna Renzi
Orontea

REVIEW QUESTIONS

1. Add to the timeline you made for the seventeenth century in chapter 13 the pieces, composers, treatises, and events discussed in this chapter.

2. Trace the development of opera in Italy and Italian opera abroad from its origins to the 1650s. Include in your answer changes of aesthetic aims and ideas as well as changes of style and procedure.

3. What connections do you see between Monteverdi's madrigals and his operas? What effects did his experience as a madrigal composer have on his operas?

4. Write an expressive recitative in the style Monteverdi used in *L'Orfeo*. Use for your text the first two lines of his madrigal *Cruda Amarilli* (NAWM 63) in either the original Italian or in the English translation. Write it for male voice and continuo, as in Orfeo's recitative *Tu se' morta* from *L'Orfeo* (in NAWM 66d), and use the latter as a model for how to write a recitative, how to fit the music to the accentuation of the poetry, and how to use gestures and dissonances for expressivity. You may write only the voice and bass line or may fill in the harmony, and you may stop after a few measures or write an entire recitative using all eight lines of the poem; the goal is to see how recitative in this style works, from the inside. (If you use the Italian, please note that in Italian, adjacent vowels elide into a single syllable. Thus the first line has eleven syllables, with the "-da" of "Cruda" elided into a single syllable with the "A-" of "Amarilli" and the "-me" of "nome" elided with the "an-" of "ancora.")

5. Given what you know about opera today, what elements of opera and its culture were already present by the mid-seventeenth century? Where did each elements come from, and how did it change between the the first operas and the 1650s? Include everything from the types of music opera contains to the types of people and institutions involved in opera productions.

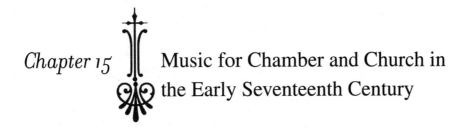

Chapter 15   Music for Chamber and Church in
the Early Seventeenth Century

CHAPTER OBJECTIVES

After you complete the reading, study of the music, and study questions for this chapter, you should be able to

1. describe the genres and styles of Italian secular vocal chamber music in the early seventeenth century;

2. describe sacred music in the Catholic, Lutheran, and Jewish traditions in the early seventeenth century; and

3. name and briefly describe the most important genres and styles of instrumental music in the early Baroque period.

CHAPTER OUTLINE

I. Introduction (HWM 328)

Chamber, church, and instrumental music of 1600–1650 maintained continuities with the past and was also influenced by the modern theatrical style.

II. Italian Vocal Chamber Music (HWM 328–32, NAWM 69)

Most secular vocal music in the early seventeenth century involved ensembles with voices and was performed in private settings or by amateurs.

A. Secular Works in Concertato Style

In the early seventeenth century, Italian composers wrote thousands of pieces for solo voice or small vocal ensemble with basso continuo and sometimes with other instruments.

1. Concerted madrigals

Concerted madrigals exemplify the blending of old (polyphonic vocal music) and new (concerto medium) in early seventeenth century chamber music.

B. Ostinato Basses

Many songs and instrumental works of the early seventeenth century used *basso ostinato,* or *ground bass.*

1. Descending tetrachord
The descending tetrachord was a common ground bass pattern, often used for laments.

2. Chacona
Bass patterns adapted from the *chacona* (Italian *ciaccona*) were used to convey happy lightheartedness.

C. Cantata

The *cantata* was a new genre for voice and continuo. Early cantatas often used strophic variations, and later ones, such as those by *Barbara Strozzi* (1619–1677), were in several sections, including both recitatives and arias, on a lyrical or dramatic text.   **Music: NAWM 69**

Biography: Barbara Strozzi

Strozzi was born in Venice and frequented intellectual circles with her father. She studied with Cavalli and was supported financially by her family and patrons. One of the most prolific composers of vocal chamber music, Strozzi published more cantatas than any other composer of the time.

D. Outside Italy

Composers outside Italy absorbed Italian influences but produced songs of distinctly national character, like the French *air de cour* and the English consort song.

III. Catholic Sacred Music (HWM 332–37, NAWM 70–71)

Composers of Catholic sacred music adopted the theatrical idiom in works like *sacred concertos,* using a dramatic medium to convey the church's message.

1. *Stile antico*
Composers utilized both the *stile moderno* (modern style) and *stile antico* (old contrapuntal style) in their works.

A. Large-Scale Sacred Concerto

Large, wealthy churches celebrated major feast days with large-scale works, often using *cori spezzati* (divided choirs).

B. Small Sacred Concerto

The *small sacred concerto* for one or more voices with organ continuo was more common and economical.

1. Lodovico Viadana
Lodovico Viadana (1560–1627) was a pioneer of the small vocal concerto, and his 1602 collection *Cento concerti ecclesiastici* (One Hundred Church Concertos) was the first volume of sacred vocal music printed with basso continuo.

2. Alessandro Grandi
Alessandro Grandi (1586–1630) composed many solo motets that used the new styles of monody.   **Music: NAWM 70**

C. Music in Convents

Music in convents was a private affair, and many church administrators forbade nuns and novices to bring outside musicians into their rehearsals and classrooms.

1. Lucrezia Vizzana

The convent Santa Cristina in Bologna was known for its music, and its most famous member, *Lucrezia Vizzana* (1590–1662), published a collection of twenty motets that incorporate elements of theatrical monody.

D. Oratorio

Oratorios originated in seventeenth-century Rome. They were religious music dramas performed outside of church services.

1. Oratorio versus opera

An oratorio uses most of the same types of music as an opera, but it has a religious subject, it is rarely staged, there is often a narrator, and it employs a chorus that changes roles.

2. Giacomo Carissimi

The leading composers of oratorios in Latin was *Giacomo Carissimi* (1605–1674), whose *Jephte* exemplifies the midcentury oratorio. **Music: NAWM 71**

IV. Lutheran Church Music (HWM 338)

Composers in both Catholic and Lutheran churches in German-speaking regions used elements of theatrical monody and concertato techniques.

1. Sacred concerto in Germany

Composers in Germany in the seventeenth century wrote large-scale concertos, but the small sacred concerto was more common. An important collection of small sacred concertos was *Opella nova* (1618 and 1626) by Johann Hermann Schein (1586–1630).

V. Heinrich Schütz (HWM 338–42, NAWM 72–73)

Heinrich Schütz (1585–1672) is renowned for applying the new Italian styles to church music and conveying the meaning of words through music.

Biography: Heinrich Schütz

Schütz's earlier musical training was sponsored by the Landgrave of Hesse, who persuaded him to study composition with Giovanni Gabrieli in Venice. Schütz spent his entire career in the service of the elector of Saxony in Dresden, where he composed church music as well as sacred and secular music for all major ceremonies.

A. Sacred Works

Schütz published most of his sacred works in a series of collections that show a variety of styles and techniques.

1. *Kleine geistliche Konzerte*

In 1636 and 1639, Schütz published his *Kleine geistliche Konzerte* (Small Sacred Concertos) for one to five solo voices with continuo that use styles of Italian monody to convey the text.   **Music: NAWM 72**

2. *Symphoniae sacrae II* and *III*

In *Symphoniae sacrae II* and *III* (1647 and 1650), Schütz published large-scale concertos that blend Gabrieli's polychoral style with Monteverdi's expressive techniques.   **Music: NAWM 73**

3. Use of musical figures

Schütz used *musical figures* to convey the meaning of the text, a practice described by his student Christoph Bernhard.

4. Historia

In *The Seven Last Words of Christ* (1650s?), Schütz incorporated elements of monody in the *historia,* a prominent genre in the Lutheran tradition that sets a biblical narrative.

5. Passions

The most common type of historia was a *Passion,* and Schütz composed three in the older German tradition.

B. Legacy

Schütz was best known in Lutheran areas of Germany. His synthesis of German and Italian elements helped to lay the foundation for later German composers.

VI. Jewish Music (HWM 342–43)

New musical developments in the seventeenth century extended to Jewish music, as well.

1. Polyphony

Polyphony was introduced into synagogue services in the seventeenth century through the efforts of Leon Modena (1571–1648) and others.

2. Salamone Rossi

Salamone Rossi (ca. 1570–ca. 1630) wrote Jewish liturgical polyphonic music that blended Jewish chant with elements of northern Italian musical style.

VII. Instrumental Music (HWM 344–51, NAWM 74–76)

Instrumental music continued to gain independence from vocal music, as instrumental composers focused on abstract genres. At the same time, they borrowed many elements of the new vocal idiom.

A. Types of Instrumental Music

1. Performing forces

Baroque instrumental music includes solo works, chamber works (for soloist or small group with continuo), and large ensemble works for two or more players per part.

2. Venue

Like Baroque vocal music, Baroque instrumental music served church, chamber, and theater.

3. Nationality

Baroque instrumental music can also be categorized by nationality.

4. Types of pieces
There are several broad types of instrumental music in the period 1600–1650:
- Pieces in improvisatory style for solo keyboard or lute (*toccata, fantasia,* or *prelude*);
- Fugal works in continuous imitative counterpoint (*ricercare, fantasia, capriccio,* or *fugue*);
- Pieces with contrasting sections (*canzona* or *sonata*);
- Settings of existing melodies (*organ verse* or *chorale prelude*);
- Pieces that vary a given melody (*variations, partita*), chorale (*chorale variations, chorale partita*), or bass line (*partita, chaconne, passacaglia*);
- *Dances* as independent pieces or linked together in a *suite.*

The mix of preferred genres changed after about 1650.

5. Mixing textures and styles
Elements of one style or type often appear in another, and composers used contrasts of style for form and expression.

B. Toccata
Toccatas and other improvisatory pieces were played on harpsichord or organ.

1. Girolamo Frescobaldi
The toccatas of *Girolamo Frescobaldi* (1583–1643) typically feature several brief sections, each focused on a different figure.   **Music: NAWM 74**

2. *Fiori musicali*
Frescobaldi used toccatas as service music in three *organ masses* in a collection titled *Fiori musicali* (Musical Flowers, 1635).

3. Johann Jacob Froberger
Johann Jacob Froberger (1616–1667) studied with Frescobaldi and wrote toccatas that alternate improvisatory passages with sections in imitative counterpoint.

Biography: Girolamo Frescobaldi
Frescobaldi was one of the first composers to focus primarily on instrumental music. As an organist at St. Peter's, he composed keyboard works and had many wealthy and prestigious patrons. His music was known across France, Flanders, and Germany even after his death, and he influenced later composers, including J. S. Bach.

C. Ricercare and Fugue
The seventeenth-century ricercare was a serious work for organ or harpsichord in which one *subject* is continuously developed in imitation. In the early seventeenth century, the term *fugue* became the name for a genre of serious piece that treated one theme in continuous imitation. **Music: NAWM 75**

D. Fantasia
The keyboard fantasia was on a larger scale and had a more complex formal organization than the ricercare.

1. English consort fantasias
   The leading genre for viol consort in England was the imitative fantasia, or fancy, which could treat one or more subjects.

E. Canzona
   The canzona features several contrasting sections, each of which treats a different theme in imitation or offers a nonimitative section for contrast.

F. Sonata
   In the seventeenth century, sonata came to refer to a work for one or two melody instruments with basso continuo. The solo writing was often idiomatic and imitated vocal style.

1. Biagio Marini
   Biagio Marini (1594–1663) worked at St. Mark's in Venice and at other posts in Italy and Germany. His solo violin sonatas resemble instrumental monody, with many idiomatic gestures. **Music: NAWM 76**

G. Settings of Existing Melodies
   Organists improvised or composed settings of liturgical melodies, such as *chorale preludes,* for use in church services

H. Variations
   Keyboard and lute composers wrote *variations,* sometimes called *partite.* The most common variation techniques were the following:
   - The melody is largely unchanged and is surrounded by contrapuntal lines (*cantus-firmus variations*).
   - The melody is in the top voice and is embellished differently in each variation.
   - Variations occur on a bass or harmonic plan rather than on a melody.

1. Chaconne and passacaglia
   The *chaconne* and *passacaglia* were variations over a ground bass in triple meter.

I. Dance Music
   Dances were used for social dancing, in the theater, and as stylized chamber music.

1. Suites
   A dance *suite* comprised several dances used for dancing or as chamber music.

J. A Separate Tradition
   Composers focused increasingly on abstract genres, and instrumental music gained stature as a tradition separate from vocal music, but with just as much expressive capability.

VIII. Tradition and Innovation (HWM 351–52)

Seventeenth-century composers developed many new genres, styles, and techniques andcombined existing genres and approaches with new ones. The innovations of this period set the pattern for several generations, but the music itself fell out of favor by the end of the century. Music of the early seventeenth century has been rediscovered in the nineteenth and twentieth centuries.

STUDY QUESTIONS

Italian Vocal Chamber Music (HWM 328–32, NAWM 69)

1. What is a *concerted madrigal*? How does it differ from sixteenth-century madrigals?

2. What is a *basso ostinato* or *ground bass*? Name and describe two different kinds of basso ostinato that Monteverdi uses. How does he use them to convey emotions?

Music to Study

NAWM 69: Barbara Strozzi, *Lagrime mie,* cantata (1650s)   ⌐CD 4|51⌐

3. In her cantata *Lagrime mie* (NAWM 69), Strozzi uses sections of recitative, aria, and arioso (a style between recitative and aria, usually more metric than recitative). Where is each kind of monody used? (Indicate by measure numbers.)

    recitative   _____

    aria   _____

    arioso   _____

    In what ways are the sections of text set as aria particularly appropriate for that style of music?

4. What musical devices does Strozzi use to represent the following words and the feelings or actions behind them?

   "lagrime" (tears)

   "respiro" (breath)

   "tormenti" (torments)

5. How is a seventeenth-century cantata like opera, and how is it different?

6. Describe Barbara Strozzi's career. How did it differ from those of her male contemporaries?

Catholic Sacred Music (HWM 332–37, NAWM 70–71)

7. What is a *sacred concerto*? What varieties of sacred concerto were written in the seventeenth century? For what circumstances and occasions was each type suited?

8. What are the *stile moderno* and *stile antico* in seventeenth-century church music?

9. Describe Lodovico Viadana's *Cento concerti ecclesiastici*. When did it appear, what did it contain, and what was its significance?

Music to Study

NAWM 70: Alessandro Grandi, *O quam tu pulchra es,* solo motet (ca. 1625)

10. How is Grandi's *O quam tu pulchra es* (NAWM 70) like a sixteenth-century motet, such as Victoria's *O magnum mysterium* (NAWM 46a), and how is it different?

11. How does Grandi's motet compare to the alternation of recitative and aria styles in the scene from Monteverdi's *L'incoronazione di Poppea* in NAWM 67? How does each work respond to its text?

12. Describe Lucrezia Vizzana's career and music. What obstacles lay in the way of women in convents who sought musical training?

13. What is an *oratorio*? From what does its name derive? How is an oratorio like an opera, and how does it differ?

Music to Study

NAWM 71: Giacomo Carissimi, *Jephte,* oratorio (ca. 1648), excerpt

    71a: *Plorate colles,* recitative   CD 5|1   CD 2|53

    71b: *Plorate filii Israel,* chorus   CD 5|2

14. Compare the excerpt from Carissimi's *Historia di Jephte* in NAWM 71 with the scene from Monteverdi's *Orfeo* in NAWM 66. What elements does each use?

How do Monteverdi and Carissimi use harmony to convey emotions?

How does each use the chorus?

Lutheran Church Music (HWM 338)

15. Describe Johann Hermann Schein's *Opella nova* and its significance.

Heinrich Schütz (HWM 338–42, NAWM 72–73)

16. Summarize Heinrich Schütz's career and his influence on later composers. What Italian influences did he absorb, and how are they reflected in his music? How does this compare with other composers of Lutheran church music?

Music to Study

NAWM 72: Heinrich Schütz, *O lieber Herre Gott* (SWV 287),   ⌠ CD 5|4 ⌡
sacred concerto from *Kleine geistliche Konzerte I* (ca. 1636)

NAWM 73: Heinrich Schütz, *Saul, was verfolgst du mich* (SWV   ⌠ CD 5|7 ⌡ | CD 2|54 |
415), sacred concerto, from *Symphonia sacrae III* (ca. 1650)

17. What Italian influences are reflected in Schütz's *O lieber Herre Gott* (NAWM 72)? What other composer used similar techniques to convey text in music?

18. How does *O lieber Herre Gott* show the effects of the Thirty Years' War?

19. How does Schütz use changes of texture and style to depict the events and text of *Saul, was verfolgst du mich* (NAWM 73)? What types of style and texture does he use?

20. What are *musical figures*? How does Schütz use them in *Saul, was verfolgst du mich* to convey the meaning of the words?

Jewish Music (HWM 342–43)

21. How did Jewish synagogue music differ from Catholic and Lutheran church music? How did the new seventeenth-century developments affect Jewish music?

22. Who was Salamone Rossi, and why is he significant?

Instrumental Music (HWM 344–51, NAWM 74–76)

23. In what ways can instrumental music in the seventeenth century be categorized? How does this compare to the sixteenth century?

24. What main types of instrumental music were practiced in the first half of the seventeenth century? How do these types compare to the forms used in the sixteenth century?

25. What main types of instrumental music were practiced in the second half of the seventeenth century? How do these types compare to those described in question 19?

26. Describe the life and career of Girolamo Frescobaldi.

Music to Study

NAWM 74: Girolamo Frescobaldi, Toccata No. 3 (ca. 1615,
rev. 1637) ⟨ CD 5|11 ⟩ ⟨ CD 3|1 ⟩

27. How is Frescobaldi's Toccata No. 3 (NAWM 74) divided into sections? Where does the style or figuration change?

28. Frescobaldi's toccata is in the Dorian mode on G (i.e., transposed up a fourth). Where are the main cadences, and on what scale degrees do they occur? How is the modal final of G established?

What clues are there that this piece is in G Dorian rather than in G Minor? (Hint: Think of the notes and chords that are more likely to occur in G Dorian than in G Minor—and the reverse—and look for them. For example, a C minor triad may occur in either, but a C major or A minor triad is unlikely in G Minor, which has an E♭ in the key signature.)

29. What was an *organ mass*? What was the function of toccatas, ricercares, and canzonas in the Catholic Mass?

Music to Study

NAWM 75: Girolamo Frescobaldi, Ricercare after the Credo   `CD 5|13`
(ca. 1635), from *Mass for the Madonna,* in *Fiori musicali*

30. Describe what happens in Frescobaldi's Ricercare after the Credo (NAWM 75). Where does the subject appear? What is the form? What is the relationship between the two sections (mm. 1–24 and 24–45)?

31. In the accompanying recording, what tuning system is used on the organ? How does this system differ from equal temperament, and what is the effect?

32. In the first half of the seventeenth century, what is the difference between a ricercare and a fantasia?

33. What is the difference between a canzona and a sonata?

Music to Study

NAWM 76: Biagio Marini, *Sonata IV per il violino per sonar con due corde,* sonata for violin and continuo (ca. 1626)   CD 5|15

34. What idiomatic violin techniques does Marini incorporate in *Sonata IV* (NAWM 76)?

35. In what ways does NAWM 76 resemble vocal music, such as Monteverdi's *Poppea* (NAWM 67) or Grandi's *O quam tu pulchra es* (NAWM 70)?

36. What kinds of variations were written in the seventeenth century? In each type, what stayed the same in each variation, and what changed?

37. What is a dance *suite*?

Tradition and Innovation (HWM 351–52)

38. In what ways did the chamber, church, and instrumental music of the early seventeenth century influence later music? How did this music fare after 1650?

TERMS TO KNOW

concerted madrigal

basso ostinato, ground bass

chacona, ciaccona

cantata

air de cour

sacred concerto

stile antico, stile moderno

cori spezzati

small sacred concerto

oratorio

musical figures

historia

Passion

toccata

fantasia

prelude

ricercare

capriccio

fugue

canzona

sonata

organ verse

chorale prelude

variations, partita

chorale variations, chorale partita

chaconne, passacaglia

dance

suite

organ mass

subject

cantus-firmus variations

NAMES TO KNOW

Barbara Strozzi

Lodovico Viadana

Alessandro Grandi

Lucrezia Vizzana

Giacomo Carissimi

Heinrich Schütz

Kleine geistliche Konzerte

Symphoniae sacrae

Salamone Rossi

Girolamo Frescobaldi

Fiori musicali

Biagio Marini

REVIEW QUESTIONS

1. Add to the timeline you made for the seventeenth century in chapter 13 the pieces and composers discussed in this chapter.

2. What new genres and styles of secular vocal music were introduced in Italy during the first half of the seventeenth century? How did they compare to the genres and styles of the sixteenth century?

3. How was sacred music affected by the new developments in secular music in the first half of the seventeenth century? What new genres or styles of sacred music emerged during this time? Include Catholic, Lutheran, and Jewish traditions in your answer.

4. What types of instrumental music were practiced during the first half of the seventeenth century? Which of these genres and styles were new, and which continued trends from the sixteenth century? Of the latter, how were the older genres or styles changed in the seventeenth century?

5. In what ways did instrumental music become increasingly independent of vocal music in the first half of the seventeenth century? In what ways did instrumental composers borrow ideas or techniques from vocal music? What was the significance for the future of instrumental music of both of these developments?

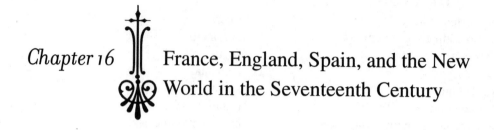

Chapter 16 France, England, Spain, and the New World in the Seventeenth Century

CHAPTER OBJECTIVES

After you complete the reading, study of the music, and study questions for this chapter, you should be able to

1. describe the differences in the political structures of France, England, Spain, and the Spanish New World, and how these differences affected music and musical style;

2. trace the origins and development of musical theater in these regions during the seventeenth century and explain what makes each national tradition distinctive;

3. define and use the most important terms and identify some of the composers and works associated with French, English, Spanish, and New World opera and vocal music in the seventeenth century; and

4. name and describe the varieties of instrumental music from France, England, and Spain in the seventeenth century, including the dance suite and the most common types of dances.

CHAPTER OUTLINE

I. Introduction (HWM 353–54)

> In the middle and late Baroque period, national styles developed, influenced by political and cultural factors, and composers merged elements from their own national style with others in their music.

II. The French Baroque (HWM 354–72, NAWM 77–78)

> French Baroque music was shaped by the centrality of dance and the role of the arts in an absolute monarchy.

A. Louis XIV

Louis XIV (r. 1643–1715) sought to assert absolute authority.

1. Art as propaganda
   Louis used the arts to project an image of supreme control.

2. The Sun King
   To identify himself with Apollo (the sun god), Louis XIV ("the Sun King") established royal academies to oversee endeavors in a variety of fields, including music.

3. Versailles
   Versailles, the king's vast country palace, was the home of the aristocracy for large parts of the year, enabling Louis to keep them under his control.

B. The Court Ballet
Louis XIV was a talented dancer, and he promoted and danced in the *court ballet,* a distinctive French genre that included solo songs, choruses, and dances.

1. Dance and political control
   French Baroque music is centered on dance and is marked by elegance and emotional restraint, characteristics reflecting Louis's political control.

C. Music at Court
Music at the French court involved 150 to 200 musicians and consisted of music for the Royal Chapel, Chamber, and *Great Stable.*

1. String orchestras
   The French created the first large ensembles of the violin family, the *Vingt-quatre Violons du Roi* (Twenty-Four Violins of the King) and the *Petits Violons* (Small Violin Ensemble). These became the model for the modern *orchestra,* whose core consists of strings with more than one player on a part.

Music in Context: The Music of the Great Stable
The musicians of the Great Stable played for all events that took place outdoors, and they were the king's best wind and brass players. Several important families of wind players, such as the Hotteterres, worked in the Great Stable and contributed to innovations in instrument building, including the modern oboe.

D. Jean-Baptiste Lully and French Opera
Jean-Baptiste Lully (1632–1687), Louis XIV's favorite musician, wrote music for ballets and created a distinctive kind of French opera.

1. Influences on French opera
   Italian opera had failed several times at the French court, and at midcentury the only successful combination of stage and music was not opera but rather Lully's and Jean-Baptiste Molière's *comédies-ballets.*

2. Tragédie en musique
   With his librettist, *Jean-Philippe Quinault* (1635–1688), Lully successfully combined drama, music, and ballet in a new French opera, *tragédie en musique* (later named *tragédie lyrique*).

3. Quinault's librettos
   Quinault's propagandistic librettos featured serious, usually mythological plots in five acts with frequent *divertissements.*

4. French overture
   Each of Lully's operas begins with an *ouverture,* or *overture,* in a format known as a *French overture.* There are two repeated sections, the first slow with dotted rhythms, the second fast and imitative. **Music: NAWM 77a**

5. Divertissements
   A divertissement appeared at the center or end of each act and provided opportunities for dances and choruses, which were very appealing to the public.

6. Adapting recitative to French
   Lully developed a French style of recitative that is often more rhythmic and more songful than Italian recitative.

7. Récitatif simple, récitatif mesuré, and air
   Lully developed two types of recitative, *récitatif simple* (simple recitative), in which the meter shifts freely between duple and triple, and *récitatif mesuré* (measured recitative), which is more songlike and measured. Lully's *airs,* songs with a rhyming text and regular meter and phrasing, were simpler than Italian arias. **Music: NAWM 77b**

8. Performance practice
   Performers emphasized the rhythmic profile of French music by using *notes inégales* and *overdotting.* They also were expected to use brief ornaments, called *agréments.*

9. Tonal organization
   Lully's music is tonal rather than modal.

10. Focus on drama
    In French opera, emphasis was placed on the dramatic declamation of words and on entertaining spectacle.

11. Lully's influence
    Lully's operas were performed well into the eighteenth century, and his followers continued to write operas that imitated his style.

Biography: Jean-Baptiste Lully
   Lully was born in Italy, and although he was a musician, it was his dancing talent that landed him a job at the French court. As Louis XIV's Superintendant of Music for the King's Chamber, Lully was the most influential musician of the seventeenth century. His greatest fame came from his operas. He was also known for creating a distinctive orchestral sound by imposing uniform bowing and coordinated ornamentation.

E. Song and Cantata
   The leading genre of French vocal chamber music continued to be the air.

1. Marc-Antoine Charpentier
   French composers, such as *Marc-Antoine Charpentier* (1634–1704), also adapted the Italian chamber cantata to French styles and taste.

F. Church Music

At midcentury, French composers borrowed genres invented in Italy, such as the sacred concerto and oratorio, but wrote in distinctively French styles.

1. *Petit motet* and *grand motet*

Composers in the royal chapel produced two types of motets on Latin texts, the *petit motet* (a sacred concerto for few voices with continuo) and the *grand motet* (a type of large-scale concerto).

2. Oratorio

Charpentier introduced the Latin oratorio into France, combining Italian and French styles of recitative and air.

3. Organ music

The French school of organ music in the seventeenth century was distinctive for its use of agréments and a strong interest in tone color.

G. Lute and Keyboard Music

During the seventeenth century, the *clavecin* displaced the lute as the main solo instrument, and *clavecinists,* such as *Elisabeth-Claude Jacquet de la Guerre* (1665–1729) and François Couperin (see chapter 18), marketed their music collections to an amateur public.

1. Agréments

Lutenists systematically developed the use of agréments, which became a fundamental element of French music.

2. Style luthé

The *style luthé* (lute style), sometimes called *style brisé* (broken style), was imitated by harpsichord composers and became a part of French style.

Biography: Elisabeth-Claude Jacquet de la Guerre

Jacquet de la Guerre was recognized by her contemporaries as one of the greatest talents of her time. She was a child prodigy who performed at King Louis XIV's court from the age of five. Best known for her harpsichord pieces and cantatas, she was the first French woman to write a ballet and an opera.

H. Dance Music

Dances formed the core of the lute and keyboard repertory.

1. Binary form

Most seventeenth-century dances were in *binary form,* a form used for dances and other instrumental genres over the next two centuries.

2. Suites

French composers grouped dances into *suites*. Typically, a suite begins with a prelude, often an *unmeasured prelude,* and continues with dances like the *allemande, courante, sarabande, gigue, gavotte,* and *minuet.* Jacquet de la Guerre's Suite No. 3 in A Minor also includes a chaconne in the form of a *rondeau,* in which a refrain alternates with *couplets.*
Music: NAWM 78

3. German versus French suites

In Germany, suites assumed a standard order, while in France, the suite consisted of a variety of dances, some with fanciful titles, in no set order.

I. Emulation of French Style

The French style was almost as influential as Italian music, and the integration of the two became one of the themes of the eighteenth century.

III. The English Baroque (HWM 372–78, NAWM 79)

English music blended its own native traditions with French and Italian styles.

1. Limited monarchy

Because England was a limited monarchy, the royal house had less money than the French court to spend on music.

A. Musical Theater

In England, native genres of dramatic music were more successful than opera.

1. Masques

Masques were court entertainment that shared many aspects of opera, but they were more like long spectacles akin to French court ballets than unified dramas.

2. Mixed genres

The first English "operas" mixed elements of spoken drama with the masque. French opera failed in the 1670s, and only two dramas sung throughout (described below) met any success in the late seventeenth century.

3. *Venus and Adonis*

John Blow (1649–1708) composed *Venus and Adonis* for the English court. Its music combines elements of Italian, French, and English styles.

B. Henry Purcell's Dramatic Music

Henry Purcell (1659–1695) was England's leading composer and a favorite at court.

1. *Dido and Aeneas*

Purcell's *Dido and Aeneas* (1689) incorporates elements of the English masque and of French and Italian opera.

2. French and Italian elements

The overture, homophonic choruses, and scene structure follow the French style, and the arias (including three on ground basses) are decidedly Italian. **Music: NAWM 79b**

3. English elements

The use of dance in *Dido and Aeneas* comes from the masque tradition, and many solos and choruses use the style of the English air. **Music: NAWM 79c**

4. English recitatives

In the recitative, Purcell fashions melodies that fit the accents, pace, and emotions of the English text. **Music: NAWM 79a**

5. Semi-operas
Purcell wrote five works in the mixed genre called *dramatic opera,* or *semi-opera.* The English did not have a native tradition of opera, or interest in supporting it, until the late nineteenth century.

Biography: Henry Purcell
Henry Purcell's entire career was supported by royal patronage. He was a prodigy as a composer and held some of Britain's most notable musical positions, including organist at Westminster Abbey. Purcell is still considered one of England's most important composers, best known for his vocal music and his ability to declaim English words properly while conveying their meaning.

C. Other English Music
England had a lively native musical culture.

1. Vocal music
English vocal music ranged from large-scale ceremonial works for chorus, soloists, and orchestra to songs for home performance and the *catch,* a humorous canon. Anthems and Services remained the principal genres of Anglican church music.

2. Instrumental music
Viol consort music, particularly In Nomines and fantasias, continued to be popular. Instrumental music was also used in social dancing, and *The English Dancing Master* (1651), published by John Playford (1623–1687), contains many folk tunes and popular airs.

3. The public concert
Public concerts were first pioneered in London in the 1670s.

IV. Spain and the New World (HWM 379–82, NAWM 80–81)

Although Spain was the richest country in Europe in 1600, by the mid-seventeenth century it lost its status as a dominant military power.

1. Spanish colonies
Spain still ruled vast colonies in the Americas, and musicians there drew directly on Spanish and wider European traditions.

A. Opera, Zarzuela, and Song
Juan Hidalgo (1614–1685) composed a distinctively Spanish opera that incorporated airs in Spanish styles and dance rhythms. Like Lully, Hidalgo also devised an enduring tradition for Spanish musical theater in the *zarzuela.*

1. *La púrpura de la rosa*
La púrpura de la rosa (The Blood of the Rose, 1701) was the first opera produced in the New World. The music by *Tomás de Torrejón y Velasco* (1644–1728) exhibits distinctive Spanish traits. **Music: NAWM 80**

2. Songs
Independent songs and those from theatrical productions circulated in manuscript throughout Spain and its possessions in Italy and the Americas.

B. Church Music

The most common sacred genre was the villancico, which combined the style of the sixteenth-century secular genre with the concertato medium. **Music: NAWM 81**

C. Instrumental Music

In seventeenth-century Spain, solo works were more common than ensemble pieces.

1. Organ music

Spanish organ music is characterized by strong contrasts of color and texture, particularly in the *tiento,* an improvisatory-style piece.

2. Harp and guitar music

Harp and guitar were the main chamber instruments, and they were used to play dance music and variations on familiar dance tunes.

V. French Style and National Traditions (HWM 382–83)

France was the most powerful of the three monarchies, and its music was imitated throughout Europe. After Purcell, foreigners dominated English music, but the public concert, an English innovation, was taken up across Europe. Spain and the New World cultivated native musical traditions, but also blended Italian and French influences with them. In the late nineteenth and twentieth centuries, French, English, and Spanish Baroque traditions began to be revived.

STUDY QUESTIONS

The French Baroque (HWM 353–54, NAWM 77–78)

1. Describe the role of the arts in Louis XIV's absolute monarchy. How did Louis's approach to the arts affect music in particular?

2. In what French musical tradition did Louis XIV participate? How did he participate? What did this genre include? Why did Louis XIV value it?

3. Describe the different types of instrumental music at the French court, and what was historically significant about them.

4. Name the composer and librettist who founded the French opera tradition, and briefly summarize the composer's career.

_____   _____

Music to Study

NAWM 77: Jean-Baptiste Lully, *Armide,* opera (1686), excerpts

    77a: Overture   [CD 5|23]   CD 2|58

    77b: Act II, scene 5: *Enfin il est en ma puissance*   [CD 5|26]   CD 2|61

5. What characteristics of the overture to Lully's *Armide* (NAWM 77a) mark it as a French overture?

6. How does the musical setting of Armide's recitative *Enfin il est en ma puissance* (NAWM 77b) reflect the form and accentuation of the text?

7. How does the musical setting reflect the dramatic situation and the emotional conflict Armide is feeling?

8. The scene ends with a minuet played by instruments and then sung by Armide. The minuet was associated at the time with surrender to love. In what ways is this appropriate to the dramatic situation? How does the use of a dance reflect the origins of French opera?

9. How does this scene from *Armide* differ from the recitative and aria of Italian opera?

10. How do improvisation and other performance practice issues in French opera differ from Italian opera?

11. In addition to opera, what other vocal genres were practiced in France in the seventeenth century?

12. Define and describe *style luthé* (or *style brisé*).

    What are *agréments*?

    On what instrument did *style luthé* and *agréments* originate? _____

    Why were they necessary or useful on that instrument?

    To what instrument were they later adapted? _____

13. What was unusual or noteworthy about the career of Elisabeth-Claude Jacquet de la Guerre?

Music to Study

NAWM 78: Elisabeth-Claude Jacquet de la Guerre, Suite No. 3 in A Minor, from *Pièces de clavecin,* keyboard suite (1687)

78a: Prelude	CD 5|31	CD 3|3
78b: Allemande	CD 5|32	CD 3|4
78c: Courante I & II	CD 5|33	CD 3|5
78d: Sarabande	CD 5|34	
78e: Gigue	CD 5|35	
78f: Chaconne	CD 5|36	
78g: Gavotte	CD 5|37	
78h: Menuet	CD 5|38	

14. What is a stylized dance? How do we know that the dances in Jacquet de la Guerre's Suite No. 3 (NAWM 78) are stylized?

15. What is distinctive about an *unmeasured prelude,* like the prelude of this suite (NAWM 78a)? Describe its character and notation.

16. What are the meter, relative speed (fast or slow), nation of origin, and character of the following dances in this suite?

	meter	speed	nation of origin	other characteristics
allemande	___	___	___	___
courante	___	___	___	___
sarabande	___	___	___	___
gigue	___	___	___	___

17. What other dances does this suite contain, and what are their characteristics?

18. What are the names of the following *agréments* in the upper melody of the Allemande (NAWM 78b), and how is each one played?

    first beat of measure 2

    first beat of measure 4

    middle of measure 6

    first beat of measure 8

19. Amateurs were the intended performers of the keyboard suite. What aspects of this suite's musical style show this to be the case? What might an amateur performer find enjoyable in performing this composition?

The English Baroque (HWM 372–78, NAWM 79)

20. How was England's musical culture different from France's in the Baroque period? What accounts for that difference?

21. What are the characteristics of the *masque* and *dramatic opera* (also called *semi-opera*)? How do they differ from Italian and French opera?

22. Briefly outline Henry Purcell's career.

Music to Study

NAWM 79: Henry Purcell, *Dido and Aeneas,* opera (1689), conclusion

    79a: Recitative: *Thy hand, Belinda*   CD 5|39   CD 3|6

    79b: Lament (ground bass aria): *When I am laid in earth*   CD 5|40   CD 3|7

    79c: Chorus: *With drooping wings*   CD 5|42

23. Compare Purcell's recitative *Thy hand, Belinda* (NAWM 79a) to Lully's recitative from *Armide* (NAWM 77b) and Monteverdi's recitatives in *L'Orfeo* (NAWM 66d) and *Poppea* (NAWM 67). How does Purcell's music follow the accentuation of the English text? How does the music convey Dido's emotions? How is this similar to or different from Lully's and Monteverdi's recitative styles?

24. Laments in Italian operas were often written over a descending ground bass, and Purcell's aria *When I am laid in earth* (in NAWM 79b) follows this tradition. Part of the expressivity comes from dissonances or conflicts in phrasing between the ostinato bass and the vocal line. Where do these dissonances or conflicts in phrasing occur?

Besides these conventions, what other devices does Purcell use to give this music the feeling of a lament?

25. In the closing chorus of *Dido and Aeneas* (in NAWM 79c), how does the music reinforce the mood of lamentation?

26. In addition to music for the stage, what other vocal and instrumental forms were popular in England in the seventeenth century?

27. How and why did public concerts of music begin in London? What is the long-range significance of these concerts?

Spain and the New World (HWM 379–82, NAWM 80–81)

28. What is a *zarzuela*? How is it similar to or different from forms of musical theater in seventeenth-century France and England?

Music to Study

NAWM 80: Tomás de Torrejón y Velasco, *La púrpura de la rosa,*   [CD 5|43]
opera (1701), excerpt

NAWM 81: Juan de Araujo, *Los coflades de la estleya,* villancico   [CD 5|47]
(late seventeenth century)

29. The excerpt from Torrejón y Velasco's *La púrpura de la rosa* (NAWM 80) contains dialogue, monologue, and chorus. How is this similar to or different from the types of vocal music in the opera excerpts by Purcell (NAWM 79), Lully (NAWM 77), Cesti (NAWM 68), and Monteverdi (NAWM 66 and 67)? What are the similarities or differences in plot and in types of characters between Spanish opera and these other types?

30. Torrejón y Velasco used strophic songs for both monologues and dialogues in *La púrpura de la rosa*. In what ways is that appropriate for the text, and for its intended audience?

31. How is this way of setting monologue and dialogue in Spanish opera different from Italian opera, French opera, and English opera? Is it similar in any way?

32. Purcell used a five-measure descending ground bass to express Dido's sadness (NAWM 79b). How does Tomás de Torrejón y Velasco use musical repetition to express passion between Venus and Adonis?

33. How are the form and texture of the villancico by Juan del Encina (NAWM 48) similar to or different from the the form and texture of Juan de Araujo's villancico *Los coflades de la estleya* (NAWM 81)? What new techniques from the Baroque era are exhibited in Araujo's villancico?

34. Where and when would Juan de Araujo's villancico have been performed? Who may have been its intended audience?

35. Describe some of the dramatic musical elements in this villancico and suggest reasons why the composer used them.

36. What kinds of instrumental music were popular in Spain in the seventeenth century?

French Style and National Traditions (HWM 382–83)

37. What impact did seventeenth-century French music have on music in other nations and in later centuries? How did seventeenth-century music from England, Spain, and the Spanish New World fare in comparison?

TERMS TO KNOW

court ballet
orchestra
comédie-ballet
tragédie en musique, tragédie lyrique
divertissement
overture, ouverture
French overture
récitatif simple
récitatif mesuré
air
notes inégales
overdotting
agréments
petit motet
grand motet
clavecin
clavecinists

style luthé, style brisé
binary form
suite
unmeasured prelude
allemande
courante
sarabande
gigue
rondeau (Baroque)
couplets (in rondeau)
gavotte
minuet
masque
dramatic opera, semi-opera
catch
zarzuela
tiento

NAMES TO KNOW

Louis XIV
Vingt-quatre Violons du Roi
Music of the Great Stable
Jean-Baptiste Lully
Jean-Philippe Quinault
Marc-Antoine Charpentier
Elisabeth-Claude Jacquet de la Guerre

John Blow
Henry Purcell
Dido and Aeneas
The English Dancing Master
Tomás de Torrejón y Velasco
La púrpura de la rosa

REVIEW QUESTIONS

1. Add to the timeline you made for the seventeenth century in chapter 13 the pieces, composers, and leaders discussed in this chapter.
2. Trace the origins and development of musical theater in France during the seventeenth century. Explain what distinguishes it from Italian opera, and describe the importance of dance in French musical theater.
3. What types of instrumental music were practiced in France during the seventeenth century? What are some elements that distinguish French from Italian instrumental style in the Baroque period?
4. What factors influenced the development of English musical theater in the seventeenth century? What genres did the English use? What did the English borrow from the French and Italian traditions?
5. Write a new setting in the style of Lully's French recitative for Dido's four lines of recitative in NAWM 79 (from "Thy hand, Belinda" through "Death is now a welcome guest"). Use as a model the opening of Armide's recitative in NAWM 68b, which is also a setting of a rhymed quatrain (from "Enfin" to "son invincible

coeur"). You may write only the voice and bass line or may fill in the harmony. Why is Purcell's recitative so different from Lully's, and what is he trying to achieve that Lully's style does not accomplish?

6. What factors influenced the development of musical theater in Spain and the New World in the seventeenth century? What genres did the Spanish use? What did the Spanish borrow from the French and Italian traditions? What other musical traditions influenced composers in Spain and the New World?

Chapter 17   Italy and Germany in the Late
Seventeenth Century

CHAPTER OBJECTIVES

After you complete the reading, study of the music, and study questions for this chapter, you should be able to

1. describe the differences in patronage between Italy and Germany and Austria in the late seventeenth century and explain how these differences affected developments in musical style in these regions;

2. describe developments in Italian opera in the late seventeenth century;

3. describe the cantata and other secular vocal genres in Italy in the late seventeenth century;

4. trace the development of ensemble music and orchestral music in Italy in this period and describe the style of Corelli; and

5. describe the different types of keyboard music in Germany and Austria in this time and describe the styles of individual composers.

CHAPTER OUTLINE

I. Introduction (HWM 384)

In Italy and Germany, musical life was supported by a variety of rulers and cities, and musicians traveled from one to another. In Italy, musicians worked in established traditions and codified new conventions, while in Germany, composers blended French, Italian, and German styles.

II. Italy (HWM 384–400, NAWM 82 83)

Opera and cantata were the leading vocal genres, but Arcangelo Corelli's sonatas and concertos are the best-known works from Italy in the late seventeenth century. The three main areas of musical development in Italy at the time were Naples (ruled by Spain), Rome (ruled by the pope), and the small states in the north.

A. Opera

By the late seventeenth century, Italian opera had spread across Italy.

1. Arias

Audiences paid to see and hear the star singers. Arias were written in a variety of forms, but the dominant form was the *da capo aria*. Arias often reflected the meaning of the text through musical motives.

B. Vocal Chamber Music

1. Cantata

Rome was the center of cantata composition in the seventeenth century. The short, contrasting sections of the midcentury cantata were replaced by alternating recitatives and arias later in the century.

2. Scarlatti cantatas

Alessandro Scarlatti (1660–1725) wrote over six hundred cantatas. His recitatives use diminished seventh chords and wide-ranging harmonies for expressive effect. **Music: NAWM 82a**

3. Da capo aria

The most common form of aria in Scarlatti's operas and cantatas is the da capo aria, in which the first section opens with a ritornello and contains two settings of the same text; the second section, to a new text, contrasts in key, figuration, and mood; and the first section repeats (with or without the opening ritornello) to produce an ABA form. The da capo aria form became the standard aria form in the eighteenth century. **Music: NAWM 82b**

4. Serenata

The *serenata* is a semidramatic piece for singers and small orchestra.

C. Church Music and Oratorio

Italian church composers in the second half of the seventeenth century continued to cultivate, and even mix, the old sixteenth-century contrapuntal style with the newer concerted styles.

1. Instrumental church music

Italian instrumental church music included sonatas and organ pieces. The Church of San Petronio in Bologna was an important center for the church sonata.

2. Oratorios

Oratorios, performed in church halls and in secular institutions, were usually in Italian verse and in two sections.

D. Instrumental Chamber Music

Italian composers continued to dominate instrumental chamber music during the seventeenth and early eighteenth centuries, as they did in opera and cantata.

1. Development of the sonata

By the later seventeenth century, the sonata became a multimovement work with contrasts between movements. By about 1660, two main types of sonata has emerged: the *sonata da camera* (or *chamber sonata*), a suite of stylized dances often opening with a prelude; and the *sonata da chiesa* (or *church sonata*), containing mostly abstract movements.

2. Trio sonata

   A *trio sonata* is played by two treble instruments with basso continuo.

3. Solo and ensemble sonatas

   Solo sonatas gained in popularity after 1700. Ensemble sonatas featured up to eight instrumental parts with continuo.

Music in Context: The Violin Workshop of Antonio Stradivarius

Antonio Stradivari (ca. 1644–1737) was the most prominent member of his renowned family of instrument makers, and today's leading string players use his instruments. Scientists have been unable to determine what makes these instruments sound so superior.

E. Arcangelo Corelli's Sonatas

Italian chamber music of the late seventeenth century is best represented in the trio and solo sonatas of *Arcangelo Corelli* (1653–1713).

1. Trio sonatas

   In his trio sonatas, Corelli treated the two violins alike, focusing on lyricism rather than virtuosity. Typical traits of Corelli's style include a *walking bass,* chains of suspensions, sequences, and a dialogue between the violins.   **Music: NAWM 83**

2. Church sonatas

   Corelli's church sonatas most often include four movements in the pattern slow–fast–slow–fast, usually consisting of a majestic first movement, a fugue, a slow duet in triple meter, and a fast dance.

3. Chamber sonatas

   Corelli's chamber sonatas typically begin with a prelude followed by two or three dance movements.

4. Solo sonatas

   Corelli's solo violin sonatas use the same format as his trio sonatas but demand more virtuosity.

5. Thematic organization

   In Corelli's sonatas, movements are based on a single subject stated at the outset, which is then expanded through sequences, variations, and modulations.

6. Tonal organization

   Corelli's music is fully tonal, and he used suspensions and sequences to achieve the sense of forward harmonic motion on which tonality depends.

7. Influence and reputation

   Corelli's sonatas served as models that composers followed for the next half century, and his compositions have become classics.

Biography: Arcangelo Corelli

Corelli studied violin and composition in Bologna, and by 1675, he was living in Rome and enjoying the support of rich patrons. He raised performance standards, and his teaching was the foundation of most eighteenth-century schools of violin playing. He composed only instrumental works, and they made him famous across Europe.

F. The Concerto

1. Music for orchestra
    In the late seventeenth century, musicians began to distinguish between chamber music for one player on a part and orchestral music for more than one on a part.

2. Instrumental concerto
    The instrumental *concerto* was a new genre that emerged in the 1680s and 1690s and became the most important Baroque instrumental genre.

3. Types of concerto
    In the *orchestral concerto,* the first violin part and bass dominated, and the texture was less contrapuntal than in the sonata. More important were the *concerto grosso,* which contrasted a small ensemble (or concertino) with a large ensemble (or concerto grosso), and the *solo concerto,* in which a solo instrument contrasted with the orchestra. In both, the full orchestra was called *tutti* (all) or *ripieno* (full).

4. Predecessors of concerto style
    The practice of contrasting solo instruments against a full orchestra had a long history, including Lully operas.

5. Corelli's concertos
    Corelli's concerti grossi were essentially trio sonatas divided between soli and tutti.

6. Giuseppe Torelli
    Giuseppe Torelli (1658–1709) was a leading composer in the Bologna school, and he treated soloists as adjuncts to the orchestra. He helped to codify the concerto as a work in three movements in the pattern fast–slow–fast.

7. Framing ritornellos
    For the fast movements of his violin concertos, Torelli often used a form like the A section of a da capo aria form, in which two passages for soloist are framed by a recurring ritornello.

G. The Italian Style
The Italian style of the last third of the seventeenth century was widely imitated and became the foundation for developments in the eighteenth century.

III. Germany and Austria (HWM 400–12, NAWM 84)

Germany was weakened by the Thirty Years' War, it had no central political power, and its professional music guilds discouraged innovation.

1. Court, city, and church musicians
    Musicians at court had the highest social standing, and their talents were used in the same fashion as by Louis XIV's court. Cities employed *Stadtpfeifer* and, in Lutheran areas, also hired church musicians. Many

musicians in Germany and Austria traveled from job to job to find the best situation.

2. Amateur musicians
   Many German towns had a *collegium musicum,* a group of amateurs that played and sang music for their own pleasure.

3. Cosmopolitan styles
   Composers in Germany often studied abroad and blended Italian, French, and native styles in new ways.

A. Opera
Opera in Italian was central to musical life in Germany and Austria, and in the eighteenth century, several of the most successful composers of Italian opera were German.

1. Opera in German
   Hamburg staged the first operas in German. Composers, among whom *Reinhard Keiser* (1674–1739) was most prominent, adopted Italian recitative and aria styles but also used a variety of French and German song styles.

B. Song and Cantata
German composers also wrote songs and cantatas in Italian and in German.

C. Catholic Church Music
German Catholic composers at the richest churches cultivated both the older contrapuntal style and the newer concerted styles with voices and instruments.

D. Lutheran Vocal Music
Orthodox Lutherans favored all available resources of choral and instrumental music, but Pietists preferred simple music and poetry that expressed the emotions of the individual believer.

1. Chorales
   New chorales continued to be composed, many intended for home devotions.

2. Concerted church music
   Orthodox Lutheran churches encouraged the sacred concerto, and composers often created concertos in several movements.

3. Dieterich Buxtehude
   Dieterich Buxtehude (ca. 1637–1707) was one of the best-known Lutheran composers of the late seventeenth century.

Biography: Dieterich Buxtehude
Buxtehude was renowned as an organist as well as a composer of organ music and sacred vocal works. He spent the majority of his career as organist at St. Mary's Church in Lübeck, where he played the organ, composed music, and performed public concerts of sacred vocal music.

E. Lutheran Organ Music
Organ music enjoyed a golden age in the Lutheran areas of Germany between about 1650 and 1750.

1. The Baroque organ
   German organ builders combined the colorful stops of the French organs and the multiple keyboards and groups of pipes used in Dutch organs.

2. Functions of organ music
   Most Protestant organ music, including chorale preludes, toccatas, and preludes with fugues, served as a prelude to part of the liturgy.

3. Toccatas and preludes
   Seventeenth-century toccatas were composed of a series of short sections in free, improvisatory style alternating with longer ones in imitative counterpoint. In the eighteenth century, the fugal and nonfugal sections became separate movements, creating a toccata (or prelude) and fugue.
   Music: NAWM 84

4. Fugue
   A fugue opens with an *exposition,* in which the subject in the tonic is imitated by the *answer* in the dominant. The other voices alternate subject and answer and other points of imitation. Some fugues have *episodes.*

5. Chorale settings
   Organ compositions based on chorales included organ chorales, chorale variations (also called chorale partite), and chorale fantasia.

6. Chorale prelude
   Another type of chorale setting is a *chorale prelude,* which uses one of the following procedures: (1) each phrase of the melody is treated in imitation; (2) each phrase is presented in long notes in the top voice and is preceded by the phrase's beginning in *diminution* in the other voices; (3) the melody is ornamented over a free accompaniment; (4) the melody is presented over an accompaniment marked by a repeating rhythmic figure not from the chorale.

F. Other Instrumental Music
   For other instrumental music, German composers borrowed genres practiced largely in Italy and France.

1. Harpsichord suite
   Froberger brought the French harpsichord style to Germany and helped establish the standard dance types for suites.

2. Orchestral suite
   Between about 1690 and 1740, German composers wrote a new type of *orchestral suite* with dances patterned on those from Lully's ballets and operas.

3. Sonata
   The solo sonata attracted more attention from German composers than the trio sonata, and the best-known works were composed by Johann Jakob Walther (ca. 1650–1717) and Heinrich Biber (1644–1704). Johann Kuhnau (1660–1722) wrote the first multimovement sonatas for keyboard instrument.

G. The German Synthesis

Composers of German-speaking lands mastered styles and genres from other nations, added elements from their own traditions, and then, in the eighteenth century, played key roles in developing the sonata and concerto.

IV. Seeds for the Future (HWM 413)

In the second half of the seventeenth century, Italian music reached new heights and Germanic composers were coming into their own. This time saw the development of tonality and the sonata and concerto, the first multimovement instrumental works not based on stringing together smaller pieces, which paved the way for later concert works. Many compositions, especially vocal music, were still written for specific events and only given a few performances. Some instrumental works, however, were played for several generations and influenced later composers.

STUDY QUESTIONS

Italy (HWM 384–400, NAWM 82–83)

1. What were the most important elements of Italian opera in the late seventeenth and early eighteenth centuries? How did drama and music relate in Italian opera of this period, and how did this compare with the ideals of the Florentine Camerata?

2. Describe the form and style of the secular Italian cantata in the late seventeenth and early eighteenth centuries. How does it compare to opera?

3. Describe *da capo aria* form. When and where was it the dominant aria form?

Music to Study

NAWM 82: Alessandro Scarlatti, *Clori vezzosa, e bella,* cantata (ca. 1690–1710), conclusion

    82a: Recitative: *Vivo penando*   CD 5|56

    82b: Aria: *Sì, sì, ben mio*   CD 5|57

4. The aria *Sì, sì, ben mio* from Scarlatti's cantata *Clori vezzosa, e bella* (NAWM 82b) follows da capo aria form. Give the primary harmonic areas for the sections listed below.

harmonic areas

A section

Opening ritornello (mm. 51–53)   _____

First vocal statement (mm. 54–59)   _____

Middle ritornello (mm. 59–60)   _____

Second vocal statement (mm. 60–73)   _____

B section (mm. 74–87)   _____

5. How does da capo aria form reflect the form of the text?

6. How does Scarlatti use form, melody, and harmony to convey the text in this aria and in the recitative that precedes it?

7. The cantata was a form of private entertainment among the elite classes in Rome (see HWM, p. 387). Why might that be? What might this group have found so appealing in the text and musical style?

8. In addition to opera and cantata, what other vocal genres (secular and sacred) were practiced in Italy in the second half of the seventeenth century?

9. What were the main types of ensemble music in the later Baroque period? How do these compare to the main types of instrumental ensemble music practiced in the sixteenth century and in the early seventeenth century?

10. What is the difference between chamber music and orchestral music? In the seventeenth century, what kinds of pieces might have been played by either type of ensemble?

11. What two main types of sonata began to be distinguished after about 1660? Describe each type as practiced by Corelli.

12. What was the most common instrumentation for sonatas in the late seventeenth century? What was a sonata in this instrumentation called?

13. Where did Arcangelo Corelli live and work? How did his career affect his music?

Music to Study

NAWM 83: Arcangelo Corelli, Trio Sonata in D Major, Op. 3, No. 2 (published 1689)

    83a: Grave   CD 6|1

    83b: Allegro   CD 6|2

    83c: Adagio   CD 6|3   CD 3|9

    83d: Allegro   CD 6|4   CD 3|10

14. What harmonic progressions do you expect a composer to use to confirm the key of D major? Do you find those in the first movement of Corelli's Trio Sonata, Op. 3, No. 2 (NAWM 83a)? Where? Using Marini's Sonata IV (NAWM 76), which is modal, as a point of comparison, what characteristics mark the Corelli movement as a tonal work, and the Marini as modal?

15. Corelli's trio sonatas are marked by sequences and by suspensions, especially chains of suspensions in sequence. For each technique, indicate by movement and measure numbers two passages in Corelli's sonata in which it is prominent.

    sequence   _____   _____

    chain of suspensions   _____   _____

    How do these techniques lend these passages a sense of forward momentum toward the next cadence?

16. Is Corelli's Op. 3, No. 2, a church sonata or a chamber sonata? What traits mark it as this type of sonata? Describe the character of each movement.

17. In what ways are Corelli's solo violin sonatas like his trio sonatas, and in what ways are they different?

18. Name and describe the three main types of concertos composed around 1700. How were Baroque principles of contrast embodied in each of them?

19. How many movements does a typical concerto by Giuseppe Torelli have, and what is the relative tempo of each movement?

Describe the typical form Torelli used in the fast movements of his violin concertos. What vocal form does it resemble?

Germany and Austria (HWM 400–12, NAWM 84)

20. What is a *collegium musicum*? What are *Stadtpfeifer*? Where and when was each of these institutions active?

21. What city was the center for opera in Germany in the last quarter of the seventeenth century, and what were the characteristics of opera there?

22. Describe the differences in the function and character of music in Orthodox Lutheran services and Pietist Lutheran services.

23. What were the components of the large German organ around 1700?

24. What role did toccatas, preludes, and chorale preludes play in the Protestant church?

25. Where and in what position was Dieterich Buxtehude employed for most of his career? What types of music did he compose for use in that position?

Music to Study

NAWM 84: Dieterich Buxtehude, Praeludium in E Major, BuxWV 141, organ prelude (late seventeenth century)

CD 6|6

26. How does Buxtehude's Praeludium in E Major (NAWM 84) fit the definition of a late-seventeenth-century toccata or prelude given in HWM, pp. 407–8? What type of texture and figuration does it use? How does it fall into sections?

27. The first fugal section of Buxtehude's Praeludium begins in m. 13. Taking the subject to be eight beats long (from the second beat of m. 13 to the downbeat of m. 15), list here the measure and staff (right-hand [top], left-hand [middle], and pedal [bottom]) of each entrance of the subject. (Note: The last one is somewhat disguised, and then the fugue blends into the following toccata section.)

	measure	staff		measure	staff
1.	_____	_____	8.	_____	_____
2.	_____	_____	9.	_____	_____
3.	_____	_____	10.	_____	_____
4.	_____	_____	11.	_____	_____
5.	_____	_____	12.	_____	_____
6.	_____	_____	13.	_____	_____
7.	_____	_____			

28. The passages between statements of the fugue subject, when the subject is not sounding, are called episodes. (Practically speaking, a passage is usually not considered an episode unless it is at least a measure long, which here is four beats.) Below, list where each episode of at least four beats begins (the beat after the subject concludes) and how many beats long each episode is.

begins in measure	number of beats	begins in measure	number of beats
_____	_____	_____	_____
_____	_____		

What does the longest episode take from the theme, and how does it treat this idea?

29. What types of organ composition in the late seventeenth century were based on chorales? In each type, how was the chorale treated?

30. Describe the *orchestral suite* of about 1690–1740 and its components.

Seeds for the Future (HWM 413)

31. Describe the historical significance of vocal and instrumental music from Italy and Germany in the late seventeenth century.

TERMS TO KNOW

da capo aria
serenata
sonata da camera, chamber sonata
sonata da chiesa, church sonata
trio sonata
walking bass
concerto (instrumental)
orchestral concerto
concerto grosso
solo concerto

tutti, ripieno
Stadtpfeifer
collegium musicum
exposition (in a fugue)
answer (in a fugue)
episode (in a fugue)
chorale prelude
diminution
orchestral suite

NAMES TO KNOW

Alessandro Scarlatti
Antonio Stradivari
Arcangelo Corelli

Giuseppe Torelli
Reinhard Keiser
Dieterich Buxtehude

REVIEW QUESTIONS

1. Add to the timeline you made for the seventeenth century in chapter 13 the pieces and composers discussed in this chapter.
2. How was Italian opera in the late seventeenth century different from Italian opera in the early seventeenth century? How did recitatives and arias change in form and style during the century? What impact did opera have on other vocal genres, like the cantata?
3. Name the varieties of instrumental ensemble music composed in the late seventeenth. Name and briefly describe an example for as many of these varieties as you can.
4. What functions did instrumental ensemble music serve in the late seventeenth century? Name the functions for as many genres as you can.
5. What did Corelli and Torelli contribute to the development of instrumental ensemble music?
6. What characteristics distinguish tonal music from modal music in the seventeenth century? What makes Scarlatti's cantata (NAWM 82) and Corelli's Trio Sonata, Op. 3, No. 2 (NAWM 83) tonal, while Monteverdi's *L'Orfeo* (NAWM 66) and Frescobaldi's Toccata No. 3 (NAWM 74) are modal?
7. As a review of this and previous chapters, trace the development of music for instrumental chamber ensembles from ca. 1500 to ca. 1700.
8. Trace the history of opera in Germany through 1700.
9. Name the varieties of keyboard music being composed in the late seventeenth and early eighteenth centuries. Name and briefly describe an example for as many of these genres as you can.
10. What functions did keyboard music serve in the late seventeenth and early eighteenth centuries? Name the functions for as many genres as you can.

11. As a review of this and previous chapters, trace the development of keyboard music from ca. 1500 to ca. 1700.

12. Compare the economic and political situation in France, Italy, and Germany in the second half of the seventeenth century, and explain how the differences between them help to explain differences in musical life in those three regions, including musical genre and style.

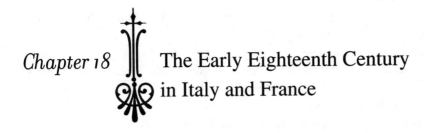

Chapter 18 The Early Eighteenth Century
in Italy and France

CHAPTER OBJECTIVES

After you complete the reading, study of the music, and study questions for this chapter, you should be able to

1. describe briefly the impact of political, economic, and social changes in western Europe in the early eighteenth century on music and culture;

2. summarize the careers, describe the musical styles, and name and describe some of the most significant works by Antonio Vivaldi, François Couperin, and Jean-Philippe Rameau;

3. compare the music of Vivaldi, Couperin, and Rameau to that of their predecessors and contemporaries; and

4. explain the historical significance of these three composers.

CHAPTER OUTLINE

I. Introduction (HWM 416)

Composers around 1700 continued traditions established in the seventeenth century. Vivaldi, Couperin, and Rameau are used in this history as case studies for Italian and French regional styles in the early eighteenth century, and Bach and Handel (chapter 19) represent the continued synthesis of several national traditions in German-speaking regions.

II. Europe in a Century of Change (HWM 416)

The eighteenth century moved from continuity with the past to radical change.

1. Realignment and revolution
    A balance of power in Europe emerged among several strong centralized states, including France, Britain, Austria, and Prussia. Late in the century, the American and French Revolutions brought winds of change.

2. Economic expansion

The middle class grew in size and in its economic status, while the aristocracy became less important.

3. Education and learning

This century also saw an increase in education, literacy, newspapers, book publishing, and discussion of current issues.

4. Demand for new music

Public audiences constantly demanded new music, which accounts for the vast output of music and the phenomenal speed at which composers worked.

5. Changing styles

Eighteenth-century music can be seen as a long argument about musical taste and style, gradually changing from Baroque to Classic styles.

III. Music in Italy (HWM 418–23)

In Italy, opera remained the most prestigious type of music, but instrumental music was gaining ground.

A. Naples

Naples, one of the largest cities in Italy, was home to a vibrant musical life.

1. Conservatories

Naples had four *conservatories* whose pupils spread Italian instrumental and vocal music across Europe.

2. Castrati

By the late seventeenth century, the leading male roles in opera were written for castrati, and one of the most famous was *Farinelli* (Carlo Broschi, 1705–1782).

3. Opera

Opera was the center of musical life in Naples. A new kind of serious Italian opera emerged in the 1720s, codified by librettist Pietro Metastasio (1698–1782).

Music in Context: The Voice of Farinelli

Farinelli's voice was legendary for its range (more than three octaves) and breath control (able to sustain a note for one full minute). He reached stardom on the operatic stage by his early thirties, then served the Spanish kings for two decades.

B. Rome

Rich Roman patrons sponsored all types of music and attracted instrumentalists from all over Italy and Germany.

C. Venice

Venice was home to all types of professional and amateur music-making, including public festivals, opera, church music and chamber music.

IV. Antonio Vivaldi (HWM 423–29, NAWM 85)

Antonio Vivaldi (1678–1741) was the best-known Italian composer of the early eighteenth century, famed especially for concertos.

1. The Pietà
   Between 1703 and 1740, Vivaldi worked at the *Pio Ospedale della Pietà,* a home and school for orphaned or abandoned girls, where he taught, composed, conducted, and maintained the instruments. He wrote about five hundred concertos, allowing those of all abilities to participate.

Biography: Antonio Vivaldi
   Vivaldi was born in Venice and trained in music and the priesthood. As master of violin (and later of concerts) at the Pio Ospedale della Pietà, he composed oratorios, sacred music, and concertos. He also received opera commissions from Venice, Florence, Rome, and elsewhere. He earned a great fortune during his career, but spent almost all of it.

A. Vivaldi's Concertos
   In his concertos, Vivaldi used a simple but flexible plan that allowed him to achieve variety through ever-changing combinations of a few basic elements.

1. Instrumentation
   Vivaldi used different groupings of solo and orchestral instruments to achieve a wide range of colors and sonorities in his concertos. All of Vivaldi's concertos feature opposition between soloist(s) and orchestra.

2. Three-movement structure
   Vivaldi used mainly the three-movement plan (fast–slow–fast), which became the standard for concertos over the next three hundred years.

3. Ritornello form
   Vivaldi used *ritornello form* for fast movements in his concertos. In this form, the full orchestra plays the ritornello, and the soloist(s) play the episodes. The opening ritornello is composed of several small units, and later ritornellos usually include only a few of those units. The opening and closing ritornellos are in the tonic, and the others confirm the keys to which the music modulates during the virtuosic and idiomatic solo episodes. **Music: NAWM 85**

4. Slow movements
   Vivaldi was the first concerto composer to make slow movements as important as fast ones.

5. Economy and variety
   Although Vivaldi created long movements from a small amount of musical material, his concertos exhibit great variety and range of expression.

6. Publications, titles, and programs
   Vivaldi wrote some concertos on commission, and to attract buyers, many were printed with fanciful titles and programs.

B. Vivaldi's Position and Influence

1. Range of styles
   Vivaldi's music reflects the variety of styles in the early eighteenth century.

2. Influence
   Vivaldi had a great influence on later composers of instrumental music, including J. S. Bach.

V. Music in France (HWM 429–31, NAWM 86)

Paris was the music capital of France, with public concerts, private patrons, and institutions.

A. Reconciling French and Italian Style

In the early eighteenth century, the relative merits of French and Italian music were debated by some and blended together by others.

B. François Couperin

Although he worked for royalty, *François Couperin* (1668–1733) earned most of his money teaching aristocrats and composing harpsichord suites (which he called "ordres") for amateur performers.   **Music: NAWM 86**

1. Chamber works
Couperin blended French and Italian styles in his chamber music. For instance, he combined the Italian sonata da chiesa with the French dance suite in his *Les Nations* (The Nations, 1726).

VI. Jean-Philippe Rameau (HWM 432–36, NAWM 87)

Jean-Philippe Rameau (1683–1764) was both a theorist who founded the theory of tonal music and a composer who was Lully's most important successor.

Biography: Jean-Philippe Rameau

Rameau was almost forty years old when he first earned fame with his theoretical treatise on harmony (*Traité de l'harmonie*, 1722). His composing took longer to be recognized, and in the 1730s he wrote his first opera. Wealthy and influential patrons supported Rameau, who despite his late start composed more ballets and operas than any other French composer of the eighteenth century.

A. Theory of Harmony

Rameau's *Traité de l'harmonie* was one of the most influential theoretical works ever written.

1. Acoustics and chords
Because of the laws of acoustics, Rameau considered the triad and seventh chord the primal elements of music.

2. The fundamental bass
Rameau asserted that the *fundamental bass* (in modern terms, the progression of chord roots) defined the harmony of a passage.

3. Tonal direction
Rameau coined the terms *tonic, dominant,* and *subdominant* and formulated the hierarchies of functional tonality. He recognized *modulation,* but considered that each piece had one principal tonic key.

4. Rameau's impact
Rameau was the first to bring these ideas together in a unified system, and since his time, they have become the primary tools for teaching musicians.

B. Operas

Rameau's attained his greatest fame from his operas, including *Hippolyte et Aricie* (1733) and *Castor et Pollux* (1737).

1. Lullistes versus Ramistes

Lully's supporters, known as Lullistes, criticized Rameau's early operas for their difficulty. Rameau was defended by Ramistes, and in the 1750s, even his former opponents praised him as the champion of French music.

2. Comparison with Lully

Rameau's theater works resembled Lully's in several ways, but they also introduced many changes.

3. Melodic and harmonic style

Rameau's melodies are often triadic, outlining the harmonies, which he drew from a rich palette of chords.

4. Instrumental music

The instrumental passages of Rameau's operas were especially original, with tone-painting, novel orchestration, and independent woodwind parts.

5. Airs and choruses

Rameau moved smoothly between recitative and aria styles and frequently included choruses.

6. Combination of elements

The conclusion of Act IV from *Hippolyte et Aricie* (NAWM 87) illustrates the high drama Rameau could achieve by combining all these musical elements.   **Music: NAWM 87**

C. Reputation

By his sixties, Rameau was the most admired musician in France, and his works exemplify French traits.

VII. A Volatile Public (HWM 437)

Changing tastes in the eighteenth century influenced the reception of Vivaldi, Couperin, and Rameau. The works of all three composers, well known during their lifetimes, were virtually forgotten by the end of the century. Through the research of nineteenth-century scholars, these musicians' works were reprinted and their place in music history was rediscovered. Meanwhile, Rameau's reputation as a theorist never waned, and his work was the foundation for most later music theory.

STUDY QUESTIONS

Europe in a Century of Change (HWM 416)

1. Describe the impact that political and social changes had on music and culture in the eighteenth century.

2. What was the eighteenth-century attitude toward new music? How did this attitude affect composers?

Music in Italy (HWM 418–23)

3. Describe musical life in Naples, Rome, and Venice in the early eighteenth century.

4. Why were castrati prized as singers in the early eighteenth century? What roles did they typically play in operas? What special qualities made Farinelli a star?

Antonio Vivaldi (HWM 423–29, NAWM 85)

5. In which city and for what institution did Antonio Vivaldi work for most of his career? Describe the institution's purpose, the role of music in it, and Vivaldi's role.

6. In what other ways did Vivaldi make money from composing, and what types of pieces were the result?

7. What is the typical pattern of movements in Vivaldi's concertos, including the number of movements and their tempo, forms, and key relationships?

8. In a typical Vivaldi concerto, what is the relationship between the soloist(s) and the orchestra? What is the role of the ritornello, and how is it used? What is the role and character of the episodes?

Music to Study

NAWM 85: Antonio Vivaldi, Concerto for Violin and Orchestra in A Minor, Op. 6, No. 2 (ca. 1710)

      85a: Allegro   CD 6|13   CD 3|12

      85b: Largo   CD 6|21

      85c: Presto   CD 6|22

9. Refer to the score and formal diagram (in HWM, p. 426, or in NAWM) of the first movement of Vivaldi's Violin Concerto, Op. 6, No. 2 (NAWM 85), to answer the following questions.

   What is the overall harmonic plan of the movement? How is this articulated by the ritornellos and episodes?

   How many different musical ideas does Vivaldi use in the opening ritornello? Describe each of them, and note (using measure numbers) where these ideas return throughout the movement.

10. The soloist plays the A material from the ritornello in the first episode and then introduces new material in the second episode. Describe this new material, what it draws from the ritornello, and how it differs.

11. Describe the other episodes. What sorts of material do they include?

12. Describe the middle movement of this concerto. How does it differ from the outer movements? What is the character of the parts for the violin solo and for the orchestra?

13. In what ways is the form of the finale of this concerto similar to the form of the first movement?

    In what ways is it different? Compare the two forms through a simplified diagram.

14. Based on your answers to the questions above, why do you think Vivaldi used ritornello form for the fast movements of hundreds of concertos? Why was it appropriate for his students at the Pietà? Why did the general public find it appealing? How did it allow him to write so much music?

15. In areas other than form, how does Vivaldi's style in this concerto differ from that of Corelli (NAWM 83), and how are they similar? Consider melodic style, rhythm, harmony, and other factors in your answer.

Music in France (HWM 429–31, NAWM 86)

16. Describe conditions for music in Paris in the early eighteenth century.

17. In what ways did French composers seek to blend the French and Italian musical traditions? Give at least three examples.

Music to Study

NAWM 86: François Couperin, *Vingt-cinquième ordre,* keyboard suite (ca. 1730), excerpts

    86a: *La visionaire*   CD 6|31   CD 3|20

    86b: *La muse victorieuse*   CD 6|33   CD 3|22

18. In what ways does Couperin's *La visionaire* (NAWM 86a) resemble a French overture, like the one from Lully's *Armide* (NAWM 77a)?

19. What sort of dance is *La muse victorieuse,* and what elements identify it as that dance? What is notable about this movement's form?

20. In what ways are these excerpts from Couperin's *Vingt-cinquième ordre* similar to and different from the dances in Jacquet de la Guerre, Suite No. 3 in A Minor (NAWM 78)?

21. Why do you think the excerpts from Couperin's *Vingt-cinquième ordre* appealed to amateur performers?

Jean-Philippe Rameau (HWM 432–36, NAWM 87)

22. Briefly trace Rameau's career. What were his various occupations? How did he earn a living? What (and who) made it possible for him to write operas and opera-ballets?

23. What were Rameau's contributions to the theory of music? What terms and concepts common today did he introduce?

Music to Study

NAWM 87: Jean-Philippe Rameau, *Hippolyte et Aricie,* opera (1733), conclusion of Act IV

⬭ CD 6|35   ⬭ CD 3|24

24. In the conclusion from Act IV of *Hippolyte et Aricie* (NAWM 87), how does Rameau use the orchestra to convey the scene, actions, and emotions?

25. How does Rameau use the chorus? How does the chorus interact with the other characters? How does this compare to the use of the chorus at the end of Carissimi's *Jephte* (NAWM 71) and Purcell's *Dido and Aeneas* (NAWM 79)?

26. Where does Rameau use accompanied recitative? Where does he use récitatif simple? Where does he use récitatif mesuré? How does each type of recitative suit the words and the dramatic situation?

27. How does Rameau use dissonance and other harmonic effects for expression and to drive the music forward? Give examples.

28. How does this excerpt compare with the scene from Lully's *Armide* in NAWM 77b? How are Rameau's approach and style similar to Lully's, and how are they different?

A Volatile Public (HWM 437)

29. How was the music of Vivaldi, Couperin, and Rameau received during their lifetimes? During later generations?

TERMS TO KNOW

conservatories

ritornello form

fundamental bass

tonic, dominant, subdominant

modulation

NAMES TO KNOW

Farinelli

Antonio Vivaldi

Pio Ospedale della Pietà

François Couperin

Jean-Philippe Rameau

Traité de l'harmonie

Hippolyte et Aricie

REVIEW QUESTIONS

1. Make a timeline for the eighteenth century and place on it the important people, writings, and events discussed in this chapter. Leave enough space to add more items as you work through the next four chapters.

2. Describe the career and music of Vivaldi. How did the circumstances of his employment relate to the music he wrote? How are his concertos similar to those of Corelli and Torelli, and how are they different?

3. Sketch a violin concerto fast movement in ritornello form in C major in the style of Vivaldi, using the first and last movements of NAWM 85 as models. Do not write the whole piece (that would take you much longer than it took Vivaldi!), but assemble the elements:

   a. Write the melody and bass line for the opening ritornello. Include in it three or four contrasting phrases of music, each two to four measures long, and label each phrase with a letter. Keep it simple, but make each phrase recognizable and appealing.

   b. Decide on the number of ritornello statements you want (four to six), and block them out on a piece of paper. The final ritornello will be in the tonic; decide which phrases of the opening ritornello you would like to include in it. The second ritornello will be in the dominant, and the others in closely related keys of your choosing (such as IV or vi). For each ritornello, indicate what key it is in and (by letter) which phrases of the opening ritornello you wish to include.

   c. Plan the episodes. For each, choose a figuration, either from the ritornello or new, and write the first measure or two of the solo line, in the key of the preceding ritornello. Plan the harmonic progression that will modulate to the key of the next ritornello.

   There you have it! Given enough time, you could write the whole movement based on this plan.

4. Describe the career and music of Rameau. How does his career differ from that of Lully? What are his most significant contributions as a theorist? How do the operas and opera-ballets of Rameau continue the tradition of Lully, and how do they differ?

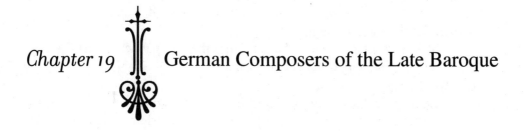

Chapter 19   German Composers of the Late Baroque

CHAPTER OBJECTIVES

After you complete the reading, study of the music, and study questions for this chapter, you should be able to

1. describe the contexts for music in Germany and Britain in the early eighteenth century;

2. summarize the careers, describe the musical styles, and name and describe some of the most significant works by Johann Sebastian Bach and George Frideric Handel;

3. compare the music of J. S. Bach and Handel to their predecessors and to each other; and

4. explain the historical significance of both composers.

CHAPTER OUTLINE

I. Introduction (HWM 438)

In the eighteenth century, German and Austrian composers rose to prominence by combining the best traits of several nations, including Italy, France, Germany, and Austria. J. S. Bach and Handel were the best-known German-speaking composers of the early eighteenth century.

II. Contexts for Music (HWM 438–40)

A. The Economics of Music in Germany and Britain

  1. German patrons
States, principalities, and independent cities of German-speaking central Europe supported music.

  2. Aristocratic musicians
Many aristocrats in eighteenth-century Germany pursued music avidly as performers and as composers.

3. English patrons
Royalty, nobility, and the public supported music in Britain.

4. Concerts and publishing
Musicians supplemented their incomes through public concerts and by selling their compositions to publishers.

B. Mixed Taste
Germans had a history of interest in music from other nations, and their synthesis of these diverse traditions gave their music wide appeal.

1. Georg Philipp Telemann
This stylistic eclecticism is exemplified by the music of *Georg Philipp Telemann* (1681–1767), a prolific composer who helped to establish the characteristic German style of his time and was regarded by his contemporaries as one of the best of his era.

III. Johann Sebastian Bach (HWM 441–57, NAWM 88–90)

Johann Sebastian Bach (1685–1750) was little known outside of Protestant Germany during his life, but he is now considered one of the greatest composers ever. He absorbed the major genres and styles of his time, blended them in new ways, and developed them further.

Biography: Johann Sebastian Bach
Bach was born in Eisenach and came from a large family of musicians. He was a virtuoso organist and keyboard player, and his first positions were as church organist at Arnstadt and Mühlhausen, where he also taught private students in performance and composition. Bach worked his way up the career ladder, serving as organist and then concertmaster in Weimar and later as music director at Cöthen. At Leipzig, he held one of the most prestigious positions in Germany as cantor of the *St. Thomas School* and civic music director. In all, Bach composed in almost every genre then current, except opera.

A. Bach at Work
Bach composed primarily to fill the needs of the positions he held.

1. The position of musicians
In the eighteenth century, composers were subject to the wishes of their employers and did not have the freedom to create exclusively what they wanted.

2. Conditions in Leipzig
In Leipzig, Bach had multiple duties, including teaching Latin and music at the school, composing and rehearsing music for services, conducting the top choir and orchestra, and providing music for civic events.

3. The craft of composition
Bach learned composition by copying and arranging other composers' music. In his own works, Bach composed by inventing the principal theme or vocal melody and then elaborating it. He often revised and reworked completed compositions.

B. Organ Music

As a church organist, Bach focused on genres employed in Lutheran services, drawing on a wide variety of models as he developed a distinctive style.

1. Preludes and fugues

By 1700, some composers were prefacing fugues with separate preludes, toccatas, or fantasias.

2. Vivaldi's influence

At Weimar, Bach arranged Vivaldi concertos for keyboard and adopted ritornello form and other of Vivaldi's traits in his own works. His fugues resemble ritornello form, with the fugue subject functioning like a ritornello.   **Music: NAWM 88**

3. Chorale settings

Bach wrote over two hundred chorale-settings for organ. His *Orgelbüchlein* (Little Organ Book), compiled at Weimar, contains short chorale preludes. In each prelude, the chorale is stated once, usually in the soprano, accompanied with counterpoint or embellished through a variety of compositional techniques. In some, images in the chorale texts are suggested through the use of musical figures.   **Music: NAWM 89**

C. Harpsichord Music

Bach wrote harpsichord music in every current genre.

1. Suites

The harpsichord suites show French, Italian, and German influences.

2. The *Well-Tempered Clavier*

Each of the two books of the *Well-Tempered Clavier* consists of twenty-four prelude and fugue pairs in each major and minor key. Each prelude assigns the player a specific technical task and illustrates different types of keyboard performance conventions and compositional practices, while the fugues comprise an array of fugal writing techniques.

3. *Goldberg Variations*

In his *Goldberg Variations,* Bach used a variety of techniques, such as canon, fugue, and *quodlibet.*

4. *Musical Offering* and *Art of Fugue*

A *Musical Offering* contains twelve pieces on a theme by Frederick the Great of Prussia, and the *Art of Fugue* systematically demonstrates all types of fugal writing.

D. Chamber Music

1. Sonatas

Bach wrote fifteen sonatas for solo instrument and harpsichord, which may have been written for the collegium musicum in Leipzig.

2. Works for unaccompanied instruments

Bach's works for unaccompanied violin, cello, or flute create the illusion of a harmonic and contrapuntal texture.

E. Orchestral Music

1. *Brandenburg Concertos*
Bach's six *Brandenburg Concertos,* dedicated to the Margrave of Brandenburg in 1721, follow Italian models but expand the forms.

2. Collegium musicum
Most of Bach's other orchestral music, including concertos and suites, was written in the 1730s for the Leipzig collegium musicum.

F. Cantatas
The Lutheran church cantata was devised around 1700 by *Erdmann Neumeister* (1671–1756) as a series of recitatives and arias meditating on a biblical text and closing with a chorale. Composers setting such cantata texts to music blended elements of chorale settings, solo song, the sacred concerto, and opera.

1. Role in church services
The church cantata was performed during the Lutheran service after the Gospel reading. Bach directed the performance of a different cantata each Sunday in Leipzig, alternating between St. Nicholas's and St. Thomas's.

2. Cantata cycles
Bach composed at least three and possibly four complete cantata cycles.

3. Chorale cantatas
Bach's second cantata cycle for Leipzig consisted of cantatas whose words and music were based on chorales. His cantata *Nun komm, der Heiden Heiland,* BWV 62, is typical: the opening chorus mixes genres (concerto and chorale motet), the movements for soloists use diverse types of aria and recitative, and the last movement is a harmonized chorale.   **Music: NAWM 90**

G. Other Church Music
Bach also composed motets, Passions, and Latin service music.

1. Passions
For the *St. John Passion* and *St. Matthew Passion,* Bach drew on elements from opera, cantata, and oratorios to recount the story of Jesus' death.

2. Mass in B Minor
Bach assembled his *Mass in B Minor* from his existing works and newly composed movements. He employed contrasting styles and demonstrated different current approaches to writing church music.

H. Bach's Synthesis
Bach synthesized into his works all the genres, styles, and forms of his time. By the last decades of his life, some considered his music old-fashioned and difficult. In the nineteenth century, his music appealed to a broader audience of connoisseurs and amateurs alike.

IV. George Frideric Handel (HWM 457–70, NAWM 91–92)

George Frideric Handel (1685–1759) won international renown and success with the public during his lifetime, and his music has been performed ever since.

Biography: George Frideric Handel [Georg Friederich Handel]

Handel was born in Germany where he studied music of German and Italian composers. In 1703, he moved to Hamburg, played in an opera orchestra, and composed his first opera. He traveled to Italy where he associated with the leading patrons and musicians. Handel's greatest successes came in London, where he served aristocratic and royal patrons, as well as a public audience. Although he wrote many instrumental works, Handel is best known for his Italian operas and English oratorios.

A. Handel and His Patrons

Handel enjoyed generous support from patrons, particularly the British monarchs who ensured Handel sizable pensions despite minimal responsibilities. Most of his musical activities, however, were for public audiences.

B. The Operas

Handel composed and directed operas for most of his career.

1. International style

In his operas, Handel combined French overtures and dances, Italian-style recitatives and arias, and German elements of counterpoint and orchestration.

2. London operas

Handel's *Rinaldo* (1711) was the first Italian opera composed for London and established his reputation there.

3. Royal Academy of Music

Handel was music director for the *Royal Academy of Music,* formed in 1718–19 by wealthy gentlemen with the support of the king.

4. Recitative styles

Simple recitative (with continuo) and *accompanied recitative* (with orchestra) were two types of recitative that emerged in Italian opera in the early eighteenth century.

5. Arias

Handel wrote arias for specific singers in a wide variety of types, including some with *coloratura* (florid ornamentation). The best music was saved for the prima donna.

6. Instrumental sections

In his operas, Handel sometimes used instrumental sinfonias or ballets.

7. Scene complexes

Handel moves the plot forward in his operas by freely combining recitative, arias, ariosos, and orchestral passages. This, and his characteristic combination of national elements, are apparent in his opera *Giulio Cesare.* **Music: NAWM 91**

8. Handel as impresario

Handel and a partner formed a new opera company in 1729, but although he continued writing operas until 1741, he never achieved the same success with opera that he had with his earlier works.

C. The Oratorios

In the 1730s, Handel devised the English oratorio, a combination of the Italian oratorio and opera traditions with French, German, and English influences.

1. Use of chorus

In his oratorios, Handel gave the chorus a more active role in the story. His choral style is dramatic but simpler and less consistently contrapuntal than Bach's.

2. *Saul*

Handel's oratorios were performed in theaters, usually during Lent, but *Saul* was premiered during the 1738–39 opera season in place of a new opera. It exemplifies the blending of genres in his oratorios.   **Music: NAWM 92**

3. *Messiah*

After the great success of *Messiah* in 1741–42, Handel stopped composing operas and focused on oratorios.

4. Performing oratorios

Oratorios were less expensive to present than operas, and they were popular with public audiences.

5. Librettos

Oratorios were meant for the concert hall, and their librettos were based on the Jewish Scriptures.

6. Borrowing and reworking

Handel, like his contemporaries, borrowed and reworked existing music, using material that was well suited to its new purpose.

D. Instrumental Works

Handel wrote a great deal of instrumental music, much of which was published in London and used in home music-making.

1. Ensemble suites

Handel's two most popular instrumental works, *Water Music* and *Music for the Royal Fireworks,* are suites for orchestra or winds that he composed for the king.

2. Concertos

Although Handel mixed tradition and innovation in his concertos, they tend toward a retrospective style.

E. Handel's Reputation

Handel became a national figure for the English, and some of his oratorios were the first pieces to have an unbroken tradition of performance from the time that they were composed to the present.

V. An Enduring Legacy (HWM 470–71)

Only a few of Bach's works were published during his life. Musicians and connoisseurs kept his works alive in musical literature and through study. In the nineteenth century, Bach's works were rediscovered and became widely known, and his reputation soared. Some of Handel's oratorios have received public performances since their premieres, making Handel the first classical composer. Although they produced music in different styles, for different purposes, and with different historical results, Bach and Handel represent the Baroque for many listeners today.

STUDY QUESTIONS

Contexts for Music (HWM 438–40)

1. Describe the political organization of Germany and England in the early eighteenth century and the impact it had on musical life in those regions.

2. How did aristocrats and the public participate in music? How did composers support themselves?

3. What differentiated the German approach to music from that of the Italians and the French? How was Georg Philipp Telemann an example of this approach?

Johann Sebastian Bach (HWM 441–57, NAWM 88–90)

4. Where did Bach work, and when? What were his duties in each position? How did his employment affect the music he composed?

5. How did Bach learn to compose? What was his typical process of composition?

6. What models did Bach draw on for his organ music? What types of organ works did he write? For each type, what are its main characteristics, and what purposes did it serve?

Music to Study

NAWM 88: Johann Sebastian Bach, Prelude and Fugue in A Minor, [CD 6|38] [CD 3|27] BMV 543, organ prelude and fugue (ca. 1715)

NAWM 89: Johann Sebastian Bach, Chorale prelude on *Durch* [CD 6|49] *Adams Fall*, BWV 637, chorale prelude (ca. 1716)

7. In what ways does the form of the fugue in Bach's Prelude and Fugue in A Minor (NAWM 88) resemble the ritornello form of Vivaldi's concertos?

8. In what ways do the melodies in both the fugue and the prelude show the influence of Italian violin style? Use the solo violin portions of Vivaldi's Op. 3, No. 6, second movement (NAWM 85), for comparison.

9. How does this Bach fugue compare to the first fugal section of Buxtehude's Praeludium in E Major (NAWM 84) in form and in other respects (see chapter 17, study questions 27–28)? Consider the way the subject is used, the length and content of the episodes, the harmonic plan, and other factors.

10. How does Bach's prelude compare to the opening section and other toccata-like passages in Buxtehude's prelude (mm. 1–12, 48–59, etc.)?

11. Based on the comparisons you have made above, write a brief summary of how Bach's prelude and fugue blends North German and Italian influences.

12. How does Bach employ musical imagery in his chorale prelude on *Durch Adams Fall* (NAWM 89) to convey the images in the chorale text?

13. When was the *Well-Tempered Clavier* written? What does it contain, and how is it ordered? What are the characteristics and purposes of this collection?

14. Describe the *Goldberg Variations, A Musical Offering,* and the *Art of Fugue.* When was each written, and what does each contain? How is each a summation of musical genres or approaches of Bach's time?

15. What types of chamber music and orchestral music did Bach write? Where were most of his works of this type written, and for what occasions?

16. Describe the Lutheran church cantata. Who devised it and when? What was the text like? From what sources might parts of the text be borrowed, and what portions were newly written? What was the music like, and from what traditions did it draw?

17. What kinds of musicians (and how many of each) did Bach have available for performing cantatas in Leipzig?

18. Where in the liturgy was the cantata performed? How did its subject matter relate to the rest of the liturgy?

Music to Study

NAWM 90: Johann Sebastian Bach, *Nun komm, der Heiden Heiland,* BWV 62, cantata (1724)

  90a: Chorus: *Nun komm, der Heiden Heiland*   [CD 6|50]   [CD 3|38]

  90b: Aria (tenor): *Bewundert, o Menschen*   [CD 6|58]

  90c: Recitative (bass): *So geht aus Gottes Herrlichkeit*   [CD 6|60]
    und Thron

  90d: Aria (bass): *Streite, siege, starker Held!*   [CD 6|61]

  90e: Accompanied recitative (soprano and alto): *Wir ehren*   [CD 6|63]
    diese Herrlichkeit

  90f: Chorale: *Lob sei Gott, dem Vater, ton*   [CD 6|64]

19. In Bach's cantata *Nun komm, der Heiden Heiland* (NAWM 90), which texts are from existing sources, and from where do they derive? Which texts are newly written? On what are they based, and what is their relationship to that source?

20. Bach wrote this cantata for the first Sunday of Advent, the four-week period preceding Christmas. How do the words relate to the season?

21. How is the chorale tune *Nun komm, der Heiden Heiland* (NAWM 42b) used in the first movement? In the final movement?

22. What French and Italian forms and textures, adapted from opera, concerto, sonata, and dance, are used in this cantata, and in which movements? What other traits from outside the German tradition do you notice?

23. Describe how Bach reflected the words and images of the text in the music in the four movements for soloists. What different types of recitative and aria are used, and why are these types appropriate to the texts?

24. On what grounds was Bach's music criticized during his lifetime?

25. What are some of the factors that have led people in later centuries to regard him as one of the greatest composer of his era?

George Frideric Handel (HWM 457–70, NAWM 91–92)

26. By the age of twenty-five, where had Handel lived, studied, and worked? What genres had he tried? What influences had he absorbed? What made his music international in style?

27. Describe Handel's relationship with his patrons. How was his career different from Bach's?

28. In which genre was Handel first successful in England? _____

Music to Study

NAWM 91: George Frideric Handel, *Giulio Cesare,* opera, (1724), Act II, scenes 1–2

    91a: Recitative, *Eseguisti*   `CD 6|65`

    91b: Da capo aria, *V'adoro pupille*   `CD 6|68`   `CD 3|46`

29. Baroque opera plots typically centered on love, drew on history or mythology, created opportunities for spectacle, and often involved secrecy and disguise. How are these elements reflected in the libretto for Handel's *Giulio Cesare,* particularly in this excerpt (NAWM 91)?

30. A typical operatic scene involved recitative followed by a da capo aria with an opening ritornello, first section, contrasting middle section, and reprise of the first section. In this excerpt, how does Handel modify this series of events? How do these changes aid the drama? How do they make the final statement of the aria's first section more than a conventional repetition?

31. How is the construction of this scene similar to or different from the conclusion of Act IV in Rameau's *Hippolyte et Aricie* (NAWM 87)?

32. What elements does Handel draw from instrumental forms, including the concerto and the dance? How does he use these elements expressively?

33. Compare this aria to Scarlatti's *Sì, sì, ben mio* (NAWM 82b). How does Handel's aria resemble Scarlatti's, and how does it differ?

34. When and why did Handel begin composing oratorios? What national styles and genres did he combine in his oratorios?

35. What language is used in Handel's oratorios? How did the language and the subject matter influence the success of his oratorios? Where were they performed, and for whom?

36. How did Handel use the chorus in his oratorios? How does this differ from the practice of Italian composers? What traditions influenced Handel in this regard?

Music to Study

NAWM 92: George Frideric Handel, *Saul,* oratorio (1738), Act II, scene 10

92a: Accompanied recitative: *The Time at length is come* [CD 6|71] [CD 3|49]

92b: Recitative: *Where is the Son of Jesse?* [CD 6|72] [CD 3|50]

92c: Chorus: *O fatal Consequence of Rage* [CD 6|73] [CD 3|51]

37. In the recitatives from Handel's *Saul* (NAWM 92a and 92b), how does the music portray Saul's rage?

38. In the following chorus (NAWM 92c), how does Handel use musical symbolism to convey the meaning of the text?

39. In this chorus, where does Handel use fugue? What other textures does he employ? Why do you think he used these elements in this way? How do the changes of texture delineate the form and convey the meaning of the text?

40. Where does Handel employ exact or near-exact repetition of entire passages? Chart the form of this chorus, noting these repetitions and the changes of texture you observed in the previous question.

41. How does Handel's choral writing in this work differ from that of Bach in the opening movement from his cantata *Nun komm, der Heiden Heiland* (NAWM 90a), and how is it similar?

42. What is the role of borrowing in Handel's music? What is borrowed in these excerpts from *Saul,* and how is this material treated?

43. What characteristics of Handel's music helped to earn it a lasting place in the repertoire of music?

An Enduring Legacy (HWM 470–71)

44. Describe the "careers" of Bach's and Handel's music after their death. What is especially notable about the posthumous reputation of each?

TERMS TO KNOW

quodlibet
simple recitative

accompanied recitative
coloratura

NAMES TO KNOW

Georg Philipp Telemann
Johann Sebastian Bach
St. Thomas Church and School,
   Leipzig
Orgelbüchlein
Well-Tempered Clavier
Goldberg Variations
A Musical Offering
Art of Fugue

Brandenburg Concertos
Erdmann Neumeister
St. John and *St. Matthew Passions*
Mass in B Minor
George Frideric Handel
Royal Academy of Music
Giulio Cesare
Saul
Messiah

REVIEW QUESTIONS

1. Add Bach and Handel and the pieces discussed in this chapter to the timeline you made for the previous chapter.
2. Trace Bach's career and explain how the circumstances of his training and employment influenced the types of music he wrote and the styles he drew upon.
3. What did Bach's instrumental music draw from German sources? What did he draw from Italian models and from French models? Describe a piece by Bach that blends at least two of these national traditions, and explain how Bach combined elements from different nations into a coherent idiom.
4. Adopting the aesthetic position of Johann Adolph Scheibe (see HWM, p. 456), describe what is wrong with Bach's Prelude and Fugue in A minor (NAWM 88) and the opening chorus of his cantata *Nun komm, der Heiden Heiland* (NAWM 92a).
5. Trace Handel's career and explain how his experiences as a composer influenced the types of music he wrote and the styles he drew upon.
6. Compare and contrast the musical ideals and styles of Bach and Handel, focusing particularly on their vocal music.
7. What was the historical significance of Bach, and Handel? What trends did each absorb, what influence did each have on later music, and in what respects did each achieve a unique musical idiom?

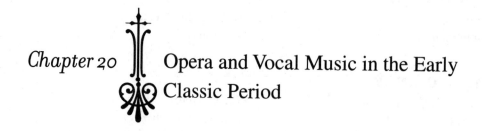

Chapter 20 Opera and Vocal Music in the Early Classic Period

CHAPTER OBJECTIVES

After you complete the reading, study of the music, and study questions for this chapter, you should be able to

1. briefly describe the intellectual, cultural, and aesthetic background to music in the early Classic period;

2. describe the characteristics that distinguish Classical music from music of earlier periods;

3. name and describe the principal styles and genres of opera and other vocal music current in the eighteenth century;

4. use and define terms appropriate to this period; and

5. name some of the composers of the period, describe their individual styles, and identify some of their works.

CHAPTER OUTLINE

I. Introduction (HWM 472)

In the mid-eighteenth century, composers created a new musical language, first developed in vocal music, based on songful melodies with light accompaniment.

II. Europe in the Mid- to Late-Eighteenth Century (HWM 472–78)

Eighteenth-century Europe was dominated politically by centralized powers with large military establishments.

1. Economic change
Urban middle classes in Europe continued to grow while landed aristocracy diminished in importance.

2. A cosmopolitan society
The eighteenth century was a cosmopolitan age because of foreign-born rulers and increased travel.

3. International musical style
    Musical life was also international, and music that combined features of many nations and thus was universally pleasing was considered to be the best music.

A. The Enlightenment
    The *Enlightenment* was an intellectual movement that valued reason and asserted the rights of every person.

1. The *philosophes*
    The philosophes were French thinkers who developed doctrines about individual human rights.

2. Humanitarianism
    Enlightenment ideals were humanitarian. Rulers patronized arts and letters and promoted social reform such as education and care for the poor.

3. Popularization of learning
    The pursuit of learning became more widespread among the middle class.

Innovations: The Public Concert
Public concerts and concert series were organized in many cities and were attended mainly by those of upper-middle and wealthy leisure classes. London was home to the Academy of Ancient Music (founded in 1726) and the Bach-Abel concerts (1765–1781). Paris had the *Concert spirituel* series (1725–90), which introduced repertoire and composers from across the continent. The Gewandhaus Orchestra in Leipzig became one of the most famous orchestras in the world. Public concerts were social events and were advertised by word of mouth and in print media. A typical concert presented a variety of vocal and instrumental genres for various ensembles.

B. Social Roles for Music
    Musicians increasingly depended upon support from the public, giving performances and teaching.

1. Musical amateurs and connoisseurs
    During the eighteenth century, amateur performers provided publishers a growing market, and music connoisseurs cultivated a taste for the best in music.

2. Musical journals and histories
    By midcentury, music magazines and histories began to appear, catering to both amateurs and connoisseurs.

III. Musical Taste and Style (HWM 478–85)

Many musical styles, old and new, national and cosmopolitan, coexisted and competed in the eighteenth century.

1. Values for music
    Critics valued music that was universal, pleasing, and entertaining, featuring a vocally conceived melody in short phrases over a spare accompaniment.

A. Terms for Styles: Galant, Empfindsam, and Classical

These values led to a new idiom known today as the *classical style*.

1. Galant style

   The new style, which originated in Italian operas and concertos, was most commonly known as *galant*.

2. Empfindsam style

   The *empfindsam style,* a close relative of the galant style, is characterized by surprising turns of harmony, chromaticism, nervous rhythms, and speechlike melody.

3. Classical music and classical style

   For historical reasons, "classsical" has come to have two meanings—as a term that covers many centuries and styles, and also refers to a late-eighteenth-century musical style.

4. What is the classical style?

   Some writers use the term "classical style" to refer only to the mature music of Haydn and Mozart, while others use it for an entire period.

5. The Classic period

   This text regards about 1730–1815 as the Classic period, during which time composers used a variety of related styles.

B. Melody, Harmony, Texture, and Form

The focus on melody in the Classic period led to a musical syntax different from earlier styles.

1. Periodicity

   The newer styles were characterized by *periodicity*. A *period* was formed by two or more phrases ending in a cadence, and a composition was made up of two or more periods.

2. Musical rhetoric

   Eighteenth-century theorists such as *Heinrich Christoph Koch* (1749–1816) frequently referred to music in rhetorical terms, believing it could move one's emotions like speech and that a composition was like an oration. Koch showed how to assemble short units into phrases, phrases into periods, and periods into larger forms.

3. Harmony

   The newer styles used a hierarchy of cadences (stronger for closing periods and weaker for internal phrases) and a hierarchy of harmonies.

4. Animation of texture

   Composers compensated for slower harmonic rhythm by animating the texture through rhythmic means like the *Alberti bass* in keyboard music.

5. Form

   By the late-eighteenth century, composers differentiated musical material according to its function in the form, with each segment of music serving as a beginning, middle, or end of a phrase, period, section, or piece.

C. Emotional Contrasts

1. New view of psychology
Unlike seventeenth-century thinkers, psychologists in the eighteenth century believed that human feelings were constantly changing.

2. Form and content
As a result, composers no longer sought to convey a single mood in a movement or section, but instead introduced emotional contrasts within sections or themes.

IV. Italian Comic Opera (HWM 485–90, NAWM 93)

Many characteristics of Classical music originated in Italian opera of the 1720s and 1730s, especially comic opera.

A. Opera Buffa
An *opera buffa* was a full-length Italian comic opera, sung throughout, with a combination of six or more serious and comic characters. Dialogue was set in rapid recitative with keyboard accompaniment.

1. Arias
The arias used short tuneful phrases, organized into periods, and accompanied by simple harmonies.

B. Intermezzo
An *intermezzo* was a type of Italian comic opera that was performed in two or three segments between the acts of a serious opera or play.

1. Pergolesi's *La serva padrona*
The best known intermezzo is *La serva padrona* (The Maid as Mistress, 1733) by *Giovanni Battistia Pergolesi* (1710–1736), who used rapid changes of melodic figuration and style to convey the shifting thoughts and moods of his characters. **Music: NAWM 93**

C. Later Comic Opera
At midcentury, the dramatist Carlo Goldoni (1707–1793) introduced more serious elements to Italian comic opera plots.

1. Ensemble finales
In an ensemble finale, all the characters were brought on stage at the end of an act to create a dramatic climax.

V. Opera Seria (HWM 490–93, NAWM 94)

Aria styles from comic opera were also used in *opera seria* (serious opera).

1. Pietro Metastasio
The Italian poet *Pietro Metastasio* (1698–1782), whose librettos were set hundreds of times, developed the standard form for opera seria.

2. Content of opera seria
The three acts of opera seria consist of alternating recitative (action) and aria (reflection) with a few duets and larger ensembles.

A. The Aria

The musical interest of Italian opera lies in the arias.

1. Da capo aria

The standard aria form was the da capo aria, featuring a large A section with two vocal statements surrounded by orchestral ritornellos based on the main melodic material; a shorter contrasting B section with a new text and in a contrasting key; and a reprise of the A section.

2. Abbreviated da capo

For some arias, composers shortened the standard da capo aria form.

3. New features

In the 1720s and 1730s, composers introduced new features to da capo arias including more than one mood in the A section, short melodic units, and the recapitulation of secondary key material in the tonic.

4. Johann Adolf Hasse

Johann Adolf Hasse (1699–1783), music director at the Saxon court in Dresden, was a leading composer of opera seria at midcentury. His vocal style follows the natural rhythms and inflections of the text. **Music: NAWM 94**

5. Faustina Bordoni

Faustina Bordoni (1700–1781), Hasse's wife, was one of the great singer-actresses of her time, performing all over Europe.

6. Vocal embellishment

Opera singers were expected to embellish the written vocal line.

VI. Opera in Other Languages (HWM 494–97, NAWM 95)

Comic operas were written in national languages and reflected national musical idioms.

A. France

1. Querelle des bouffons

The *Querelle des bouffons* was a debate between French intellectuals about French and Italian opera.

2. Jean-Jacques Rousseau

Jean-Jacques Rousseau (1712–1778) praised Italian opera, especially its emphasis on melody and expression of emotions.

3. Opéra comique

Opéra comique is French light opera in which songs alternate with spoken dialogue. The songs were either existing popular tunes (vaudevilles) or newly composed (ariettes).

4. Serious plots

By the later eighteenth century, some opéras comiques were based on serious plots, such as "rescue" opera.

B. England

1. Ballad opera

The *ballad opera* consisted of spoken dialogue and songs that set new words to borrowed tunes. Over time, composers wrote more original music.

2. *The Beggar's Opera*
Ballad operas became popular with the success of *The Beggar's Opera* (1728) with libretto by *John Gay* (1685–1732).   **Music: NAWM 95**

C. Germany and Austria

1. Singspiel
Singspiel was an opera in German with spoken dialogue, musical numbers, and usually a comic plot.

D. Opera and the Public
Public audiences supported national opera traditions, reinforcing Enlightenment preferences for music that was simple and had wide appeal.

VII. Opera Reform (HWM 497–500, NAWM 96)

From midcentury on, Italian opera underwent reforms that reflected Enlightenment thought.

1. Jommelli and Traetta
Two of the most important figures in opera reform were Niccolò Jommelli (1714–1774) and Tommaso Traetta (1727–1779), who combined French and Italian traits to create a cosmopolitan type of opera.

A. Christoph Willibald Gluck
Christoph Willibald Gluck (1714–1787), working with librettist *Raniero de Calzabigi* (1714–1795), reformed opera by making music serve the poetry and advance the plot, while synthesizing French, Italian, and German operatic styles.

1. *Orfeo ed Euridice*
In Gluck's *Orfeo ed Euridice,* recitatives, arias, and choruses intermingle in large unified scenes.   **Music: NAWM 96**

2. French operas
Gluck brought his new style to Paris and composed several successful French operas, including *Iphigénie en Aulide* (Iphigenia in Aulis, 1774), *Armide* (1777), and *Iphigénie en Tauride* (Iphigenia in Tauris, 1779).

3. Gluck's influence
Gluck's operas became models for many other operas, especially in Paris.

VIII. Song and Church Music (HWM 500–5, NAWM 97)

Secular vocal chamber music was performed in intimate settings across Europe and, along with opera, influenced changes in church music.

A. Song
Songs for home performance were composed for amateurs to sing and play. Secular songs emerged in different regions—like the romance in France and ballad in England.

1. The Lied
Many collections of *Lieder* (German songs) were published in the second half of the century and were syllabic settings of strophic poetry in a simple style.

2. Johann Friedrich Reichardt

By century's end, *Johann Friedrich Reichardt* (1752–1814) and others made the structure of the Lied more flexible and the accompaniment more independent.

3. The virtues of song

Eighteenth-century song embodied values the Enlightenment held most dear.

B. Church Music

Church music of this era was no longer the driving force for innovations and was valued more for its traditionalism.

1. Catholic music

Catholic music took over the musical idioms and genres of opera.

2. Lutheran music

In Lutheran areas, service music was in the new galant style, and the oratorio became the principal medium of North German composers.

3. English church music

In England, composers focused on the traditional service and anthem in Baroque styles.

4. New World

In the New World, church musicians drew on their respective national styles.

5. New England hymnody

New England Puritans used metrical psalms in worship. In the eighteenth century, singing schools trained amateurs and created a demand for new music.

6. William Billings

William Billings (1746–1800) was the most prominent composer of sacred music in New England, writing in a variety of genres, including plain hymns, anthems, and *fuging tunes*. He wrote in a style best suited to his needs, remaining independent from normal rules of counterpoint. **Music: NAWM 97**

7. Moravians

Moravians, German-speaking Protestants, were familiar with European trends and used organ, strings, and other instruments in their services.

IX. Opera and the New Language (HWM 505)

The new musical idioms of the mid- to late-eighteenth century had their sources in vocal music. These new styles then had a tremendous impact on instrumental music. Compositions from this period in music history are now little known, but at the time, they were part of the debate on changing styles and aimed at pleasing a growing audience.

STUDY QUESTIONS

Europe in the Mid- to Late-Eighteenth Century (HWM 472–78)

1. What was the Enlightenment? How did the wider cultural climate of the eighteenth century affect music?

2. According to Johann Joachim Quantz and others (quoted in HWM, p. 474), what were the characteristics of the best music?

3. How did economic and political changes stimulate greater public interest in music, and how did musical life change in response to this growing interest?

4. What circumstances encouraged the growth of public concerts? Where did public concerts begin, and to what cities did they spread? What were concerts and concert programs of the late eighteenth century like?

Musical Taste and Style (HWM 478–85)

5. What distinguishes the new classical styles (including *galant* and *empfindsam*) from Baroque style and from each other?

6. What is the difference between classical music and classical style? Why do we use the same term with different meanings?

7. According to Heinrich Christoph Koch, how is a melodic *period* put together? What role does harmony play? How does this process resemble that of an orator formulating a sentence or making a speech?

8. In late-eighteenth-century music, how does the material relate to the form? How are units of music put together into movements or compositions?

9. What changed in the view of human psychology between the seventeenth century and the late eighteenth century? How did this affect music?

Italian Comic Opera (HWM 485–90, NAWM 93)

10. What are the characteristics of an *opera buffa*? What are the arias like? How does the aria by Leonardo Vinci excerpted in HWM, Example 20.3 (pp. 494–95), exemplify some of these characteristics?

Music to Study

NAWM 93: Giovanni Battista Pergolesi, *La serva padrona,* intermezzo (1733), excerpt

93a: Recitative: *Ah, quanto mi sta male*   ⬡ CD 7|1   ⬡ CD 3|55

93b: Aria: *Son imbrogliato io*   ⬡ CD 7|3   ⬡ CD 3|57

11. What is funny in Uberto's recitative soliloquy in this scene from Pergolesi's *La serva padrona* (NAWM 93a)? How do his vocal line, the changes of harmony, and the interjections of the string orchestra convey yet parody his emotions?

12. What characteristics of the new Classic-era styles (as described in the first section of this chapter) appear in Uberto's aria (NAWM 93b)?

13. How does Pergolesi use these new Classic-era styles or methods to convey and also parody Uberto's emotions?

14. Imagine that you are in the audience at the Teatro San Bartolomeo in Naples on September 5, 1733. What work did you probably come to the opera house to see?

    Give a general description of how and when *La serva padrona* is performed on the stage during that evening.

    What is the purpose of the intermezzo *La serva padrona*? How does it affect your enjoyment of what you saw at the theater?

15. What are the characteristics of the *opera seria* libretto as established by Pietro Metastasio? What moral lessons did his operas aim to teach?

16. What are the musical characteristics of opera seria?

17. Describe and chart the typical form of an aria in an opera seria. What alterations in this form were made by some composers? Why did composers choose to make these alterations? What do the indications "da capo" and "dal segno" indicate to the performer?

Opera Seria (HWM 490–93, NAWM 94)

Music to Study

NAWM 94: Johann Adolf Hasse, *Cleofide,* opera seria (1731),　　　 ⌐ CD 7|7 ⌐
excerpt: Act II, scene 9: *Digli ch'io son fedele*

18. The story of Hasse's *Cleofide* was adapted from one of Metastasio's librettos. How is the form and content of Act II, scene 9 (NAWM 94), and the general plot of this opera representative of Metastasio's librettos?

19. Compare Cleofide's aria *Digli ch'io son fedele* to the standard da capo form you charted in question 17. Where does each section begin and end? In what respects does it follow this form? Where and why does it deviate?

20. Where does material from the opening ritornello (mm. 1–10) return later in the aria, either in the vocal statements or in later ritornellos, and how is it changed? What might account for these changes?

21. In what ways does the B section contrast with the A section? Why does Hasse use two contrasting sections?

22. What characteristics of the new Classic-era styles (as described in the first section of this chapter) appear in the music of both sections of this aria?

23. The embellished melody in the upper staff of Example 20.5 in HWM (p. 493) was transcribed from a performance of this aria from *Cleofide*. How does the embellished line relate to the written melody in the staff below? What can you deduce from this example about how singers embellished arias in opera seria?

Opera in Other Languages (HWM 494–97, NAWM 95)

24. Describe the development of light opera in eighteenth-century France. How was it influenced by Italian opera?

Music to Study

NAWM 95: John Gay, *The Beggar's Opera,* ballad opera (1728), [CD 7|12] excerpt from scene 13

25. In what ways does *The Beggar's Opera* (NAWM 95) differ from Italian opera and French comic opera? In what ways is it similar? What is this type of musical theater called? What did John Gay do to "compose" this work?

26. In what ways does *The Beggar's Opera* (NAWM 95) reflect Enlightenment ideals?

27. Can you think of any modern-day examples of this type of composition?

28. In what ways is eighteenth-century Singspiel similar to or different from Italian comic opera, French opéra comique, and English ballad opera? What are the distinctive features of each national tradition?

29. What was the importance of comic opera for later developments in music of the late eighteenth and nineteenth centuries?

Opera Reform (HWM 497–500, NAWM 96)

30. How did Jommelli and Traetta seek to reform Italian opera in the 1750s? How did this reform reflect Enlightenment ideals?

Music to Study

NAWM 96: Christoph Willibald Gluck, *Orfeo ed Euridice,* opera ⸤ CD 7|14 ⸣
(1762), excerpt from Act II, scene 1

31. Describe the differences in the melody, harmony, form, and orchestration between
the excerpts from Gluck's *Orfeo ed Euridice* (NAWM 96), Lully's *Armide*
(NAWM 77b), and Hasse's *Cleofide* (NAWM 94).

	Orfeo ed Euridice	*Armide*	*Cleofide*
melody			
harmony			
form			
orchestration			

32. In Gluck's view, what was the proper relationship between the words and the music in opera? How did Gluck accomplish his reform objectives in the excerpt from *Orfeo ed Euridice* (NAWM 96)?

How does this differ from Hasse's *Cleofide* as composed and performed?

33. What dramatic musical devices does Gluck use to set the scene and portray the characters (the Furies in the underworld, and Orfeo, who has come down to bring back his beloved Euridice)?

Song and Church Music (HWM 500–5, NAWM 97)

34. In what ways is J. F. Reichardt's *Erlkönig* (excerpted in HWM, Example 20.7, p. 501) typical of eighteenth-century Lieder? How do songs like this one reflect the values of the Enlightenment?

35. How was eighteenth-century church music influenced by opera? Where did older styles continue, and why?

Music to Study

NAWM 97: William Billings, *Creation,* from *The Continental*
Harmony (ca. 1794), fuging tune

36. What is a *fuging tune*? What characteristics of Billings's *Creation* (NAWM 97) are typical of fuging tunes? What characteristics are typical of his personal style?

37. For what purposes did William Billings compose *Creation*? Why are fuging tunes in general and *Creation* in particular suitable for such purposes?

38. What is William Billings's significance in American music history?

Opera and the New Language (HWM 505)

39. Summarize briefly how opera and vocal music were influenced by and helped to disseminate the new musical idioms in the early Classic period.

TERMS TO KNOW

Enlightenment
classical style
galant style
empfindsam style
periodicity
period
Alberti bass
opera buffa

intermezzo
opera seria
Querelle des bouffons
opéra comique
ballad opera
Singspiel
Lied (pl. Lieder)
fuging tune

NAMES TO KNOW

Heinrich Christoph Koch
La serva padrona
Giovanni Battista Pergolesi
Pietro Metastasio
Johann Adolf Hasse
Faustina Bordoni
Jean-Jacques Rousseau

The Beggar's Opera
John Gay
Christoph Willibald Gluck
Raniero de Calzabigi
Orfeo ed Euridice
Johann Friedrich Reichardt
William Billings

REVIEW QUESTIONS

1. Add to the timeline you made for the eighteenth century the composers and pieces discussed in this chapter. (See Review Question to chapter 18.)

2. How did the Enlightenment ideals of reason and naturalness help to create a climate in which the older Baroque styles were replaced by simpler, immediately pleasing styles with wide appeal?

3. What parallels did eighteenth-century writers observe between music and rhetoric? How does Cleofide's aria (NAWM 94) resemble a speech, and how does the theme from C. P. E. Bach's sonata movement (Example 20.1 in HWM, p. 483) resemble a speech?

4. If you are familiar with jazz improvisation on a standard tune, what comparisons can you draw between jazz performance and the improvised embellishments in opera seria, exemplified in Example 20.5 in HWM, p. 493? What is similar about the two approaches to improvisation, and what differs?

5. Example 20.5 in HWM, p. 493, was transcribed from a performance of *Cleofide*. Using this example as a model, add vocal embellishments to the written vocal line of Leonardo Vinci's *T'aggio mmidea* (Example 20.3 in HWM, pp. 486–87). Be creative. Remember that the singers were the center of attention in opera, and audiences paid to hear improvised vocal gymnastics.

6. Describe the varieties of comic opera in the eighteenth century in Italy, France, England, and Germany.

7. Trace the development of serious opera from the 1730s to the 1770s, including both opera seria and reform opera. How does the reform opera of Gluck and Calzabigi differ from opera seria?

8. Describe the diversity of church music styles in the New World in the early Classic period. How were they similar to and different from national church music styles in Europe?

Chapter 21   Instrumental Music: Sonata, Symphony, and Concerto at Midcentury

CHAPTER OBJECTIVES

After you complete the reading, study of the music, and study questions for this chapter, you should be able to

1. name and describe the principal instrumental genres current in the mid- to-late-eighteenth century;

2. diagram and describe rounded binary form, sonata form (as described in the 1780s and in the nineteenth century), and concerto first-movement form; and

3. name some of the composers of the period, describe their individual styles, and identify some of their works.

CHAPTER OUTLINE

I. Introduction (HWM 506)

The new musical idiom of the mid-eighteenth century, developed primarily in opera, became pervasive in instrumental music, which gained new independence. This time saw a rise in works for piano, string quartet, and symphony, as well as the development of sonata form.

II. Instruments and Ensembles (HWM 506–10)

Instrumental music served a variety of social roles, including private performance in the home, at concerts, and as entertainment music for parties.

1. The piano
   The most popular keyboard instrument at the time was the *pianoforte,* or *piano,* which allowed greater variety of dynamics and expression.

2. Chamber ensembles
   Ensembles were written for numerous instruments, including those with the keyboard in a dominant role. The *string quartet,* also common, was a social activity meant for the enjoyment of the performers and their companions.

3. Wind instruments and ensembles
   The clarinet, oboe, bassoon, and flute were the standard wind instruments by the 1780s; they were rarely played by amateurs.

4. Orchestra
   The late-eighteenth-century orchestra was much smaller than today's and was led by the leader of the violins. At midcentury, all the essential musical material was given to the strings, and the winds were used for doubling and filling in harmonies; later, the winds gained more independence.

III. Genres and Forms (HWM 510–14)

The major genre of keyboard music was the sonata, and the main genres for orchestral music were the concerto and the *symphony*. Sonatas, symphonies, and chamber works typically had three or four movements in related keys and contrasting moods and tempos, and concertos had three.

1. Continuity and change
   Although these instrumental genres were quite similar to their Baroque counterparts, they reflected the new galant style and used new forms.

2. Preference for major mode
   Music from the Classic period favored the major mode as the home key and used the minor mode for contrast.

A. Sonata Form
   The typical form for first movements in the Classic period is now known as *sonata form.*

1. Koch on first-movement form
   In his *Introductory Essay on Composition* (1793), Heinrich Christoph Koch described first-movement form as an expanded binary form in two sections, both normally repeated. The first, with one main period, presents the movement's main idea in the tonic, modulates to the dominant or relative major, and then affirms the new key. The second section, with two main periods, modulates back to the tonic, then restates material from the first section in the tonic.

2. Later view of sonata form
   By the 1830s, theorists described the form in three sections (*exposition, development,* and *recapitulation*). There may also be a slow introduction before the exposition or *coda* after the recapitulation.

3. Changes in first-movement form
   Koch's approach, emphasizing phrase structure and tonal plan, works better for music before 1780, and the later view, emphasizing the thematic content, is a better fit for music after 1800.

B. Other Forms
   Composers also used other forms, including *slow-movement sonata form, variations form, minuet and trio form,* and *rondo form* (which alternates a main theme with *episodes*). Each of these forms expands upon binary form, and all use similar compositional approaches.

IV. Keyboard Music (HWM 514–19, NAWM 98–99)

Keyboard works were in great demand by amateurs in the middle and late eighteenth century, and sonatas were widely regarded as the most challenging.

A. Domenico Scarlatti

Domenico Scarlatti (1685–1757), son of Alessandro Scarlatti, worked in Portugal and Spain and composed many keyboard works.

1. Sonatas

In his 555 keyboard sonatas, Scarlatti typically used *rounded binary form.*

2. Style

Although Scarlatti's style in the sonatas was not galant, he did use a great variety of figuration.   **Music: NAWM 98**

B. Carl Philipp Emanuel Bach

Carl Philipp Emanuel Bach (1714–1788) composed in many vocal and instrumental genres, but he is best known for his keyboard works and his *Essay on the True Art of Playing Keyboard Instruments* (1753–62).

1. Sonatas

C. P. E. Bach composed many sets of keyboard sonatas that exhibit the galant style as well as the empfindsam style.

2. Empfindsam characteristics

In many slow movements of his keyboard sonatas, Bach used the empfindsam style, characterized by constantly changing rhythms, sudden surprising changes of harmony, texture, or dynamic level, and instrumental evocations of recitative.   **Music: NAWM 99**

V. Orchestral Music (HWM 519–23, NAWM 100–102)

Music for orchestra grew in importance during the eighteenth century.

A. Symphony

The symphony, which originated in Italy around 1730, was the major orchestral genre of the mid- to late-eighteenth century.

1. Italian origins

The symphony originated from the opera sinfonia (overture), the orchestral concertos of Torelli and others, church sonatas in northern Italy, and the orchestral suite.

2. Giovanni Battista Sammartini

The first symphonies were written by composers in northern Italy like *Giovanni Battista Sammartini* (ca. 1700–1775), whose three-movement works contained a variety of contrasting ideas.   **Music: NAWM 100**

3. Mannheim

The *Mannheim* orchestra, led by *Johann Stamitz* (1717–1757), was renowned for its discipline, technique, dynamic range, and crescendos.

4. Johann Stamitz

Stamitz was the first composer to use consistently four movements and a theme after the modulation.   **Music: NAWM 101**

5. Vienna and Paris

Vienna and Paris were also important centers of symphonic activity.

B. Symphonie Concertante

The *symphonie concertante,* popular in Paris and elsewhere from around 1770 to 1830, was a genre that combined virtuoso playing by soloists with an orchestra.

C. Concerto

The solo concerto was also a popular vehicle for virtuosos *Johann Christian Bach* (1735–1782) was among the first to compose piano concertos.

1. Three-movement plan

Concertos were typically three-movement works in a fast–slow–fast format.

2. Concerto first-movement form

The first-movement form of concertos was a combination of Baroque ritornello form (orchestral ritornellos alternated with solo episodes) and Classic sonata form (contrasts in key and thematic material).   **Music: NAWM 102**

3. Cadenza

By the late eighteenth century, the soloist improvised a cadenza just before the final orchestral ritornello.

D. Entertainment Music

A great deal of instrumental music was written for entertainment purposes.

VI. The Singing Instrument (HWM 524)

In the eighteenth century, composers absorbed the new styles of vocal music with existing traditions within the instrumental repertory to create new genres and forms. Individual compositions had wide and instant appeal, but they were replaced quickly and often by new music. The prolonged popularity of a few composers, such as C. P. E. and J. C. Bach, was overshadowed later by Haydn and Mozart.

STUDY QUESTIONS

Instruments and Ensembles (HWM 506–10)

1. Which instruments and ensembles were most common in the mid-eighteenth century? Where and by whom was instrumental music performed?

2. How large was the typical orchestra in the mid-eighteenth century? How were the strings divided, and about how many of each type were there? In addition to the strings, what other instruments were members, about how many of each were there, and what was their function? Who conducted, and how did this differ from earlier practice?

Genres and Forms (HWM 510–14)

3. Which instrumental genres were most popular by the mid-eighteenth century? In what ways were these genres similar to and different from their Baroque counterparts?

4. Diagram a sonata first-movement form as described by Koch. Below that, diagram it as described by theorists of the 1830s and later, and show the correspondences between these two descriptions by indicating which elements of the later description parallel particular elements of the Koch model.

5. Name and describe other forms used in instrumental music from the Classic period. How does each relate to or expand upon binary form?

Keyboard Music (HWM 514–19, NAWM 98–99)

Music to Study

NAWM 98: Domenico Scarlatti, Sonata in D Major, K. 119, keyboard sonata (ca. 1740s) [CD 7|22] [CD 3|61]

NAWM 99: Carl Philipp Emanuel Bach, Sonata in A Major, H. 186, Wq. 55/4: keyboard sonata (1765), second movement, Poco adagio [CD 7|26] [CD 3|65]

6. In the first half of his Sonata in D Major, K. 119 (NAWM 98), Scarlatti introduces a string of ideas with contrasting figuration and function. For each of the following passages (indicated by measure numbers), indicate the implied key when it is tonally stable or "mod." if it changes key, and briefly describe the figuration (e.g., arpeggios, scales, octaves, repeated notes or chords, trills, stepwise melody, or a combination of these).

   Some of these ideas return in the second half, and some do not. For those that do, indicated where in the second half they begin and in what key they are presented.

	Mm.	Implied key	Figuration	Where in 2nd half?
a.	1–5	_____	_____	_____
b.	6–13	_____	_____	_____
c.	14–17	_____	_____	_____
d.	18–35	_____	_____	_____
e.	36–55	_____	_____	_____
f.	56–64	_____	_____	_____
g.	65–72	_____	_____	_____
d'.	73–95	_____	_____	_____

7. Based on your answers above, describe the form of Scarlatti's sonata. Does it resemble Koch's first-movement form? Or, is it something else altogether?

8. For whom did Scarlatti write this keyboard sonata? Describe what you think may have made this piece appropriate and enjoyable for his patron. How does Scarlatti suggest his patron's nationality?

9. What elements of the second movement of C. P. E. Bach's Sonata in A Major (NAWM 99) are typical of his empfindsam style?

10. Compare the melodic writing in this sonata movement to the vocal embellishments added to Hasse's aria from *Cleofide* (NAWM 94) as shown in the upper staff of Example 20.5 in HWM, p. 493. Although the melodic range in the sonata is too wide for a singer, how does Bach create the sense in this instrumental work of a vocal melody, like a slow aria?

11. Bach's Sonata in A Major was a great success among the amateur music-making public. Based on this movement, why do you think that was the case?

Orchestral Music (HWM 519–23, NAWM 100–102)

12. Where (in what region) and when did the *symphony* originate? What characteristics does the Classic symphony share with Baroque instrumental genres? What genres or forms were its "parents," and what did it draw from them?

Music to Study

NAWM 100: Giovanni Battista Sammartini, Symphony in F Major, [CD 7|28] No. 32, symphony (ca. 1740), first movement, Presto

NAWM 101: Johann Stamitz, Sinfonia a 8 in E-flat Major, Op. 11, [CD 7|31] No. 3, symphony (mid-1750s), first movement, Allegro assai

NAWM 102: Johann Christian Bach, Concerto for Harpsichord [CD 7|36] or Piano and Strings in E-flat Major, Op. 7, No. 5, keyboard concerto (1770), first movement, Allegro di molto

13. How does the first movement of Sammartini's Symphony in F Major, No. 32 (NAWM 100) compare in style to the aria from Pergolesi's *La serva padrona* in NAWM 93 or the Scarlatti sonata in NAWM 98? What elements does it have in common with each?

14. Which description of sonata form or first-movement form applies better to this movement, that of Koch or that of theorists of the 1830s and later? Why?

15. What are some of the techniques that made the Mannheim orchestra famous, and how are they used in the first movement from Stamitz's Sinfonia a 8 in E-flat Major (NAWM 101)?

16. Compare Stamitz's first movement to that of Sammartini (NAWM 100). How are they similar, and how are they different, in instrumentation, style, and form?

17. For what occasions and in what settings might Sammartini's and Stamitz's symphonies have been performed? What characteristics of each piece led you to that conclusion?

18. What traits mark J. C. Bach's keyboard concerto first movement (NAWM 102) as galant in style?

19. In this concerto movement, what elements of the opening orchestral ritornello return later, and where does each return?

20. When the keyboard solo enters, how does it vary what has already been presented, and what new material does it introduce? Which of these variants and new ideas are later recapitulated, and where?

21. In what ways is the form of this first movement a blend of ritornello form and sonata form? Why is this concerto first-movement form appropriate for the public concerts for which Bach wrote this piece?

The Singing Instrument (HWM 524)

22. How did instrumental music change during the middle decades of the eighteenth century? How were the instrumental works of the composers treated in this chapter received during their lifetimes, and in later eras?

TERMS TO KNOW

pianoforte, piano
string quartet
symphony
sonata form
exposition, development,
  recapitulation, coda
slow-movement sonata form

variations form
minuet and trio form
trio
rondo form
episode (in a rondo)
rounded binary form
symphonie concertante

NAMES TO KNOW

Domenico Scarlatti
Carl Philipp Emanuel Bach
Giovanni Battista Sammartini

Mannheim
Johann Stamitz
Johann Christian Bach

REVIEW QUESTIONS

1. Add to the timeline you made in chapter 18 the important people, writings, pieces, and events discussed in this chapter.
2. What did comic opera styles (see chapter 20) contribute to instrumental music in the second half of the eighteenth century?
3. What social functions were served by the various instrumental works discussed in this chapter? Which were concert pieces, and which were for amateur or private performance?
4. What elements of form do all or most of the instrumental works in NAWM 98–102 have in common? (For instance, do they all have similar harmonic plans? Do they repeat musical material in similar ways? What elements does each share with the standard model of sonata form?) Can you distill from these five movements a short list of formal strategies that are shared by all or most of these pieces?
5. How did the new musical idioms of the eighteenth century make possible the rise of instrumental music to a position equal to that of vocal music?

Chapter 22   Classic Music in the Late Eighteenth Century

CHAPTER OBJECTIVES

After you complete the reading, study of the music, and study questions for this chapter, you should be able to

1. trace the careers of Haydn and Mozart and the development of their musical idioms;

2. describe the principal genres and forms practiced by Haydn, Mozart, and their contemporaries; and

3. name several important works by each of these composers and describe some works by each in their mature styles.

CHAPTER OUTLINE

I. Introduction (HWM 525)

The most successful composers of the late eighteenth century wrote music that pleased a wide range of listeners. Haydn and Mozart synthesized styles to create music that continues to appeal to audiences and performers today.

II. Joseph Haydn (HWM 526–46, NAWM 103–104)

Joseph Haydn (1732–1809), the most celebrated composer of his day, is best remembered for his symphonies and string quartets.

Biography: Joseph Haydn

Haydn was trained in music as a choirboy in Vienna, where, as a young adult, he barely supported himself as a freelance musician. His first steady job was as music director for Count Morzin. In 1761, he entered the service of the Esterházy princes, which allowed him to hear his music in excellent performances and to experiment with new ideas. His publications brought him fame throughout Europe. During the early

1790s, he lived mostly in London, where he composed, gave concerts, and taught, before returning to Vienna.

A. Haydn's Patrons: The Esterházy Princes

Haydn composed whatever the Esterházy princes demanded. He also conducted, trained, and supervised all musicians, and maintained instruments.

1. Eszterháza

Beginning in 1766, Haydn worked mostly at *Eszterháza,* the country estate built by *Prince Nikolaus Esterházy* (r. 1762–90), where he composed opera, sacred vocal works, orchestral pieces, chamber music, and music for marionette plays. Visitors kept him up-to-date on current developments in music.

2. Publication

Unauthorized publications of Haydn's works made him famous but earned him no money. His 1779 contract allowed him to sell his music to others.

3. London

After Nikolaus died in 1790, Haydn received a pension, moved to Vienna, and then worked in London with impresario *Johann Peter Salomon* during two extended stays between 1791 and 1795.

B. Haydn's Style

In his time, Haydn's style was recognized as highly individual. He earned broad appeal with his compositions by combining the familiar with the unexpected.

1. Sources

Haydn's idiom was created from a synthesis of diverse styles, including galant, empfindsam, and learned (counterpoint). His works also employed a wide range of elements, including opera buffa style, hymns, and folksongs.

2. Sophistication within apparent simplicity

Many of Haydn's melodies, like the theme from the finale of the string quartet nicknamed *The Joke,* seem simple but are actually quite sophisticated. **Music: NAWM 103**

3. Economy and novelty

Combining economy of material with constant novelty is typical of Haydn.

4. Rhythm, phrasing, and harmony

In Haydn's music, rhythm, phrasing, and harmony work together to give the music shape and continuity, despite relatively short melodic units.

5. Expansion, delay, and drama

Haydn used unexpected expansions of phrase, period, or section for both expressive and formal purposes.

6. Wit

Haydn created wit by playing on performers' and listeners' expectations.

7. Differentiation of function
Stylistic conventions make it easy to distinguish between gestures that signal the beginning, middle, or end of a phrase, period, or section, and between themes, transitions, and cadential extensions. Haydn used these differences to make his music easy to follow.

8. Double appeal
Haydn's music appeals at once to the least experienced listener and also rewards the connoisseur.

C. Compositional Process
Haydn's compositional process combined improvisation and calculation.

D. Symphonic Form
Haydn's symphonies set the pattern for later composers through their high quality, wide dissemination, lasting appeal, and individuality.

1. Four-movement structure
Haydn's symphonies typically have four movements—fast sonata-form (often with slow introduction), slow movement, minuet and trio, and fast finale. This format became the standard for later composers.

2. *Oxford* Symphony
Haydn's Symphony No. 92 in G Major (*Oxford*) illustrates many elements that characterize his symphonic techniques.   **Music: NAWM 104**

3. First-movement form
In the first movement, Haydn created contrasts between stable themes and unstable transitions to help us follow the form.   **Music: NAWM 104a**

4. Exposition
Each thematic area in the exposition contains a variety of ideas.

5. Development
In the development, Haydn used a variety of techniques to manipulate motives from the exposition.

6. Recapitulation
Haydn sometimes disguised or played down the appearance of the recapitulation, which repeats all themes in the tonic (sometimes altered) and often amplifies the transition.

7. Slow movement
In the second movement, Haydn usually offered songlike themes and simple forms to contrast with the drama and complexity of the first movement.   **Music: NAWM 104b**

8. Minuet and trio
The minuet and trio provides relaxation, since it is shorter than the second, written in a more popular style, and in a form that is easy to follow.
Music: NAWM 104c

9. Finale
The final movement, usually a sonata form, rondo, or *sonata-rondo,* closes the symphony with a further build-up of tension, climax, and release.   **Music: NAWM 104d**

E. The Symphonies

Haydn mastered the symphony early on, but his approach changed over time.

1. Early symphonies, 1757–67

Haydn's earliest symphonies were typically in three movements, scored for strings and pairs of oboes and horn, and had themes made of elements that were easily broken up and recombined. For his early Esterházy symphonies, Haydn sought novelty and variety.

2. Symphonies of 1768–72

Beginning about 1768, Haydn treated the symphony as a serious work that was longer, had greater extremes in dynamic level, a richer harmonic palette, wider ranging modulations, and more contrapuntal textures than his previous symphonies. The agitated, minor-key character of some has been linked to the literary movement *Sturm und Drang* (storm and stress).

3. Symphonies of 1773–81

Beginning around 1773, Haydn composed symphonies in a more popular style that was immediately intelligible yet serious, stirring, and impressive.

4. Symphonies for public concerts

In the 1780s, Haydn increasingly composed for the public, combining popular and learned styles in symphonies scored for strings, flute, and pairs of oboes, bassoons, and horns.

5. *London* Symphonies

Haydn's twelve *London* Symphonies have more daring harmonic movements, intensified rhythmic drive, more memorable themes, and expanded orchestra. He also used appealing features to please both music lovers and experts.

F. String Quartets

Haydn was the first great master of the string quartet (a genre intended for amateurs), and the evolution of these works parallels that of the symphonies.

1. Early quartets

Haydn's first ten quartets resembled divertimentos and were so titled.

2. Opp. 9, 17, and 20

In Opp. 9, 17, and 20, Haydn established the same four-movement pattern as in the symphony, but with the minuet often before the slow movement and a unique approach to sonata-form movements.

3. Opus 33

The six Op. 33 quartets (1781) are lighthearted, witty, and tuneful with fast or metrical jesting minuets titled *scherzo*. The humor in these works is aimed at the performers.

4. Later quartets

Each of Haydn's late quartets had individual features and juxtaposed diverse styles and emotions.

G. Keyboard Sonatas and Trios

Keyboard sonatas and trios were written for amateurs to play in private, and they usually feature three movements in fast-slow-fast format.

H. Vocal Works

Haydn considered his vocal works his most successful, believing, like his contemporaries, that vocal music was more important than instrumental music.

1. Operas

Haydn's many Italian operas (most of them comic) were successful in their day but are now rarely performed.

2. Masses

Haydn's most important works for church were six late festive masses (1796–1802) that blend traditional elements with a new prominence for orchestra and elements drawn from symphonic style and forms.

3. Oratorios

While in England, Haydn heard some of Handel's oratorios. His own late oratorios *The Creation* (1798) and *The Seasons* (1801), both on librettos by *Baron Gottfried van Swieten,* show Handel's influence and became standards for choral societies.

I. Achievement and Reputation

Although he left an enormous body of work, Haydn's reputation rests primarily on the later quartets, symphonies, and oratorios, only a small fraction of his total output. His best music still elicits awe and admiration.

III. Wolfgang Amadeus Mozart (HWM 546–64, NAWM 105–107)

Wolfgang Amadeus Mozart (1756–1791) toured as a child prodigy in the 1760s and, unable to find a suitable position, spent his mature years as a free agent in Vienna.

Biography: Wolfgang Amadeus Mozart

Mozart was born in *Salzburg*. He composed, performed on harpsichord, and improvised at a very young age, and his father took him and his sister Nannerl on tours across Europe as child prodigies. In 1781, Mozart moved to Vienna and made a good income composing, teaching private students, performing, and selling his works to publishers. He was a master in every medium and is considered one of the greatest musicians of the Western tradition.

A. Child Prodigy

Mozart was exposed at a young age to a wide range of music, which influenced his composing throughout his life.

1. Leopold Mozart

Mozart's father *Leopold Mozart* (1719–1787) was a violinist, composer, and author, who devoted himself to educating his children in music and other subjects.

2. Touring
   From 1762 to 1773, the Mozarts went on tour across Europe, performing and composing for very famous and influential people.
3. Absorbing influences
   Mozart became familiar with every kind of music being written or heard in western Europe, and his work became a synthesis of national styles.
4. Paris
   In Paris, Mozart was influenced by music of Johann Schobert (ca. 1735–1767), which simulated orchestral effects on the harpsichord.
5. London
   In London, Mozart met Johann Christian Bach, whose use of thematic contrast and infusion of features from Italian opera into instrumental works became hallmarks of Mozart's style.
6. Italy and Vienna
   In trips to Italy (between 1769 and 1773), Mozart studied counterpoint and composed his first two opere serie. In Vienna (1773), he became acquainted with current styles in serenade, string quartet, and symphony.

B. Freelancing
   Mozart's adult career illustrates the growing tension between steady employment and freelancing at a time when most musicians had to combine the two to survive financially.
1. Salzburg
   Mozart was dissatisfied with his position in Salzburg, but he was unable to find another in his travels to Italy, Vienna, Germany, and Paris.
2. Gaining independence
   Mozart experienced independence and success in Munich with *Idomeneo* (1781) and left Salzburg for Vienna.
3. Vienna
   For ten years, Mozart earned his living as a freelance musician in Vienna by composing, teaching, performing, organizing concerts, and publishing.
4. Success or failure?
   Near the end of his life, Mozart was still active freelancing, but he was not very good at managing his expenses and requested assistance from friends.

C. Mature Style
   Mozart's most famous works came from his time in Vienna and show a synthesis of form and content and of galant and learned styles.
1. Haydn, Bach, and Handel
   Mozart's music was enriched by influences from three of the century's greatest composers: Haydn, whom he knew personally, and J. S. Bach and Handel, whose music he discovered through Baron Gottfried van Swieten.

D. Piano Music
   Mozart wrote sonatas, fantasias, variations, rondos, and piano duets for his pupils, for domestic music-making, and for publication.

1. Sonata in F Major, K. 332
   The first movement of Mozart's Sonata in F Major, K. 332, exemplifies his style at the beginning of his Vienna period.   **Music: NAWM 105**
2. Themes
   Mozart's themes tend to be songlike, perhaps reflecting Italian influence.
3. Contrasting styles
   Composers of the time used diverse styles (referred to as *topics*) to delineate form, convey feelings, and provide variety, and Mozart's skill in doing so was unparalleled.

E. Chamber Music
1. Mozart's *Haydn* Quartets
   Mozart's six *Haydn* quartets (dedicated to Haydn) show a mature capacity to absorb the essence of Haydn's technique of pervasive thematic development with substantial equality between the four instruments.
2. Quintets
   Many of Mozart's other chamber works are also classics, including his string quintets and works for solo wind and strings.

F. Serenades and Divertimentos
   Mozart composed serenades and divertimentos for entertainment, but he treated them as serious music.

G. Piano Concertos
1. Vienna concertos
   Mozart composed seventeen piano concertos as vehicles for his own public performance and intended them to please the entire range of listeners.
2. First movement
   The first movements blend elements of ritornello and sonata-form procedures, like J. C. Bach's concertos, but they also contain several individual features.   **Music: NAWM 106**
3. Slow movement and finale
   The slow movement resembles a lyrical aria, and the finale is typically a rondo or sonata-rondo on themes with a popular character.
4. Balance of elements
   Mozart always maintained a balance of musical interest between the orchestral and solo portions in his concertos.

H. Symphonies
   Mozart's early symphonies were mostly in three movements and intended to open concerts or theatrical events, and his later symphonies were in four movements and were often the main feature on concert programs.
1. Vienna symphonies
   Mozart's six Vienna symphonies have ambitious dimensions, greater demands on performers, harmonic and contrapuntal complexity, and climatic final movements. Each of these symphonies has its own special character.

2. Finales

As in Haydn's late symphonies, the finales of Mozart's late symphonies balance the serious opening movement.

I. Operas

Mozart eagerly sought opportunities to compose operas and wrote six before moving to Vienna.

1. *Die Entführung*

Mozart's operatic fame in Vienna and beyond was established by the Singspiel *Die Entführung aus dem Serail* (The Abduction from the Seraglio, 1782).

2. Da Ponte operas

For his last three Italian comic operas, *The Marriage of Figaro* (1786), *Don Giovanni* (1787), and *Così fan tutte* (1790), Mozart collaborated with *Lorenzo Da Ponte* (1749–1838), whose librettos followed the conventions of opera buffa but lifted them to a higher level.

3. *Don Giovanni*

Da Ponte and Mozart were the first to create an opera about Don Juan that took the character seriously. **Music: NAWM 107**

4. Mixing styles

Don Giovanni mixes the styles of opera seria and comic opera to develop three levels of characters: the noble class from opera seria styles; the lower class from opera buffa styles; and the class or character (like Don Giovanni) who passes easily between the two levels. References to familiar styles and departures from their conventions are crucial to Mozart's depiction of characters and their feelings.

5. *The Magic Flute*

Mozart's *The Magic Flute* (*Die Zauberflöte,* 1791), a Singspiel, contains many eighteenth-century musical styles and traditions as well as references to the teachings and ceremonies of Freemasonry.

J. Church Music

Mozart's masses are written in the modern symphonic-operatic style, alter-nating chorus and soloists.

1. Requiem

Mozart's Requiem was unfinished at his death and was completed by his student and collaborator Franz Xaver Süssmayr (1766–1803).

K. Achievement and Reputation

Although Mozart never found the secure position he sought, his music eventually found a secure place among performers and listeners.

IV. Classic Music (HWM 564–65)

Among the composers of the time, only Haydn and Mozart achieved widespread and enduring fame and composed such complex music. By the early nineteenth century, certain works by them had become classics.

STUDY QUESTIONS

Joseph Haydn (HWM 526–46, NAWM 103–104)

1. Who was Haydn's principal patron? What was Haydn required to do as part of his employment? What sorts of music did he compose for this patron, and how did that change over time?

2. What other sources of income did Haydn have during his service with this patron? How did this affect the music he composed?

3. Trace Haydn's career after 1790, including his sources of income and his major compositions.

Music to Study

NAWM 103: Joseph Haydn, String Quartet in E-flat Major, Op. 33, [CD 8|1] [CD 3|67]
No. 2 (*The Joke*), Hob. III: 38 (1781), fourth movement, Presto

4. The melody of the finale to Haydn's String Quartet in E-flat Major (NAWM 103) sounds as if it might come from an opera buffa. How does this melody resemble the melodies in the excerpt from Pergolesi's *La serva padrona* (NAWM 93)?

Pergolesi parodied Uberto's emotions in NAWM 93 (see chapter 20, question 13). What similar techniques does Haydn use in this finale (NAWM 103) to create humor?

5. Besides its wit, what characteristics of Haydn's style are exemplified in this quartet movement? Give examples for each trait.

6. String quartets were written primarily for amateurs to play for their own pleasure. Describe what makes this finale well suited for that purpose.

7. Haydn is also known for appealing to connoisseurs. Describe what makes this finale well suited for that purpose.

8. What are the standard four movements of a Haydn symphony, and what are the main characteristics of each?

Music to Study

NAWM 104: Joseph Haydn, Symphony No. 92 in G Major (*Oxford*), Hob. I:92, symphony (1789)

> 104a: First movement, Adagio–Allegro spiritoso   `CD 7|51`   `CD 4|1`
>
> 104b: Second movement, Adagio cantabile   `CD 7|61`
>
> 104c: Third movement, Menuetto, Allegretto   `CD 7|65`
>
> 104d: Finale, Presto   `CD 7|70`

9. Below are listed characteristics of Haydn's idiom as described in HWM, pp. 531–35. Give a specific example for each characteristic from any movement of Haydn's *Oxford* Symphony (NAWM 104).

a. synthesis of styles

b. economy with novelty

c. rhythm and harmony used to sustain continuity

d. expansion of a phrase or delay of a cadence

e. creating a sense of drama

f. wit

10. In the exposition of the finale of Haydn's Symphony No. 92 (NAWM 104d), how are the following sections distinguished from each other? Mention these and other features you find significant: harmonic stability or instability; key (when stable); use of chromaticism; phrasing (clearly articulated or continuous and overlapping); dynamics; orchestration; and melodic content.

first theme area (mm. 1–31)

transition (mm. 32–78)

second theme area (mm. 79–97)

closing theme (mm. 98–113)

Notice how many different ways there are to follow the form. A listener may attend to any of these distinguishing features and will still be able to follow the course of the music clearly. This is one of the ways in which Classic-era music is notable for its intelligibility to a wide range of listeners.

11. The recapitulation repeats material from the exposition, but with some changes. What is different in the recapitulation, in comparison to the exposition?

12. What happens in the development in terms of harmony and key?

How are orchestration and dynamics used in the development?

What ideas from the exposition are used in the development, where do they appear, and how are they changed from the exposition?

13. Using questions 10-12 above as guidelines, how does the first movement of Haydn's Symphony No. 92 (NAWM 104a) differ from the finale NAWM 104d) in the ways Haydn differentiates between elements of the exposition, changes those elements in the recapitulation, and structures the development?

14. Chart the form of the slow movement of Haydn's Symphony No. 92 (NAWM 104b), and give the key of each main section.

How do the opening motives of the first two sections relate?

What elements of both sections appear in the coda (mm. 94–111)?

What vocal form(s) and style(s) does this movement recall or imitate? How does the melodic style compare to that of Hasse (NAWM 94) or C. P. E. Bach (NAWM 99)?

15. Chart the form of the third movement (NAWM 104c). How does this relate to binary form?

16. How is dance style evident in this movement? How does Haydn create humor?

17. Compare the first movement of Haydn's *Oxford* Symphony (NAWM 104a) with the first movements from Sammartini's Symphony in F Major (NAWM 100) and Stamitz's Sinfonia a 8 in E-flat Major (NAWM 101). Based on your observations, what generalizations can you make about the development of the symphony from midcentury to the late eighteenth century?

18. Describe how Haydn's employment influenced the development of his musical idiom, especially his symphonies and quartets. Refer to questions 1–3 above and to HWM, p. 539-43.

19. What elements in Haydn's keyboard music parallel his symphonies and quartets composed around the same time? Which of these elements made the piano more suitable than the harpsichord for playing his music?

20. Briefly describe Haydn's late Masses and oratorios. What music influenced Haydn's music in each genre, and how is this influence evident?

Wolfgang Amadeus Mozart (HWM 546–64, NAWM 105–107)

21. Describe Mozart's career and the influences on his music to 1781. Why was his music so diverse in styles?

22. How did Mozart make a living in Vienna?

23. How did Mozart become acquainted with the music of Haydn, J. S. Bach, and Handel? How was he influenced by the music of these composers?

| *Music to Study*

NAWM 105: Wolfgang Amadeus Mozart, Piano Sonata in F Major, ⎡CD 7|79⎤ K. 332 (300k), piano sonata (1781–83), first movement, Allegro

24. What is the form of the first movement of Mozart's Piano Sonata in F Major, K. 332 (NAWM 105)? Chart the form and harmonic plan, indicating the major themes, sections, and points of articulation with measure numbers.

25. List the diverse musical styles Mozart uses in this movement. What associations outside music does each of these styles carry?

How do the changes of style relate to the movement's form? How do they highlight the harmonic plan of the movement?

How do the various styles relate to expression or mood?

Why do you think Mozart chose to use so many different styles?

How does knowing what those styles refer to affect your own understanding of Mozart's piano sonata?

26. What are the characteristics of the quartets and symphonies Mozart wrote in Vienna? How do they compare to Haydn's works in the same forms?

Music to Study

NAWM 106: Wolfgang Amadeus Mozart, Piano Concerto in A Major, K. 488, (1786), first movement, Allegro

27. In the first movement of Mozart's Piano Concerto in A Major (NAWM 106), which segments of the opening orchestral ritornello return later in the work, and where does each return? How is each segment varied on its return?

28. How does the form of this first movement compare with the first movement of J. C. Bach's concerto in NAWM 102 (see chapter 21, questions 19–20)?

29. Compare Mozart's melodic style, as exemplified by this movement and by the first movement of his Piano Sonata in F Major (NAWM 105), with Haydn's melodic style in the *Oxford* Symphony (NAWM 104). What do they have in common? How are they different?

30. In a Classic-period concerto, what is a *cadenza*?

Where does it fall in the form, and how is it prepared harmonically?

The cadenza in NAWM 106 is Mozart's own. How would you describe it, in terms of melodic figuration, harmony, and treatment of the instrument?

What other compositions that you have studied incorporate improvisation in performance? What does this suggest about the composer's and performer's role in the creation of music in the eighteenth century?

31. What are Mozart's five best-known operas of his Vienna period, and in what year was each premiered?

    _____   _____

    _____   _____

    _____   _____

    _____   _____

    _____   _____

Music to Study

NAWM 107: Wolfgang Amadeus Mozart, *Don Giovanni,* opera   `CD 8|24`   `CD 4|29`
(dramma giocoso, 1787), Act I, scenes 1–2

32. In what ways is Leporello's opening aria in *Don Giovanni* (NAWM 107) similar to Uberto's aria from Pergolesi's *La serva padrona* (NAWM 93)? Why is this musical style appropriate for Leporello? How does Mozart use musical gestures, conventions, and styles to convey information about this character and his feelings?

33. In what ways does Donna Anna's singing style resemble the style of opera seria? Why is this musical style appropriate for her character?

34. How does Mozart use musical gestures, conventions, and styles to convey information about the character and feelings of Don Giovanni and the Commendatore?

35. What does the form of this scene have in common with instrumental forms of the Classic period? (See your answer to chapter 21, Review Question 4.)

36. In what ways does Mozart play against convention or foil usual expectations in the opening two scenes of *Don Giovanni*? What musical devices does he use to achieve these effects? Why are his choices appropriate to the drama?

Classic Music (HWM 564–65)

37. Describe the reception of Haydn's and Mozart's music during their lives. How has their music fared over the past two hundred years? How does their reception differ from that of their contemporaries, or of other eighteenth-century composers (see the final questions for chapters 18–21)? What were the secrets of their success?

TERMS TO KNOW

sonata-rondo
Sturm und Drang

scherzo

NAMES TO KNOW

Joseph Haydn
Prince Nikolaus Esterházy
Eszterháza
Johann Peter Salomon
Oxford Symphony
London Symphonies
The Creation
The Seasons
Baron Gottfried van Swieten
Wolfgang Amadeus Mozart

Salzburg
Leopold Mozart
Mozart's *Haydn* quartets
Die Entführung aus dem Serail
Lorenzo Da Ponte
The Marriage of Figaro
Don Giovanni
Così fan tutte
The Magic Flute (*Die Zauberflöte*)

REVIEW QUESTIONS

1. Add Haydn, Mozart, and the major events and works discussed in this chapter to the timeline you made for chapter 18.
2. Compare the careers of Haydn and Mozart, including the circumstances of their lives and the genres and styles they cultivated. What are the main similarities between their careers, and what are the major differences? What impact did these differences have on the types and styles of music they composed?
3. Briefly describe each of the following genres as practiced by Mozart and Haydn in terms of form, style, content, and social function: symphony, string quartet, piano sonata, concerto, and opera.
4. Describe the principal characteristics of Haydn's mature style in his instrumental works. Use NAWM 103–104 and other works described in HWM as examples for your discussion, referring to and describing passages from them as appropriate.
5. Building on question 4 immediately above, what aspects of Haydn's style did Mozart absorb into his own? And in what ways does Mozart's mature music differ from that of Haydn? Use NAWM 105–107 and other works described in HWM as examples for your discussion, referring to and describing passages as appropriate.
6. Describe the elements of the music of Haydn and Mozart that gave it appeal to a wide range of listeners in their day and over the next two centuries. What would a composer living today have to do to adapt their recipe for present-day audiences, and what difficulties might lie in the way?

Chapter 23 ‖ Revolution and Change

CHAPTER OBJECTIVES

After you complete the reading, study of the music, and study questions for this chapter, you should be able to

1. describe some of the influences on the culture and music of the late-eighteenth and early-nineteenth centuries;
2. briefly recount Beethoven's career and the circumstances of his life;
3. list the main characteristics of his music before 1802, between 1802 and 1814, and after 1814, and why some aspects of his musical style changed during these periods; and
4. name several important works and describe at least one complete movement for each period listed in the previous objective.

CHAPTER OUTLINE

I. Introduction (HWM 568)

The late eighteenth and early nineteenth centuries were a time of political and economic revolution, reflected in the career of Beethoven, whose life and highly individual and dramatic musical works changed society's concept of music and of composers.

II. Revolution, War, and Music, 1789–1815 (HWM 568–71)

A. The French Revolution

The French Revolution, inspired by Enlightenment ideals and social reform, took place in three phases over ten years.

1. Napoleon Bonaparte

Napoleon Bonaparte became leader of the Republic in 1799, crowned himself emperor in 1804, conquered most of Europe, carried out some of the goals of the Revolution, and was defeated in 1814–15.

2. Effects of the revolution
Although the Revolution ultimately failed, its ideas, which included the possibility of freedom, reform, and a new concept of nation, spread across Europe.

B. Music and the Revolution
The French Revolutionary government supported large choral works and opera with librettos on themes of the Revolution or concerns of the time.

1. Paris Conservatoire
Founded by the government in 1795, the *Paris Conservatoire* was the first modern conservatory, becoming the model for others throughout Europe.

C. The Industrial Revolution
The Industrial Revolution transformed traditional ways of life and brought unprecedented prosperity to urban and merchant classes.

III. Ludwig van Beethoven (HWM 571–93, NAWM 108–110)

The career and music of *Ludwig van Beethoven* (1770–1827) reflect these revolutionary changes in the decades around 1800.

1. Division into three periods
Beethoven's career is usually divided into three periods: (1) 1770–1802, when he mastered the musical language and genres of his time; (2) 1803–1814, when he achieved a new level of drama and expression; and (3) 1815–1827, when his music became more introspective and difficult.

Biography: Ludwig van Beethoven
Beethoven was born in Bonn where he studied piano and violin with his father and other musicians. In 1792, Beethoven moved to Vienna where he took lessons from Haydn and found aristocratic patrons. After overcoming a crisis in 1802 related to a gradual loss of hearing, Beethoven wrote music of greater depth and scope that soon made him the most popular composer alive. He was able to devote himself entirely to composition and write at his own pace. After 1815, Beethoven became increasingly withdrawn from society.

A. Bonn and the First Decade in Vienna
Beethoven's first period consists of his youth in Bonn and his first decade in Vienna.

1. Teachers, patrons, and publishers
While in Vienna, Beethoven studied with Haydn and others and made a living through performing as a pianist, teaching, publishing, and patrons.

2. Piano sonatas
In his piano sonatas, Beethoven made increasing demands on the performer and often used contrasts of style to delineate the form and broaden the expressive range.

3. *Pathétique* Sonata
Beethoven's *Sonate Pathétique* includes a dramatic, fantasia-like slow introduction that recurs twice in the first movement and a serious and

intense sonata-rondo finale with thematic and harmonic connections to the other two movements.   **Music: NAWM 108**

4. Op. 18 String Quartets
Beethoven's first string quartets (Op. 18) were published in 1800, and they demonstrate Beethoven's individuality in their use of themes, surprising modulations and turns of phrase, and formal structure.

5. First Symphony
In his First Symphony in C Major (1800), Beethoven used the model of Haydn's and Mozart's late symphonies, yet also distinguished his own style in distinctive ways.

B. Circumstances in the Middle Period

1. Reputation and patrons
Around 1803, Beethoven began to compose in a new, more ambitious style. He was able to do so because he had established a strong reputation in German-speaking lands, and the combination of financial, social, and creative support freed him to follow his own inspiration.

2. Publishers
Publishers competed for Beethoven's music, and he could afford to take the time to revise his works.

3. Sketches
Beethoven composed with great deliberation, keeping notebooks with sketches and creating music in which each part was related to the whole.

4. Deafness
In 1802, Beethoven realized that his hearing loss was permanent. After contemplating suicide, he resolved to continue for the sake of his art, writing movingly of his suffering in an unsent letter called the *Heiligenstadt Testament*.

5. Music as drama
One way of viewing Beethoven's music after 1802 is as a narrative or drama, perhaps reflecting the struggle of his own life.

6. Style characteristics
Typically, Beethoven was economical in his material (like Haydn), but often expanded or reworked the form in novel ways.

C. *Eroica* Symphony
Beethoven's *Eroica* Symphony (1803–4), the first work to exemplify fully his new approach, is longer than any previous symphony with a title celebrating a hero.

1. First movement
In the first movement, the transformations of the first theme's main motive and its interaction with a leaping figure from the first theme group can be interpreted as a story of a hero's challenge, struggle, and final victory.   **Music: NAWM 109**

2. Other movements
The other movements are also large and dramatic: a funeral march, a fast scherzo, and a variations finale with fugal and developmental episodes.

3. References to French Republic
Beethoven first titled the work "Bonaparte," but changed the title after Napoleon crowned himself emperor. His plan to honor Napoleon may explain the references to French Revolutionary marches and hymns in the second movement.

4. Reception
With the *Eroica* Symphony, Beethoven challenged listeners to engage music deeply and thoughtfully rather than merely seeking to be entertained.

D. Other Works of the Middle Period
Over the next decade, Beethoven probed new possibilities in traditional genres and forms, composing some of his most popular works.

1. *Fidelio*
Fidelio, Beethoven's only opera, expresses humanitarian ideals of the French Revolution and went through three revisions before it was a success.

2. Chamber music
Chamber music had traditionally been intended for enjoyment in the home, but Beethoven increasingly tested the limits of amateur players in the *Razumovsky* Quartets, Op. 59, and other works.

3. Concertos
The concertos from Beethoven's middle period are composed on a grander scale with the soloist often coequal with the orchestra.

4. Fifth Symphony
Beethoven's Fifth Symphony (1807–8) portrays struggle and ultimate triumph by moving from C minor to C major and developing the famous opening four-note figure that recurs in various guises in the other three movements.

5. *Pastoral* Symphony
Beethoven's Sixth Symphony (*Pastoral*) has five movements, each with a title suggesting a scene from life in the country.

6. Peak of popularity
By 1814, Beethoven had changed audience expectations for what instrumental music can do and was celebrated as the greatest living composer.

E. Circumstances in the Late Period
At the height of his renown, Beethoven's deafness, family problems, ill health and larger political and economic changes forced him into greater isolation, slowed the pace of composition, and prompted a change in focus and style.

F. Characteristics of the Late Style
Most of Beethoven's late works were addressed to connoisseurs, becoming more introspective and concentrated, with extremes from the sublime to the grotesque in works that invoked but altered classical conventions.

1. Variation technique
Beethoven's late variations go beyond a traditional approach to reexamine the most basic elements of the theme.

2. Continuity

In his late style, Beethoven emphasized continuity by blurring divisions between phrases and movements. He also achieved continuity in the *song cycle,* a genre he created.

3. New sonorities

Beethoven's search for new expressive means in his late works gave rise to new sonorities, insisting on the composer's vision at the expense of performer freedom and audience comfort.

4. Uses of traditional styles

In his late works, Beethoven frequently used familiar styles and genres, either for expressive purposes or to reflect on tradition.

5. Imitation and fugue

Beethoven frequently used imitative counterpoint, especially fugue, in his late works. **Music: NAWM 110a**

6. Reconceiving multimovement form

Beethoven's reflections on tradition include reconceiving the number and arrangement of movements. **Music: NAWM 110**

7. String Quartet in C-sharp Minor, Op. 131

The arrangement of forms, keys, and tempos in the String Quartet in C-sharp Minor, Op. 131, illustrates how Beethoven simultaneously invokes and departs from tradition in his late works.

8. Unity

While Beethoven varied the traditional sequence of movements, he sought ways to integrate them more closely.

9. Appeal to connoisseurs

Beethoven's late sonatas and quartets are for connoisseurs who are likely to appreciate the complex compositional techniques and the intertwining of tradition and innovation.

G. Last Public Works

Like his late private works, Beethoven's last two large public works re-examine the traditions of their respective genres.

1. *Missa solemnis*

Beethoven's *Missa solemnis* was not a liturgical work, but a mass for concert performance shaped as a unified five-movement symphony.

2. Ninth Symphony

In his Ninth Symphony (1824), Beethoven combined tradition and innovation, disparate styles, and profound emotional expression. The first three movements are on a grand scale. The finale refers back to the previous movements and includes solo voices and chorus in an extended movement that draws on tradition yet is unprecedented in shape and scope.

IV. Beethoven's Centrality (HWM 593–94)

Beethoven became a cultural hero, and his life story helped to define the Romantic view of the creative artist as social outsider. Many of Beethoven's compositions were immediately popular and have remained so ever since. They invited attentive listening and new approaches to theoretical analysis. Beethoven could afford to compose as he pleased, and his self-expressive music changed the image of what a composer is and does.

STUDY QUESTIONS

Revolution, War, and Music, 1789–1815 (HWM 568–71)

1. What effects did the French Revolution and Napoleonic wars have on politics and culture in Western Europe at the end of the eighteenth century?

2. What types of music, and what musical institutions, did the French Revolutionary government support, and what was their significance?

Ludwig van Beethoven (HWM 571–93, NAWM 108–110)

3. Why is Beethoven's career often divided into three periods? Provide the dates and important biographical information for each period and a brief characterization of each.

First period

Second period

Third period

4. How did Beethoven make a living in Vienna? How was his situation different from that of Haydn's and Mozart's? How did Beethoven's situation affect his choice of genres and the number of total works he composed?

Music to Study

NAWM 108: Ludwig van Beethoven, Piano Sonata in C Minor, CD 8|29　CD 4|34
　Op. 13 (*Pathétique,* 1797–98), third movement, Rondo, Allegro

5. In what ways is the finale of Beethoven's *Pathétique* Sonata (NAWM 108) like traditional rondos?

In what ways is it different?

6. What are some of the effects Beethoven uses to make this rondo dramatic?

7. Compare the later repetitions of the rondo refrain to its initial presentation. What changes are made? How do these changes contribute to the dramatic quality of the music?

8. Compare the rondo's first episode (mm. 25–61) to the reprise of this episode near the movement's end (mm. 134–69). In the reprise, how is it changed from its initial presentation? How does this reflect the influence of sonata form?

9. Compare Beethoven's melodic style in this movement with Mozart's in the first movement of his Piano Sonata in F Major (NAWM 105). How do these composers differ in their approach to melody?

Compare how they delineate phrases and sections. Describe those similarities and/or differences.

10. Using your answers in question 9 and your other observations about musical style (such as sonority, use of imitation, etc.), give a general description of the differences between the piano music of Beethoven and of Mozart.

11. What was Beethoven's reputation as a pianist and composer by the early 1800s? How did he relate to his patrons and publishers?

12. What is the *Heiligenstadt Testament*? What does it discuss, and what attitudes does Beethoven express? What does Beethoven say in it about his relations with other people and about the role of his art in his life?

Music to Study

NAWM 109: Ludwig van Beethoven, Symphony No. 3 in E-flat `CD 8|36` `CD 4|41`
   Major, Op. 55 (*Eroica*, 1803), first movement, Allegro con brio

13. What are some features of the first movement of Beethoven's *Eroica* Symphony (NAWM 109) that his audiences would have found unusual?

14. What in the sketches for this movement (shown in NAWM, pp. 285–90) can help us to clarify some of these unusual features? How do these sketches illuminate Beethoven's process of composition?

15. According to HWM and NAWM, the principal theme is treated as a person in a drama, struggling against other players and triumphing in the end. How does Beethoven use changes in the principal motive (mm. 3–8) to convey struggle and triumph?

16. What other musical devices (form, meter, orchestration, harmony, etc.) does Beethoven use in this movement to suggest a heroic struggle ending in triumph? How do the very long development and coda contribute to this effect?

17. Why do the authors of HWM emphasize the heroic aspects of the first movement of Beethoven's Symphony No. 3? What kinds of evidence do they rely on to build their case?

Are you persuaded? Do you agree, or disagree? Using the same information, what other conclusions can you draw about the first movement of Beethoven's Symphony No. 3?

18. What do Beethoven's *Eroica* Symphony and his opera *Fidelio* owe to the arts and politics of France in the Revolutionary period?

19. How does Beethoven's Fifth Symphony portray the progress from struggle to triumph?

20. How does music of Beethoven's Sixth Symphony (the *Pastoral*) suggest scenes from life in the country?

21. What personal, family, and political circumstances affected Beethoven's personality and his music after 1814?

22. For each of the following aspects of music, how does Beethoven's late style differ from Haydn, Mozart, and his own earlier style?

 a. intended audience

 b. juxtaposition of disparate elements

 c. variation technique

 d. continuity

 e. sonority

 f. evocations of tradition

 g. imitation and fugue

 h. multimovement form

Music to Study

NAWM 110: Ludwig van Beethoven, String Quartet in C-sharp Minor, Op. 131
(1826), excerpts

110a: First movement, Adagio ma non troppo e molto   [CD 8|52]   [CD 4|57]
espressivo

110b: Second movement, Allegretto molto vivace   [CD 8|54]   [CD 4|59]

23. Refer to the forms, keys, tempo markings, and meters for the seven movements of
Beethoven's Op. 131 in HWM, p. 590. How does this sequence of movements relate to the traditional four-movement plan of a string quartet? Where, in this quartet, are those traditional four movements, and what is the function of the added
movements?

24. The key scheme of the quartet is unusual, and there is a correspondence between
the keys used for each movement and the important pitches in the subject and answer of the opening fugue (NAWM 110a). Write out the following notes for the
subject in violin I (mm. 1–4) and the answer in violin II (mm. 4–8):

	first note (same as last note)	highest note	lowest note	longest and loudest note
subject in violin I	_____	_____	_____	_____
answer in violin II	_____	_____	_____	_____

Of these notes, circle the ones that are used as the key of one of the movements in
the quartet, as listed in HWM, p. 590.

From the evidence in the previous question, can you suggest a reason that
Beethoven might have chosen to have the answer in the subdominant rather than in
the dominant as expected?

25. In what ways is the first movement like a traditional fugue? What traditional fugal techniques does Beethoven use, and where is each one used? What is unusual about this fugue?

26. How does the second movement (NAWM 110b) differ from the first in mood and character? What aspects of the music create these contrasts?

27. Where in the first movement is there a suggestion of the key of the second movement?

    Where in the second movement is there a recollection of the key of the first movement?

28. Compare the second movement of Beethoven's String Quartet in C-sharp Minor (NAWM 110b) with the finale from Haydn's String Quartet in E-flat Major (NAWM 103). Haydn and Beethoven were both known for including some unusual features in their music. In what ways are they similar in their use of unusual features? How do they differ? How do the forms compare?

29. In what ways does this quartet exemplify the characteristics of Beethoven's late style as you described them in question 22 above?

30. What does Beethoven's *Missa solemnis* owe to Handel, and what does it owe to Haydn? How does it differ from most earlier masses?

31. What is unusual about Beethoven's Ninth Sysmphony? What is the expected form for a finale of a symphony? Describe the sequence of events in the finale. What form (or forms) does Beethoven use in this movement? Can you suggest a reason for why he organized the finale in this way?

Beethoven's Centrality (HWM 593)

32. Describe the reception of Beethoven's music in his own time and over the last two centuries.

33. What impact did Beethoven have on later composers, performers, and theorists? How has his approach to composition and musical expression influenced how we conceive of and hear music today?

TERMS TO KNOW

Beethoven's three periods
song cycle

NAMES TO KNOW

Paris Conservatoire
Ludwig van Beethoven
Sonate pathétique
Heiligenstadt Testament
Eroica Symphony
Fidelio

Beethoven's Fifth Symphony
Pastoral Symphony
String Quartet in C-sharp Minor,
  Op. 131
Missa Solemnis
Beethoven's Ninth Symphony

REVIEW QUESTIONS

1. Write an essay in which you recount Beethoven's career, including the changing circumstances of his life, his major style periods, and major compositions of each period.
2. What other composers particularly influenced Beethoven's music, and what did he absorb from each? In what ways is his music similar to or different from Mozart's and Haydn's? What accounts for these similarities and differences?
3. You have examples in NAWM 108, 109, and 110 of movements from each of Beethoven's three periods. For each of these works, describe the form and other significant features of the movements in NAWM and explain what makes this work characteristic of its period.
4. Take the first eight measures of the Haydn string quartet movement you have studied (NAWM 103) and recompose it to feature one or more of the characteristics of Beethoven's late style. You can change as many notes and rhythms as you wish, as well as dynamics, articulations, registration, and any other aspect. You may recast it for piano or for another ensemble if you prefer. Try to make it sound as much like Beethoven as possible. Then write a short statement explaining what aspects of Beethoven's late style you have tried to imitate and how you have done so.

Chapter 24 The Romantic Generation:
Song and Piano Music

CHAPTER OBJECTIVES

After you complete the reading, study of the music, and study questions for this chapter, you should be able to

1. describe some of the differences between music of the Classic and Romantic periods, particularly in their aesthetic orientation;
2. describe the variety of contexts in which songs and piano music were performed in the first half of the nineteenth century;
3. describe the German Lied, English drawing-room ballad, and American parlor song of the period, name some of the principal composers, characterize their styles, and describe representative songs; and
4. name some of the principal composers of piano music from the early to middle nineteenth century, characterize their styles, trace influences upon them, and describe representative piano works by them.

CHAPTER OUTLINE

I. Introduction (HWM 595)

Unlike music from earlier centuries, most nineteenth-century music was composed for home music-making or performance in public venues.

II. The New Order, 1815–1848 (HWM 595–602)

The upheavals of 1789–1815 changed the map of Europe. In the nineteenth century, interest in national cultures grew, and composers incorporated national traits in vocal and instrumental music.

1. The Americas
As Latin America nations became independent and the United States expanded west, the new nations began to create their own national identities through music and literature.

A. The Decline of Patronage

As aristocratic patronage declined, more musicians made their living as free agents, often specializing in one instrument as *virtuosos,* or in one medium as composers.

B. Middle-Class Music-Making

Although larger institutions used music as a means of social control, music-making in middle class homes was a form of entertainment, a diversion from social pressures, and a means of personal expression.

1. Separate spheres

In the middle and upper classes, boys went to school and men to work while women and girls maintained the home and pursued activities such as music.

C. The Piano

Manufacturing and design improvements for the piano made it ideal for home music-making and public concerts.

1. Women and the piano

Although some women were professional pianists, most women played the piano in the home for enjoyment.

D. The Market for Music and the New Idiom

Amateur musicians demanded new music, and composers supplied it in great quantities, creating a boom in music publishing.

1. The new musical idiom

Composers writing for the public sought to make their music accessible and appealing to amateurs by composing beautiful melodies and colorful harmonies. They competed for sales by creating music with novel and individual features. These characteristics defined a new idiom, known today as the early Romantic style.

Innovations: Musical Instruments in the Industrial Revolution

Manufacturing innovations during the Industrial Revolution made musical instruments more widely available and less costly. The design of the piano was improved, and the new capabilities were exploited by composers and performers. Harps were developed that could be played in any key. New brass instruments were invented, and valves were added to trumpets and horns, enabling them to produce all the notes of the chromatic scale. Modern wind-instrument design, improved percussion construction, and the invention of the saxophone all originated in the nineteenth century.

III. Romanticism (HWM 602–5)

The new idiom paralleled Romanticism in literature and art and came to be called *Romantic*.

1. "Romantic" as a term

The word "romantic" derived from the medieval romance, and in the nineteenth century it was applied to literature, music, and art that focused on the individual and on expression of the self.

2. "Romantic" as a period

By the mid- to late nineteenth century, a distinction was drawn between the Classic period in music and the Romantic period, beginning ca. 1815.

3. Romanticism as reaction

As a reaction against a changing society, Romantics sought refuge in the past and in Nature, and pursued novelty and high ideals.

4. Music as the ideal Romantic art

Some writers thought that because music was free from the concreteness of words and visual images, it could evoke emotions that words could not.

5. Absolute, characteristic, and program music

Romantic writers drew new distinctions among instrumental works. *Absolute music* refers to nothing but itself. A *character piece* depicts or suggests a mood, personality, or scene and is known as *characteristic* (or *descriptive*) *music*. *Program music* recounts a narrative or events, often explained in a *program*.

6. Music and the literary

Literature was central to the work of most composers in both vocal and instrumental music.

IV. Song (HWM 605–14, NAWM 111–115)

Songs ranged from simple to virtuosic and were performed most often by voice and piano. The German Lied was the most influential nineteenth-century song repertoire. British and American parlor songs were also significant.

A. The Lied

The Lied tradition extends back to the eighteenth century, but its popularity grew after 1800.

1. The lyric

The chief poetic genre, the lyric, was a short, strophic poem on one subject that was meant to be sung.

2. The ballad

The *ballad,* a form of long narrative poem written in imitation of folk ballads, inspired composers to use more varied themes and textures and to write a piano part that was as important in expressing the poetry as the voice.

3. Song collections and song cycles

Lieder composers often grouped their songs into collections and into cycles.

B. Franz Schubert

The characteristics of the Romantic Lied are exemplified in the songs of *Franz Schubert* (1797–1828), who wrote over six hundred Lieder.

1. Song texts

Schubert set poetry by many writers, including Goethe, and wrote two song cycles on poems by Wilhelm Müller: *Die schöne Müllerin* (The Pretty Miller-Maid, 1823) and *Winterreise* (Winter's Journey, 1827).

2. Form
   Schubert always chose forms that suited the shape and meaning of the text. For example, he used *modified strophic form* to depict contrast or change.

3. Melody
   Schubert composed beautiful melodies that capture a poem's character and situation.

4. Accompaniment
   The figuration of the accompaniment always fits the poem's mood and the personality of the protagonist.

5. *Gretchen am Spinnrade*
   In *Gretchen am Spinnrade* (Gretchen at the Spinning Wheel), the piano suggests the spinning wheel and Gretchen's agitation as she thinks of her beloved.   **Music: NAWM 111**

6. Harmony
   Schubert used harmony as an expressive device, often modulating by third rather than by fifth.

7. *Der Lindenbaum*
   In *Der Lindenbaum* from *Winterreise,* Schubert conveys the meaning of the poem through form, melody, accompaniment, and harmony.
   Music: NAWM 112

8. Schubert's achievement
   Schubert's songs set the standard that later song composers strove to match.

Biography: Franz Schubert
   After studying music as a child, Schubert became a schoolmaster, working in his father's school for several years. His true love was music, and he composed in his free time with astonishing speed. He never held a salaried music position and gained most of his income from publication. Best known for his Lieder, Schubert was a prolific composer in all genres.

C. Robert and Clara Schumann
   Robert Schumann (1810–1856), Schubert's first important successor as a Lieder composer, wrote more than 120 songs in 1840, the year of his marriage, including the song cycle *Dichterliebe* (A Poet's Love).

1. Music and poetry
   Schumann thought that music should capture a poem's essence in its own terms and that voice and piano should be equal partners, as shown by relatively long preludes, interludes, and postludes for the piano. In *Im wunderschönen Monat Mai* from *Dichterliebe,* Schumann uses unresolved harmonies to create a sense of longing.   **Music: NAWM 113**

2. Clara Schumann
   Clara Schumann (1819–1896) wrote several collections of Lieder, using an approach to song that paralleled Robert's.

Biography: Robert Schumann and Clara Schumann

After university studies in law, Robert aimed to become a concert pianist, studying with Clara's father. While Robert suffered a career-ending injury and turned to composition and to criticism, founding the journal *Neue Zeitschrift für Musik,* Clara became one of the leading concert pianists in Europe. After their marriage in 1840, Clara toured less but continued to perform and compose while raising eight children. Her husband suffered physical and psychological illnesses and was confined to an asylum for the last two years of his life. After his death, Clara performed, taught, and edited and promoted Robert's music.

D. British and North American Song

Drawing-room ballads and *parlor songs* in Great Britain and in North America are usually strophic or in verse-refrain form, and the piano supports the singer. The most famous drawing-room ballad, and perhaps the most widely known song of the century, was *Home! Sweet Home!* by *Henry R. Bishop* (1786–1855). **Music: NAWM 114**

1. Canada

The most notable song composer in Canada was James P. Clarke (1807/8–1877), who composed the song cycle *Lays of the Maple Leaf.*

2. Stephen Foster

The leading American song composer of the nineteenth century was *Stephen Foster* (1826–1864), the first American to earn a living solely as a composer. In his songs, he combined elements of British, American, German, Italian, and Irish music. **Music: NAWM 115**

3. Continuum of taste

In the early nineteenth century, both parlor songs and German Lieder were written for middle-class markets, and there was not yet a firm distinction between popular and serious music.

V. Music for Piano (HWM 615–29, NAWM 116–120)

Piano music served three overlapping purposes: amateur enjoyment, public performance, and teaching (including *études,* or studies).

A. Schubert

Schubert wrote marches, dances, and lyrical works suitable for the amateur market and larger works, including eleven sonatas and the *Wanderer Fantasy* (1822), for more accomplished performers.

1. Sonatas

Schubert's sonatas typically feature lyrical themes that resist development and often use three keys in the exposition, rather than two.

B. Felix Mendelssohn

Felix Mendelssohn (1809–1847), one of the leading German Romantic composers, blended styles from Bach, Handel, Mozart, Beethoven, and his own contemporaries.

1. *Songs without Words*

   Mendelssohn's best-known piano works are his *Lieder ohne Worte* (Songs without Words), which capture the lyrical qualities of Lieder and exemplify his belief that music can express what words cannot.

Biography: Felix Mendelssohn

Mendelssohn was a prodigy, composing seriously by age eleven. He was supported by his family, who had the financial means to provide the best teachers and who were at the center of Berlin's intellectual life. Mendelssohn achieved success as a composer, pianist, conductor, and music director, and was the founder of the Leipzig Conservatory.

C. Clara Schumann and Fanny Mendelssohn Hensel

Clara Schumann and *Fanny Mendelssohn Hensel* (1805–1847) had contrasting careers as pianist-composers. Schumann played in public concerts and published much of her music. The equally talented Fanny Mendelssohn composed for performances in her home and published only a few of her works.

D. Robert Schumann

Schumann's publications up to 1840 were all for solo piano, mostly short character pieces in colorfully named collections.

1. Extramusical associations

   Schumann gave titles to his piano pieces to suggest extramusical associations. In his writings, Schumann personified different facets of himself through the imaginary characters Florestan, Eusebius, and Meister Raro, and we can see traces of their personalities in his music. **Music: NAWM 116**

E. Fryderyk Chopin

Fryderyk Chopin (1810–1849) composed almost exclusively for piano. He wrote for performers and audiences of all levels and opened new possibilities for the piano.

1. Études

   Chopin's twenty-seven études were the first with significant artistic content and were often played in concert, inaugurating the genre of the *concert étude.*

2. Preludes

   Chopin wrote twenty-four preludes that, like his études, pose specific performance problems.

3. Waltzes, mazurkas, and polonaises

   Chopin's *waltzes, mazurkas,* and *polonaises* were often composed for his students. His waltzes evoke the Viennese ballroom, his polonaises assert the spirit of Poland, and his mazurkas capture the popular Polish ballroom dance. Chopin and other nineteenth-century performers often used *rubato,* holding back or hurrying the tempo, as an expressive technique. **Music: NAWM 117**

4. Nocturnes

Chopin's *nocturnes* are slow works with embellished melodies over sonorous accompaniments.   **Music: NAWM 118**

5. Ballades and scherzos

Chopin's *ballades* and scherzos are longer and more demanding than his other one-movement piano works.

6. Sonatas

Chopin composed three piano sonatas, each in four movements.

7. Chopin's achievement

Chopin's greatest achievement was producing a whole new repertory of idiomatic sounds and figurations for the piano.

Biography: Fryderyk Chopin

Chopin was born near Warsaw in Poland. After studying at the Conservatory, he toured as a concert pianist. His pieces with Polish character were very popular. In 1831, he moved to Paris where he met the leading musicians and entered the highest social circles. He made a living by teaching, publishing, and performing at private concerts and salons.

F. Franz Liszt

Franz Liszt (1811–1886) was the most astounding piano virtuoso of his era and one of its most important composers. In Paris, he met many of the most notable writers, painters, and musicians of his day.

1. Solo recitals

Liszt toured all over Europe, giving solo piano *recitals* (a concept and term he pioneered) and changing the way pianists performed in concert.

2. Influences

Liszt was influenced by Hungarian music, by Viennese and Parisian virtuosos, and by Chopin.

3. Paganini and virtuosity

Liszt was also influenced by violinist *Nicolò Paganini* (1782–1840), who raised both the technique and mystique of the virtuoso. Liszt's *Un sospiro* shows that same level of technique applied to the piano.   **Music: NAWM 119**

4. Harmony

Un sospiro also illustrates Liszt's innovative uses of chromatic harmony.

5. Character pieces and sonata

Liszt composed numerous character pieces. His innovative Sonata in B Minor combines aspects of three movements in one extended movement.

6. Paraphrases and transcriptions

Much of Liszt's piano music consists of operatic paraphrases and *transcriptions* of vocal and instrumental music.

7. Liszt's reputation

Liszt established most of the traditions of the modern recital, developed new playing techniques, and opened new possibilities in harmony, form, and expression.

Biography: Franz Liszt

Liszt had an enormous impact on music as a piano virtuoso, composer, conductor, and teacher. He studied piano and composition in Vienna and Paris, taught piano at age sixteen, and pursued a career as a concert virtuoso until 1848. He devoted the rest of his career to composing, conducting, and teaching. He worked in Weimar and Rome, where he took minor orders in the Catholic Church.

G. Louis Moreau Gottschalk

Louis Moreau Gottschalk (1829–1869) was the first American composer with an international reputation. His music was designed to appeal to the middle-class audience and the amateur performer.   **Music: NAWM 120**

VI. The Romantic Legacy (HWM 629–308)

Songs and piano music were the leading genres of the early nineteenth century, and their melody-centered style affected every other genre. Home music-making, rare today, was the leading market for this music. Lieder and parlor songs by Schubert, Schumann, and Foster defined the genres and served as models for later composers. Schubert, Mendelssohn, Schumann, Chopin, and Liszt composed pieces that redefined piano music and became central to the repertory. Music by women was treated differently in the nineteenth century, and current research is bringing this music to light. Most of our attitudes about music come from the Romantic era.

STUDY QUESTIONS

The New Order, 1815–1848 (HWM 595–602)

1. How did European musical life change in response to political, economic, and social changes in the first half of the nineteenth century?

2. What purposes did home music-making serve in the nineteenth century? How did it relate to women's social roles?

3. How did nineteenth-century pianos differ from earlier keyboard instruments, including eighteenth-century pianos? What advancements were made in how other instruments were constructed, and what impact did they have on music?

4. What factors spurred the growing market for sheet music? What types of music were in particular demand? How did composers attempt to appeal to buyers, and what changes did this bring about in musical style?

Romanticism (HWM 602–5)

5. Describe the ideas and ideals of the Romantic movement in the early nineteenth century. How was Romanticism reflected in music? How did nineteenth-century music come to be called "Romantic"?

6. Define the following terms, making clear how each differs from the others:

   program music

   characteristic or descriptive music

   absolute music

7. What are some of the connections between music and literature in the nineteenth century?

Song (HWM 605–14, NAWM 111–115)

8. What types of poetry did Lieder composers set, and how did composers respond to them? What were the influences on the poets and on the music?

9. Briefly summarize Schubert's career. How did he make a living in Vienna? How was his situation different from Beethoven's? How did Schubert's situation affect his choice of genres?

Music to Study

NAWM 111: Franz Schubert, *Gretchen am Spinnrade,* D. 118,　　⌈CD 8|62⌉　⌈CD 4|67⌉
Lied (1814)

NAWM 112: Franz Schubert, *Winterreise,* D. 911, song cycle　　⌈CD 8|68⌉　⌈CD 4|73⌉
(1827), excerpt: *Der Lindenbaum*

10. In *Gretchen am Spinnrade* (NAWM 111), how does Schubert use the piano to depict the scene and Gretchen's actions? How do these same devices suggest Gretchen's mood?

11. Diagram the form of this song, including the key(s) for each section.

12. For each stanza, how does Schubert use harmony and melody to portray Gretchen's changing emotions? Include the choice of key, stability of key or rapid modulation, melodic character, range, and dynamic level.

13. What characteristics make *Gretchen am Spinnrade* representative of the Romantic idiom?

14. *Gretchen am Spinnrade* was one of Schubert's most famous Lieder. Describe who would have performed this song. Where would it have been performed? Why do think this Lied was so appealing at the time? Why do you think it has continued being performed since his death?

15. Diagram the form of *Der Lindenbaum* (NAWM 112) in the same manner you did for *Gretchen am Spinnrade* (see question 11 above). Write down the key or keys of each stanza and of each piano interlude, and indicate which stanzas or sections have the same melody and which are different.

16. How does Schubert use melody, harmony, piano figuration, and key to move from the distant past to the recent past and, finally, to the present? What sections of the music initiate those changes in time?

17. Compare the melody of *Der Lindenbaum* with *Gretchen am Spinnrade*. Describe the differences between them.

    Why do you think Schubert choose such contrasting melodies for these Lieder?

18. Briefly describe the careers and historical significance of Robert and Clara Schumann. What genres did each of these composers choose? Why did they compose in these genres? How did each of them earn money aside from composition?

Music to Study

NAWM 113: Robert Schumann, *Dichterliebe,* Op. 48, song cycle   ⟨ CD 8|72 ⟩
(1840), excerpt: No. 1, *Im wunderschönen Monat Mai*

19. The text of *Im wunderschönen Monat Mai* (NAWM 113) speaks of new love. How
does Robert Schumann's music imply, through melody and harmony, that this love
is unrequited—as yet all "longing and desire" and no fulfillment? How are the
opening piano prelude and closing postlude crucial in conveying this meaning?
What role do the key and the beginning and ending harmonies play?

20. Compare Schumann's *Im wunderschönen Monat Mai* (NAWM 113) with Schubert's *Der Lindenbaum* (NAWM 112). In what general ways are these examples
representative of early-nineteenth-century Lieder?

Schubert and Schumann treat the relationship between piano and voice differently.
Describe these differences and give specific measure numbers from each song to
illustrate your points.

21. How do these examples of nineteenth-century German Lied from the nineteenth century differ from an eighteenth-century example, J. F. Reichardt's *Erlkönig* (excerpted in HWM, Example 20.7, p. 501)?

How are they similar?

22. What were the social functions of *parlor songs*? How are parlor songs like Lieder in social role and musical attributes, and how do they differ?

Music to Study

NAWM 114: Henry R. Bishop, *Home! Sweet Home!*, theatrical [CD 8|73]
song and drawing-room ballad (parlor song), (1823)

NAWM 115: Stephen Foster, *Jeanie with the Light Brown Hair*, [CD 8|75]
parlor song (1853)

23. In the space below, diagram the form of Bishop's *Home! Sweet Home!* (NAWM 114). Write down the key or keys of each verse, refrain, and piano interlude. How does this compare to the songs by Schubert and Schumann (NAWM 111–113)?

24. How is *Home! Sweet Home!* (NAWM 114) representative of Romanticism?

25. In what setting was this song originally performed? Why do you think this song was so popular as a drawing-room ballad?

26. Aside from the fact that it was composed in the nineteenth century, how is Stephen Foster's *Jeanie with the Light Brown Hair* (NAWM 115) representative of Romanticism?

27. In what setting was *Jeanie with the Light Brown Hair* originally performed? Why do you think people found this song so appealing in 1854?

28. Compare the musical style of Stephen Foster's *Jeanie with the Light Brown Hair* (NAWM 115) with Bishop's *Home! Sweet Home!* (NAWM 114). Aside from the fact that both have English texts, how are these songs similar to one another, and how do they differ?

    What do they have in common with German Lieder? How do they differ from Lieder?

Music for Piano (HWM 615–29, NAWM 116–120)

29. What purposes did piano music serve in the nineteenth century?

30. How do Schubert's sonatas differ from those of earlier composers, such as Mozart and Beethoven?

31. In what ways do Mendelssohn's *Lieder ohne Worte* resemble songs? Use as an example the excerpt from Mendelssohn's Op. 19, No. 1, in Example 24.5 in HWM, p. 617.

Music to Study

NAWM 116: Robert Schumann, *Fantasiestücke,* Op. 12 (1837), character pieces

    116a: No. 2: *Aufschwung* (Soaring)   `CD 8|76` `CD 4|77`

    116b: No. 3: *Warum?* (Why?)   `CD 8|84`

32. How does Schumann achieve the effect of soaring in *Aufschwung* (NAWM 116a)? Describe the form, and explain how it helps to convey the piece's emotional content.

33. *Warum?* (NAWM 116b) is described in HWM, p. 620, as "a kind of fragment . . . implying that there may be more to the story." How does Schumann achieve that sense of incompleteness in this piece?

34. What features of *Aufschwung* and *Warum?* are typical of character pieces?

35. How do these pieces intersect with the composer's personal life and literary interests?

36. How is a cycle of character pieces like *Fantasiestücke* like a song cycle, such as *Winterreise* (NAWM 112) or *Dichterliebe* (NAWM 113)?

37. What textures and figuration does Schumann use in these piano pieces that are different from those used by Classic-era composers such as C. P. E. Bach (NAWM 99), J. C. Bach (NAWM 102), or Mozart (NAWM 105)? How do these differences reflect changes in the piano? How do they reflect changes in artistic aims or ideals?

38. Briefly summarize the careers of Felix Mendelssohn and Fanny Mendelssohn Hensel. How did their careers differ from those of Robert and Clara Schumann? What were some reasons for these differences?

39. Briefly summarize Fryderyk Chopin's career and historical significance. What genres did he specialize in?

Music to Study

NAWM 117: Fryderyk Chopin, Mazurka in B-flat Major, Op. 7, No. 1 (ca. 1832), mazurka (dance)　　[CD 8|86]

NAWM 118: Fryderyk Chopin, Nocturne in D-flat Major, Op. 27, No. 2 (1835), nocturne (character piece)　　[CD 8|89]　[CD 4|85]

40. Describe the Polish elements of Chopin's Mazurka in B-flat Major, Op. 7, No. 1 (NAWM 117).

41. The NAWM commentary notes that these elements were "a way to assert Polish national identity." Where and by whom were stylized dance pieces like this mazurka performed? How did this and other stylized dance pieces reinforce Polish national identity?

42. How does Chopin embellish the melodic line of his Nocturne in D-flat Major, Op. 27, No. 2 (NAWM 118)? How do his melodies resemble the style of Italian opera?

43. How is chromaticism used in Chopin's nocturne?

44. What elements of style, sound, and texture distinguish Chopin's mazurka and nocturne from Schumann's *Fantasiestücke* (NAWM 116) and from earlier keyboard styles? Describe Chopin's style, based on these examples.

45. Briefly summarize Franz Liszt's career and historical significance. What genres of keyboard music did he cultivate?

46. Who was Nicolò Paganini? What was his significance for Liszt's career?

Music to Study

NAWM 119: Franz Liszt, *Trois études de concert* (Three Concert Études) (1845–49), No. 3, *Un sospiro* (A Sigh)   [CD 9|1]   [CD 4|92]

47. What technical problem for the player is the focus of Liszt's étude *Un sospiro* (NAWM 119)? How is it addressed at the outset? How does the texture change over the course of the piece, to raise new problems for the performer?

What can we learn about Liszt's performing abilities from this piece?

48. How does Liszt develop or vary the opening melodic idea over the course of the piece?

49. How does Liszt use equal divisions of the octave in the harmony, melodies, and form of *Un sospiro*?

50. What elements of style, sound, and texture distinguish Liszt's étude from Chopin's nocturne (NAWM 118), from Schumann's *Fantasiestücke* (NAWM 116), and from earlier keyboard styles? Describe Liszt's approach to writing for the piano, based on this example.

51. Briefly summarize Louis Moreau Gottschalk's career and explain his significance to the history of American music.

Music to Study

NAWM 120: Louis Moreau Gottschalk, *Souvenir de Porto Rico*
   (Marche des Gibaros), Op. 31 (1857–58), character piece

52. What events does Gottschalk's *Souvenir de Porto Rico* (NAWM 120) depict, and how are they suggested in the music? What elements are used to suggest the locale, the people, and their actions?

53. What are the *tresillo, cinquillo,* and *habanera* rhythms? For each one, define it and indicate examples of its use in *Souvenir de Porto Rico* (by measure number). If you know other music that uses these rhythms, name one or two examples for each.

54. Of all the pieces we have studied in this chapter, which one most closely resembles the style and purpose of *Souvenir de Porto Rico*?

    Why did you choose this piece? Refer to specific passages (with measure numbers) to explain your choice.

55. Who was the intended audience for *Souvenir de Porto Rico (Marche des Gibaros)*? Why do you think this piece appealed to its audience?

The Romantic Legacy (HWM 629–30)

56. Briefly describe the reception of the songs and piano music discussed in this chapter, in its own time and over the last two centuries. What impact did the new Romantic style and aesthetic viewpoint have on later music? How does it continue to influence how we think about music today?

TERMS TO KNOW

virtuosos
Romantic, Romanticism
absolute music
characteristic (or descriptive) music
character piece
program music, program
ballad
modified strophic form
parlor songs
étude

concert étude
waltz
mazurka
polonaise
rubato
nocturne
ballade (for piano)
recital
transcription

NAMES TO KNOW

Franz Schubert
Die schöne Müllerin
Der Winterreise
Robert Schumann
Dichterliebe
Clara Schumann
Neue Zeitschrift für Musik
Home! Sweet Home!
Henry R. Bishop

Stephen Foster
Felix Mendelssohn
Lieder ohne Worte (Songs without
    Words)
Fanny Mendelssohn Hensel
Fryderyk Chopin
Franz Liszt
Nicolò Paganini
Louis Moreau Gottschalk

REVIEW QUESTIONS

1. Make a timeline for the nineteenth century, placing on it the composers and most significant pieces discussed in this chapter. Add to it the three periods of Beethoven's career and his most important works, as discussed in chapter 23. Make your timeline large enough to allow further additions, as you will be adding to it in later chapters.

2. Trace the development of the German Lied from the late eighteenth century through the mid-nineteenth century. Name some of the prominent composers in the genre and explain how each contributed to its development.

3. Compare the German Lied to the British and North American parlor song. How are they similar or different in terms of subject matter, harmonic palette, melodic style, form, and level of difficulty? Where, by whom, and for whom were they performed?

4. Trace the history of piano music in the first half of the nineteenth century. Include in your discussion the changed character of the piano and the genres composers used, as well as describing the styles and works of the most prominent composers for the instrument.

5. What impact did women have on music in the early nineteenth century? What roles did they play in the demand, creation, production, performance, and consumption of music? Is this similar to or different from earlier periods in music history?

6. Summarize the similarities and differences between music in the Classic era and music in the Romantic period. Focus especially on piano music, comparing the sonatas by C. P. E. Bach and Mozart (NAWM 99 and 105) with the piano music in this chapter (NAWM 116–120). Include social and economic aspects as well as questions of musical style.

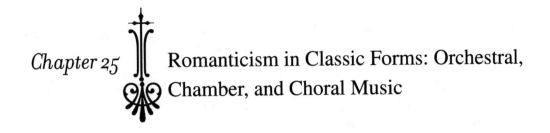

Chapter 25 Romanticism in Classic Forms: Orchestral, Chamber, and Choral Music

CHAPTER OBJECTIVES

After you complete the reading, study of the music, and study questions for this chapter, you should be able to

1. describe the changes to the orchestra in the nineteenth century and its impact on composers;

2. describe the variety of approaches to composing for orchestra in the first half of the nineteenth century, identify some of the most important symphonic composers of that period, and briefly describe one or more characteristic works for each one;

3. name some of the principal composers of chamber music in the first half of the nineteenth century, characterize their styles, trace influences upon them, and describe representative works; and

4. describe the social roles for and varieties of choral music in the nineteenth century, name some of the most important composers of choral music in the first half of the century, and describe examples.

CHAPTER OUTLINE

I. Introduction (HWM 631)

The nineteenth century saw a growth in public concerts accompanied by the emergence of musical classics. Living composers were aware that their own music could achieve a similar permanence and sought to balance tradition and individuality in their orchestral, chamber, and choral works, joining Romantic content to Classic genres and forms.

II. Orchestral Music (HWM 632–45, NAWM 121–122)

A. The Nineteenth-Century Orchestra

Central to public concert life was the orchestra, which was used in concert series, operas houses, theaters, cafés, and dance halls.

1. Size and composition
Orchestras grew from about forty players (usually all men) at the beginning of the century to as many as ninety at its close. A greater variety of instruments provided a much wider range of color.

2. Conductors
Orchestras were now led by *conductors,* who used a baton to beat time and cue entrances. By the 1840s, some conductors had become stars.

B. Audiences and Concerts

1. Audience
Orchestras now drew primarily a middle-class audience.

2. Concert programming
Nineteenth-century concert programs offered a diversity of works, including a mix of vocal and instrumental music for soloists and ensembles.

C. The Rise of the Classical Repertoire
By 1870, three-quarters of the concert repertoire was by composers of past generations. These works were considered masterpieces that combined craft with emotional depth with lasting appeal.

1. The effect on performers
Although many conductors and virtuosos also composed, they gradually shifted to performing the classics more than their own music, permanently altering the nature of performers' work and training.

2. The effect on composers: Beethoven's legacy
Orchestral composers after Beethoven knew that their works would be compared to his and must meet a similar standard while offering something new.

D. The New Romantic Style: Schubert
Schubert maintained the form of the symphony while infusing it with a greater focus on tuneful melodies, colorful harmonies and instrumental color, strong contrasts, and heightened emotions. For him and other Romantics, themes became the most important aspect of any form.

1. *Unfinished* Symphony
In his *Unfinished* Symphony, Schubert used secondary material for symphonic development while focusing the thematic areas on memorable, lyrical melodies like those of his songs and piano works.

2. The "Great" Symphony in C Major
In his "Great" Symphony in C Major, Schubert blended Romantic lyricism and Beethovenian drama within an expanded Classic form.

E. Programmatic Romanticism: Berlioz
Following precedents he found in Beethoven's Fifth and Sixth Symphonies, *Hector Berlioz* (1803–1869) wrote programmatic symphonies shaped around a series of emotions that tell a story.

1. *Symphonie fantastique*
Berlioz conceived his *Symphonie fantastique* (1830) as a musical drama whose words are not sung but are written in a program given to the audi-

ence. The main theme or *idée fixe* (fixed idea) represents the obsessive image of the hero's beloved and appears in every movement, transformed to suit the drama. Throughout the five movements, Berlioz bends the standard structure of the symphony to serve narrative and autobiographical purposes. He also uses the recurring theme and orchestral color to express emotional content in music.   **Music: NAWM 121**

2. *Harold en Italie*
Berlioz's second symphony, *Harold en Italie* (Harold in Italy, 1834), features solo viola and was inspired by a poem and his own visit to Italy. His later symphonies depart even further from the traditional model.

3. Berlioz's achievement
Berlioz's radical approach influenced how other composers composed program music and used instrumental color, harmony, expression, and form.

Biography: Hector Berlioz
Berlioz, a flute and guitar player, taught himself to compose in his teens and eventually studied at the Paris Conservatoire. After winning the Prix de Rome in 1830, he composed *Symphonie fantastique,* an attempt to express his obsession for Harriet Smithson in the context of a Beethovenian symphony. Many of Berlioz's compositions were inspired by literature. His music was far too radical to earn him a steady income, so he turned to writing music criticism, organizing his own concerts, and conducting.

F. Classical Romanticism: Mendelssohn
Mendelssohn's mature symphonies follow Classic models and show the strong impact of Romanticism.

1. *Italian* Symphony
The *Italian* Symphony (No. 4, 1833) uses tuneful themes in Italian styles, accommodating them within the developmental structures of Classic forms.

2. Overtures
Mendelssohn's imaginative use of figuration and orchestral color for musical depiction in his *Midsummer Night's Dream Overture* (1826) set the standard for all subsequent concert overtures.

3. Piano concertos
Mendelssohn was a virtuoso pianist, yet his four piano concertos emphasize musical content over technical display.

4. Violin concerto
In his Violin Concerto in E Minor (1844), Mendelssohn linked the three movements and reworked concerto form, finding new ways to reinterpret yet continue the tradition.   **Music: NAWM 122**

G. New Wine in Old Bottles: Robert Schumann
Robert Schumann modeled his symphonies on those of Schubert and Mendelssohn. His Symphony No. 4 in D Minor is an integrated cycle in four movements played without a break, exemplifying the strong interest of Romantics in taking a new and distinctive approach to tradition.

H. The Romantic Legacy

Schubert, Berlioz, Mendelssohn, and Schumann each found a distinctive way to join Romantic elements with the symphonic tradition, and they influenced later composers of orchestral music.

III. Chamber Music (HWM 645–49, NAWM 123)

A. Chamber Works in Classic Forms

In the nineteenth century, chamber works were increasingly played in concerts by professional ensembles and were often treated as seriously as symphonies, requiring an engagement with the past.

1. Schubert

Schubert's late chamber works are conceived more as dramatic pieces of concert music than as entertaining diversions for amateur players. In his String Quintet in C Major (1828), Schubert treats all five instruments as equals, develops the musical ideas in a symphonic way, and presents contrasting moods and styles within and between movements.

2. Mendelssohn

In his most characteristic chamber works, Mendelssohn used Classic genres and forms as vessels for Romantic material.

3. Robert Schumann

Schumann built on the tradition of Haydn, Mozart, and Beethoven without simply imitating them. His Piano Trios from 1847 were his most influential chamber works.

B. Beyond Women's Domains

Women were discouraged from composing large public concert works, but pieces with piano were accepted as extensions of private music-making.

1. Fanny Mendelssohn Hensel

In her Piano Trio, Op. 11, Fanny Mendelssohn Hensel demonstrated mastery of the genre and the ideal of chamber music as conversation among peers.

2. Clara Schumann

In her Piano Trio in G Minor, Clara Schumann combined traits from Baroque, Classic, and Romantic models.   **Music: NAWM 123**

C. Chamber Music and the Classical Tradition

Although chamber music was regarded as a conservative medium by mid-century, its composers offered something new and distinctive.

IV. Choral Music (HWM 650–57, NAWM 124)

Church choirs were increasingly made up of amateurs, and most choruses outside of church were organized primarily for the enjoyment of the singers themselves. Choral music was a lucrative business for publishers, who issued great quantities of music. Three main types of choral music in the nineteenth century were (1) oratorios and similar works for large chorus, soloists, and orchestra; (2) short choral works on secular texts; and (3) sacred pieces for church or home performance.

A. Amateur Choirs

Amateur choruses were typically organized as *choral societies* and were common all over Germany, Switzerland, England, France, and the United States. Choral singing had entertainment, ethical, spiritual, and communal values.

   1. Festivals

Large amateur choruses played a central role at music festivals, where singers from across a region gathered to perform.

B. Oratorios and Other Large Works

Choral societies were important for maintaining interest in Handel and Haydn oratorios and for reviving Bach's vocal music, beginning with Mendelssohn conducting the *St. Matthew Passion* in 1829.

   1. Mendelssohn's oratorios

Mendelssohn rooted his oratorios *St. Paul* and *Elijah* in Baroque tradition while creating something new and up-to-date.   **Music: NAWM 124**

   2. Berlioz's Requiem and *Te Deum*

Berlioz's Requiem and *Te Deum* are of huge dimensions and belong to a patriotic rather than a liturgical tradition.

C. Partsongs

The *partsong* was the choral parallel to the Lied or parlor song, and nearly every composer in Europe composed them. The music served an immediate purpose for amateur choirs and home music-making and has been largely forgotten.

D. Church Music

Church music was a vehicle for worship but also for amateur singers at home and in public gatherings.

   1. Catholic music

Catholic composers produced concerted liturgical music, elaborate works in up-to-date operatic styles, and *a cappella* (unaccompanied) choral music in a Palestrina-inspired style.

   2. Protestant churches

Protestant churches saw developments building on music of the past, with a flood of new music and a revival of older works.

   3. Russian Orthodox music

Dmitri Bortnyansky (1751–1825) helped to found a new choral style of Russian church music inspired by the modal chants of the Orthodox liturgy.

   4. The United States

In the United States, church music was divided by race; African-American churches developed their own styles, while in predominantly white churches two trends in congregational singing diverged.

   5. Shape-note singing

Southerners participated in *shape-note singing* in church and in revival meetings, singing works by the Yankee tunesmiths and others in a similar style that often featured open fifths and parallel fifths and octaves.

6. Lowell Mason

Lowell Mason (1792–1872) regarded the style of the Yankee tunesmiths and shape-note singers as crude and composed tunes whose harmonies followed the rules of proper European music of the time.

E. The Tradition of Choral Music

Although choral music of the nineteenth century did not lead stylistic developments, it was heard and performed by enormous numbers of people.

V. Romanticism and the Classical Tradition (HWM 657–58)

In the first half of the nineteenth century, composers blended elements of Romanticism into Classic frameworks from the eighteenth century. A classical repertoire was established, and some new works by Schubert, Berlioz, Mendelssohn, Schumann, and others won wide popularity and became classics in their own right. Other works were forgotten quickly and were revived only with the help of later performers and critics. Some utilitarian music of the time, such as Viennese waltzes and sacred music by Bortnyansky and Mason, has won a surprising permanence.

STUDY QUESTIONS

Orchestral Music (HWM 632–45, NAWM 121–122)

1. What were the roles of orchestral music in the nineteenth century? Where was it performed? Who was its audience, and what was its status? How did this differ from eighteenth-century orchestral music?

2. What was the composition of a mid-nineteenth century orchestra? Who led it, and how? How was this different from an eighteenth-century orchestra?

3. Describe the emergence of the classical repertoire in the nineteenth century. What changed in concert programming? What were the causes? What impact did these changes have on composers, performers, and audiences in the nineteenth century?

4. How do Schubert's symphonies differ in approach from those of Beethoven?

5. What does Schumann praise in Schubert's "Great" Symphony in C major (see the passage in HWM, p. 637)? What aspects of Romanticism does Schumann notice in this symphony?

6. In what ways was Berlioz's musical training and career similar to and different from those of Schubert, Schumann, and Mendelssohn? (Refer to chapter 24, questions 9, 18, and 38.)

Music to Study

NAWM 121: Hector Berlioz, *Symphonie fantastique,* program symphony (1830), fifth movement, "Dream of a Witches' Sabbath"

CD 9|16   CD 5|1

7. Diagram the form of the fifth movement of Berlioz's *Symphonie fantastique* (NAWM 121). What eighteenth-century form or forms do you see traces of in your diagram?

8. Where does the *idée fixe* (shown in NAWM, p. 429) appear in this movement? Where does the *Dies irae* chant appear? How are these themes used and transformed to fulfill the program (in NAWM, pp. 427–28)?

9. In what ways is the program of *Symphonie fantastique* representative of Romanticism?

10. What special instruments and instrumental effects does Berlioz use, and how do they suit the program? What other aspects of the music help to support the program?

11. Berlioz was influenced by Beethoven's symphonies while writing his *Symphonie fantastique*. Describe characteristics of the fifth movement that resemble Beethoven's approach to symphonic writing. In what ways does Berlioz depart from or go beyond Beethoven?

12. What was Berlioz's significance for later generations?

13. Describe Mendelssohn's approach to the symphony. How did his idea of the symphony and its purpose differ from Berlioz's? Why do you think they came to different solutions for writing symphonies?

Music to Study

NAWM 122: Felix Mendelssohn, Violin Concerto in E Minor,   [CD 9|30]   [CD 5|15]
   Op. 64, violin concerto (1844), third movement, Allegretto
   non troppo–Allegro molto vivace

14. The third movement of Mendelssohn's Violin Concerto in E Minor (NAWM 122)
    is diagrammed as a rondo or sonata-rondo in NAWM, p. 450. In the space below,
    diagram the form again using the terminology and sections of sonata form, to
    show how this movement also follows sonata-form procedures.

15. What other characteristics of the third movement (besides form) are representative
    of Classic ideals and traits?

16. How does this movement reflect the ideals and musical characteristics of Roman-
    ticism?

17. Describe Schumann's approach to symphony composition, using his Symphony
    No. 4 as an example. How did his approach relate to his piano music and songs?
    What did he draw from Beethoven, Schubert, and Mendelssohn?

Chamber Music (HWM 645–49, NAWM 123)

18. Describe the variety of performance contexts for chamber music. Who performed it, and where? How is this similar to or different from chamber music from earlier periods?

19. How did Schubert, Mendelssohn, and Robert Schumann each approach chamber music? What did each seek to achieve in his chamber music, what models did he draw upon or reject, and how does his chamber music compare to his symphonies, songs, and piano music?

Music to Study

NAWM 123: Clara Schumann, Piano Trio in G Minor, Op. 17, piano trio (1846), third movement, Andante

CD 9|41   CD 5|26

20. According to the commentary in NAWM (p. 456), the A section of the third movement of Clara Schumann's Piano Trio in G Minor (NAWM 123) "resembles a nocturne." Compare this section with Chopin's Nocturne in D-flat Major (NAWM 118) and describe their similarities. Refer to specific measure numbers for both pieces in your answer.

21. Aside from the date it was composed, what makes the third movement of Schumann's Piano Trio an example of Romantic music? How is its musical style and performance context similar to or different from the musical style and performance context of other examples of chamber music we have studied in this anthology, such as the string quartets by Haydn (NAWM 103) and Beethoven (NAWM 110)?

Choral Music (HWM 650–57, NAWM 124)

22. Describe the different functions of choral music in the nineteenth century. Who performed choral music? Where? What types of music were written for different uses and choirs? Which of these uses and types of music are still part of musical life today?

23. What are *choral societies*? What effect did they have on the composition and performance of choral music in the nineteenth century?

Music to Study

NAWM 124: Felix Mendelssohn, *Elijah,* Op. 70, oratorio (1846, [CD 9|45]
rev. 1847), Chorus, *And then shall your light break forth*

24. What traits in the final chorus of Mendelssohn's *Elijah* (NAWM 124) are reminiscent of Baroque music? What contrapuntal devices are used?

What elements in this movement are typical of nineteenth-century music, or of Mendelssohn in particular?

How do these Baroque and Romantic style traits help to depict the text and convey the emotions suggested in the text?

25. Mendelssohn's *Elijah* was one of most popular new choral works in the nineteenth century. Judging from this movement, why do you think it was such a success? Given what you know about the social roles of choral music in the nineteenth century, why might Mendelssohn have chosen to write in this genre?

26. What do partsongs have in common with parlor songs? Refer specifically to the refrain from Elizabeth Stirling's *All among the Barley* (Example 25.8 in HWM, p. 653) and any song example from chapter 24 to illustrate your answer.

27. Describe nineteenth-century developments in Catholic, Lutheran, Anglican, and Russian Orthodox church music. How did each tradition draw on the past?

28. What are the differences between Guido of Arezzo's solmization system (see chapter 2) and *shape-note singing*? What do they have in common? What is the historical significance of shape-note singing?

29. What did Lowell Mason criticize in the music of the Yankee tunesmiths (such as William Billings) and the shape-note tradition, and how did his own music correct those faults? Cite specific passages in Billings's *Creation* (NAWM 97), *Amazing Grace* as it appears in *The Sacred Harp* (Figure 25.6 in HWM, p. 655), and Mason's *Bethany* (Example 25.9 in HWM, p. 656) as examples.

Romanticism and the Classical Tradition (HWM 657–58)

30. How did Schubert, Berlioz, Mendelssohn, Robert Schumann, Clara Schumann, and Fanny Mendelssohn Hensel relate to the classical repertoire that was forming during the nineteenth century? How was their music received in their lifetimes, and since?

31. What utilitarian music from the first half of the nineteenth century has found a permanent place in musical life? To what might you attribute its success?

TERMS TO KNOW

conductor
idée fixe
choral societies

partsong
a cappella
shape-note singing

NAMES TO KNOW

Unfinished Symphony
"Great" Symphony in C Major
Hector Berlioz
Symphonie fantastique
Harold en Italie
Italian Symphony

Schumann, Symphony No. 4
  in D Minor
Schubert, String Quintet in C Major
Elijah
Dmitri Bortnyansky
Lowell Mason

REVIEW QUESTIONS

1. Add to the timeline you made for the last chapter the composers, the most significant pieces, and important writings discussed in this chapter.
2. How are Classic and Romantic orchestral music similar, and how are they different? Use examples from the orchestral works you know by Stamitz (NAWM 101), Haydn (NAWM 104), Berlioz (NAWM 121), and Mendelssohn (NAWM 122) to illustrate these similarities and differences. Include consideration of the size and composition of the orchestra, forms and genres used, the artistic aims of the composers, and matters of style and procedure.
3. Describe the symphonic works of Schubert, Berlioz, Mendelssohn, and Schumann and explain how each of them found an individual path. For each composer, what aspects of past music—especially the legacy of Beethoven—did he continue, what did he reject, and what did he do that was innovative or distinctive?
4. What are the distinctive features of chamber music in the nineteenth century? How is it similar to or different from chamber music in the eighteenth century?
5. Name the varieties of choral music composed in the nineteenth century and describe one or more examples of each type. What were the social roles and contexts for choral music in the nineteenth century? How did this affect the types and styles used by choral composers? What roles did amateurs play in choral performance, and how might this have affected the relative prestige of choral music in comparison to orchestral music?
6. Write a short essay describing the role that women played in music as patrons, dedicatees, composers, and performers from the Middle Ages through the nineteenth century. List the major social, political, and economic changes that affected how women participated in musical culture. Name historically significant women who had a major impact on composers, performers, patrons, and institutions. You will add to this essay in later chapters.

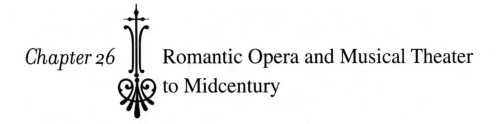

Chapter 26 — Romantic Opera and Musical Theater to Midcentury

CHAPTER OBJECTIVES

After you complete the reading, study of the music, and study questions for this chapter, you should be able to

1. trace the history of opera and musical theater in Italy, France, Germany, and the United States in the first half of the nineteenth century and distinguish between the characteristics of each national tradition;

2. name the most significant composers of opera and musical theater in each nation and describe the style and approach of each of them; and

3. define and use terminology associated with nineteenth-century opera and musical theater.

CHAPTER OUTLINE

I. Introduction (HWM 659)

In the first half of the nineteenth century, Italian composers dominated the stage, new types of opera were cultivated in France and Germany, and the minstrel show became the first musical export from North America to Europe.

II. The Roles of Opera (HWM 659–60)

Opera appealed both to the elite and middle class, who attended the opera, and to the public at large. Librettists addressed issues that spoke to the broader audience and used a variety of subjects and settings. The music itself now became the most important element of an opera's success, and it was heard on and off the stage in arrangements at home and in concerts.

III. Italy (HWM 660–68, NAWM 125)

In the early nineteenth century, Rossini, Donizetti, and Bellini created a new Italian tradition in opera, and their works have been performed ever since.

A. Gioachino Rossini

Gioachino Rossini (1792–1868), the most popular and influential opera composer of his generation, blended aspects of opera buffa and opera seria into his operas and established new conventions for Italian opera.

1. Bel canto style

Rossini helped establish *bel canto* opera, in which the voice is the most important element.

2. General style

Rossini's operas are known for their tunefulness, snappy rhythms, clear phrases, spare orchestration, and simple harmonic schemes.

3. Scene structure

Rossini and his librettists developed a scene structure in which all solos, ensembles, and choruses contributed to advancing the plot. A typical solo scene consists of an orchestral introduction and *scena* (orchestrally accompanied recitative) followed by an aria in two main sections, a slow, lyrical *cantabile* and a fast, brilliant *cabaletta*. A *tempo di mezzo* often separates these sections. Ensembles and finales have similar forms.

4. *The Barber of Seville*

The Barber of Seville (1816) combines features of opera buffa with bel canto tradition. Rosina's aria *Una voce poco fa* conveys her character through changes of style.   **Music: NAWM 125**

5. Serious operas

Although Rossini is now best known for his comic operas, his serious operas were equally significant in his day.

6. *Guillaume Tell*

Rossini's *Guillaume Tell* (William Tell, 1829) was performed five hundred times during the composer's lifetime, and it combines conventions he had helped to establish in Italian opera with characteristics of French grand opera.

7. Overtures

Many of Rossini's opera overtures are also performed in the concert hall.

Biography: Gioachino Rossini

Rossini trained at the Bologna Conservatory and was commissioned to write his first opera at age eighteen. In 1815, he was appointed musical director of the Teatro San Carlo in Naples, but also composed for other cities. Because he had to compose very quickly, he often reworked music from his previous works to create new operas. Later, he moved to Paris and became director of the Théâtre Italien, adapting his Italian works for the French stage and writing one new opera in French (*Guillaume Tell*). Rossini stopped writing operas when he was barely forty and lived the last forty years of his life in financial comfort, composing other genres.

B. Vincenzo Bellini

Vincenzo Bellini (1801–1835) preferred serious dramas with fast action.

1. Style

Bellini is known for long, highly embellished, intensely emotional melodies, as in the cantabile section of *Casta diva,* the *cavatina,* or entrance aria, for the title character in *Norma* (1831).

C. Gaetano Donizetti

Gaetano Donizetti (1797–1848) was one of the most prolific Italian composers of his generation. He effectively captured character, situation, and feeling in music while constantly moving the drama forward.

1. *Lucia di Lammermoor*

Lucia di Lammermoor (1835) is one of Donizetti's most famous operas. Lucia's "mad scene" uses a *reminiscence motive* to refer to earlier scenes and flexibly adapts Rossini's standard scene-structure by blurring boundaries between sections.

D. Classics of Italian Opera

The most successful operas of Rossini, Bellini, and Donizetti were performed in opera houses all over Italy and in other nations, and they were among the first operas ever to reach the status of permanent classics.

IV. France (HWM 668–72)

Opera remained the most prestigious musical genre in France.

1. French opera under Napoleon

French opera was centered in Paris and shaped by politics. Under Napoleon only the Opéra, the Opéra-Comique, and the Théâtre Italien were allowed to present operas.

2. Restoration and the July Revolution

The Opéra received government support, including a new theater with gas lighting. After the 1830 Revolution, the theater was leased to Louis Véron, who found additional sponsors.

A. Grand Opera

Grand opera was designed to appeal to middle-class audiences with exciting historical plots and spectacular stage effects.

1. Eugène Scribe and Giacomo Meyerbeer

Véron, librettist *Eugène Scribe* (1791–1861), and composer *Giacomo Meyerbeer* (1791–1864) were the leaders of grand opera.

2. *Les Huguenots*

Meyerbeer's *Les Huguenots* (1836) is typical of French grand opera, combining glorious singing and entertaining spectacle (including an enormous cast, a ballet, and dramatic scenery and lighting effects) with a serious artistic statement.

3. Impact of grand opera

Meyerbeer's approach to grand opera was admired and emulated by later composers such as Richard Wagner.

4. Berlioz, *Les Troyens*
   Berlioz's *Les Troyens* (1856–58) drew on grand opera and older French opera traditions.

B. Opéra Comique
   Opéra comique, which used spoken dialogue instead of recitative, featured comic or romantic plots and was on a smaller scale than grand opera.

C. Ballet
   Ballet continued to be popular in France, and dancer Marie Taglioni (1804–1884) introduced a new style of Romantic ballet. Composers typically wrote music for ballets after the dance had already been choreographed.

V. Germany (HWM 673–75, NAWM 126)

Singspiel was at the root of German opera, and composers intensified its national features while absorbing Romantic elements from French opera.

A. Carl Maria von Weber
   Der Freischütz, by *Carl Maria von Weber* (1786–1826), established German Romantic opera.

1. German Romantic opera
   German Romantic opera draws plots from medieval history or legend, involves the supernatural, is often set in the country, addresses good versus evil, and uses a folklike style, chromatic harmony, and orchestral color for dramatic expression.

2. *Der Freischütz*
   Der Freischütz includes rustic choruses, marches, dances, airs, and arias in Italian style. The story revolves around the subjects of love, good versus evil, magic, and the supernatural.

3. Wolf's Glen Scene
   In the famous Wolf's Glen Scene, Weber uses *melodrama* (spoken dialogue over music), daring chromatic harmonies, and orchestral effects to convey the eerie events.   **Music: NAWM 126**

VI. The United States (HWM 675–78)

A. Opera in the Americas
   Opera was an important part of musical life in the Americas.

1. Theater companies
   Theater companies and touring troupes in North America performed spoken plays, ballad operas, and adaptations of foreign-language operas.

2. European opera
   Opera performed in foreign languages took hold more slowly in the United States.

3. Opera as popular entertainment
   The music of opera was heard by a wide public, in home music-making and in public concerts.

B. American Opera

There was virtually no demand for American operas in the nineteenth century, despite attempts by American composers.

C. Minstrel Shows

Minstrelsy was the most popular form of musical theater in the United States from the 1830s through the 1870s.

1. Origins

Minstrelsy grew from solo comic performances to performances between acts of a play to independent minstrel shows. Some minstrel songs are still sung today.

2. Minstrel songs

Minstrelsy was the first of many forms of entertainment in which white musicians have borrowed from the music of African Americans.

VII. Opera as High Culture (HWM 678)

Most musical theater in the first half of the nineteenth century sought to include elements that would appeal to all possible listeners. By the later nineteenth century, new operas were staged less frequently, and the standard repertory came to predominate. Today opera is very expensive to stage and serves as a status symbol. Lighter forms of musical theater have vanished, but their descendants are a vital part of today's musical life.

STUDY QUESTIONS

The Roles of Opera (HWM 659–60)

1. Look back at your answer to question 1 in chapter 24. What impact did the changes you described there have on opera in the nineteenth century? Who attended opera? Who else heard operatic music, and what roles did it play? How did opera change to suit these new circumstances?

Italy (HWM 660–68, NAWM 125)

2. Briefly trace the career of Rossini.

3. Describe Rossini's operatic style and his typical scene structure.

Music to Study

NAWM 125: Gioachino Rossini, *Il barbiere di Siviglia,* comic   (CD 9|48)
     opera (1816), Act I, no. 7, *Una voce poco fa*

4. Diagram the form of the scene from Rossini's *Il barbiere di Siviglia* in NAWM 125, including indications of instrumental and vocal sections, melodic and thematic repetitions, and changes of tempo, style, and figuration. How does this compare to the typical structure of a solo scene in a Rossini opera? How do the changes of style, tempo, and figuration help to convey what Rosina is saying and feeling?

5. How does Rossini's style compare to the operatic styles of Pergolesi (NAWM 93), Hasse (NAWM 94), Gluck (NAWM 96), and Mozart (NAWM 107)? Pay particular attention to the forms used, the melodic style, and the way the voice is accompanied.

6. What did audiences value in Rossini's operatic style? Refer to specific aspects of this scene from *Il barbiere di Siviglia* to illustrate your general points.

7. Who were the two most important composers of Italian opera in the 1830s? What changes did they bring to Italian opera? Why did their operas appeal to audiences?

Why are these composers and Rossini considered important today?

France (HWM 668–72)

8. How did political and economic changes affect opera and musical theater in France from the French Revolution to the mid-nineteenth century?

9. What theater was associated with *grand opera,* and who was its director?

theater _____   director _____

Who were the librettist and composer for *Les Huguenots*?

librettist _____   composer _____

10. What are the characteristics of grand opera? In what ways does *Les Huguenots* ex-emplify the style? How did its creators seek to appeal to the public?

11. Describe the characteristics of French ballet in the 1830s and 1840s.

Germany (HWM 673–75, NAWM 126)

Music to Study

NAWM 126: Carl Maria von Weber, *Der Freischütz,* opera
(1817–1821), Act II, finale, Wolf's Glen Scene

12. What distinguishing characteristics of German Romantic opera plots in the early nineteenth century are exemplified in Weber's *Der Freischütz* as a whole and in the Wolf's Glen Scene (NAWM 126) in particular?

13. In the first half of the scene, before Caspar begins to cast the bullets, how does Weber use music to depict the Wolf's Glen? What devices or musical elements does he use to convey the characters and feelings of Caspar, Samiel, and Max?

14. What is *melodrama*? Where and how is it used in the Wolf's Glen Scene? Why do you think it might be more effective here than recitative?

15. A series of supernatural events occur as the first six bullets are cast. Briefly describe each event and how Weber depicts it in the music. What musical effects does he use to create a feeling of the supernatural? (Note: In examining the harmony, remember that the clarinets in A sound a minor third lower than written; the horns in D a minor seventh lower than written; and the trumpets in D a whole step higher than written.)

Bullet #1:

Bullet #2:

Bullet #3:

Bullet #4:

Bullet #5:

Bullet #6:

The United States (HWM 675–78)

16. What were the roles of opera in the United States? What operas were most popular? Why was there little support for operas by American composers?

17. What was *minstrelsy*? What aspects of minstrelsy might account for its popularity?

18. Briefly describe the origins and history of minstrelsy. Why was it historically significant?

Opera as High Culture (HWM 678)

19. Briefly describe what changed in the world of opera after about 1850 and what roles operas from the first half of the nineteenth century have continued to play.

TERMS TO KNOW

bel canto
scena
cantabile
cabaletta
tempo di mezzo

cavatina
reminiscence motive
grand opera
melodrama
minstrelsy

NAMES TO KNOW

Gioachino Rossini
The Barber of Seville
Guillaume Tell (William Tell)
Vincenzo Bellini
Gaetano Donizetti

Eugène Scribe
Giacomo Meyerbeer
Les Huguenots
Carl Maria von Weber
Der Freischütz

REVIEW QUESTIONS

1. Add the composers, major works, and significant events discussed in this chapter to the timeline you made for chapter 24.
2. Describe the operas and operatic styles of Rossini, Bellini, and Donizetti, noting similarities and differences among them. Use examples from HWM (Example 26.2) and NAWM 125 to illustrate your points.
3. What types of opera were written for production in Paris in the first half of the nineteenth century? Trace the emergence of the new types of opera, briefly describe what makes each type distinctive, and explain how French opera differs from Italian opera.
4. How does the German Romantic opera of Weber differ from Italian and French opera in the first half of the nineteenth century? Use examples from the works excerpted in NAWM or described in HWM to support your answer.
5. How do opera and musical theater in the United States differ from all the European opera styles we studied in this chapter?
6. Compare the early Romantic operas by Rossini (NAWM 125) and Weber (NAWM 126) to eighteenth-century operas by Hasse (NAWM 94), Gluck (NAWM 96), and Mozart (NAWM 107). In what ways are they similar, and in what ways are they different in terms of form, vocal style, instrumentation, use of orchestra and chorus, presentation of the drama, and portrayal of characters? Write a short essay describing these similarities and differences.

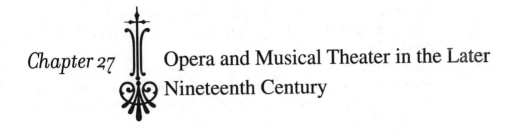

Chapter 27 Opera and Musical Theater in the Later Nineteenth Century

CHAPTER OBJECTIVES

After you complete the reading, study of the music, and study questions for this chapter, you should be able to

1. describe the impact that political and technological changes had on musical life in the later nineteenth century and specifically on opera;

2. distinguish between Italian, German, French, Russian, and other styles of opera and musical theater in the later nineteenth century; and

3. identify some of the most important composers associated with these national styles of opera and musical theater, explain their historical significance, and describe characteristic excerpts from their works.

CHAPTER OUTLINE

I. Introduction (HWM 679)

The second half of the nineteenth century saw a continuation of national traditions in Italian, German, and French opera, the rise of a Russian school in opera and ballet, and growing traditions of musical theater in other lands.

II. Technology, Politics, and Nationalism (HWM 679–83)

Europe and the United States became industrial powerhouses during the latter nineteenth century.

1. 1848 revolutions
A series of revolutions swept Europe in 1848–49, but they failed to produce permanent changes.

2. Political reforms
During the second half of the nineteenth century, most European governments granted more political rights to their people.

3. Nationalism

The French Revolution and the Napoleonic Wars popularized the concept of *nationalism,* which continued to grow throughout the nineteenth century.

4. National unification

Nationalism could be used to support governments of states that were already unified or to challenge a foreign government that was not allowing national unification.

5. Cultural nationalism

In some places, cultural nationalism—pride in a people's language, literature, and art—was crucial to forging a new nation, while in others, it worked against political unity.

6. Other themes in the arts

Other themes in the arts include realism, exoticism, fantasy, the distant past, and enjoyment of the outdoors.

Music in Context: Nationalism and Exoticism

In music, nationalism meant that some composers cultivated melodic and harmonic styles or chose subjects that carried associations with their own ethnic group, while others invented those "national" styles. Composers in Russia and Eastern Europe searched for a native voice independent of Austria, Germany, and Italy. Many composers also wrote music that evoked a distant land or foreign culture. This was called *exoticism,* and its history extends back into the eighteenth century.

III. Opera (HWM 683)

Opera became increasingly associated with nationalism throughout the later nineteenth century, although many composers blended traditions.

1. Rise of the operatic repertory

A core operatic repertory emerged in the later nineteenth century. In response, composers took more time to write new operas, seeking to create something original and distinctive.

2. Other changes

As audiences and performing spaces for opera grew, orchestras grew larger and singers needed more powerful voices. New genres of lighter opera emerged.

IV. Giuseppe Verdi (HWM 683–88, NAWM 127)

Giuseppe Verdi (1813–1901) was the dominant figure in Italian music for the fifty years after Donizetti.

1. Nationalism

Although Verdi supported and became identified with the Italian Risorgimento (resurgence), his operas are not overtly nationalist.

Biography: Giuseppe Verdi

Verdi studied music as a child and in Milan, then took his first post in Busseto, where he was married. He suffered great personal losses with the deaths of his two children and wife before moving to Milan to begin his opera career. He poured himself into his music, composing several works that quickly became part of the permanent opera repertory. Later Verdi slowed his production of new operas, eventually retiring and living off the royalties from his music. He was persuaded by his publisher to come out of retirement to write his two last operas.

A. Approach to Opera

Verdi captured character, feeling, and situation in memorable melodies. He also had strict training in harmony and counterpoint, knowledge of past music, and an ear for colorful orchestration.

  1. Librettos

Verdi preferred stories that were already successful plays, with action, contrast, unusual characters, and strong emotions.

B. Style

Verdi's early operas built on the conventions of Rossini, Bellini, and especially Donizetti. *Rigoletto* (1851), *Il trovatore* (The Troubadour, 1853), and *La traviata* (The Fallen Woman, 1853) reached new heights of musical characterization, melodic invention, and dramatic intensity.

  1. *La traviata*

Many features of Verdi's mature works are embodied in *La traviata*. **Music: NAWM 127**

C. Later Operas

In his later operas, Verdi still used traditional forms but often reshaped them to suit the dramatic situation, achieving greater continuity.

  1. *Otello* and *Falstaff*

Verdi based his last two operas on plays by Shakespeare. In *Otello* (1887), he realized a sense of continuity in music and action most completely, and in the comic opera *Falstaff* (1893), he transformed the ensemble.

D. Verdi's Reception

Verdi experienced phenomenal success in his own lifetime, and in recent decades there have been more operas in the permanent repertory by him than by any other composer.

V. Later Italian Composers (HWM 688–89)

Few operas by composers after Verdi have had as much lasting success as Verdi's operas did.

  1. Verismo

Two operas that did enter the repertory are the *verismo* operas *Cavaleria rusticana* (Rustic Chivalry, 1890) and *I Pagliacci* (The Clowns, 1892).

A. Giacomo Puccini

Giacomo Puccini (1858–1924) was the most successful Italian opera composer after Verdi. He blended Verdi's focus on vocal melody with elements of Wagner's approach. In Puccini's operas, arias, choruses, and ensembles are usually part of a continuous flow rather than set off as independent numbers.

VI. Richard Wagner (HWM 690–98, NAWM 128)

Richard Wagner (1813–1883) was the outstanding composer of German opera and one of the crucial figures in nineteenth-century culture. He brought German Romantic opera to its height, invented the *music drama,* and developed a chromatic idiom that influenced later composers.

Biography: Richard Wagner

Wagner's early instrumental works show a devotion to Beethoven. In the early 1830s, he began writing operas, gaining his first great success in 1842 in Dresden, where he directed opera, conducted, and composed at the Saxon court. After fleeing Germany during the 1848–49 insurrection, Wagner settled in Switzerland, where he wrote his most important essays and began *Der Ring des Nibelungen.* He found a patron in King Ludwig II of Bavaria, who sponsored his later operas. Wagner built the festival theater at Bayreuth where several of his operas were performed, including the *Ring* cycle.

A. Writings

In a series of essays, Wagner argued that the function of music was to serve dramatic expression.

1. Gesamtkunstwerk

Wagner believed that poetry, scenic design, staging, action, and music work together to form what he called a *Gesamtkunstwerk* (collective artwork). In his music dramas, vocal lines are part of a complete texture in which the orchestra plays a leading role.

2. Anti-Semitism

In his essay *Das Judentum in der Musik* (Jewishness in Music, 1850), Wagner drew on and strengthened an anti-Semitic strain in German culture, while attempting to obscure his deep debt to Meyerbeer and Mendelssohn, who were Jewish.

B. Operas

Wagner drew on Meyerbeer for his grand opera *Rienzi* (1842) and was influenced by Weber for *The Flying Dutchman* (1843).

1. *The Flying Dutchman*

Characteristics that became typical of Wagner's later music were established in *The Flying Dutchman,* including writing his own librettos based on Germanic legend and the use of recurring musical themes.

2. *Tannhäuser* and *Lohengrin*

In *Tannhäuser* (1845) and *Lohengrin* (1850), Wagner again wrote his own librettos from Germanic legends and developed recurring themes and introduced a new kind of semi-declamatory vocal style.

C. Music Dramas

1. *Der Ring des Nibelungen*

Wagner's *Der Ring des Nibelungen* (The Ring of the Nibelungs, completed 1874) is a cycle of four music dramas linked by common characters and musical motives: *Das Rheingold* (The Rhine Gold), *Die Walküre*

(The Valkyrie), *Siegfried,* and *Götterdämmerung* (The Twilight of the Gods).

2. *Tristan, Meistersinger,* and *Parsifal*
Wagner's other music dramas are *Tristan und Isolde* (1857–59), *Die Meistersinger von Nürnberg* (1862–67), and *Parsifal* (1882).

3. The *Leitmotiv*
A *Leitmotiv,* or *leitmotive,* is a theme or motive associated with a particular person, thing, emotion, or idea, and Wagner organized each music drama around a variety of leitmotives.

4. Leitmotives in *Tristan und Isolde*
Tristan und Isolde illustrates Wagner's idea of music drama and the use of leitmotives, which differs from the use of reminiscence motives by Weber or Verdi. Leitmotives are the basic musical material of the score. They are usually short and are often characterized by particular instruments, registers, harmonies, or keys.   **Music: NAWM 128**

D. Wagnerian Harmony
In *Tristan,* Wagner produced an ambiguous kind of tonality that expresses unfulfilled desire by evoking yet evading traditional harmonic expectations.

E. Wagner's Influence
More has been written about Wagner than about any other musician, and his writings and music dramas affected virtually all later opera and had an impact on the other arts as well.

VII. France (HWM 698–701, NAWM 129)

France did not have a single dominant composer of opera, and Paris had a variety of musical theaters for the production of new works.

A. Grand Opera, Ballet, and Lyric Opera
Grand opera continued to be prominent, and ballet grew in popularity as an independent art. Opéra comique developed into *lyric opera,* which featured romantic plots and a focus on melody.

1. Gounod's *Faust*
The most famous lyric opera is *Faust* by Charles Gounod (1818–1893).

B. Exoticism
Several operas exploited an interest in exoticism.

1. Bizet's *Carmen*
Georges Bizet (1838–1875) combined exoticism and realism in *Carmen,* which is set in Spain. It provoked outrage among some at its premiere, but has become one of the most popular operas of all time.   **Music: NAWM 129**

C. Lighter Fare
1. Opéra bouffe
Opéra bouffe, inaugurated in the 1850s by Jacques Offenbach (1819–1880), satirized operatic and social conventions.

2. Cabarets and revues

Paris was also famous for its popular musical theaters, such as *cabarets,* the *cafés-concerts,* and music halls that offered *revues.*

VIII. Russia (HWM 701–9, NAWM 130)

Opera was first performed in Russia in 1731 by an Italian troupe, and until the nineteenth century, most of the star singers and composers there were Italian.

A. Russian Nationalism

Russian nationalism in opera was both a way to proclaim a national identity and a tool of propaganda for the absolutist government.

1. Mikhail Glinka

Mikhail Glinka (1804–1857) was the first Russian composer recognized as an equal of his Western contemporaries. He was valued in the West for the Russian flavor of his operas *A Life for the Tsar* (1836) and *Ruslan and Lyudmila* (1842), but his countrymen valued him for being the first to claim a place for Russia in the international musical world.

B. Looking West

There were two main camps among Russian composers: those who pursued professional training in the Western mode, and those who opposed academic study as a threat to their originality.

1. Rubinsteins and conservatories

Anton Rubinstein (1829–1894) founded the St. Petersburg Conservatory with a program of training on the Western model, and his brother Nikolay Rubinstein (1835–1881) founded the Moscow Conservatory on similar lines.

C. Piotr Il'yich Tchaikovsky

Piotr Il'yich Tchaikovsky (1840–1893) was the leading Russian composer of the nineteenth century, and he sought to reconcile the nationalist and internationalist tendencies in Russian music.

1. Operas

In his two most important operas, *Eugene Onegin* (1879) and *The Queen of Spades* (1890), Tchaikovsky used a variety of Russian styles and materials, not only folk music, to provide national flavor.

2. Ballets

Tchaikovsky wrote the most famous and frequently performed ballets in the permanent repertory, including *The Nutcracker* (1892).

D. The Mighty Handful

Standing against the professionalism of the conservatories were five composers dubbed *the Mighty Handful.*

1. Mily Balakirev and César Cui

Mily Balakirev (1837–1910), the leader and informal teacher of the group, published two collections of folk songs but wrote little for the stage. César Cui (1835–1918) wrote operas, but none entered the permanent repertory.

2. Aleksander Borodin
   Aleksander Borodin (1833–1887) was a chemist whose unfinished opera *Prince Igor* (1869–87) used contrasting musical styles to evoke two ethnic groups.

E. Modest Musorgsky
   Modest Musorgsky (1839–1881) is widely considered the most original of the Mighty Handful, and his opera *Boris Godunov* (1868–69; revised 1871–74) echoes the realism prominent in nineteenth-century Russian literature.

1. Melodic style
   Musorgsky followed the rhythm and pacing of speech and sought a melodic profile like that of Russian folk songs. **Music: NAWM 130**

2. Harmony
   Musorgsky's harmony is essentially tonal, but he often juxtaposes distantly related or coloristic harmonies, sometimes joined by a common tone.

3. Block construction
   Musorgsky and many other Russian composers juxtapose large blocks of material instead of using traditional development.

F. Nikolay Rimsky-Korsakov
   Nikolay Rimsky-Korsakov (1844–1908) became a professor at the St. Petersburg Conservatory, abandoning the anti-academic stance of the Mighty Five.

1. Professionalism
   Rimsky-Korsakov's professionalism guaranteed the continuation of a distinctively Russian school through his activities as editor, conductor, and teacher.

2. Operas
   Rimsky-Korsakov used Russian subjects for his operas and, in many of them, alternated a diatonic style used for the everyday world with a lightly chromatic style used for the fantastic or magical world.

3. Whole-tone and octatonic collections
   Rimsky-Korsakov often used the *whole-tone scale* and the *octatonic scale* (respectively, scales composed of all whole tones or of whole and half steps in strict alternation) in the fantastic style.

G. Russian Influence
   In less than a century, Russian music went from being peripheral to being a major current in Western music.

IX. **Other Nations (HWM 709–12, NAWM 131)**

   Opera continued to spread to other nations.

A. Bohemia
   In Bohemia, opera was a nationalist project, part of an effort to foster stage works in Czech.

1. Bedřich Smetana

   The eight operas of *Bedřich Smetana* (1824–1884) form the core of the Czech operatic repertory, and his comic opera *The Bartered Bride* (1866) secured his international reputation.

2. Antonín Dvořák

   Antonín Dvořák (1841–1904) wrote twelve operas based on Czech village life, Czech fairy tales, and Slavic history.

B. Opera in Other Lands

   Opera in Poland, Spain, Britain, and the New World took varying paths, depending on individual circumstances in each nation.

C. Operetta

   Lighter forms of musical theater flourished in nearly every country. The *operettas* of Johann Strauss (1825–1899) in Vienna and of *W. S. Gilbert* (librettist) and *Arthur Sullivan* (composer, 1842–1900) in England satirized operatic conventions.   **Music: NAWM 131**

D. The Variety of Musical Theater

   A great variety of musical theater flourished throughout Europe and the Americas, from opera to the American variety shows known as *vaudeville*. In all these endeavors, the focus was on pleasing the audience and making as much money as possible.

IX. Music for the Stage and Its Audiences (HWM 713)

While Verdi and Wagner brought the opera of their nations to a peak, some works by composers outside of Italy and Germany also entered the permanent repertory. Nationalism was a major concern in nineteenth-century opera, and it continues to affect the reception of much of this music in both positive and negative ways. The split between elite and popular musical theater became permanent during this period. Yet almost every expressive device in the musical language was first created in opera, and those devices still carry meaning today in film, television, and other media.

STUDY QUESTIONS

Technology, Politics, and Nationalism (HWM 679–83)

1. What is nationalism? What political events and cultural beliefs inspired nationalism in Europe in the nineteenth century? What impact did nationalism have on music in the nineteenth century?

2. What is *exoticism*? How does it differ from nationalism, and how is it similar?

Opera (HWM 683)

3. Describe how opera production in the later nineteenth century differed from opera production in the earlier part of the century. How did the repertory change? How did opera houses, singers, and orchestras change? What effects did these changes have on opera composers?

Giuseppe Verdi (HWM 683–88, NAWM 127)

4. Briefly summarize Verdi's biography and career, including significant operas and their dates. What makes Verdi's career so extraordinary when compared with other nineteenth-century opera composers?

Music to Study

NAWM 127: Giuseppe Verdi, *La traviata,* opera (1853), scena and ⟨CD 9|69⟩ CD 5|30
duet from Act III

5. Sketch the form of the scena and duet from Act III of Verdi's *La traviata* in NAWM 127, providing terms for each section.

6. The form of this excerpt by Verdi is more expansive than the form of the excerpt from Rossini's *Il barbiere di Siviglia* in NAWM 125. What happens in the plot to explain this scene structure? What does its place in the drama as a whole have to do with its structure?

7. How does Verdi use various musical forces, textures, and types to further the drama in this scene? How does this compare with the textures and types used in the excerpt from Rossini's *Il barbiere di Siviglia*?

8. Compare the dialogue in the opening part of this scene from *La traviata* (mm. 1–34) to the dialogue in recitative in the excerpt from Mozart's *Don Giovanni* in NAWM 107 (scene 2). Describe the melodic styles, the interaction of characters, and the role of the orchestras in each. What effect does Verdi achieve, and how is it different from the effect that Mozart creates?

9. In the Andante section of the scene, *Parigi, o cara,* how does Verdi's melodic style compare to the slow section of Rosina's aria *Una voce poco fa* in Rossini's *Il barbiere di Siviglia* (NAWM 125)?

10. In the Allegro section of the scene, *Ah! Gran Dio!,* how does Verdi's melodic style compare to that of the cabaletta in the excerpt from Rossini? Why do you think Verdi used the melodic style that he did? Do you think his choice is effective? Explain your answer.

Later Italian Composers (HWM 688–89)

11. What is *verismo*? Name composers associated with it and some notable examples of it.

12. Describe Puccini's approach to opera. Why was it difficult for composers of Italian opera in the later nineteenth century to become as successful as Verdi, and what were the secrets of Puccini's success?

Richard Wagner (HWM 690–98, NAWM 128)

13. Summarize Wagner's career. How did he make a living? What composers were important influences on his music, and for his opera in particular?

14. What does *Gesamtkunstwerk* mean? What is its importance for Wagner?

15. What is a *music drama*? How does a music drama differ from a Romantic opera?

16. Why did Wagner attack "Judaism in music"? How have his anti-Semitic views interacted with wider German culture and history? How have they affected his reputation?

17. Who wrote the librettos for Wagner's operas? _____

18. Name (in English or German) and give the dates for Wagner's last three Romantic operas:

_____   _____

_____

19. Name (in English or German) his seven music dramas. Indicate by (R) which are part of his cycle *The Ring of the Nibelungs,* and give the dates for the others:

    _____

    _____

    _____

    _____

Music to Study

NAWM 128: Richard Wagner, *Tristan und Isolde,* opera (music drama) (1857–59), excerpt from Act I, scene 5   `CD 9|78`   `CD 5|39`

20. How do text, action, scenery, and music reinforce each other in the scene from Wagner's *Tristan und Isolde* in NAWM 128? How is this like, and how is it different from, the scene from Verdi's *La traviata* in NAWM 127?

21. In the section of *Tristan und Isolde* from measures 132–88, how do the singers' melodies relate to the melodies in the orchestra? Where does the musical continuity lie, with the singers or with the orchestra, and how is continuity achieved?

    How does this compare to the scene from *La traviata*?

22. How do Wagner's vocal melodies here and throughout the scene compare to those of Rossini and Verdi in NAWM 125 and NAWM 127? Include observations on phrasing and overall shape as well as on vocal embellishment. What are the main characteristics of Wagner's vocal style?

23. What is a *leitmotive*? How are they used in this scene?

24. How does the harmonic language used for the sailors (e.g., at mm. 196–203, "Hail! King Mark, hail!") differ from that used for Tristan and Isolde after they have drunk the love potion? Why is this contrast appropriate, and how does it heighten the drama?

25. What aspects of Wagner's music and ideas were especially influential on later composers?

France (HWM 698–701, NAWM 129)

26. What is *lyric opera*? How does it differ from grand opera and opéra comique, and what does it share with each?

Music to Study

NAWM 129: Georges Bizet, *Carmen,* opera (1873–74), Act I,
No. 10, seguidilla and duet

      [CD 10|1]   [CD 5|47]

27. Sketch the form of Act I, No. 10, from Bizet's *Carmen* (NAWM 129).

Why is this particular form effective for this scene?

How does this compare to the scenes from *La traviata* (NAWM 127) and *Tristan und Isolde* (NAWM 128)?

28. How does Bizet portray Don José's changing emotions in this scene? How does Don José's music throughout the scene compare with Carmen's? How do we know from his music that she has succeeded in seducing him?

29. How do the style, phrasing, and overall shape of Bizet's vocal melodies compare to those of Verdi in *La traviata* and Wagner in *Tristan und Isolde*?

30. What makes *Carmen* an example of realism and exoticism? Refer to the scene in NAWM 129 specifically to illustrate your points.

31. What is *opéra bouffe,* when did it come into existence, and what social roles did it serve?

    Who was a major composer of *opéra bouffe*? _____

32. What other lighter forms of musical theater were available to Parisian audiences? What did these forms offer that others, including opera, did not?

Russia (HWM 701–9, NAWM 130)

33. What was the role of Glinka in the creation of a Russian national music?

34. What was Tchaikovsky's approach to the issue of musical nationalism? How did he invest his operas with national character?

35. What was the Mighty Handful? Who took part? What were their general goals?

Music to Study

NAWM 130: Modest Musorgsky, *Boris Godunov,* opera (1868–69, [CD 10|6] revised 1871–74), Coronation scene

36. What is unusual about the harmony in the Coronation scene from Musorgsky's *Boris Godunov* (NAWM 130)? Cite and describe some unusual progressions.

37. How does the form of this scene differ from the forms of the excerpts from Verdi's *La traviata* (NAWM 127), Wagner's *Tristan und Isolde* (NAWM 128), and Bizet's *Carmen* (NAWM 129)? How does Musorgsky's approach to presenting and developing musical ideas differ from theirs? How does this effect how the listener experiences the story?

38. How do the vocal lines in this scene from *Boris Godunov* compare to the vocal styles in the other nineteenth-century operas you have studied, by Verdi, Wagner, and Bizet?

39. How does Boris's vocal line in measures 114–31 show the influences of genuine Russian folk melody, like the one Musorgsky used at measure 50?

40. Why is *Boris Godunov* an example of Russian nationalism, while Bizet's *Carmen,* which uses musical elements associated with Spain, is an example of exoticism?

41. How did Rimsky-Korsakov depict the fantastic and supernatural in his operas? Describe the *whole-tone* and *octatonic* scales and explain why he found them useful.

Other Nations (HWM 709–12, NAWM 131)

42. Name nationalist opera composers active in nations other than Italy, France, Germany, and Russia in the late nineteenth century. Briefly describe what motivated them to write nationalist music and what makes their music nationalist.

Music to Study

NAWM 131: Arthur Sullivan, *The Pirates of Penzance,* operetta (comic opera) (1879), Act II, No. 17, *When the foeman bares his steel*

43. How do Gilbert and Sullivan create humor in *When the foeman bares his steel* (NAWM 131) from their operetta *The Pirates of Penzance*? What does their audience have to know to get the jokes?

44. Point out a few conventions from serious opera that Gilbert and Sullivan refer to in this scene, and for each, provide an example from the NAWM excerpts you have studied so far that illustrates the convention.

45. What other works excerpted in NAWM create comedy in a similar way?

46. Why did so few composers native to the United States compose opera in the nineteenth century?

47. What other kinds of musical theater were popular in the United States?

Music for the Stage and Its Audiences (HWM 713)

48. What works, ideas, and events in the realm of opera in the period 1850–1900 have had the greatest continuing significance?

TERMS TO KNOW

nationalism

verismo

music drama

Gesamtkunstwerk

Leitmotiv, leitmotive

lyric opera

opéra bouffe

cabaret

café-concert

revue

whole-tone scale (or collection)

octatonic scale (or collection)

operetta

vaudeville

NAMES TO KNOW

Giuseppe Verdi

La traviata

Giacomo Puccini

Richard Wagner

Der Ring des Nibelungen

Tristan und Isolde

Georges Bizet

Carmen

Mikhail Glinka

Piotr Il'yich Tchaikovsky

The Mighty Handful

Mily Balakirev

Aleksander Borodin

Modest Musorgsky

Boris Godunov

Nikolay Rimsky-Korsakov

Bedřich Smetana

Antonín Dvořák

W. S. Gilbert

Arthur Sullivan

REVIEW QUESTIONS

1. Add the composers and major works discussed in this chapter to the timeline you made for chapter 24.
2. Describe the operas and operatic styles of the two most famous opera composers of the nineteenth century, Verdi and Wagner. Note similarities and differences between them, and use examples from NAWM to illustrate your points.
3. Explain the difference between nationalism and exoticism in opera, providing examples from NAWM.
4. How did composition and production of opera and other musical theater in the United States differ from Europe? What accounts for these differences?
5. What effect did the break between popular and elite traditions in musical theater have on audiences, composers, and performers in the late nineteenth century? What effect does it have on audiences, composers, and performers today?
6. Review the operas we have studied in NAWM since the 1720s. Choose character types, plot situations, scene structures, and musical styles that you find particularly old-fashioned, humorous (even if the composer did not intend them to be), or unbelievable and draft a scenario (summary) of an operetta scene that satirizes those elements. Then write a short essay explaining why you chose the operas and conventions you did and how you would create comedy from them. Remember to describe both the plot AND the music of your operetta scene.

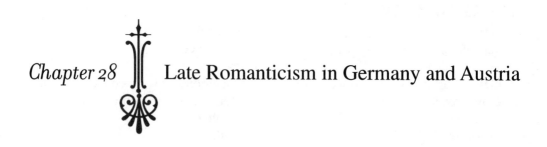

Chapter 28 Late Romanticism in Germany and Austria

CHAPTER OBJECTIVES

After you complete the reading, study of the music, and study questions for this chapter, you should be able to

1. describe the dichotomies composers in Germany and Austria had to address when writing music in the late nineteenth century;

2. identify some of the most important composers in Germany and Austria in the late nineteenth century and suggest what makes each composer individual; and

3. briefly describe one or more characteristic works by each of these composers and explain how it illustrates a balance between the past and the present.

CHAPTER OUTLINE

I. Introduction (HWM 715)

The second half of the nineteenth century saw a widening gulf between classical and popular music, debate and division within German music, and a new importance gained by other national traditions.

II. Dichotomies and Disputes (HWM 715–18)

Music since 1850 is more varied than music of earlier eras.

1. Classical repertoire
By 1850, concert programs increasingly focused on musical classics.

2. Revival of past music
Scholars unearthed and published music of the past, especially from their own nations, issuing editions of complete works and performing editions.

3. Old versus new
Performers and audiences had available to them a variety of old and new music, which satisfied the desire to hear new pieces as well as familiar ones.

4. Brahms versus Wagner
Brahms and Wagner represented two sides of a dispute regarding absolute versus program music, tradition versus innovation, and classical genres and forms versus new ones. Yet partisans on both sides shared common goals and composed *classical music.*

5. Nationalism and internationalism
Nationalism was as strong a force in instrumental music, song, and choral music as it was in opera. It was not an attempt to break free of the Western tradition but a way to join it and become part of the international repertoire.

6. Classical versus popular music
There was a growing gulf between classical and popular music later in the century, and composers tended to specialize in one or the other.

7. Negotiating the fault lines
Composers had to make choices between old and new genres and styles, absolute and program music, nationalist and internationalist elements, and classical and popular music.

III. Johannes Brahms (HWM 718–26, NAWM 132)

Johannes Brahms (1833–1897) used virtually all musical languages of his time and drew heavily on elements from past classics, integrating them into music that appealed to a wide range of listeners.

Biography: Johannes Brahms
Brahms studied piano, cello, and horn as a child, developing a love for past composers as well as for folk and popular music. He was close with Robert and Clara Schumann, who were instrumental in launching his career. Brahms made his living as a concert pianist, conductor, composer, and editor. He was the leading German composer of his time in every field except opera and an important influence on twentieth-century music.

A. Orchestral Works
Brahms felt Beethoven as an almost overwhelming influence and waited to write symphonies until he could create something fresh while following Beethoven's example.

1. Symphonies
Brahms wrote four symphonies.

2. First Symphony
Brahms's First Symphony (1876) fully absorbs Beethoven's influence but also blends in other models and new ideas. His middle movements are often in keys a third away from the main key of the symphony, instead of in the dominant or subdominant.

3. Third Symphony
Brahms often used wide melodic spans, cross-relations, and metric ambiguity, which are illustrated in his Third Symphony (1883).

4. Fourth Symphony

The finale of Brahms's Fourth Symphony (1885) is a chaconne, a set of variations on a bass ostinato adapted from a Bach cantata. By blending elements from the past with the present, Brahms created music that sounds individual.   **Music: NAWM 132**

5. Concertos

Brahms also created a distinctive sound in his concertos, which are symphonic in conception.

B. Chamber Music

As in his symphonies, Brahms blends references to past music with his individual style in his chamber music.

1. Piano Quintet

Throughout all of his work, including his Piano Quintet (1864), Brahms used what Schoenberg called *developing variation,* in which a musical idea is varied to create a string of interrelated but different ideas, producing both unity and variety.

C. Piano Music

Brahms developed a highly individual piano style, marked by broken-chord figuration, cross-rhythms, and melodies doubled in octaves, thirds, or sixths. He wrote three early sonatas (1852–53), then focused on variations. In the 1880s and 1890s, Brahms issued perhaps his greatest contribution to keyboard literature, six collections of intermezzos, rhapsodies, and other short pieces.

D. Songs

Brahms used Schubert as his model for songwriting. In his songs, as in his piano music, Brahms wrote music that is both accessible for amateurs and interesting for the connoisseur.

E. Choral Works

All of Brahms's choral music was composed for amateur performers, yet it appeals to connoisseurs.

1. *A German Requiem*

Ein deutsches Requiem (A German Requiem, 1868) uses Biblical passages rather than the liturgical Requiem text, and combines Baroque procedures with rich Romantic harmonies.

F. Brahms's Place

Brahms, though often called a conservative, was a model for twentieth-century composers in creating new, individual music that drew deeply on the past.

IV. The Wagnerians (HWM 727–35, NAWM 133)

1. The New German School

The "New German School" was a term for composers (including Wagner, Liszt, Berlioz, Anton Bruckner, Hugo Wolf, and Richard Strauss) who believed that music could be linked to the other arts.

A. Liszt

Liszt moved to Weimar in 1848 and focused on composition.

1. Symphonic poems

Liszt composed thirteen *symphonic poems,* programmatic works for orchestra whose content and form were suggested by a person, a story, an artwork, or something else outside music, identified by the title and usually by a program.

2. Thematic transformation

Liszt used *thematic transformation,* a process of transforming a theme or motive into new themes, to provide unity, variety, and narrative-like logic to a composition.

3. Sonata in B Minor

Liszt's Sonata in B Minor (1853) shows his use of thematic transformation with four themes in one extended movement.

4. Choral music

In his choral works, Liszt reinterpreted the past, often deriving melodies from plainchant.

5. Liszt's influence

Liszt's symphonic poems, chromatic harmonies, and thematic transformation influenced other composers.

B. Anton Bruckner

Anton Bruckner (1824–1896) absorbed Wagner's style and ideas into the traditional symphony and wrote church music that united the technical resources of nineteenth-century music with a reverent approach to sacred texts.

1. Symphonies

Bruckner wrote eleven symphonies, none explicitly programmatic.

2. Influences

Bruckner was influenced by Beethoven's Ninth Symphony, Wagner, and his own experience as on organist.

3. Fourth Symphony

Bruckner's Fourth Symphony (1874–80) opens like Beethoven's Ninth, and its continuous development of musical ideas is characteristic of Beethoven and Wagner.

4. Choral music

Bruckner's religious choral music blends modern elements with influences from the Cecilian movement.

C. Hugo Wolf

Hugo Wolf (1860–1903) is best known for adapting Wagner's methods to the German Lied.

1. Lieder

Wolf's 250 Lieder treat the poem as an equal partner to the music, reflecting Wagner's notion of a collective artwork. The musical continuity is often in the piano, while the voice has a speechlike arioso, as in Wagner's operas. The intense chromaticism often means all twelve notes appear in a phrase, an effect later termed *chromatic saturation*.

D. Richard Strauss

Richard Strauss (1864–1949) was a dominant figure in German musical life as a composer and conductor and is remembered for his symphonic poems, operas, and songs.

1. Symphonic poems

Strauss's chief models for program music were Berlioz and Liszt. His symphonic poems cover a broad spectrum from the representational to the philosophical.

2. *Don Juan*

Don Juan (1888–89) is Strauss's first mature work, and most of the piece evokes general moods rather than following a specific plot.

3. *Till Eulenspiegel*

Strauss's *Till Eulenspiegel* (1894–95) is a representational symphonic poem. Like other program music, it uses a program to explain novel musical sounds and forms, yet the music makes sense on its own terms.

4. *Also sprach Zarathustra*

Although the general course of the program for *Also sprach Zarathustra* (1896) is philosophical, moments are directly representational.

5. *Don Quixote*

Strauss used variation form for *Don Quixote* (1897), transforming the beginnings of the two main themes into new melodic characters. **Music: NAWM 133**

V. Reaching the Audience (HWM 735–36)

Each of the composers discussed in this chapter pursued a different path, but all succeeded in reaching an audience and securing a permanent place in the classical repertoire.

STUDY QUESTIONS

Dichotomies and Disputes (HWM 715–18)

1. How did the revival and preservation of past music affect the composition and performance of new classical music in the second half of the nineteenth century? What types and styles of music did composers of the time have at their disposal?

2. Besides the dichotomy between new and older music, what other dichotomies and disputes were significant in music of the time, especially in Germany and Austria?

Johannes Brahms (HWM 718–26, NAWM 132)

3. Briefly summarize Brahms's biography and career. Why was he such a popular composer during his lifetime? How did his life as a composer differ from others you have studied?

4. In what genres did Brahms compose? What were some of the trademarks of his style?

Music to Study

NAWM 132: Johannes Brahms, Symphony No. 4 in E Minor, Op. 98, (1884–85), fourth movement, Allegro energico e passionato

[CD 10|18] [CD 5|52]

5. What elements of or references to past music does Brahms incorporate in the fourth movement of his Symphony No. 4 in E Minor (NAWM 132)?

6. How did Brahms learn about this past music? What composers influenced his musical style?

7. Why would we not mistake this movement for one composed long before Brahms? What does Brahms do with this past material to make it sound like his own style? (Refer to the description of his First and Third Symphonies, chamber music, piano music, and songs in HWM, pp. 720–24, for some of the most common characteristics in Brahms's music.)

8. Who coined the term *developing variation* and applied it to Brahms's music? What is developing variation, and where does it occur in the fourth movement of Brahms's Symphony No. 4?

9. What was Brahms's approach to texture on the piano, and how did it differ from the approaches of Schumann, Chopin, or Liszt?

The Wagnerians (HWM 727–35, NAWM 133)

10. What was "The New German School"? To whom did it refer?

11. What did the New German School composers believe music could and should do? How does this differ from the philosophy of supporters of absolute music as expressed by Eduard Hanslick (see HWM, p. 727)?

12. Liszt composed thirteen symphonic poems. What do these works have in common? When did he compose them? Where was he living, and what else was he doing to earn a living when he composed most of these works?

13. Liszt used thematic transformation in some of his symphonic poems. What is it, and why is it appropriate for this type of composition? How does he use it in *Les Préludes*? How does it reflect Liszt's philosophy of music, as articulated in the excerpt in HWM, p. 727?

14. What are the distinctive features of Bruckner's symphonies? What did he draw from Beethoven? From Wagner?

15. What texts did Hugo Wolf choose for his songs? What was his approach to the relationship of music and poetry?

16. In what ways is the relationship between the voice and accompaniment, melodic style, harmonies, and texture of Wolf's *Lebe wohl*! (shown in Example 28.7 in HWM, p. 732) similar to and different from those elements in Wagner's *Tristan und Isolde* (NAWM 128)?

17. What kinds of program did Richard Strauss use in his symphonic poems? Name and describe one work of each type (other than *Don Quixote*).

Music to Study

NAWM 133: Richard Strauss, *Don Quixote,* Op. 35, symphonic   CD 10|25   CD 5|59
    poem (1897), themes and variations 1–2

18. How does Strauss characterize Don Quixote and Sancho Panza in the themes of his *Don Quixote* (NAWM 133)? What musical devices does he use to depict their personalities?

19. How are these themes treated and varied in the first two variations given in NAWM 133? What does this suggest, in terms of the story? What other musical elements contribute to the story? Why is variation form appropriate to the tale?

20. How does the variation form of NAWM 133 differ from Brahms's use of variation form in the fourth movement of his Symphony No. 4 (NAWM 132)?

21. How does Strauss achieve unity in this symphonic poem when he retains so little of the music from Don Quixote's and Sancho Panza's themes?

Reaching the Audience (HWM 735–36)

22. How did Brahms, Liszt, Bruckner, Wolf, and Strauss create their own individual voices yet also compose music that appealed to an audience?

TERMS TO KNOW

classical music
developing variation
symphonic poems

thematic transformation
chromatic saturation

NAMES TO KNOW

Johannes Brahms
Brahms's Fourth Symphony
Ein deutsches Requiem (A German
    Requiem)
The New German School
Anton Bruckner

Hugo Wolf
Richard Strauss
Don Juan
Till Eulenspiegel
Also sprach Zarathustra
Don Quixote

REVIEW QUESTIONS

1. Add the composers and major works discussed in this chapter to the timeline you made for chapter 24.
2. Stage a debate with your classmates based on the writings in HWM, p. 727, in which one side defends Eduard Hanslick's statements about music and the other supports Liszt's. Start by using examples from NAWM and then explore how their views can be applied to music today, including their impact on composers, performers, audience members, educators, and students.
3. How did Brahms and Strauss respond to the German symphonic tradition? What elements from the past did they continue in their music, what aspects did they further intensify or develop, and what did they introduce that was new and individual?
4. What are some cultural, historical, social, economic, and technological reasons for the dichotomies and debates discussed at the beginning of the chapter? Which of these dichotomies and debates are still present in music today?

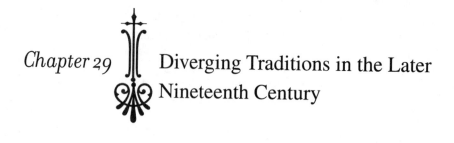

Chapter 29 Diverging Traditions in the Later Nineteenth Century

CHAPTER OBJECTIVES

After you complete the reading, study of the music, and study questions for this chapter, you should be able to

1. name some of the most prominent classical European composers active outside of Germany and Austria in the later nineteenth century, describe some of their music, characterize their styles, and explain their relation to the dichotomy between musical nationalism and internationalism; and

2. explain why the United States had such a diverse musical culture in the later nineteenth century, name some of the most prominent composers active there, and describe their music.

CHAPTER OUTLINE

I. Introduction (HWM 737)

Composers outside of Germany and Austria drew both on the German tradition and on the music of their own nations, increasing the diversity of classical music. Other streams in musical life included entertainment music, popular song, folk music, and utilitarian music.

II. France (HWM 737–41)

1. Concert life in Paris
Concerts in Paris focused on classical symphonic music and on new French works in the same vein.

2. Politics
Concert series, composers, and even musical styles were often associated with political movements.

3. Schools
Music schools reflected a diversity of ideologies and educational concerns, from technical training to the study of history.

452

4. Renewal
   Before the emergence of impressionism in Paris, there was a cosmopolitan tradition and a more specifically French tradition.

B. César Franck
   César Franck (1822–1890) blended traditional counterpoint and classical forms with Liszt's thematic transformation, Wagnerian harmony, and Romantic cyclic unification through thematic return.

1. Keyboard music
   Franck's keyboard music reflects the thematic and harmonic methods of Liszt and Wagner and the organ music of Bach and the French Baroque.

2. Chamber and symphonic music
   Franck's chamber and symphonic works are cyclic and employ thematic transformation.

C. Gabriel Fauré and the French Tradition
   The other tendency in French music drew primarily on earlier French composers from Couperin to Gounod. The refined songs, piano pieces, and chamber works of *Gabriel Fauré* (1845–1924) embody the qualities of the French tradition.

1. Harmony
   Fauré's works are marked by lyrical melodies, lack of virtuosic display, and harmony that does not drive toward a tonic resolution but uses chromaticism to create a sense of repose or even stasis.

III. Eastern and Northern Europe (HWM 741–47)

Some composers from eastern and northern Europe active in the later nineteenth century were able to secure a place in the classical canon.

A. Tchaikovsky
   Tchaikovsky was by far the most successful of these composers, and his works transcended nationalism.

1. Fourth Symphony
   Tchaikovsky's Fourth Symphony (1877–78) has a private program conveyed in the music with a recurring horn motive. The first movement has a key scheme based on a circle of minor thirds, reflecting the interest among Russian composers in equal divisions of the octave.

2. Sixth Symphony
   Tchaikovsky's Sixth Symphony also contains novel musical elements, including a waltz in quintuple time and a closing slow movement.

B. The Mighty Handful
   The instrumental music of the composers known as the Mighty Handful is better known in the West than their operas.

1. Borodin
   Borodin's chamber and orchestral works are characterized by songlike themes, transparent orchestral texture, modally tinged harmonies, and spinning out an entire movement from a single thematic idea.

2. Musorgsky

Musorgsky's principal nonoperatic works are the symphonic fantasy *Night on Bald Mountain* (1867); *Pictures at an Exhibition* (1874), a suite of character pieces for piano; and three song cycles.

3. Rimsky-Korsakov

Rimsky-Korsakov is best known for his programmatic orchestral works, such as the exoticist *Sheherezade* (1888).

C. Bohemia: Smetana and Dvořák

Like the Russians, Smetana and Dvořák are better known outside their native land for their instrumental music than for their operas.

1. Smetana

Smetana sought to create a national music in his String Quartet No. 1, *From My Life* (1876), and in his cycle of six symphonic poems titled *Má Vlast* (My Country, ca. 1872–79).

2. Dvořák

Many of Dvořák's instrumental works are in an international style, but he also wrote pieces that use elements from Czech traditional music. His best-known symphony is No. 9 in E Minor (*From the New World*, 1893), written during his time spent in the United States and drawing elements from the music of American Indians and African Americans.

D. Norway: Edvard Grieg

Edvard Grieg (1843–1907) wrote music that incorporated the modal melodies, harmonies, and dance rhythms of his native Norway, as well as music that was not nationalist.

E. Britain: Edward Elgar

Edward Elgar (1857–1934), the first English composer in more than two hundred years to enjoy wide international recognition, adopted the universal language of the classical tradition.

F. Finding a Niche

Only a few composers outside of Germany and Austria won a broad audience, often by capitalizing on their national identity.

IV. The United States (HWM 747–55, NAWM 134–135)

Musical life in the United States was influenced by its ethnic diversity as well as by the rapidly emerging distinctions between classical, popular, and folk music.

A. The Classical Tradition

1. Immigration and institutions

German musicians who immigrated to the United States played in orchestras, taught music at all levels, and dominated the teaching of composition and theory in conservatories and universities.

2. Theodore Thomas

Theodore Thomas (1835–1905), one of the most famous immigrant musicians, played violin, founded his own orchestra, programmed both classics and lighter music on the same concerts, and was the first conductor of the Chicago Symphony Orchestra.

   3. American composers
   Native-born composers, many of whom studied in Germany, were able to pursue careers that combined composition with performing and teaching. Among the most prominent were George Whitefield Chadwick (1854–1931) and Edward MacDowell (1860–1908), who incorporated American elements in some of their works.

   4. Amy Beach
   Amy Marcy Beach (1867–1944) was internationally recognized as one of America's leading composers. Some of her music had an ethnic flavor, but most of it engaged the traditions of the German classics.   **Music: NAWM 134**

B. Band Music
   Wind and brass bands maintained the mix of serious and popular music that had once been common in orchestra concerts as well.

   1. Spread of bands
   The earliest American bands were attached to military units, but in the nineteenth century amateur local bands became common everywhere.

   2. Professional bands
   The period between the Civil War and World War I was the heyday of professional bands, including the one founded by the most successful bandmaster, *John Philip Sousa* (1854–1932).

   3. Repertory
   The repertory of nineteenth-century bands consisted of marches, dances, arrangements of arias and songs, transcriptions of pieces by classical composers, and virtuosic display pieces.   **Music: NAWM 135**

   4. Marches
   The standard *march* form at midcentury included a brief introduction, two repeated *strains,* a trio, and a da capo repetition of the march up to the trio.

   5. Sousa marches
   In most of his marches, including *The Stars and Stripes Forever,* Sousa preferred a nonrepetitive march form, which created a more dramatic effect.

C. Popular Song
   In the later nineteenth century, there was a widening gulf between *art songs,* which had precisely notated parts and were meant to be appreciated as art, and *popular songs,* which were meant to entertain listeners and amateur performers.

   1. Subjects
   Popular songs were written on a variety of topics and were used for every possible cause.

2. Conventions

Popular songs depend on the interplay of novelty with convention, such as the standard form of verse and refrain. The refrain was sometimes scored in parts and became known as the *chorus*. The key to success was creating a catchy phrase that could be repeated and varied.

3. Tin Pan Alley

Tin Pan Alley was the name for a district in New York City where, beginning in the 1880s, numerous publishers specializing in popular songs were located.

D. Music of African Americans

1. Traits of African-American music

Although African slaves came from many diverse ethnic groups, their music shared many common elements, such as *call and response,* improvisation, syncopation, layered rhythms, and bending pitches.

2. Spirituals

The African-American form of music with the greatest impact in the nineteenth century was the *spiritual*. By the end of the nineteenth century, spirituals were simultaneously folk music, popular songs, and a source for melodic material for classical composers.

V. Reception and Recognition (HWM 755)

By the end of the nineteenth century, the split between classical and popular music had widened and there were numerous competing currents in each tradition. National flavor helped composers gain a niche, and performers, audiences, and critics tended to favor works that brought a distinctive new personality into the tradition. The division between classical and popular streams in the United States is especially interesting because most of the American works from the second half of the nineteenth century that have become permanent classics grew from indigenous popular traditions, rather than as an offshoot of the international classical mainstream.

STUDY QUESTIONS

France (HWM 737–41)

1. Describe concert life and the music schools in Paris in the second half of the nineteenth century. How were they affected by politics? How did they relate to music of the past, and composers of the present?

2. According to HWM, what were the two most significant compositional trends in the later nineteenth century in French music before impressionism? For each trend, name a composer whose music illustrates it and describe his music. What influences did they absorb, and how did they achieve distinctive styles?

Eastern and Northern Europe (HWM 741–47)

3. How did Tchaikovsky approach the symphony? How do his Fourth and Sixth Symphonies compare to the symphonies of Beethoven and Brahms?

4. What did Dvořák suggest composers native to the United States do to write "truly national music"? How are his ideas reflected in his own *New World* Symphony?

5. Name at least three nineteenth-century composers (other than Tchaikovsky and Dvořák) from different countries in eastern and northern Europe, identify a representative instrumental work by each, and explain how each created an individual voice.

Based on these examples, what conclusions can you draw about how composers reached an audience in the late nineteenth century?

The United States (HWM 747–55, NAWM 134–135)

6. Explain the differences between the traditions of classical music, popular music, and folk music, focusing on the roles of notation, composition, and performance in each.

7. What roles did German immigrants play in musical culture in the United States in the second half of the nineteenth century?

8. How was Amy Beach's life and career similar to and different from Clara Schumann's and Fanny Hensel's?

Music to Study

NAWM 134: Amy Marcy Beach, Piano Quintet in F-sharp Minor, 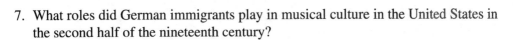 Op. 67, piano quintet (1907), third movement, Allegro agitato

9. How does Beach's approach to form in the third movement of her Piano Quintet (NAWM 134) compare to the approaches of Beethoven (NAWM 108–110), Liszt (NAWM 119), Mendelssohn (NAWM 122), Clara Schumann (NAWM 123), and Brahms (NAWM 132)? What traditional elements does she use, and how does she depart from traditional models?

10. Compare the melodies beginning in measures 13 and 215 of the third movement of Beach's Quintet. What do these melodies have in common? Do other melodies in the third movement have similar characteristics? If so, give measure numbers and explain their relationship to measures 13 and 215.

11. Describe the melodic material and figuration. What elements and characteristics reveal the influence of European composers? What traits suggest other influences or Beach's individual voice?

12. What was the significance of brass and wind bands in the United States? What roles did they serve? Who performed in them?

13. What was the repertory for bands? Describe the typical program of a concert by John Philip Sousa's band.

Music to Study

NAWM 135: John Philip Sousa, *The Stars and Stripes Forever,* CD 10|38
   march (1897)

14. Chart the form of Sousa's march *The Stars and Stripes Forever* (NAWM 135).
   How does it differ from the traditional form of marches before his time? Why did
   he prefer the new form?

15. What elements in *The Stars and Stripes Forever* do you think made the piece so
   popular and appealing to audiences?

16. Why did Sousa publish piano arrangements of his marches? How does the piano
   arrangement of *The Stars and Stripes Forever* differ from the version for band?
   (Hint: Listen to the band performance on the recording while following the piano
   arrangement in NAWM, and note the differences.) What can you conclude about
   the different audiences and functions of marches for band and marches for piano?

17. What were the characteristics of popular song in the United States in the late nineteenth century? What was its purpose? Who was it aimed at? How was it marketed?

18. How is popular song of the late nineteenth century similar to or different from song in the early part of the nineteenth century?

19. According to HWM, what traits of African-American music have been traced back to Africa? (We will return to these in later chapters.)

Reception and Recognition (HWM 755)

20. Describe how European classical music and American classical and popular music from the second half of the nineteenth century has been received over the past century. How do the situations in Europe and the United States differ?

TERMS TO KNOW

march

strain

art song

popular song

Tin Pan Alley

call and response

spiritual

NAMES TO KNOW

César Franck

Gabriel Fauré

Edvard Grieg

Edward Elgar

Amy Beach

John Philip Sousa

REVIEW QUESTIONS

1. Add the composers and major works discussed in this chapter to the timeline you made for chapter 24.

2. Summarize the individual approaches to instrumental music taken by composers working outside of Germany and Austria. What do these composers and their works have in common? How are they different?

3. Compose the melody for a popular song in the style of the late nineteenth century. Try to make it musically and topically appropriate for that time period, and follow the typical form of the time. Make a list of the stylistic traits you are trying to emulate. What does this style have in common with popular song today? (Alternatively, compose the melody for one strain of a march, using Sousa's *The Stars and Stripes Forever* as a model, and answer the same questions.)

4. Write two letters to a family member or friend, telling them about the musical culture around you in the second half of the nineteenth century. Write one from the point of view of a performance major who loves classical music and studies at a conservatory in New York City and the other from the point of view of a music lover and amateur performer working full time in business or a trade in a smaller city or town. What opportunities allow you to participate in music as a composer, performer, or listener? How does this compare with your own experiences in the early twenty-first century?

Chapter 3o The Early Twentieth Century

CHAPTER OBJECTIVES

After you complete the reading, study of the music, and study questions for this chapter, you should be able to

1. identify some of the factors that led to a diversity of musical style and technique in the twentieth century that was greater than in any previous era;

2. list the different types of vernacular music popular in the early twentieth century and name some of the most prominent composers and performers active in each tradition, characterize their styles, and describe some of their music;

3. name some of the most prominent composers of the first modern generation in the classical tradition, characterize their styles, describe some of their music, and note the ways in which their music reflects national identity and their own individual voices; and

4. describe the avant-garde movement in the early twentieth century, some characteristic works, and how the avant-garde differs from other trends of the time.

CHAPTER OUTLINE

I. Introduction (HWM 758)

The early twentieth century was a time of rapid change in technology, society, and the arts, and music became increasingly diverse in style and approach.

II. Modern Times, 1898–1918 (HWM 758–64)

The rapid pace of change in the early twentieth century prompted both an optimistic sense of progress and nostalgia for a simpler past.

1. New technologies
Of crucial importance for music was electrification, which offered new technologies for reproducing music and a new form of entertainment with musical accompaniment: movies.

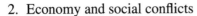

2. Economy and social conflicts
   The growth of industry fostered an expanding economy, which had both positive and negative social consequences.

3. United States
   In the early twentieth century, the United States became a world power. The influx of European immigrants and African Americans from the south into cities in the north had a profound impact on music.

4. New views on the human mind
   Theories on the sources of human behavior and how to control it played a strong role in literature and the other arts.

5. The arts
   Artists increasingly regarded their work as an end in itself to be appreciated for its own sake, seeking novel content and techniques and measuring their success not by wide popular appeal but by the esteem of intellectuals and fellow artists. The symbolist poets used intense imagery and disrupted syntax to suggest events and feelings rather than describing them.

6. From impressionism to cubism
   In most of the new artistic movements, including impressionism, cubism, and expressionism, artists no longer placed a high value on beauty or on pleasing the viewer. Instead, they valued originality and substance, demanding that the viewer work to understand and interpret the image.

7. Effects on music
   All of the trends mentioned above had an effect on musical culture.

Innovations: Recorded Sound and Its Impact
   Recording technology had the most significant impact on musical culture of any innovation since the printing press. In 1877, Thomas Edison made the first sound recording with his mechanical phonograph, which he later modified with wax cylinders and a motor. In 1887, Emile Berliner recorded on a flat disc, which simplified the duplication process. The technology was not well suited for orchestral music, but early discs featured famous singers who achieved for the first time the kind of immortality only composers had experienced. In the 1920s, new electrical methods of recording and reproduction increased sales and competition. Companies continued to develop new improvements, including the LP (1946), magnetic tape (1950s), and the CD (1983). The development of recordings irrevocably altered the way we listen to music and exposed composers (and others) to musical styles and ideas outside their ordinary experiences

III. Vernacular Musical Traditions (HWM 765–70, NAWM 136)

The impact of prosperity and technology on music, and the growing importance of the United States, are apparent in vernacular music.

A. Popular Song and Stage Music
   Popular song was performed, published, sold, and heard more than any other genre of music.

1. Operettas and revues
   Many of the best-known popular songs came from stage shows, including revues and operettas.
2. Musicals
   The *musical,* a type of stage show featuring songs and dance numbers, was established in London in the 1890s and found a home on Broadway in New York, where George M. Cohan (1878–1942) set the pattern for the American musical.

B. Music for Silent Films
   Before the 1920s, the music accompanying silent films was played live by a pianist, an organist, or an instrumental ensemble.
1. Cue sheets and film scores
   Film music ranged from cue sheets for live musicians to the film score, music composed to accompany one particular film.

C. Band Music
   The tradition of military and amateur wind bands remained strong across Europe and North America.
1. Concert repertoire
   The twentieth century saw a growing effort to establish a repertoire of serious classical works for band worthy of comparison to the orchestral repertoire.
2. African-American bands
   Brass bands, black churches, and dance orchestras were among the main training grounds for African-American musicians.

D. Ragtime
   Ragtime, featuring syncopated rhythm over a regular, marchlike bass, was a style popular from the 1890s through the 1920s.
1. Cakewalk, rags, and ragtime songs
   In the late nineteenth and early twentieth centuries, ragtime encompassed piano music, ensemble music, and songs, including the cakewalk, instrumental pieces called *rags,* and songs in ragtime rhythms.
2. Scott Joplin
   The leading ragtime composer was *Scott Joplin* (1867–1917), best known for his piano rags. A typical rag, such as Joplin's *Maple Leaf Rag* (1899), uses march form in duple meter and presents a syncopated melody over a steady bass.   **Music: NAWM 136a**

E. Early Jazz
   The 1910s saw the early development of *jazz.*
1. New Orleans
   The dance bands of New Orleans interwove musical styles from Haitian, Cuban, and Creole music with African traditions and European styles, gradually producing a new kind of music, later known as jazz.
2. Manner of performance
   Jazz players extemporized arrangements that distinguished one performer or performance from another. Jazz style is marked by anticipated

beats, swinging rhythms, and other features, as in the playing of *Jelly Roll Morton* (1890–1941).   **Music: NAWM 136b**

F. Classics of Vernacular Music
Many vernacular pieces became classics in their own traditions.

IV. Modern Music in the Classical Tradition (HWM 770–71)

Musicians and audiences in the early 1900s expected that most concert music they performed or heard would be at least a generation old, and they judged new music by the standards of the classics. In competing with past composers, living composers sought to secure a place for themselves by offering something new and distinctive while continuing the tradition. Composers were expected to write music that was true to their national identity and drew from regional traditions yet spoke to an international audience. The result was music of tremendous variety.

V. Germany and Austria (HWM 771–80, NAWM 137)

German-speaking composers found ways to intensify elements from their heritage and create music at once familiar and new.

A. Gustav Mahler
Gustav Mahler (1860–1911) was the leading Austro-German composer of symphonies after Brahms and Bruckner and one of the great masters of the song for voice and orchestra. He made a living as a conductor, directing the Vienna Opera and New York Philharmonic.

1. Songs in the symphonies
Mahler used voices in four of his symphonies and sometimes incorporated melodies from his own songs.

2. Symphony as world
Mahler's symphonies often convey a sense of life experience, as if telling a story or depicting a scene through a variety of musical topics.

3. Instrumentation and sound
Mahler's works typically require an enormous number of performers that he combines in imaginative ways, producing a vast palette of sounds and effects from gigantic to delicate.

4. Programmatic content
Mahler's symphonies often imply a program.

5. Fourth Symphony
Mahler's Fourth Symphony is typical in featuring strong contrasts between and within movements. In the first movement, Mahler interweaves classical references, Romantic fantasy, and modern style, sometimes ironically, to create a musical metaphor for contradictions of modern life.

6. *Kindertotenlieder*
The irony of *Nun will die Sonn' so hell aufgeh'n* from *Kindertotenlieder* (Songs on the Death of Children, 1901–4) is heightened by an understated restraint and at times by an emotional mismatch between text and music.   **Music: NAWM 137**

7. *Das Lied von der Erde*

Das Lied von der Erde (The Song of the Earth, 1908) is a song cycle for tenor and alto soloists with orchestra that alternates between the frenzied activity of life and sad resignation at having to part from it.

B. Strauss Operas

After his success with symphonic poems, Richard Strauss turned to opera, using leitmotives and associating certain keys with particular characters.

1. *Salome*

To dramatize the strange subject, actions, and emotions of *Salome,* Strauss heightened the polarities inherent in tonal music between dissonance and consonance, tension and resolution. The harmonically complex and dissonant music in this opera inspired some later composers to abandon tonality altogether.

2. *Elektra*

In *Elektra* (1906–8), Strauss again combined intensified chromaticism, dissonance, and tonal instability with diatonic and tonally stable passages.

3. *Der Rosenkavalier*

In *Der Rosenkavalier* (The Cavalier of the Rose, 1909–10), set in eighteenth-century Vienna, simple diatonic music dominates and chromaticism suggests enchantment.

4. Style and rhetoric

Strauss used a wide range of styles and effects to engage the audience's emotions directly.

VI. Claude Debussy (HWM 780–85, NAWM 138)

Claude Debussy (1862–1918) blended influences from Wagner, French tradition, Russian composers, medieval music, music from Asia, and elsewhere to create strikingly individual works that had an impact on almost all later composers.

1. Impressionism and symbolism

Debussy's music is often called impressionist, but it is closer to symbolism.

Biography: Claude Debussy

Debussy began studying at the Paris Conservatoire at the age of ten. He was influenced by works of Russian composers and Wagner as well as by new artistic movements in Paris. By 1908, he was France's leading modern composer, making his living as a music critic and through an income from his publisher. Debussy exercised an enormous influence on his contemporaries and later generations.

A. Piano Music

Symbolist traits are evident in Debussy's piano music. Each motive is associated with a texture, harmony, scale, dynamic level, and range, creating a succession of distinct musical images. Debussy usually maintained a tonal focus but emphasized the pleasure of sound rather than conventional resolution. Many of Debussy's piano pieces have evocative titles.

B. Orchestral Music

Debussy's orchestral works require a large ensemble, which he used to offer a variety of tone colors and textures. His best-known orchestral works are *Prélude à "L'après-midi d'un faune"* (Prelude to "The Afternoon of a Faun," 1891–94), *Nocturnes* (1897–99), and *La Mer* (The Sea, 1903–5).

1. *Nuages*

Nuages from *Nocturnes* exemplifies the interaction of motive with timbre, scale type, and other elements.   **Music: NAWM 138**

C. Songs and Stage Music

Debussy composed songs to texts by several major French poets, as well as music for dramatic projects, including ballet and one opera, *Pelléas et Mélisande* (1893–1902).

D. Debussy's Influence

The changes that Debussy introduced in harmony and orchestration and his emphasis on sound itself made him one of the most influential composers in the history of music.

VII. The First Modern Generation (HWM 785–95, NAWM 139–140)

A number of other major composers from nations across Europe combined tradition and innovation, national identity and personal style.

A. France: Ravel

The music of *Maurice Ravel* (1875–1937) encompasses a variety of influences while carrying a distinctive stamp.

1. Distinctive traits

Unlike Debussy, Ravel usually treated colorful harmonies as dissonances needing resolution, and he attached major sevenths to tonic and subdominant chords.

2. Varied influences

Ravel also absorbed ideas from older French music, the Classic tradition, Viennese waltz, Gypsy style, blues, and Spanish idioms to create a diverse set of original works.

B. Spain: Falla

Spanish composer *Manuel de Falla* (1876–1946) combined specific national elements with the neoclassic approach popular after World War I to produce music that is both nationalist and more broadly modern.

C. England: Vaughan Williams and Holst

After centuries of domination by foreign styles, English composers in the early twentieth century sought a distinctive voice for English art music, often drawing on folk songs.

1. Gustav Holst

Gustav Holst (1874–1934) was influenced by English song and Hindu sacred texts, but is best known for a non-nationalist work, *The Planets* (1914–16).

2. Ralph Vaughan Williams
Ralph Vaughan Williams (1872–1958) was more national in style than Holst, drawing inspiration from folk song, English hymnody, and earlier English composers. Like several modern English composers, he wrote both art music and utilitarian music, using elements from each tradition in the other.

D. Czech Nationalism: Janáček
Leoš Janáček (1854–1928), the leading twentieth-century Czech composer, created a specifically national style through a distinctive melodic idiom based on peasant speech and song and through procedures more similar to Musorgsky's or Debussy's than to Germanic tradition. His operas dominated the Czech stage between the world wars and later became part of the international repertoire.

E. Finland: Sibelius
In the 1890s, *Jean Sibelius* (1865–1957) established his reputation as Finland's leading composer through symphonic poems on Finnish topics, then wrote seven symphonies and the Violin Concerto for an international audience. He created a distinctive sound marked by modal melodies, simple rhythms, repetition, ostinatos, pedal points, and strong contrasts.

1. Form
Sibelius reworked sonata form in novel ways and used formal devices such as "rotational form" and "teleological genesis." His music was popular in Finland, Britain, and the United States, but his continued use of diatonic melodies and tonality hurt his reputation on the Continent, and he stopped composing by the late 1920s.

F. Russia: Rachmaninov and Scriabin
The works of Rachmaninov and Scriabin illustrate the wide variety of personal styles in this period.

1. Sergei Rachmaninov
Sergei Rachmaninov (1873–1943), a virtuoso pianist, is best known for his piano music. His music retains elements from the Romantic tradition.

2. Prelude in G Minor
Rachmaninov's Prelude in G Minor (1903) illustrates his ability to create innovative textures and individual melodies within traditional harmonies and ABA' form.   **Music: NAWM 139**

3. Alexander Scriabin
Alexander Scriabin (1872–1915) began by writing in the manner of Chopin and gradually evolved an innovative harmonic vocabulary in which a complex chord serves as a kind of tonic.

4. *Vers la flamme*
Scriabin's unique harmonic process is illustrated in the tone poem for piano, *Vers la flamme* (Toward the Flame), Op. 72.   **Music: NAWM 140**

G. Tonal and Post-tonal Music
Strauss, Ravel, Vaughan Williams, Rachmaninov, and other composers active through the 1930s and later wrote tonal music. Others, including

Debussy, Falla, Janáček, and Scriabin, wrote in *post-tonal* idioms that moved beyond common practice tonality.

VIII. The Avant-Garde (HWM 795–99)

While some composers were developing new sounds within the classical tradition, others challenged the very notion of classics and sought to focus on the present, creating the *avant-garde* movement.

A. Erik Satie

Erik Satie (1866–1925) used wit in his music to upend convention. His early piano pieces challenged Romantic pretension through deliberate plainness and modal, nonfunctional harmony

1. Piano works

Between 1900 and 1915, Satie wrote several sets of piano pieces that satirize classical traditions through surreal titles, parodistic music, and satirical commentary printed in the score.

2. Larger works

Satie's larger works, such as his ballet *Parade* (1916–17), question the listener's expectations and fix our attention on the present. His antisentimental spirit influenced later avant-garde composers.

B. Futurism

The Italian *futurists* favored machines and noise over traditional instruments and pitches. Like Satie, they focused on the experience of listening in the present moment and rejected the music and aesthetics of the past.

IX. Late Romantic or Modern? (HWM 799)

The music of the early twentieth century was remarkably diverse, and its reception has varied. Most vernacular music of the time quickly fell out of fashion, but some popular songs and band works endured, and some traditions, like ragtime, have been revived. All the classical composers of this generation combined nineteenth-century elements with twentieth-century sensibilities, which has made some of their music very popular. While some music by these composers may sound late Romantic in spirit or technique, all of it is modern in its overwhelming sense of measuring itself against the past.

STUDY QUESTIONS

Modern Times, 1898–1918 (HWM 758–64)

1. How did the roles of composer, performer, and listener in early-twentieth century musical culture differ from the early nineteenth century? What developments initiated those changes? What role did technology play?

2. Name some of the significant movements in art and poetry in the early twentieth century. What new ideals did they hold for art?

Vernacular Musical Traditions (HWM 765–70, NAWM 136)

3. Describe the musical comedy, or *musical*. How does it compare to opera and operetta?

4. What roles did music serve in the silent film era? Who provided music for film?

5. What impact did opera and operetta have on film music in the early twentieth century? How does this compare with the impact opera and operetta had on symphonic music in the eighteenth and the nineteenth century?

6. What was the significance of brass and wind bands for women and African Americans in the early twentieth century?

7. What problem did some bandleaders see with the band repertoire, and what was the response?

Music to Study

NAWM 136: Scott Joplin, *Maple Leaf Rag,* piano rag (1899)

    136a. Performed by Scott Joplin (piano roll)   CD 10|43

    136b. Performed by Jelly Roll Morton (1938 recording)   CD 10|47

8. What is *ragtime*? From what traditions did it derive? How is Scott Joplin's *Maple Leaf Rag* (NAWM 136) typical of the style?

9. What style characteristics of Scott Joplin's *Maple Leaf Rag* reflect its original function as dance? How does it compare in form and style to a march by Sousa (see NAWM 135)?

10. Compare the performances of *Maple Leaf Rag* by Scott Joplin and Jelly Roll Morton. How do they differ? In what ways is Joplin's performance typical of the ragtime tradition, and Morton's typical of early jazz?

Modern Music in the Classical Tradition (HWM 770–71)

11. Why was there such a great variety of music in the classical tradition in the early twentieth century? What problems did composers face, and how did they seek a solution?

Germany and Austria (HWM 771–80, NAWM 137)

12. How did Gustav Mahler earn a living as a musician? To what genres and styles of music was he exposed?

13. Describe the characteristics of Mahler's symphonies that distinguish them from earlier symphonies by other composers. How are these characteristics exemplified in the Fourth Symphony, as excerpted and discussed in HWM, pp. 774–75? How does Mahler use the symphony to, as he said, "construct a world"?

Music to Study

NAWM 137: Gustav Mahler, *Kindertotenlieder,* orchestral song cycle (1901), No. 1, *Nun will die Sonn' so hell aufgeh'n*

[CD 10|51] [CD 5|65]

14. How does Mahler suggest the loneliness and sadness of a parent grieving the death of a child in *Nun will der Sonn' so hell aufgeh'n* (NAWM 137)? Consider melody, harmony, counterpoint, and instrumentation in your answer.

15. How does Mahler achieve a sense of irony in this song? When the protagonist utters the final line, "Hail to the joy-light of the world!" what in the music indicates that this is ironic rather than sincere?

16. How is Mahler's use of the orchestra in this song similar to or different from Wagner's use of the orchestra in the excerpt from *Tristan und Isolde* (NAWM 128)?

17. Based on the descriptions of Strauss's *Salome* (1905) and *Der Rosenkavalier* (1909–10) in HWM (pp. 777–80), what is distinctive about each of these operas? What do they have in common with Strauss's orchestral music?

18. How did Strauss achieve a high level of dissonance in *Salome* without abandoning tonality?

Claude Debussy (HWM 780–85, NAWM 138)

19. Briefly describe Claude Debussy's life and career and the significant influences on his music.

Music to Study

NAWM 138: Claude Debussy, *Nocturnes,* symphonic poem (1897–99), No. 1: *Nuages* (Clouds)

[CD 10|59] [CD 5|73]

20. How does Debussy's treatment of the English-horn motive in *Nuages* (NAWM 138) differ from motivic development as practiced in the nineteenth century? If motivic development suggests a drama or story, with the motives as characters, in what ways is *Nuages* almost visual rather than dramatic? How is this like symbolist poetry?

21. How does Debussy's treatment of harmony differ from linear progressions of tension and resolution characteristic of most nineteenth-century music? Give specific examples from *Nuages* that illustrate your points.

22. If the form is ABA', what is the relationship of the final A' (mm. 80–102) to the first A section (mm. 1–63)?

23. How does Debussy use the orchestra in *Nuages*? How is this similar to or different from Wagner, Mahler, and Strauss? •

24. Why is Debussy's treatment of motives, harmony, form, and use of orchestra described above appropriate for evoking the image of clouds in this symphonic poem? How are the clouds evoked, and what happens to them during the piece?

25. How is the concept and the technique of the symphonic poem *Nuages* different from the concept and the technique of the symphonic poem *Don Quixote* (NAWM 138)?

The First Modern Generation (HWM 785–95, NAWM 139–140)

26. How and why did the following composers use national styles and idioms in their music? For each, how was his approach to national material similar to or different from how and why composers used national styles and idioms in the middle of the nineteenth century? In what ways did each transcend nationalism and seek an international modern idiom?

Maurice Ravel

Manuel de Falla

Ralph Vaughan Williams

Leoš Janáček

Jean Sibelius

Music to Study

NAWM 139: Sergei Rachmaninov, Prelude in G Minor, Op. 23, `CD 10|67`
No. 5 (1901), piano prelude

NAWM 140: Alexander Scriabin, *Vers la flamme,* Op. 72 (1914), `CD 10|72`
tone poem for piano

27. How does Rachmaninov's treatment of harmony in his Prelude in G Minor (NAWM 139) compare with Debussy's in *Nuages* (NAWM 138)?

28. What aspects of this prelude make it an appropriate piece for a touring virtuoso pianist? What does it have in common stylistically with Liszt's *Un sospiro* (NAWM 119)?

29. *Vers la flamme* (NAWM 140) is not tonal in a traditional sense. What kinds of chords does Scriabin use? How does he create a sense of tonal motion? What chord progressions (or root progressions) does he use most often? How does this compare with Rachmaninov? With Debussy?

30. What is the relationship between the opening passage of the piece and the closing passage (mm. 107–37) in terms of theme, rhythm, and harmony? How is a sense achieved of ending on a kind of tonic chord?

31. Describe the rhythm of this piece. Does it suggest a strong forward motion, or a static hovering? How is the effect achieved?

32. What is *post-tonal* music? Of the composers surveyed in this chapter, which wrote post-tonal music? Which of the pieces in NAWM 136–140, if any, would you describe as post-tonal, and why?

The Avant-Garde (HWM 795–99)

33. When and where did the *avant-garde* movement in art first appear? What were its aesthetic goals?

34. What is avant-garde about Erik Satie's music? Name and describe two pieces that best illustrate your points.

35. What do the Italian *futurists* have in common with Satie? How do they differ?

Late Romantic or Modern? (HWM 799)

36. What do all the classical composers discussed in this chapter have in common? What makes their music modern rather than late Romantic?

TERMS TO KNOW

musical
ragtime
rag
jazz

post-tonal
avant-garde
futurists, futurism

NAMES TO KNOW

Scott Joplin
Jelly Roll Morton
Gustav Mahler
Kindertotenlieder
Salome
Elektra
Der Rosenkavalier
Claude Debussy
Nocturnes

Maurice Ravel
Manuel de Falla
Gustav Holst
Ralph Vaughan Williams
Leoš Janáček
Jean Sibelius
Sergei Rachmaninov
Alexander Scriabin
Erik Satie

REVIEW QUESTIONS

1. Make a new timeline for the twentieth century and place on it the composers and major works from the vernacular and classical traditions discussed in this chapter.

2. Scott Joplin's piano rags were stylized dances; they were intended for performance and not for actual dancing. For him, the border between popular and classical traditions was not very wide. In the past few decades, some classical pieces (including the first movement of Beethoven's Fifth Symphony) have been remixed and sold as party music. What does a composition need in order to make the change to a different function—for example, from a popular setting to a classical, or concert, setting? What is the purpose of doing this? Who benefits from it? What are those benefits?

3. Write an essay tracing the developments and manifestations of nationalism from the middle of the nineteenth century through the early twentieth century. In your essay, include composers, compositions, dates, and other historical figures. How did issues of and approaches to nationalism differ from nation to nation and composer to composer?

4. What elements of the nineteenth-century musical tradition did Mahler, Debussy, Rachmaninov, and Scriabin continue in their music; what aspects did they further intensify or develop; and what did they introduce that was new and individual?

5. Beethoven's music conveys a sense of drama and forward motion toward a goal, as in the first movement of his *Eroica* Symphony (NAWM 109). Some of the music studied in this chapter conveys a different sense of harmonic and rhythmic stasis, or of movement, that is not directed toward a goal. Compare the works you have studied by Debussy and Scriabin (NAWM 138 and 140) with Beethoven. and with each other, in order to show what musical techniques these later composers use to avoid tension, negate forward momentum, and create a musical experience of being present in the moment, rather than striving toward a goal.

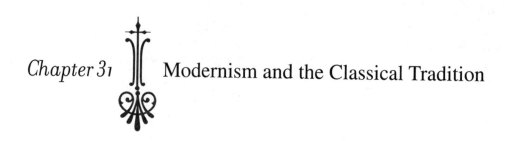

Chapter 31 — Modernism and the Classical Tradition

CHAPTER OBJECTIVES

After you complete the reading, study of the music, and study questions for this chapter, you should be able to

1. summarize the careers and describe the music of Arnold Schoenberg, Alban Berg, Anton Webern, Igor Stravinsky, Béla Bartók, and Charles Ives; and

2. describe the connections between modernism and the classical tradition in representative works by these composers.

CHAPTER OUTLINE

I. Introduction (HWM 801–2)

Modern composers in the classical tradition all faced a common challenge of writing new works deemed worthy of performance alongside classics. Beginning shortly before World War I, *modernists* broke radically from the musical language of the past while maintaining strong links to tradition. Arnold Schoenberg, Alban Berg, Anton Webern, Igor Stravinsky, Béla Bartók, and Charles Ives wrote tonal music in late Romantic styles and then devised new and distinctive post-tonal idioms that won them a central place in the world of modern music.

II. Arnold Schoenberg (HWM 802–14, NAWM 141–142)

Arnold Schoenberg (1874–1951) moved beyond tonality to atonality and then to the twelve-tone method.

Biography: Arnold Schoenberg

Schoenberg was born in Vienna, where he studied violin as a boy and received minimal instruction in theory and composition. After moving to Berlin, where he worked at a cabaret and taught composition, he returned to Vienna, where he taught Alban Berg and Anton Webern and was acquainted with expressionist painters. Schoenberg formulated the twelve-tone method in the 1920s. After the Nazis came to power, he emigrated to the United States, where he taught at UCLA. Schoenberg was one of the most influential composers of the twentieth century.

A. Tonal Works
Schoenberg began by writing tonal music in the late Romantic style.

  1. Developing variation
  After turning toward chamber music, Schoenberg applied the principle of *developing variation* to his own works.

  2. Nonrepetition
  Schoenberg believed in the principle of nonrepetition between and within pieces. He sought not to repeat the past but to build on it.

B. Atonal Music
Schoenberg's experimentation in novel harmonic progressions led him to what he called the emancipation of dissonance, since dissonances were freed of the need to resolve to consonance, and in 1908, he began to compose pieces that others called *atonal*.

  1. Coherence in atonal music
  To organize atonal music, Schoenberg relied on developing variation, the integration of harmony and melody, and chromatic saturation, as well as gestures from tonal music.

  2. Pitch-class sets
  Schoenberg generated the melodies and harmonies for a composition from a *set,* or *pitch-class set*.

  3. Chromatic saturation
  Atonal music can also be shaped through *chromatic saturation,* the appearance of all twelve pitch-classes within a segment of music.

  4. Atonal works
  Schoenberg's one-character opera *Erwartung* (1909) exemplifies *expressionism,* which portrayed extreme emotions through dissonances and exaggerated gestures, and pushed nonrepetition to an extreme.

  5. Return to form
  After *Erwartung,* Schoenberg turned back to motives, themes, and long-range repetition, evoking traditional forms and the functions of tonality in new ways.

  6. *Pierrot Lunaire*
  Schoenberg's *Pierrot lunaire* (Moonstruck Pierrot, 1912), a song cycle for woman's voice and chamber ensemble, has expressionist features (such as *Sprechstimme*) while using many traditional elements.   **Music: NAWM 141**

Music in Context: Expressionism
In the late 1800s, some German and Austrian painters embraced expressionism, which developed from the subjectivity of Romanticism. Expressionist painters aspired to convey the inner experience, representing real objects in grossly distorted ways and using intense color and dynamic

brushstrokes. Schoenberg and Berg, two leading exponents of expressionism in music, deployed angular melodies, fragmented rhythms, and discordant harmonies to convey extreme and irrational states of mind.

C. Twelve-Tone Method

Schoenberg developed the *twelve-tone method* to lend formal coherence to atonal music without text.

1. The method

The basis of twelve-tone composition is a *row* or *series* that can be used in its original, or *prime,* form but also in *inversion,* in *retrograde* order, and in *retrograde inversion.*

2. Sets, saturation, and structure

Twelve-tone music combined developing variation with the systematic use of sets and chromatic saturation. In his twelve-tone compositions, Schoenberg presented and developed motives and themes, using tonal forms and genres of Classic and Romantic music, but twelve-tone rows stand in for the keys.

3. Piano Suite

Schoenberg's Piano Suite illustrates some of his methods, such as the division of the row into segments (here, three *tetrachords* or groups of four notes) that are used as sets; analogies between rows and keys; and references to tonal music.   **Music: NAWM 142**

4. Twelve-tone regions and modulation

In many works, Schoenberg designed the row so that its two *hexachords* (six-note segments) are shared with an inverted form (in a different order). He then treated each transposition of the prime form, its related inversion, and retrogrades as a tonal region analogous to a key.

D. Late Tonal Works

Some of Schoenberg's works from the 1930s and 1940s are tonal, including "recompositions" of eighteenth-century music.

E. Schoenberg as Modernist

The problems Schoenberg addressed as a modernist and the way he faced them did much to shape musical practice in the twentieth century.

1. The Second Viennese School

Schoenberg and his students Alban Berg and Anton Webern are known as the Second Viennese School.

III. Alban Berg (HWM 814–16, NAWM 143)

Alban Berg (1885–1935) adopted Schoenberg's atonal and twelve-tone methods but achieved greater popular success by infusing his music with the familiar forms, expressive gestures, and characteristic styles of tonal music.

1. *Wozzeck*

Wozzeck (1917–21) is an atonal, expressionist opera in three acts of continuous music with each act linked by orchestral interludes. Berg highlights the drama and organizes the music through the use of leitmotives, pitch-class sets identified with the main characters, and traditional forms. The use of tonal effects and familiar types of music helped him to convey strong emotions in a language listeners could understand. **Music: NAWM 143**

2. Twelve-tone works

   In his twelve-tone works, Berg often chose rows that allowed for tonal-sounding chords and chord progressions.

3. Violin Concerto

   Berg designed the row of the Violin Concerto (1935) with four interlocking minor and major triads, which gives this twelve-tone work a familiar sound.

IV. Anton Webern (HWM 816–19, NAWM 144)

Anton Webern (1883–1945) was trained as a musicologist and absorbed ideas about music history that influenced his development as a composer.

1. View of music history

   Webern believed that twelve-tone music was the inevitable result of music's evolution throughout history.

2. Works and style

   Webern also passed through the stages of late Romantic chromaticism, atonality, and twelve-tone organization. He sought to write deeply expressive music, yet his music is extremely concentrated. His works are usually brief, spare in texture, often canonic, and without tonal references.

3. Symphony, Op. 21

   The first movement of Webern's Symphony, Op. 21 (NAWM 144), illustrates Webern's use of twelve-tone procedures, canons, instrumentation, form, and *Klangfarbenmelodie*. In this movement, he integrates twelve-tone concepts with Classical formal principles and procedures from Renaissance polyphony.

4. Influence

   Webern has never gained wide popularity, but his reputation and his influence on other composers grew steadily after World War II.

V. Igor Stravinsky (HWM 819–29, NAWM 145–146)

Igor Stravinsky (1882–1971) started as a Russian nationalist and became a cosmopolitan, and through his music, elements of Russian music became part of a common international modernist practice.

Biography: Igor Stravinsky

Stravinsky was raised in St. Petersburg and studied composition privately with Rimsky-Korsakov. In the early 1910s, Sergei Diaghilev commissioned him to write ballets for the Ballets Russes (Russian Ballet) in Paris, which made Stravinsky famous. After World War I, he composed in the neoclassical idiom that would characterize his music for thirty years. After the outbreak of World War II, he moved to the United States, settling in Hollywood. Most of his late works are serial and many are religious. Stravinsky wrote some of the most successful music of the twentieth century and influenced three generations of composers.

A. Russian Period

Stravinsky's most popular works are three ballets from early in his career, composed for the Ballets Russes.

1. *The Firebird*

   The Firebird (1910) stems from Russian nationalism and from Rimsky-Korsakov's exoticism.

2. *Petrushka*

   Some of Stravinsky's distinctive stylistic traits emerge in *Petrushka* (1910–11), including repetitive melodies and rhythms over static harmony; blocks of sound that interrupt and alternate with each other without transitions; and sharp dissonances that are often octatonic or derived from superimposed triads. Stravinsky evokes a carnival atmosphere by borrowing and elaborating Russian folk tunes and Viennese waltzes.

3. *The Rite of Spring*

   In *The Rite of Spring*, Stravinsky borrowed folk melodies, placing them in a primitivist context that caused a riot at the premiere.

4. Stravinsky trademarks

   The typical characteristics of Stravinsky's mature idiom can be heard in *The Rite of Spring*.   **Music: NAWM 145**

5. Undermining meter

   Stravinsky reduced meter to pulse through unpredictable accents and silences and rapidly changing meters, which helped to convey a sense of primitivism in *The Rite of Spring*.

6. Ostinatos and juxtaposed blocks

   Stravinsky uses ostinatos to create static blocks of sound, which he juxtaposes.

7. Layering

   He frequently layers two or more independent strands of music on top of each other.

8. Discontinuity and connection

   Stravinsky plays off the obvious surface discontinuities of his music with subtle connections between blocks of sound.

9. Dissonance

   Most of the dissonance used in Stravinsky's music is based on scales from Russian classical music, including diatonic and octatonic scales.

10. Timbre linked with motive and variation

    Stravinsky often identified a musical idea with a particular timbre, or used changes of timbre to provide variety.

11. Stark timbres

    Stravinsky preferred dry rather than lush or resonant timbres.

12. Small-ensemble works
   Having developed these techniques and stylistic trademarks, Stravinsky used them throughout his career. During World War I, Stravinsky turned towards small combinations of instruments to accompany stage works.

B. Neoclassical Period
   In his ballet *Pulcinella* (1919), Stravinsky applied the methods distilled in *The Rite of Spring* to arrangements of eighteenth-century pieces by Pergolesi and others.

   1. Neoclassicism defined
   This marked his turn to *neoclassicism,* a broad movement from the 1910s to the 1950s in which composers revived, imitated, or evoked the styles, genres, and forms of eighteenth-century music.

   2. Uses of neoclassicism
   Neoclassicism allowed Stravinsky to use the tools he had developed in his Russian period while claiming a place in the classical tradition of the West. Stravinsky's neoclassical music adopts an anti-Romantic tone, reflecting a preference for balance, objectivity, and absolute music.

   3. *Symphony of Psalms*
   Stravinsky's neoclassicism and its continuity with his earlier style are both evident in his *Symphony of Psalms* (1930).   **Music: NAWM 146**

   4. Neotonality
   Symphony of Psalms is *neotonal,* using reiteration or other means to establish a tonal center, rather than traditional functional harmony.

   5. Schoenberg and Stravinsky
   Both Schoenberg and Stravinsky sought to revitalize traditional forms in an entirely new musical language.

C. Serial Period
   From about 1953 on, Stravinsky adapted techniques from *serial music* (an extension of twelve-tone methods) to his characteristic idiom. His particular genius lay in assimilating new ideas into his own personal sound.

D. Influence
   Through Stravinsky, elements that had been nurtured in Russian music and traits he had introduced became commonplaces of modern music, making him one of the most influential composers of the century.

VI. Béla Bartók (HWM 829–36, NAWM 147)

Béla Bartók (1881–1945) created an individual modernist idiom by synthesizing elements of Hungarian, Romanian, and Bulgarian peasant music with elements of the classical tradition.

   1. Classical and modern influences
   Bartók drew on the classical tradition from Bach to Brahms for his early compositions, then absorbed influences from Strauss, Debussy, Schoenberg, and Stravinsky.

2. Peasant music

Bartók's search for an innately Hungarian music led him to collect and study peasant music, often with fellow composer Zoltán Kodály (1882–1967). He arranged peasant tunes, created original works based on them, and also blended characteristics of them with those of classical and modern music.

3. Stylistic evolution

Bartók first achieved a distinctive personal style around 1908. In the decade after World War I, he pushed the limits of dissonance and tonal ambiguity. His later works have become the most widely known. His *Mikrokosmos* (1926–37) is a series of graded piano pieces that encapsulates his style.

Biography: Béla Bartók

Bartók took music lessons from a young age and studied piano and composition in Budapest. A virtuoso pianist, he performed all over Europe and edited keyboard music by Bach, Haydn, Mozart, and others. As an ethnomusicologist, he collected folk music, edited and published it, and wrote about it. He composed his most famous pieces shortly before World War II. In 1940, Bartók immigrated to the United States, settling in New York.

A. Bartók's Synthesis

Bartók synthesized peasant music with classical music by emphasizing what the traditions have in common—a pitch center, diatonic scales, and motives that are repeated and varied—and what is most distinctive about each—the classical tradition's forms and counterpoint, and the irregular meters, modal scales, melody types, ornamentation, and other traits of specific peasant traditions.

1. Use of neotonality

Music for Strings, Percussion and Celesta (1936) exemplifies Bartók's synthesis and personal style. His approach to neotonality is novel, yet alludes both to the chordal motions and tonic-dominant polarities of classical music and to the ways peasant melodies establish a tonal center.
Music: NAWM 147

2. Melodic structure

Bartók's melodies reflect procedures of varying small motives that are typical both in classical music and in peasant music of Hungary and Bulgaria, and sometimes mix modes, as do some Hungarian songs.

3. Form and counterpoint

Forms and contrapuntal procedures used by Bartók, such as fugue, sonata, rondo, canon, inversion, and cyclic form, come from the classical tradition.

4. Peasant elements

Bartók also used elements from traditional peasant styles, including Bulgarian dance meters, the ornamental style of Serbo-Croatian song, and melodies over drones.

B. Bartók as Modernist

Through his synthesis of classical and peasant traditions, Bartók created new works with a strong personal identity and rich connections to past music.

VII. Charles Ives (HWM 836–43, NAWM 148)

Charles Ives (1874–1954) composed in four distinct traditions—American vernacular music, Protestant church music, European classical music, and experimental music—and in his mature music combined elements of all four to convey rich musical meanings.

Biography: Charles Ives

Ives began his musical training as a child, then studied music theory and composition at Yale with Horatio Parker. He was a church organist as a teenager and young adult. When his music failed to attract positive reviews, he focused on his insurance business. He still composed in the evenings and on weekends, but published nothing until the 1920s. By the time of his death, most of his major works had been performed and published. Ives is now widely regarded as the first to create a distinctly American body of art music.

A. Sources for Ives's Style

1. Vernacular music

Ives grew up surrounded by American vernacular music, and he composed many pieces in the styles of the day.

2. Church music

As a child and a professional church organist, Ives sang, heard, and played all styles prominent in American Protestant church music.

3. Classical music

Ives was well versed in European classical music, which he played and studied.

4. Experimental works

Ives wrote *experimental music* in which he preserved most of the traditional rules but changed other rules in order to see what would happen. He wrote several pieces that were *polytonal* (in two or more keys) and others that explored new ways to construct chords, layer multiple rhythms, or establish a tonal center. His experimental pieces were private studies and were not published or performed for decades, but one, *The Unanswered Question* (1908), later became well known.

B. Syntheses

From 1902 on, Ives wrote only in classical genres, but he brought into his music the styles and sounds of the other traditions he knew.

1. Cumulative form

In some of his works, such as the *Third Symphony,* Ives used *cumulative form,* which uses the procedures of thematic fragmentation and development of European sonata form but reverses the normal course of events so that the themes are developed before they appear in full near the end.

2. American program music

Many of Ives's later pieces, such as *Three Places in New England,* are programmatic, celebrating aspects of American life and using American tunes and styles to convey meanings. Some pieces layer multiple borrowed tunes in a musical *collage* to suggest the process of remembering.

3. Stylistic heterogeneity

Ives frequently mixed styles within a single piece to evoke a wide range of extramusical references and also to articulate the musical form.

4. *General Booth*

Ives synthesized all four of these musical traditions in his song *General William Booth Enters into Heaven* (1914).   **Music: NAWM 148**

C. Ives's Place

Although Ives had little influence on others until after World War II, his work has had a tremendous impact on younger generations of American musicians.

VIII. Composer and Audience (HWM 843)

Modernist composers have a central place in the canon of music, but they are more admired by critics, composers, and scholars than they are loved by audience members. On the other hand, the sounds that offended audiences generations ago are now familiar. The music of Schoenberg, Berg, Webern, Stravinsky, Bartók, and Ives has found a small but growing and apparently permanent place in the repertoire.

STUDY QUESTIONS

1. What were the aims of modernist composers? What did they have in common with modernist artists?

Arnold Schoenberg (HWM 802–14, NAWM 141–142)

2. Briefly summarize Schoenberg's career. What was unusual about his training? How did he earn a living?

3. What was Schoenberg's early music like, and which composers most influenced it?

4. What are the principle of developing variation and the principle of nonrepetition? How was Schoenberg's interest in these ideas manifest in his music and in his career?

5. What is *atonal* music? What did Schoenberg mean by "the emancipation of the dissonance"?

6. What sorts of musical problems did Schoenberg need to solve when writing atonal music? How did he use pitch-class sets, chromatic saturation, and form to solve those problems?

Music to Study

NAWM 141: Arnold Schoenberg, *Pierrot lunaire,* Op. 21, melodrama (song cycle) for speaker and chamber ensemble (1912), excerpt

> 141a. No. 8: *Nacht* (Night)   [CD 11|1] [CD 6|1]

> 141b. No. 13: *Enthauptung* (Beheading)   [CD 11|4] [CD 6|4]

NAWM 142: Arnold Schoenberg, Piano Suite, Op. 25, (1921–23), excerpt

> 142a: Prelude   [CD 11|8] [CD 6|8]

> 142b: Minuet and Trio   [CD 11|9] [CD 6|9]

7. What is *Sprechstimme*? How is it notated, and how is it performed?

What effect does *Sprechstimme* create in the two numbers from *Pierrot lunaire* in NAWM 141? Why is it appropriate for conveying the text?

8. In *Nacht* (NAWM 141a), how is the opening motive (E-G-E♭) used during the course of the piece? Where does it *not* appear in some form? How do this motive and the way Schoenberg uses it relate to the text?

9. In addition to this motive, how else do *Nacht* and *Enthauptung* (NAWM 141b) create a sense of unity and form, without tonality?

10. What musical gestures does Schoenberg use to express or illustrate the text in these two songs?

11. What is *expressionism*? What characteristics of these two songs mark them as expressionist works?

12. What gestures, figuration, or other features does Schoenberg use in his Piano Suite, Op. 25 (NAWM 142), that remind you of Baroque keyboard music, especially a keyboard suite (see NAWM 78 and 86)? What do the Prelude (NAWM 142a) and Minuet and Trio (NAWM 142b) have in common with Baroque pieces in the same genres?

13. For the questions below, refer to the eight forms of the row Schoenberg uses in his Piano Suite (Example 31.2 in HWM, p. 811, and NAWM, p. 842).

    What tetrachord begins on the last three sixteenth notes of the right hand in measure 10 of the Prelude? What form of the row do these notes belong to?

    How about the next two tetrachords in the right hand, beginning on D in measure 11? Which tetrachords are these? What form of the row do they belong to?

    Continue from the last four sixteenth notes in the left hand of measure 11, including both hands through the beginning of measure 13. What different forms of the row are used during this span of time, and where do they appear?

14. In what ways is Schoenberg's use of rows in this passage and throughout the Piano Suite analogous to procedures in tonal music? How does he recreate the structural functions of tonality? How does he relate harmony and melody?

15. Where did Schoenberg think his atonal and twelve-tone music fit in the history of music? Where did he get his inspiration from? (Refer to the Source Readings in HWM, p. 804.) Choose two of the composers he names as influences and, for each one, describe a passage in the Piano Suite or *Pierrot lunaire* that draws one or more elements from that composer's music.

Alban Berg (HWM 814–16, NAWM 143)

16. In what ways is Berg's *Wozzeck* similar to a Wagnerian opera? How does it use forms adapted from instrumental music? What other aspects of this music are likely to sound familiar to listeners?

Music to Study

NAWM 143: Alban Berg, *Wozzeck,* Op. 7, opera (1917–22),   [CD 11|12] [CD 6|12]
   Act III, scene 3

17. Berg called Act III, scene 3, of *Wozzeck* (NAWM 143), "Invention on a Rhythm." The rhythmic idea is presented in the right hand of the piano at the beginning of the scene (mm. 122–25) and immediately repeated. Wozzeck then states it in augmentation and with a new melody (mm. 130–36). (Notice that the attacks are in the same rhythm, even though one note is sustained through what was originally a rest.) List below the appearances of this rhythm in measures 138–54, by the measure in which each statement begins and the instrument(s) or voice that carry it.

Measure	Instrument(s) or Voice	Measure	Instrument(s) or Voice
1. ____	_____	6. ____	_____
2. ____	_____	7. ____	_____
3. ____	_____	8. ____	_____
4. ____	_____	9. ____	_____
5. ____	_____	10. ____	_____

How does the constant reiteration of this rhythm convey the dramatic situation?

18. Where does Berg imitate a polka? A folk song? How does he suggest these types of tonal music, despite using an atonal language?

19. Where do major and minor triads occur in the row for Berg's twelve-tone Violin Concerto (shown in Example 31.5 in HWM, p. 816)? Why did Berg introduce triads into a twelve-tone work?

Anton Webern (HWM 816–29, NAWM 144)

Music to Study

NAWM 144: Anton Webern, Symphony, Op. 21, symphony (1927–28), first movement, Ruhig schreitend ⌞ CD 11|15 ⌟

20. Which characteristics of Webern's style, as described in HWM, pp. 817–19, are evident in the first movement of his Symphony, Op. 21 (NAWM 144)?

21. What is *pointillism*? In what way is this movement pointillistic?

22. How does Webern use pitch symmetry to establish a sense of tonal location in the exposition?

23. In what ways is the exposition like a traditional sonata-form exposition? In what ways is it different?

24. The pitch-canons in the exposition return in the recapitulation, which starts with the viola's high A in measure 42. The commentary on p. 874 of NAWM points out where the voices of canon 1 appear. Using as a guide Example 31.6 (in HWM, p. 818), which shows the notes of both canons in the exposition, where do the first twelve notes of the leading voice of canon 2 appear in the recapitulation? Indicate the notes, the instrument, and the measure number. Then do the same for the following voice.

leading voice

following voice

Igor Stravinsky (HWM 819–29, NAWM 145–146)

25. Summarize Stravinsky's career, including where he lived, brief descriptions of his style in each period, and his significance to music history.

Music to Study

NAWM 145: Igor Stravinsky, *The Rite of Spring,* ballet (1911–13), excerpt

    145a: *Danse des adolescentes* (Dance of the Adolescent Girls)   CD 11|19   CD 6|15

    145b: *Danse sacrale* (Sacrificial Dance)   CD 11|23

NAWM 146: Igor Stravinsky, *Symphony of Psalms,* choral symphony (1930), Part I   CD 11|31

26. How does Stravinsky evoke the primitive in *The Rite of Spring* (NAWM 145)? What musical elements does he use in these excerpts, and how does he use them?

27. What traits that became Stravinsky trademarks are evident in these excerpts? For each trait, indicate (with measure numbers) and briefly describe a passage that exemplifies it.

28. Within what is essentially a static texture of repeating figuration and almost constant pulsation, how does Stravinsky achieve variety?

29. How does Stravinsky create the effect of building intensity towards the end of each excerpt?

30. What makes the melodies beginning at measures 43, 89, and 119 of *Danse des adolescentes* (NAWM 145a) sound like folk tunes?

31. What elements of Stravinsky's *Symphony of Psalms*, Part I (NAWM 146), recall past music? What past style-period does Stravinsky deliberately avoid? Why?

32. How does Stravinsky establish pitch centers in this movement? Why is this movement described as *neotonal* rather than tonal?

33. What characteristics of Stravinsky's style do you find in both *The Rite of Spring* and *Symphony of Psalms*?

Why are these style characteristics appropriate both for evoking the primitive and for creating a neoclassical style?

34. How does Stravinsky's look back to the past in his *Symphony of Psalms* compare to Schoenberg's in his Piano Suite (NAWM 142)? What do their approaches have in common? How do they differ?

Béla Bartók (HWM 829–36, NAWM 147)

35. In addition to composing, what were Bartók's activities in music, and what significance did these activities have for music history?

Music to Study

NAWM 147: Béla Bartók, *Music for Strings, Percussion*   [CD 11|36]   [CD 6|19]
    and Celesta, symphonic suite (1920), third movement, Adagio

36. What elements drawn from east European folk music does Bartók use in the third
    movement of *Music for Strings, Percussion and Celesta* (NAWM 147)?

37. Where does Bartók use the following techniques derived from the Western classi-
    cal tradition?

    imitation and canon

    ostinato

    inversion and retrograde of melodic material

    rhythmic diminution of material

    recollection of material presented earlier in this or other movements

38. Bartók's synthesis of the folk and art music traditions creates something new within
    the realm of the orchestral repertory. List the ways in which this movement offers
    new sounds and ideas, in comparison with nineteenth-century symphonic music.
    (You may use NAWM 109, 121, 122, 132, and 133 as points of comparison.)

39. How is Bartók's use of folk music traditions in the third movement of *Music for Strings, Percussion and Celesta* (NAWM 147) different from Musorgsky's in *Boris Godunov* (NAWM 130)? How do they differ in their use of these traditions as well as in their purposes for using these traditions?

Charles Ives (HWM 836–43, NAWM 148)

40. What was Ives's musical background and training? What were some prominent influences on his music? What was his significance for American music?

Music to Study

NAWM 148: Charles Ives, *General William Booth Enters into Heaven,* song (1914)

41. Compare Ives's song *General William Booth Enters into Heaven* (NAWM 148) with Schubert's Lied *Gretchen am Spinnrade* (NAWM 111). Aside from differences in language and general style traits, what do these two songs have in common in terms of conveying the text? What does each composer do to express the emotions of the scene?

42. What experimental elements does Ives use in *General Booth*? Describe them, indicating passages by measure number.

   How do these elements affect your experience of the work? In your opinion, how do they affect the work's meaning?

43. What is the form of the song? Describe the process of introducing and developing the main ideas.

44. What different musical styles does Ives use or allude to in this song? How does he use contrasts of style and changes of figuration in the piano to distinguish each phrase or section from the previous one? How does his approach resemble or differ from Mozart's use of diverse styles (see NAWM 105 and chapter 22, question 25)?

45. How does this song illustrate Ives's thoughts about American music as stated in the Source Reading in HWM, p. 840?

46. What do Ives and Bartók have in common in terms of how they incorporate national elements into their music? How do they differ?

Composer and Audience (HWM 843)

47. What do Schoenberg, Berg, Webern, Stravinsky, Bartók, and Ives have in common as composers of modern music? How have audiences, scholars, and other composers reacted to their music?

TERMS TO KNOW

modernism, modernists
atonality, atonal
set, pitch-class set
pitch-class
chromatic saturation
expressionism
Sprechstimme
twelve-tone method
row, series
prime, inversion, retrograde,
  retrograde inversion

tetrachord
hexachord
Klangfarbenmelodie
neoclassicism
neotonal, neotonality
serial music
experimental music
polytonal, polytonality
cumulative form
collage

NAMES TO KNOW

Arnold Schoenberg
Pierrot lunaire
The Second Viennese School
Alban Berg
Wozzeck
Anton Webern
Igor Stravinsky
The Firebird

Petrushka
The Rite of Spring
Symphony of Psalms
Belá Bartók
Music for Strings, Percussion
  and Celesta
Charles Ives

REVIEW QUESTIONS

1. Add the composers and major works discussed in this chapter to the twentieth-century timeline you made for chapter 30.
2. Compare the atonal music of Schoenberg's *Pierrot lunaire* (NAWM 141) to the music you know by Wagner, Mahler, and Strauss (NAWM 128, 133, and 137). How does Schoenberg continue the late-Romantic German tradition, and what does he introduce that is new? How does Schoenberg's twelve-tone music, as exemplified in the Piano Suite (NAWM 142), continue and extend nineteenth-century procedures?
3. How does the music of Berg and Webern resemble that of Schoenberg, and how docs it differ? How do they compare to one another? How does the music of each one compare to the music you know by Wagner, Mahler, and Strauss?
4. Trace the career of Igor Stravinsky, naming major pieces and describing the changes in his style. What distinctive characteristics of his music, established in *The Rite of Spring,* continued throughout his career, and how are these traits embodied in his neoclassical music?
5. How does Bartók achieve an individual style within the Western art music tradition by integrating traditional procedures with elements abstracted from East European folk music? Describe how this synthesis works in *Music for Strings, Percussion and Celesta.* How does Bartók's synthesis compare with Ives's synthesis of traditional compositional procedures and American vernacular musics.
6. What do all the examples for this chapter (NAWM 141–148) have in common as modern works? How do they differ from one another?

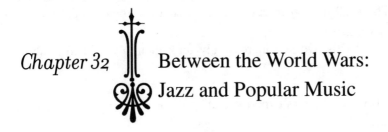

Chapter 32 Between the World Wars:
Jazz and Popular Music

CHAPTER OBJECTIVES

After you complete the reading, study of the music, and study questions for this chapter, you should be able to

1. recount briefly the political, economic, social, and technological changes in Western Europe and the United States between the two World Wars and their impact on jazz and popular music;

2. describe popular song and musical theater in the United States between the wars and name important songwriters;

3. explain the differences between blues, New Orleans jazz style, and big-band jazz, identify some of the most significant composers, arrangers, and performers associated with each, and name significant works by them; and

4. describe music for films from the first sound pictures to World War II.

CHAPTER OUTLINE

I. Introduction (HWM 844)

The period between World Wars I and II saw a remarkable series of changes in musical life and continued diversification in musical styles.

II. Between the Wars (HWM 844–48)

Popular music, jazz, and music of earlier times flourished as people sought an escape from the aftermath of World War I.

1. New nations and ideologies
New nations changed the face of Europe, and totalitarian rulers had an impact on musical life.

2. Economy
The European economy was weak after World War II, while the United

States and Canada prospered, fostering a golden age for American music. The 1929 stock market crash triggered a worldwide depression.

3. Roles for women

During the 1920s, women increasingly took their place in the public sphere.

A. The Arts

The 1920s were a time of experimentation in the arts.

1. The 1930s

As a result of the worldwide depression of the 1930s, many artists sought to make their work accessible to all people and relevant to the problems of the time.

B. New Technologies

New technologies enabled the preservation and distribution of music in performance and created a new mass market and new commercial possibilities.

1. Recordings

The popular music industry shifted its attention from sheet music to recordings, and better recording technology influenced performance styles.

2. Radio

Musicians also profited from exposure over the radio, as stations relied on live performers.

3. Diffusion of music

Recordings and radio made music available to almost everyone and increased the size of audiences for all kinds of music.

III. American Musical Theater and Popular Song (HWM 848–51)

The 1920s were an especially rich time for American popular music. The most successful songwriters of this period were equally at home writing for Tin Pan Alley, musical theater, and movie musicals.

A. Musical Theater

1. Revues

Revues, shows made up primarily of musical numbers that often included many performers, were popular in larger cities.

2. Musicals

Musicals were collaborations, with different artists creating the music, lyrics, book (spoken words), choreography, staging, sets, and costumes. Some were primarily vehicles for star entertainers, but there was increasing interest in plot-driven musicals with close integration between music and story.

3. *Show Boat*

Show Boat (1927), with music by *Jerome Kern* (1885–1945) and book and lyrics by Oscar Hammerstein II, is an integrated musical that brings together a number of traditions and musical styles that all serve dramatic ends.

B. Tin Pan Alley: The Golden Age
Most Tin Pan Alley songs had one or more verses followed by a thirty-two-measure chorus where songwriters placed their catchiest rhythms and melodic ideas.

1. Irving Berlin
Irving Berlin (1888–1989), one of America's most prolific and best-loved popular songwriters, wrote sentimental and patriotic lyrics and tunes.

2. Cole Porter
Cole Porter (1891–1964) wrote both lyrics and music for his songs and is remembered for his use of sophisticated lyrics that use double meanings.

IV. The Jazz Age (HWM 851–59, NAWM 149–151)

African-American music and musicians played an increasingly influential role in the 1920s, as blues and jazz gained wide currency and jazz became an emblem for social liberation.

A. Blues
The *blues* were one of the most influential genres of early-twentieth-century America, and its music expresses the feelings suggested by the words through a variety of elements, including *blue notes*. Two distinct blues traditions, now known as classic blues and delta blues, emerged in the 1910s and 1920s.

1. Classic blues
Classic blues were performed primarily by African-American women singers and accompanied by piano or small group.

2. Twelve-bar blues
The classic blues singers joined aspects of oral tradition with elements of popular song. In his publications, *W. C. Handy* (1873–1958) standardized what is now called the *twelve-bar blues* form, which is illustrated in *Back Water Blues* by *Bessie Smith* (1894–1937).   **Music: NAWM 149**

3. Delta blues
Delta blues came primarily from the Mississippi Delta region, is associated primarily with male African-American singers and guitarists, and is rooted in oral traditions. As African Americans migrated north, several delta blues singers moved to Chicago and made recordings that influenced later performers.

B. Jazz in the 1920s
Jazz in the 1920s featured syncopated rhythm, novel vocal and instrumental sounds, and improvisation or music in improvisatory style. Jazz was a player's art, fostered by recordings and radio.

1. New Orleans jazz
New Orleans jazz, the leading style just after World War I, centered on group variation of a given tune. The style was developed in New Orleans by musicians such as cornettist *Joe "King" Oliver* (1885–1938) and trumpeter *Louis Armstrong* (1901–1971).

2. King Oliver and Louis Armstrong

Oliver formed King Oliver's Creole Jazz Band in Chicago, joined by Armstrong, who also recorded with his own group. The recordings of these bands embody the New Orleans jazz style. The ensemble is divided into the "front line" of melody instruments and the *rhythm section*. After presenting a tune, the group repeats its harmonic progression in a series of *choruses,* each featuring different instruments. Armstrong's recording of Oliver's *West End Blues* features both his virtuoso trumpet playing and his *scat singing*.   **Music: NAWM 150**

C. Big Bands

By the 1930s, *big bands* were popular. Bands were divided into three sections (brass, reeds, and rhythm), and an arranger wrote down their music.

1. The swing era

Swing was a popular dance craze in America, and the number of swing bands exploded in the 1930s.

D. George Gershwin

1. Jazz in art music

George Gershwin (1898–1937) successfully combined jazz and art music in several works, including the "jazz concerto" *Rhapsody in Blue* (1924) and his opera *Porgy and Bess* (1935).

2. Musicals and popular songs

Gershwin also wrote popular songs and musicals. The chord progression from his song *I Got Rhythm* became popular as a vehicle for jazz improvisation and composition.   **Music: NAWM 151**

E. Jazz in Europe

Jazz spread to Europe, and by the 1920s jazz groups were forming there. Guitarist Django Reinhardt (1910–1953) formed one of the most successful and musically innovative European jazz bands.

V. Duke Ellington (HWM 859–62, NAWM 152)

Duke Ellington (1899–1974) was a leading figure in jazz and one of the most influential American composers.

1. Cotton Club years

From 1927 to 1931, Ellington developed his individual style and began to gain national recognition at the Cotton Club in Harlem. His works and arrangements highlighted the individual sounds of his musicians.

2. Touring

In the 1930s, Ellington's band spent most of their time touring.

3. The 1940s

The early 1940s is widely considered the peak of Ellington's creative abilities. *Cotton Tail*, a *contrafact* (new tune based on a borrowed harmonic progression) based on *I Got Rhythm,* illustrates his music from this era.   **Music: NAWM 152**

4. Beyond category

Ellington believed that jazz could serve as art music as well as dance and entertainment music.

Biography: Duke Ellington

Born in Washington, D.C., Ellington studied piano from the age of seven. By seventeen he had formed his own band, which he moved to New York in 1923. His band was known around the world through recordings and international tours.

VI. Film Music (HWM 862–64)

1. Sound in film

New technologies in the late 1920s made it possible to synchronize recorded sound with film. There are two categories of music in film; (1) music heard or performed by the characters in the film, called *diegetic music* or *source music,* and (2) background music, called *nondiegetic music* or *underscoring*.

2. On-screen performances

Movies often included musical numbers as interludes or for dramatic reasons.

3. Movie musicals

The 1930s were the "Golden Age" of the Hollywood musical.

4. Hollywood film scores

In the 1930s, the Hollywood studios fostered film scores that were fully integrated into the dramatic action, guiding the viewer's emotional responses and giving depth to the events on screen. An important early example is the score for *King Kong* (1933) by *Max Steiner* (1888–1971), which used leitmotives and was coordinated with the action on screen.

VII. Mass Media and Popular Music (HWM 864)

Through new technologies, American popular music, jazz, and film music reached audiences throughout the Western world, and by the 1970s canons of classics had developed for this music, centered around music that was popular between the wars.

STUDY QUESTIONS

Between the Wars (HWM 844–48)

1. Describe the economic, social, political, artistic, and technological changes between World War I and World War II and their effects on music.

American Musical Theater and Popular Song (HWM 848–51)

2. What is the difference between a musical that is a vehicle for a star performer and an integrated musical? Name and describe an example of the latter.

3. Name some of the most important American popular songwriters in the 1920s and 1930s, and describe their approach to writing popular song. Why was their music significant in its time, and what is its significance today?

The Jazz Age (HWM 851–59, NAWM 149–151)

Music to Study

NAWM 149: Bessie Smith, *Back Water Blues,* blues (1927)   〔 CD 11|49 〕

NAWM 150: King Oliver [Joe Oliver], *West End Blues,* blues (recorded 1928), as performed by Louis Armstrong and His Hot Five

    150a: Original sheet music (not on recording)

    150b: Transcription of recording by Louis Armstrong and   〔 CD 11|50 〕
        His Hot Five

NAWM 151: George Gershwin, *I Got Rhythm* from *Girl Crazy,*   〔 CD 11|55 〕 〔 CD 6|32 〕
  Broadway show song (1930)

4. Refer to the standard twelve-bar blues form shown in Figure 31.4 in **HWM,** p. 852. How is Bessie Smith's *Back Water Blues* (NAWM 149) typical of the form?

5. How is the music typical of blues style, both as written and as performed by Bessie Smith and James P. Johnson?

6. How are the topics and word choices of *Back Water Blues* typical of blues lyrics?

7. What makes *Back Water Blues* an example of the classic blues?

8. In the sheet music for *West End Blues* (NAWM 150a), how does King Oliver adapt the blues to the format of a Tin Pan Alley popular song? How does he create variety?

9. Between World Wars I and II, how did amateur performers learn about new music? Where did they hear it? In this context, what may have been the functions of the sheet music in NAWM 150a? How is this similar to or different from the functions of sheet music in the nineteenth century?

10. How is the performance of *West End Blues* by Louis Armstrong and His Hot Five (NAWM 150b) typical of the New Orleans jazz style?

11. Which elements of the group's performance are present in the sheet music version (NAWM 150a)? Explain the differences.

12. What comparisons can you draw between Armstrong's performance of *West End Blues* and the improvised embellishments in an opera seria aria, exemplified in Example 20.5 in HWM, p. 493 (this is a transcription of a live performance of NAWM 94)? What is similar about the two approaches to improvisation, and what makes them different?

13. What elements of blues form make it an appropriate vehicle for improvisation?

14. How is Gershwin's *I Got Rhythm* (NAWM 151) typical of the standard Tin Pan Alley song form? How does it differ from typical blues form?

15. Compare the music for the verse of *I Got Rhythm* with its refrain. What harmonic, rhythmic, and melodic elements create a contrast between the two sections? How do these contrasts suggest a change of mood? Why is the chorus more memorable than the verse?

16. What are "rhythm changes"? What element of music does it refer to, and what is its relationship to Gershwin's *I Got Rhythm*?

Write out the "changes" for each section of the chorus (AABA) of *I Got Rhythm* (beginning in m. 29). Each space represents one measure, so in the first space, you would write B♭ and B♭6 (i.e., with an added sixth), in the second you would write Cm7 and F7, and so on.

A   ____   ____   ____   ____   ____   ____   ____   ____

A   ____   ____   ____   ____   ____   ____   ____   ____

B   ____   ____   ____   ____   ____   ____   ____   ____

A'   ____   ____   ____   ____   ____   ____   ____   ____

     ____   ____

17. How does a big band differ from the ensemble typical of New Orleans style jazz? How do their performance contexts differ?

Duke Ellington (HWM 859–62, NAWM 152)

18. Give a brief summary of Duke Ellington's career. What were his most significant achievements?

Music to Study

NAWM 152: Duke Ellington, *Cotton Tail,* jazz composition   (CD 11|58)   [CD 6|35]
    (contrafact) (1940)

19. What aspects of Ellington's *Cotton Tail* (NAWM 152) are typical of big band music?

20. What elements of *Cotton Tail* did Ellington compose in advance? What elements were left to improvisation? How does this differ from the performance of *West End Blues* (NAWM 150)?

21. *Cotton Tail* (NAWM 152) is a *contrafact.* How does this compare with a *contrafactum* such as *O Welt, ich muss dich lassen,* described in HWM (pp. 214–15)? In each case, what was borrowed from an existing piece of music? What was the purpose of using existing music to create new compositions in these cases?

22. Compare the harmonies of *Cotton Tail* with the harmonic progression from *I Got Rhythm* (see question 16 above). How does Ellington modify the harmonic progression from *I Got Rhythm* in *Cotton Tail*?

23. Aside from harmony, what other musical elements does Ellington retain from the chorus of Gershwin's *I Got Rhythm* (NAWM 151) for the tune *Cotton Tail*?

Film Music (HWM 862–64)

24. What is the difference between *diegetic* and *nondiegetic music* in film?

25. Describe Max Steiner's score for *King Kong*. What musical devices did he use? What music did he use as models? Why is this film score significant?

Mass Media and Popular Music (HWM 864)

26. How did technology and mass media facilitate the emergence of a repertoire of classics in popular music and jazz?

TERMS TO KNOW

blues

blue notes

twelve-bar blues

New Orleans jazz

rhythm section

chorus (in a jazz performance)

scat singing

big bands

swing

contrafact (in jazz)

diegetic music, source music

nondiegetic music, underscoring

NAMES TO KNOW

Show Boat

Jerome Kern

Irving Berlin

Cole Porter

W. C. Handy

Bessie Smith

King Oliver

Louis Armstrong

George Gershwin

I Got Rhythm

Duke Ellington

Max Steiner

REVIEW QUESTIONS

1. Add the composers, performers, and major works discussed in this chapter to the twentieth-century timeline you made for chapter 30.

2. Summarize the historical background for music between the World Wars. What role did blues and jazz play in this context? Where, by whom, for whom, and for what purposes was it performed? How did it intersect with classical traditions?

3. Write your own blues poetry to set to music. What are common topics of the blues? What form does it need to be in? How many syllables should each line have? Write your own melody that fits this poetry and the harmonic progression of the twelve-bar blues. Describe the musical setting for a performance of your song. How many people will perform it? What instruments will be used? What musical elements need to be planned in advance? What musical elements can change in performance? After performing it, write a short essay describing the similarities and differences between blues songs and other song types we have studied in this course (such as the Lied, aria, Tin Pan Alley song, and parlor-room ballad).

4. Take the tune that you wrote in Review Question 3 above and recompose it in New Orleans jazz style and in the big-band style of Duke Ellington. Change as many elements of the music (notes, rhythms, scoring, form) as you wish. When you have finished, write a short statement explaining what aspects of New Orleans jazz and big band styles you have tried to imitate and how you have done so. Compare this process with a similar one in chapter 23, Review Question 4, in which you recomposed a Haydn theme to sound like Beethoven's late style. In what ways was the process different? In what ways was it similar?

5. Write an essay on the impact of recording technologies on musical composition and performance. For example, consider what the differences are between a live performance and a recording of a live performance. How do you experience each of these as a listener? In these situations, what is the composition? Is there one? How do these questions affect how we think about musical composition and performance? How do they affect the acts of composition and performance?

Chapter 33   Between the World Wars:
The Classical Tradition

CHAPTER OBJECTIVES

After you complete the reading, study of the music, and study questions for this chapter, you should be able to

1. describe briefly the differences in the political situations in France, Germany, the Soviet Union, and the Americas during the interwar period, and explain the impact of politics on the patronage of music in the classical tradition;

2. name some of the most prominent classical composers active in France, Germany, the Soviet Union, and the Americas between the two World Wars, characterize their musical styles, and explain how politics influenced their ideas about music; and

3. summarize the diversity of musical styles in the classical tradition during the interwar period.

CHAPTER OUTLINE

I. Introduction (HWM 865)

Between the world wars, music in the classical tradition continued to diversify and became increasingly tied to political concerns and ideologies.

II. Music, Politics, and the People (HWM 865–67)

Music has long been linked to politics, as we have seen in earlier chapters.

1. Classical music as autonomous

In the nineteenth century, some writers claimed that classical music was an autonomous art that should be admired for its own sake, but it never fully escaped politics.

2. Links to politics

The period between the world wars brought new links between music and politics. Believing that music must be relevant to social needs, some composers tried to make their music more accessible to audiences and amateurs, while nationalism continued strong in many countries.

3. Government sponsorship

Most governments sponsored musical activities directly. The connections between musical style and politics varied with the political situation in each nation.

III. France (HWM 867–70)

In France, musical life had long been connected with politics, and many concert sponsors had a political purpose.

1. Notions of classicism

During and after World War I, neoclassicism became the prevailing trend in France, allied with patriotism. Conservatives identified classicism with balance, order, discipline, and tradition while composers on the left saw the classic as encompassing a variety of styles and genres, regardless of nationality.

A. Les Six

"Les Six" (The Six) was a group of French composers who sought to escape the old political dichotomies and wrote highly individual works that drew on a wide range of influences, including neoclassicism. The most successful were Honegger, Milhaud, and Poulenc.

1. Arthur Honegger

Arthur Honegger (1892–1955) is best known for *Pacific 231* (1923), an orchestral impression of a train, and for his opera-oratorio *King David* (premiered 1923).

2. Darius Milhaud

Darius Milhaud (1892–1974), prolific in every genre, blended neoclassicism with other influences from jazz to Schoenberg.

3. Francis Poulenc

Francis Poulenc (1899–1963) drew especially on the Parisian popular chanson tradition associated with cabarets and revues.

IV. Germany (HWM 870–76, NAWM 153)

Music and politics were linked closely in Germany under the Weimar Republic (1919–1933), and the Nazis (1933–1945) attacked modern music and banned leftists and Jews from public life.

A. New Objectivity

The *New Objectivity* (Neue Sachlichkeit) of the 1920s opposed complexity and favored music that was widely accessible, objective in expression, and connected to current concerns.

1. Ernst Krenek

Jonny spielt auf (1927) by Ernst Krenek (1900–1991) embodied ideals of New Objectivity and was attacked by the Nazis for its use of jazz.

B. Kurt Weill

Kurt Weill (1900–1950), a supporter of New Objectivity, sought to enter-tain everyday people rather than the intellectual elites.

1. *Mahagonny*

Weill and playwright Bertolt Brecht collaborated on *Rise and Fall of the City of Mahagonny* (1930), an allegorical opera about the failures of capitalism.

2. *The Threepenny Opera*

Weill's and Brecht's *The Threepenny Opera* (1928), adapted from *The Beggar's Opera* (see chapter 20), parodied American hit songs and was a great success before being banned as decadent by the Nazis in 1933.

3. Career on Broadway

After emigrating to the United States, Weill wrote successful Broadway musicals in the spirit of New Objectivity.

C. Paul Hindemith

Paul Hindemith (1895–1963), among the most prolific composers of the century, was also important as a teacher and performer.

1. Works of the Weimar period

During the Weimar period, Hindemith moved from expressionism to writing neotonal music that avoided Romantic expressivity and focused on purely musical procedures.

2. *Gebrauchsmusik*

By the late 1920s, Hindemith began composing *Gebrauchsmusik* (music for use), especially music for young or amateur performers that was modern and challenging yet rewarding to perform.

3. *Mathis der Maler*

Hindemith's opera *Mathis der Maler* (Matthias the Painter, 1934–35), written after the Nazis came to power, examines the role of the artist in relation to politics. From the 1930s on, Hindemith wrote in a more Ro-mantic style and developed a new harmonic method that he called "har-monic fluctuation," in which phrases start with relative consonance, move toward greater dissonance, and return to consonance. **Music: NAWM 153**

4. Later works

Hindemith emigrated to Switzerland in 1938, then to the United States in 1940 before returning to Europe in 1953. His notable later works include *Ludus tonalis* (Tonal Play, 1942), *Symphonic Metamorphosis* (1943), and Symphony in B-flat for band (1951).

D. Music under the Nazis

The Nazis established a Reich Music Chamber to which all musicians had to belong. The Nazis attacked most modern music, but there was no coherent Nazi style of new music: the government focused more on per-formance than on composition, exploiting the great nineteenth-century German composers as symbols of alleged German superiority.

1. Carl Orff
Carl Orff (1895–1982) is best known for *Carmina burana* (1936) and his contributions to music education.

V. The Soviet Union (HWM 876–80, NAWM 154)

In the Soviet Union, the government controlled every realm of life, including the arts.

1. Composers' organizations
During the early 1920s, the Association for Contemporary Music promoted modernism and contacts with the West, and the Russian Association of Proletarian Musicians supported simple tonal music with wide appeal. Both were replaced in 1933 by Stalin's Union of Soviet Composers.

2. Socialist realism versus formalism
Beginning in 1934, Soviet authorities promulgated *socialist realism,* which called for accessible, melodic, folklike music on patriotic or inspirational topics, and condemned "formalism."

A. Sergey Prokofiev
Sergey Prokofiev (1891–1953) made his initial reputation as a radical modernist. After touring outside Russia, he accepted commissions from the Soviet regime for works in a more popular style, and he returned permanently in 1936. During World War II, he turned to absolute genres, and his music was labeled as "formalist" by authorities in 1948.

B. Dmitri Shostakovich
Dmitri Shostakovich (1906–1975) spent his entire career within the Soviet system, reaching international fame at a young age.

1. *Lady Macbeth of Mtsensk*
Shostakovich achieved great success with *Lady Macbeth of the Mtsensk District* (1934), but he and his opera were attacked in the official press two years later.

2. Fifth Symphony
Shostakovich's Fifth Symphony, modeled on Mahler and Tchaikovsky, outwardly conformed to socialist realism, but could be heard as conveying emotions experienced in a totalitarian regime.   **Music: NAWM 154**

3. Seventh Symphony
The Seventh Symphony (1941) is a programmatic work on the heroic defense of Leningrad that some hear as a complaint against Stalin's repression.

4. Later works
In 1948, Shostakovich was denounced, and he wrote music for the regime and also some for himself. The apparent double meanings in Shostakovich's music reflect the fact that he could never say precisely what he felt under Soviet rule.

VI. The Americas (HWM 880–83, NAWM 155)

Composers of the Americas often found that creating a distinctive national style helped them gain attention from an international audience.

A. Canada

Canada had a thriving musical life that developed along patterns similar to those in the United States.

1. Claude Champagne

Claude Champagne (1891–1965) was the first Canadian composer to achieve an international reputation.

B. Brazil

Art music was well established in Brazil by the late nineteenth century.

1. Heitor Villa-Lobos

Heitor Villa-Lobos (1887–1959), the most important Brazilian composer, drew together traditional Brazilian elements with modernist techniques.

2. *Chôros* and *Bachianas brasileiras*

In *Chôros* (1920–28), Villa-Lobos blended Brazilian vernacular styles and modernist techniques, and in *Bachianas brasileiras* (1930–45), he pays tribute to Bach with a blend of Baroque and Brazilian folk elements.

C. Mexico

Beginning in 1921, the Mexican government supported bringing the arts to a wide public and promoted nationalism drawing on native Indian cultures.

1. Carlos Chávez

Carlos Chávez (1899–1978), the first composer associated with the new nationalism, wrote ballets and symphonic works with Aztec elements.

2. Silvestre Revueltas

Silvestre Revueltas (1899–1940) combined melodies modeled on Mexican folk and popular music with a modernist idiom.   **Music: NAWM 155**

VII. The United States (HWM 883–91, NAWM 156–158)

American composers and performers developed new links with Europe, as many studied with Nadia Boulanger in France and several European composers immigrated to the United States. The period between the wars saw several new currents among American composers, including experimentalist and Americanist trends.

A. Edgard Varèse

Born and trained in France, *Edgard Varèse* (1883–1965) moved to New York in 1915 and composed music influenced by Debussy, Schoenberg, and Stravinsky.

1. Spatial music and sound-masses

Beginning in the 1920s, Varèse imagined music as *spatial,* in which *sound masses* characterized by timbre, register, rhythm, and pitch, change and interact in unconventional ways, while percussion is on an equal footing with other instruments.

2. Electronic music
   After World War II, Varèse used electronic means to create new sounds.

B. Henry Cowell
   In his experimental pieces, *Henry Cowell* (1897–1965) tried out new techniques (such as *tone clusters* and playing directly on the strings of the piano), new textures, and new procedures. During and after the 1930s, Cowell created a more accessible musical language, often incorporating American, Irish, or Asian elements. Cowell promoted and published music by modernist and ultramodernist composers.

C. Ruth Crawford Seeger
   Ruth Crawford Seeger (1901–1953) experimented with dissonant counterpoint, rhythmic independence of parts, and serial techniques, then turned from composition to editing and arranging American folk songs.

   1. String Quartet
      In her String Quartet (1931), Crawford combines the string quartet tradition with her constant search for new procedures.   **Music: NAWM 156**

D. Aaron Copland
   Aaron Copland (1900–1990) became the most important American composer of his generation through his own compositions and his work for the cause of American music.

   1. Early works
      Jazz elements and strong dissonances figure prominently in Copland's early works.

   2. Americanist style
      In the 1930s and 1940s, Copland sought to appeal to a larger audience by reducing his modernist technique to its essence and combining it with simple textures and diatonic melodies and harmonies.

   3. *Appalachian Spring*
      Copland's Americanist idiom is exemplified in the ballet *Appalachian Spring* (1943–44). His use of widely spaced sonorities, open octaves and fifths, and diatonic dissonance became a musical emblem for America.
      Music: NAWM 157

   4. Later works
      Although Copland employed a variety of styles in his later works, including some twelve-tone methods, he retained his unique artistic identity.

E. William Grant Still
   William Grant Still (1895–1978) incorporated specifically American idioms into art music and broke numerous racial barriers.

   1. *Afro-American Symphony*
      Still's *Afro-American Symphony* (1930) encompasses African-American musical elements within the traditional framework of a European four-movement symphony.   **Music: NAWM 158**

F. Virgil Thomson
   Virgil Thomson (1896–1989) was a composer and critic who sought to write music that was simple, direct, playful, and focused on the present.

1. *Four Saints in Three Acts*

    Thomson collaborated with Gertrude Stein on the opera *Four Saints in Three Acts* (1927–28), an absurdist work that uses a variety of musical styles and idioms in surprising juxtapositions.

2. Other works

    Much of Thomson's other music is more overtly Americanist.

G. Diversity of Styles

Art music in America during the interwar period encompassed a variety of styles as composers sought a place in the crowded classical repertoire.

VIII. What Politics? (HWM 891–92)

Although art music of the interwar period includes some of the most widely performed classical works of the twentieth century, many listeners and musicians have largely forgotten the political circumstances in which most of it was created. Today, many musicians and historians are challenging the notion that classical music is an autonomous art and seek to understand the circumstances surrounding its creation. What seems most important about classical music of this period is its great variety.

STUDY QUESTIONS

Music, Politics, and the People (HWM 865–67)

1. From whom did composers in the classical tradition get financial support after World War I?

2. Why did some composers turn to more accessible styles during the interwar period?

France (HWM 867–70)

3. What political meanings were associated with neoclassical music in France during and after World War I? Why did neoclassicism become the prevailing trend in France?

4. Name the composers of "Les Six." Describe the relationship among these six composers. What did they have in common? How does this group compare with the Mighty Five in Russia (chapters 27 and 29)?

5. Based on information in HWM, how does the music and musical style of Milhaud compare with the music and musical style of Poulenc?

Germany (HWM 870–76, NAWM 153)

6. What is *New Objectivity,* and what impact did it have on music? Where and when was this idea developed? Why was it supported there at that time? How did Krenek's opera *Jonny spielt auf* exemplify New Objectivity?

7. Briefly describe Weill's career and his musical style. How does his musical style achieve the goals of New Objectivity? What did he hope to achieve dramatically with his particular musical style?

8. Briefly summarize Hindemith's career. How did it differ from Weill's?

9. What is *Gebrauchsmusik*? How is it similar to and differ from New Objectivity?

Music to Study

NAWM 153: Paul Hindemith, *Un cygne,* from *Six Chansons*   `CD 11|64`
   (1939), choral partsong

10. In Hindemith's *Un cygne* (NAWM 153), where do consonant harmonies (triads or open fifths) appear from measure 1 through measure 11? Indicate them by measure number, beat, and notes they contain:

Measure	Beat	Notes	Measure	Beat	Notes

11. How does Hindemith proceed from one consonant harmony to the next?

12. What kinds of dissonance does Hindemith use? Name the dissonant intervals that seem to appear most frequently.

13. How does Hindemith's method of "harmonic fluctuation" create a sense of harmonic conflict and resolution?

14. How does the harmonic motion of *Un cygne* help to convey its text?

How does the harmonic motion of *Un cygne* help to delineate its musical form?

15. Why is *Un cygne* well suited for amateur performers?

16. What motivated Hindemith to compose music for amateurs such as *Un cygne*?

17. What kinds of music did the Nazis support in Germany? What did they condemn or ban? What effect did this have on German composers and performers?

The Soviet Union (HWM 876–80, NAWM 154)

18. According to Soviet doctrine, what was *socialist realism*? How could composers achieve it? What was "formalism," and why did the Soviets oppose it?

19. Briefly describe Prokofiev's career. How did he relate to the Soviet state, and how was his music affected?

20. Describe Shostakovich's career and music. How did it differ from Prokofiev's?

21. What characteristics of Shostakovich's *Lady Macbeth of Mtsensk* displeased the Soviet authorities, as related by the article from *Pravda* excerpted in HWM, p. 879. Translating the negative words of the article into neutral or positive ones, what elements of musical modernism is the author describing?

Music to Study

NAWM 154: Dmitri Shostakovich, Symphony No. 5, Op. 47   ⟮ CD 11|66 ⟯
    (1937), second movement, Allegretto

22. In what ways does the scherzo movement from Shostakovich's Symphony No. 5 (NAWM 154) resemble the minuet movement from Haydn's Symphony No. 92 (NAWM 104c)? How does it differ? What is comic or witty about each?

23. Shostakovich was influenced by Mahler's music. In chapter 30, question 15, you explored the idea of musical irony (emotional mismatch between text and music) in Mahler's orchestral song *Nun will die Sonn' so hell aufgeh'n* (NAWM 137). In what ways does the second movement from Shostakovich's Symphony No. 5 create a similar tone? How is Shostakovich able to convey sarcasm and satire in instrumental music, which does not have a text?

24. Of the modernist traits you listed in question 21 above, which are present in this Shostakovich movement? Which did he avoid? In what ways, if any, does this movement conform to the doctrine of socialist realism? In what ways, if any, does it seem not to conform?

The Americas (HWM 880–83, NAWM 155)

25. According to HWM, who were the most important composers active in Canada, Brazil, and Mexico during the interwar period? How did their music reflect their nationality, and what influences did each absorb from other nations?

Music to Study

NAWM 155: Silvestre Revueltas, *Sensemayá* (1938), symphonic poem

26. Although Revueltas does not use a strong tonal center in his symphonic poem *Sensemayá* (NAWM 155), how does he suggest tonal areas? How does this help to delineate form?

27. What other musical elements does Revueltas rely on to create a coherent form? Refer to specific measures in the score when you describe these elements.

28. What extramusical elements does Revueltas rely on to create a meaningful form?

29. How do the musical elements you described above in questions 26–27 help to convey the program in *Sensemayá*?

30. How does Revueltas's choice of instruments and performing techniques help to convey the program in *Sensemayá*? Refer to specific measures to illustrate your points.

31. How is the use of national musical elements in *Sensemayá* similar to or different from the use of national musical elements in Bartók's *Music for Strings, Percussion and Celesta* (NAWM 147) and Ives's *General Booth* (NAWM 148)?

The United States (HWM 883–91, NAWM 156–158)

32. How did twentieth-century European composers interact with and influence American composers writing in the classical tradition between the world wars?

33. Describe Varèse's approach to composition in the 1920s and 1930s. How did he conceive of music? What resources does he use, and how does he deploy them? In what ways does his approach to music build on the approaches of Debussy and Stravinsky?

34. What musical resources did Cowell introduce in his piano music? For each one, name at least one piece that uses it.

35. Describe Cowell's musical activities outside of composition and their significance to music history.

36. Summarize Ruth Crawford Seeger's life and career. How was she influenced by the New Deal? What do her activities have in common with the ideals of Soviet socialist realism? How do they differ?

Music to Study

NAWM 156: Ruth Crawford Seeger, *String Quartet 1931* (1931),   ⸢ CD 11|83 ⸣   ⸢ CD 6|50 ⸣
string quartet, fourth movement, Allegro possibile

37. Describe the form and the procedures Crawford uses in the fourth movement of her *String Quartet 1931* (NAWM 156). What is novel in her design? Among the other modernist works you have studied (NAWM 140–148 and 153–155), which ones does it resemble, and it what ways?

38. In what ways is the "rotation" technique in this movement of Crawford's quartet similar to and different from Schoenberg's manipulations of twelve-tone rows?

39. How is her treatment of texture similar to or different from other works from the string quartet repertoire represented in NAWM 103 (Haydn) and NAWM 110 (Beethoven)? In what other ways does she continue or depart from the traditions of the string quartet, as described in HWM, chapters 22 and 23?

40. Who first published this string quartet? What does this tell you about the audience for "ultramodern" compositions in the 1940s?

41. Briefly describe the variety of styles Aaron Copland employed throughout his career as a composer. What style is he best known for? What is his significance for American music? Why is he one of the best-known American composers of the century?

Music to Study

NAWM 157: Aaron Copland, *Appalachian Spring* (1943–44, orchestrated 1945), ballet suite, excerpt: Variations on *'Tis a Gift to Be Simple*

CD 11|86   CD 6|53

NAWM 158: William Grant Still, *Afro-American Symphony* (Symphony No. 1) (1930), symphony, first movement, Moderato assai

CD 12|1   CD 6|63

42. How does Copland evoke the activities and spirit of rural America in the first part of the excerpt from *Appalachian Spring* in NAWM 157 (mm. 1–170)?

43. In what ways does the Shaker hymn *Simple Gifts* (shown in NAWM, p. 1187) convey simplicity? How does Aaron Copland reinforce that simplicity in his use of the tune in *Appalachian Spring* (beginning in m. 171)?

44. What kinds of harmonies does Copland use in this excerpt (including the entire passage in NAWM)? What traits of his harmonies and melodies convey an "American sound"?

45. What aspects of this excerpt suggest the influence of Stravinsky? What traits distinguish Copland's style from Stravinsky's? Use the excerpts from *The Rite of Spring* and *Symphony of Psalms* (NAWM 145–146) for comparison.

46. How does this excerpt from *Appalachian Spring* illustrate Copland's ideas about the purpose of music?

47. The first movement of Still's *Afro-American Symphony* (NAWM 158) unites symphonic and African-American traditions. What elements does it draw from symphonic tradition?

48. What elements does Still incorporate from African-American traditions, including those illustrated in NAWM 136, 149, 150, and 152?

49. Why do you think Still chose to incorporate elements from African-American musical traditions in his *Afro-American Symphony*? How is this similar to and different from Copland's use of a Shaker tune in *Appalachian Spring*?

What Politics? (HWM 891–92)

50. In what ways were some of the best-known and most widely performed classical works created between the world wars shaped by political or social concerns? Why do you think the political context for these works has been forgotten or deemphasized?

TERMS TO KNOW

New Objectivity
Gebrauchsmusik
socialist realism

spatial music
sound masses
tone clusters

NAMES TO KNOW

Names Related to European Music

Les Six
Arthur Honegger
Darius Milhaud
Francis Poulenc
Kurt Weill
The Threepenny Opera

Paul Hindemith
Mathis der Maler
Sergey Prokofiev
Dmitri Shostakovich
Lady Macbeth of the Mtsensk District
Shostakovich's Fifth Symphony

Names Related to Music in the Americas

Claude Champagne
Heitor Villa-Lobos
Carlos Chávez
Silvestre Revueltas
Edgard Varèse
Henry Cowell

Ruth Crawford Seeger
Aaron Copland
Appalachian Spring
William Grant Still
Afro-American Symphony
Virgil Thomson

REVIEW QUESTIONS

1. Add the composers and major works discussed in this chapter to the twentieth-century timeline you made for chapter 30.
2. Music and politics intersected in a variety of ways between the two world wars. Write a brief essay outlining the connections that the NAWM examples by Hindemith, Shostakovich, Revueltas, Crawford, Copland, and Still have to politics, including both governmental actions and broader social concerns. How would you characterize these intersections? How is each composer's political environment, and musical response to it, unique?
3. Describe the relationships between modernism and popular styles in music of the interwar period, using NAWM 153–158 to illustrate your points.
4. Compare the lives and careers of American composers Copland, Revueltas, Crawford, and Still to their contemporary Duke Ellington. What do they have in common in terms of their education, careers, and aesthetics? How do they differ?
5. Write an essay in which you trace the roles of women in the classical music tradition in the nineteenth and early twentieth centuries. Refer to Review Question 5, chapter 24. How did Ruth Crawford Seeger's life and career differ from Clara Schumann's, Fanny Mendelssohn Hensel's, and Amy Beach's? How was it similar? What changes in society made it possible for Crawford to achieve what she did?

Chapter 34   Postwar Crosscurrents

CHAPTER OBJECTIVES

After you complete the reading, study of the music, and study questions for this chapter, you should be able to

1. identify some of the factors that have led to a diversity of musical style, technique, and patronage in Europe and the Americas after World War II;

2. briefly describe the different styles of popular music that developed after World War II, and name some of the most important musicians associated with each style;

3. trace the new developments in jazz from the 1940s through the 1960s, name the most significant musicians associated with those developments, and describe their individual styles;

4. name some of the most significant composers of and trends in the classical tradition between the mid-1940s and the 1960s, explain what is individual about each one, and describe pieces by some of the major composers of the century; and

5. describe some of the effects that these new trends in the classical tradition had on music notation and on the roles of the composer, performer, and listener.

CHAPTER OUTLINE

I. Introduction (HWM 893)

In the twenty-five years after the end of World War II, the creation of new popular music traditions and of more diverse styles of art music accelerated.

II. The Cold War and the Splintering Tradition (HWM 893–96)

The people involved in the diversification of music after World War II had experienced a global depression and the worst war ever, and they responded in a variety of ways.

1. The Cold War
   International relations after World War II were framed by the Cold War. Both sides of this conflict used music performance and composition as arenas for competition.

2. Economic expansion
   The United States, Western Europe, and Japan enjoyed rapid economic growth.

3. Greater access to music
   Technological innovations, increased education, and government and private support made music more accessible to a greater number of people.

4. Independence and civil rights
   As nations in Asia and Africa won independence, there was a growing interest in music of the non-Western world in the West and in American popular music around the world. Music played a significant role in the Civil Rights movement.

5. Musical pluralism
   The postwar period was one of unprecedented experimentation and diversification in music.

III. Popular Music (HWM 896–902)

After World War II, musicians took the traditions of popular music, Broadway musicals, and jazz in separate directions.

1. Identity through music
   Young people had more disposable income, and *pop music* was marketed to them. As popular music split into niche markets tracked by *charts* (rankings of the best-selling records), the music people listened to marked their identity as strongly as their clothing and behavior.

A. Country Music
Country music blended traditional music of the southern hill country, derived from Anglo-American ballads and fiddle tunes, with cowboy songs, Tin Pan Alley, blues, swing, and gospel songs. Singers accompanied themselves on guitar, often with others singing harmony or backed by a band with fiddles and guitars.

B. Rhythm-and-Blues and Rock and Roll
Rhythm-and-blues was a black urban blues-based style with insistent rhythm emphasizing the offbeats and often using electric guitar and bass. At first intended for an African-American audience, it reached white teenagers through radio and recordings.

1. Rock and roll
   Rock and roll emerged in the 1950s from a blending of rhythm-and-blues with country music and quickly became popular. *Elvis Presley* (1935–1977) was its first megastar. By 1960, it was simply called *rock* and was outselling every other kind of music.

C. The Sixties

    1. The Beatles

       The Beatles, the most popular rock band of the 1960s, embraced a wide variety of musical styles and experimented with recording technology, appealing to connoisseurs as well as a general audience.

    2. Rock branches out

       As bands sought an individual sound, they developed many new styles within the broad tradition of rock.

    3. Folk and protest music

       Rising interest in American folk songs led to a new kind of popular music that drew on folk traditions, called *folk music* even though most songs were newly composed. Songs, often linked to social and political struggles, were deliberately simple with one or more singers and guitar or banjo and sometimes audience participation.

    4. Soul

       In the 1960s, *soul,* a blend of rhythm-and-blues and gospel styles, was the leading African-American tradition of popular music.

    5. Motown

       Motown, a Detroit record company owned by Berry Gordy (b. 1929), produced popular music derived from soul that appealed to both black and white audiences.

    6. Tex-Mex and salsa

       Latino-Americans produced their own styles of music, including Tex-Mex and *salsa.*

    7. Pluralism and hybrids

       The diversity of popular traditions shows the pluralism of modern society, yet all these traditions had common roots in prewar popular song, jazz, and blues.

IV. Broadway and Film Music (HWM 902–905)

  A. Broadway Musicals

    1. Musicals

       Broadway musicals maintained their traditions after World War II, and those that were successful tended to become Hollywood films.

    2. Rodgers and Hammerstein

       Richard Rodgers (1902–1979) and Oscar Hammerstein II (1895–1960) produced some of Broadway's best-loved shows, beginning with *Oklahoma!* (1943).

    3. Leonard Bernstein

       Leonard Bernstein (1910–1990) was a conductor and classical composer as well as a major presence on Broadway, best known for his musical *West Side Story* (1957).

4. Later Broadway
In the 1960s, Broadway musicals diversified their subject matter and adapted styles from other traditions.

B. Film Music
Film music also diversified in the postwar years, as composers chose styles and sounds that were appropriate to the subject and mood. Popular music, jazz, and rock were also featured in postwar films.

V. From Bebop to Free Jazz (HWM 905–908, NAWM 159)

From 1940 to 1970, several new styles of jazz emerged while older styles continued. There was a growing sense of jazz history and of jazz as an art music.

A. Bebop
Bebop (*bop*) emerged in the early 1940s in New York City and was built around virtuosic soloists supported by small combos.

1. Characteristics
A typical bebop combo had a rhythm section and one or more melody instruments. Bebop combined traditional jazz elements with complex harmony and rhythm, chromaticism, and more improvisation, and it was meant for attentive listening, not dancing.

2. *Anthropology*
A characteristic example of bebop is *Anthropology,* by *Charlie "Bird" Parker* (1920–1955) and *Dizzy Gillespie* (1917–1993). **Music: NAWM 159**

B. After Bebop
In the 1950s, musicians pioneered new jazz styles, seeking paths for individual expression by extending the methods and ideas of bebop. A major figure in several trends was *Miles Davis* (1926–1991).

1. Avant-garde jazz
Ornette Coleman (b. 1930) and his quartet introduced *free jazz,* and *John Coltrane* (1926–1967) developed a personal avant-garde style.

C. Jazz as a Classical Music
By 1970, the jazz world had developed its own roster of classics, and it was treated as a kind of classical music, studied in written histories and in college courses and ensembles.

VI. Heirs to the Classical Tradition (HWM 908–909)

During the postwar years, living composers shared less and less common ground, with little consensus on style, aesthetic, or purpose.

A. The New Patronage
Most composers had to find new sources of patronage to make a living.

1. The university as patron
In the United States and Canada, many composers were employed as teaching faculty in universities, colleges, and conservatories.

VII. Traditional Media (HWM 909–917, NAWM 160–162)

Many postwar composers used traditional media, developing an individual style within the classical tradition.

A. Olivier Messiaen

Olivier Messiaen (1908–1992), the most important French composer born in the twentieth century, was also an organist and teacher who taught many important younger composers.

1. Religious themes

Messiaen composed many pieces on religious subjects, such as the *Quatuor pour la fin du temps* (Quartet for the End of Time, 1941).

2. Music as contemplation

Messiaen sought to embody ecstatic contemplation in music, focusing on a few ideas that are juxtaposed rather than developed. **Music: NAWM 160**

3. Birdcalls

Messiaen often notated birdsongs and used them in several compositions.

4. Modes of limited transposition

Messiaen used what he called "modes of limited transposition" to create contemplative music.

5. Harmonic stasis

Messiaen used repeated chord series to create a sense of stasis or meditation.

6. Duration, not meter

Messiaen treated rhythm as a matter of duration, not meter, sometimes using repeated patterns of duration like those of medieval isorhythm.

7. Additive and nonretrogradable rhythms

Messiaen also used devices he called "added values," which produce units of irregular length, and "nonretrogradable rhythms," which are the same in forward and backward order, to emphasize duration over meter.

8. Beautiful sounds

Messiaen preferred beautiful timbres and colorful harmonies.

B. Benjamin Britten

The English composer *Benjamin Britten* (1913–1976) was concerned primarily with communicating ideas in his music, especially humanitarian concerns.

1. Music for amateurs

Most of Britten's choral music was conceived for church and cathedral choirs, schools, and amateur choruses,

2. Homosexuality

Britten was a homosexual, and several of his operas have themes related to homosexuality.

3. *Peter Grimes*

Britten established his reputation with *Peter Grimes* (1944–45), the first English opera since Purcell to enter the international repertory. **Music: NAWM 161**

4. *War Requiem*

Britten's pacifism is expressed in his *War Requiem* (1961–62).

C. Tonal Traditionalism

Many twentieth-century composers developed individual styles without departing radically from the past.

1. Samuel Barber

The American composer *Samuel Barber* (1910–1981) offered a novel blend of traditional tonality with modern resources.   **Music: NAWM 162**

D. Stylistic Mixtures

The wide dissemination of music all over the world encouraged composers to mix styles and traditions.

1. Latin America: Ginastera

Alberto Ginastera (1916–1983) of Argentina drew on both nationalism and international sources.

2. Third Stream

Some American composers merged jazz and classical music to create what Gunther Schuller (b. 1925) called "third stream."

3. Michael Tippett

Michael Tippett (1905–1998) synthesized historical, ethnic, and non-Western styles and materials.

VIII. Serialism (HWM 917–920)

A. The Spread of Serialism

After World War II, young composers in Germany and elsewhere adopted twelve-tone methods, adapting them to their own purposes.

1. Politics and institutional support

Government and university support for serial music was crucial, since there was never a large audience for it.

2. Individualism

The ideas fostered in centers for new music inspired experiments by composers in many countries.

B. Extensions of Serialism

Beginning in the late 1940s, composers applied serial procedures of twelve-tone music to parameters other than pitch, such as duration and dynamics, resulting in *total serialism*.

1. Milton Babbitt

Milton Babbitt (b. 1916) first applied serial principles to duration in his Three Compositions for Piano (1947). His music grew even more complex because of the maximum interrelatedness of its musical materials, exemplified in his Third String Quartet (1970).

2. Pierre Boulez

Composers in Europe explored new serialist ideas, independent of Babbitt. *Pierre Boulez* (b. 1925) wrote the first European work of total serialism but soon relaxed the technique's rigidity in works like *Le marteau sans maître* (1954).

3. The listener
Totally serial compositions are logical, but they may give listeners an impression of randomness and have appealed principally to a small set of enthusiasts.

IX. Nonserial Complexity and Virtuosity (HWM 920–922)

In the postwar years, a new generation of extraordinarily proficient performers encouraged composers to write pieces to challenge their skills.

1. Luciano Berio
The series of works by *Luciano Berio* (1925–2003) titled *Sequenza* were each for a different unaccompanied solo instrument, composed for a specific virtuosic performer.

2. Elliott Carter
Elliott Carter (b. 1908), who also wrote music only the most proficient performers could play, developed what he called "metric modulation." In his String Quartet No. 2 (1959), Carter gives each instrumental part a distinctive personality that interacts with the others.

X. New Sounds and Textures (HWM 922–931, NAWM 163–165)

One prominent strand in twentieth-century music was the exploration of new musical resources.

A. New Instruments, Sounds, and Scales
Some composers built new instruments or explored new scales.

1. John Cage
Throughout his career, *John Cage* (1912–1992) challenged the core concepts of music and brought into music what had been excluded from it. In the late 1930s and 1940s, he focused on new sounds.

2. Prepared piano
Cage's experimentation with timbre culminated in his invention of the *prepared piano,* essentially, a one-person percussion ensemble.

3. Harry Partch
Harry Partch (1901–1974) developed new instruments that could play in a scale based on pure intervals.

4. George Crumb
George Crumb (b. 1929) used ordinary instruments and objects to create new sounds. His unusual effects provide material for juxtaposition and variation and usually convey meanings through association. **Music: NAWM 163**

B. Non-Western Styles and Instruments
Composers explored music of other cultures with respect for its uniqueness.

1. Asian influences
Several Western composers became fascinated with Asian instruments, sounds, and textures.

2. Japan: Takemitsu

By midcentury, many Asian composers, such as *Tōru Takemitsu* (1930–1996), were writing music in the European classical tradition.

C. Electronic Music

Electronic recording, production, and manipulation of sounds were first explored in art music but ultimately became more significant for popular music, especially after 1970.

1. Musique concrète

Tape recorders became widely available in 1950, allowing composers to create *musique concrète* using recorded sounds that were transformed through tape and electronic procedures.

2. Electronic sound

Some new sounds were produced electronically, beginning with electronic instruments like the Theremin and the Ondes Martenot.

3. Electronic music studios

Electronic music studios made possible a whole new realm of sounds.

4. *Gesang der Jünglinge* and *Poème electronique*

Some composers used recorded sounds alongside electronic ones, as in *Gesang der Jünglinge* (Song of the Youths, 1955–56), by *Karlheinz Stockhausen* (b. 1928), and Varèse's *Poème electronique* (Electronic Poem, 1957–58).

5. Synthesizers

Electronic sound synthesizers made the process of recording and mixing much easier, and in the mid-1960s, popular artists also began using them.

6. Role of performers

The electronic medium gave composers complete, unmediated control over their compositions.

7. Tape and live performance

Since audiences expect to have performers to watch and respond to, composers began to create works that combined prerecorded tape with live performers, as in Babbitt's *Philomel* (1964).   **Music: NAWM 164**

D. Music of Texture and Process

Inspired by Varèse's concept of spatial music and by electronic music, some composers wrote pieces based on interesting and novel textures, organized by gradual or sudden processes of change.

1. Iannis Xenakis

Iannis Xenakis (1922–2001) was among the first to write such music for acoustic instruments, in works such as *Metastaseis* (1953–54).

2. Krzysztof Penderecki

Krzysztof Penderecki (b. 1933) wrote *Threnody: To the Victims of Hiroshima* (1960), one of the best-known pieces based on texture and process, which uses high clusters, glissandos, and special effects on string instruments to create music that sounds electronic. He also used this technique in dramatic works.   **Music: NAWM 165**

3. György Ligeti

György Ligeti (b. 1923) created music that was in constant motion, yet static both harmonically and melodically.

E. New Thinking

These pieces using new sounds and textures demand new thinking about music from their listeners as much as from their composers.

XI. The Avant-Garde (HWM 931–936, NAWM 166)

1. Modernist, experimentalist, avant-garde

In some discussions of twentieth-century music, all postwar developments are lumped together as avant-garde. But modernist, experimental, and avant-garde composers have different motivations—respectively, seeking a place in the classical repertoire, trying new methods for their own sake, and challenging accepted aesthetics while focusing on the present.

A. John Cage

John Cage, the leading composer of the postwar avant-garde, created opportunities for experiencing sounds as sounds and not as the composer's intentions.

1. Chance

Cage used *chance* operations to make some of the decisions normally made by the composer in his *Music of Changes* for piano (1951) and other works. **Music: NAWM 160**

2. Indeterminacy

Different from chance is *indeterminacy,* in which the composer leaves unspecified certain aspects of the music, such as the precise notes and rhythms or the coordination of parts. By using chance and indeterminacy, Cage invites the listener to simply hear sound as sound and not expect the music to communicate meaning.

3. Blurring the boundaries

Beginning in the 1950s, Cage created pieces that blurred the boundaries between music, other arts, and the rest of life.

B. Indeterminacy in Works of Other Composers

Many composers adopted indeterminacy in some form under Cage's influence.

1. Witold Lutosławski

Witold Lutosławski (1913–1994) made selective use of indeterminacy to create certain effects, while insisting on his authorship of the entire composition.

2. Significance of indeterminacy

Pieces that use indeterminacy utilize new kinds of notation and are never performed the same way twice, drawing into question the nature of a musical "work."

C. Music as Theater and Performance Art

John Cage inspired others to challenge accepted definitions of music and art.

1. Fluxus

Performance art came into its own in the 1960s, spearheaded by Fluxus, a loose group of avant-garde artists in Europe and the United States.

2. Temporary art

Performance art had no place in the concert repertoire but prompted questions about what music is and what it is for.

XII. Quotation and Collage (HWM 936–938)

Many composers of varying orientations quoted existing music, using evocations of older music to carry new meanings.

1. Peter Maxwell Davies

Peter Maxwell Davies (b. 1934) drew on older music and distorted it to emphasize the gulf between modern times and the distant past.

2. Rochberg, Foss, Crumb

George Rochberg (b. 1918), Lukas Foss (b. 1922), and George Crumb wrote works that incorporate past music for expressive reasons.

3. Stockhausen

Stockhausen used borrowed material in several works to relate music of the present to that of the past in a new way.

4. Berio's *Sinfonia*

One of the richest pieces based on borrowed material is the third movement of Luciano Berio's *Sinfonia* (Symphony, 1968–69).

5. Role of the familiar

Music based on quotation gives the audience something familiar to grasp and provides a new experience of that music.

XIII. Band and Wind Ensemble Music (HWM 938–940, NAWM 167)

Band music underwent a striking transformation in the postwar era with the creation of a large repertoire of serious works for band.

1. Concert bands

Schools, colleges, and professional organizations promoted the concept of the *concert band* as a vehicle for serious concert music.

2. Commissioning serious works

Major composers, including Schoenberg, Milhaud, and Hindemith, received commissions to write works for concert band.

3. Wind ensemble

In 1952, Frederick Fennell (1914–2005) founded the first *wind ensemble,* in which each instrumental part was essential and most were played by soloists.

4. Works for winds

Ensembles, commissions, and widespread performances attracted many composers to write for winds.

5. *Music for Prague 1968*

Works for band reflect the same range of styles and concerns as contemporary orchestral works. For example, *Music for Prague 1968* by Karel Husa (b. 1921) was written in a university context and uses quoted material, twelve-tone methods, indeterminacy, and a focus on texture.
Music: NAWM 167

6. The problem of prestige

Despite the size and quality of the repertoire, wind music still lacks the status of music for strings or orchestra.

XIV. Roll Over, Beethoven (HWM 940)

Since 1970, popular music has grown even more central to musical life. There are now classical repertoires of pop music, musicals, jazz, and film music, with works from the period 1945–1970 at their core. Postwar art music has not fared as well, finding few listeners when it was new and having no larger an audience today. Yet many of the new sounds and techniques of this period have become common currency for later composers in classical, popular, and film music.

STUDY QUESTIONS

The Cold War and the Splintering Tradition (HWM 893–96)

1. What were some of the most significant political, social, economic, and technological changes after World War II that had an impact on music? Why was music between 1945 and 1970 so diverse?

Popular Music (HWM 896–902)

2. Describe the characteristics of *country music*. From what traditions did it derive? Who was its target audience?

3. Describe the origins and style of *rhythm-and-blues*. Who was its original audience? What other group grew interested, and why? What later styles of popular music grew out of rhythm-and-blues, and how did they differ from it?

4. What is the relationship between country music, rhythm-and-blues, and *rock and roll*? Describe the origins of rock and trace changes in rock from its early years to the 1960s. Name some of the most important rock musicians during these years and describe why they are significant to music history. To whom did their music appeal?

5. In addition to country music, rhythm-and-blues, and rock, what other traditions of popular music were strong in the 1950s and 1960s? What were the distinctive qualities of each? What was the audience for each, and how was it adapted to suit that audience?

Broadway and Film Music (HWM 902–905)

6. Name two of the major composers on Broadway in the period 1940–1970, name one show by each, and explain what made them innovative or interesting.

7. What different styles and traditions were used in film music in the period 1940–1970? Why was film music so diverse during this period?

From Bebop to Free Jazz (HWM 905–908, NAWM 159)

8. Where and when did *bebop* originate? What are its essential characteristics?

Music to Study

NAWM 159: Charlie Parker and Dizzy Gillespie, *Anthropology* (1945), bebop tune and solo

   159a: Lead sheet (at concert pitch)

   159b: Transcription of Charlie Parker's solo (transposed for alto saxophone)   [CD 12|8]   [CD 6|70]

9. What is the relationship between the harmonic progression of *Anthropology,* as notated on the lead sheet (NAWM 159a), and those of Gershwin's *I Got Rhythm* (NAWM 151) and Ellington's *Cotton Tail* (NAWM 152)?

10. What style traits typical of bebop are heard in the recording of *Anthropology* and are evident in Parker's solo (NAWM 159b)?

11. How is improvisation in the recording of *Anthropology* similar to or different from improvisation in the recordings of *West End Blues* (NAWM 150) and *Cotton Tail* (NAWM 152)?

12. What parts of *Anthropology* were composed before it was recorded? How and why does *Anthropology* differ from *Cotton Tail* in this respect?

13. What is the social function of *Anthropology*? Where and for whom would it be performed? How is this different from New Orleans and big band jazz?

14. What are the differences between sheet music (see NAWM 150a) and a lead sheet (see NAWM 159a) in what they contain and how they are used?

15. Describe other trends in jazz after bebop, and name a prominent figure associated with each style.

Heirs to the Classical Tradition (HWM 908–909)

16. How did composers earn a living in the years after World War II? How did the situation differ between Europe and North America? What effects do you think this has had on composition?

Traditional Media (HWM 909–917, NAWM 160–162)

17. Briefly summarize Messiaen's career and significance.

Music to Study

NAWM 160: Olivier Messiaen, *Quartet for the End of Time*
(1940–41), Quartet for violin, clarinet, violoncello, and piano,
first movement, *Liturgie de cristal*

18. Describe Messiaen's use of rhythm in *Liturgie de cristal,* the first movement of
Quartet for the End of Time (NAWM 160), refering to specific measures and instruments to illustrate your points. Is there a regular meter? Is there a sense of momentum toward a goal?

19. *Liturgie de cristal* features birdsongs in the clarinet and in the violin. How does
Messiaen imitate these birdsongs?

20. How does Messiaen use his musical material? What happens to it over the course
of the movement? How is it repeated or varied?

21. What is the form of *Liturgie de cristal*? How does Messiaen create the form?

22. How do the musical material, the form, and the treatment of rhythm suggest mystical contemplation?

23. Imagine you are at the very first performance of this quartet. Who is in the audience with you? How do your surroundings influence your experience of the work?

24. What were Britten's goals for his music? How did his goals differ from those of Messiaen? From those of Schoenberg and Webern?

25. How is Britten's pacifism reflected in his *War Requiem*?

Music to Study

NAWM 161: Benjamin Britten, *Peter Grimes* (1944–45), opera   CD 12|17
Act III, scene 2, *To hell with all your mercy!*

NAWM 162: Samuel Barber, *Hermit Songs,* Op. 29 (1952–53),   CD 12|23   CD 6|76
song cycle No. 8, *The Monk and His Cat*

26. In the concluding scene of *Peter Grimes* (NAWM 161), how does Britten portray Grimes's madness through musical means, including reminiscences of earlier material?

27. What musical elements (including motives, chords, keys or collections of pitches, timbres, and so on) are associated with the townspeople (the chorus) and with the sea (the figuration in the orchestra)?

28. How does Britten create the effect of events happening simultaneously, but remaining separate from one another? What does this tell us about the relationship between Grimes and those around him? What does it suggest about the relationship between the townspeople and the sea?

29. This opera premiered shortly after World War II ended in Europe. In what ways might the events of war and its aftermath affect an audience's experience of the work?

30. In Barber's song *The Monk and His Cat* (NAWM 162), what are the monk and cat doing? What is their general mood?

31. Although this is clearly secular music from the twentieth century, what references does Barber make to sacred music from a much earlier time? How does he use rhythm, meter, melody, and harmony to evoke the monk's environment?

32. Like other modern composers, Barber and Britten sought to contribute something new and individual to the repertoire of musical classics, while drawing on the past tradition. How did their approaches to this challenge differ from those of the modernist composers discussed in chapter 31? Which approach do you think is more successful? Why?

Serialism (HWM 917–920)

33. Why did many composers take up serialism in the period after World War II? What institutions promoted or sponsored it? What purposes did it serve?

34. What is Milton Babbitt saying in the excerpt from his article "Who Cares If You Listen?" in HWM, p. 916? What is his view of contemporary music and its relationship to the wider musical public?

How does his view relate to the employment of composers as college and university teachers? How does he view the roles of the audience member and the performer?

Do you agree with his views? Why or why not?

35. How did Babbitt apply serialism to rhythm in his Third Quartet (see the discussion of Example 34.3 in HWM, pp. 918–19)?

Nonserial Complexity and Virtuosity (HWM 920–922)

36. What effect do total serialism and other highly complex styles of music have on musical training and performance? How do Berio's *Sequenzas* and Carter's String Quartet No. 2 resemble Babbitt's music, and what is distinctive about each of them?

New Sounds and Textures (HWM 922–931, NAWM 163–165)

37. What is the *prepared piano*? Who invented it? How does it relate to the exploration of new sounds?

38. What did Harry Partch reject in Western music, and what materials did he use instead?

NAWM 163: George Crumb, *Black Angels: Thirteen Images from the Dark Land* (1970), electric string quartet

163a: Image 4, *Devil-Music*   CD 12|26

163b: Image 5, *Danse macabre*   CD 12|27

39. What new playing techniques for string instruments does Crumb use in these two movements from *Black Angels* (NAWM 163)? (Hint: Check the footnotes that explain how to perform certain effects; these footnotes sometimes appear on a different page.) What additional instruments and sounds does he call for, beyond the four instruments of the string quartet? List all the new playing techniques, instruments, and other sounds you can find. For each one, put down one or a few words that describe how the device sounds and what emotional effect it conveys.

40. Crumb quotes or refers to earlier music several times. List these quotations and references along with the instrument that plays them. What is the effect of these references to earlier music within the context of Crumb's music? In your opinion, what might these references mean?

41. What are the programmatic ideas in *Black Angels,* and how are they conveyed? How does music like this compare to earlier program music?

42. Describe the differences between nineteenth-century exoticism, as in Bizet's *Carmen* (NAWM 129) and Borodin's *Prince Igor* (see HWM, p. 704), and uses of non-Western styles and instruments in the twentieth century.

43. What is *musique concrète*? When and where was it developed? How did musique concrète change the role of the composer and the performer?

Music to Study

NAWM 164: Milton Babbitt, *Philomel*: Section I (1964), monodrama for soprano, recorded soprano, and synthesized sound, Section I

CD 12|26   CD 6|79

44. How does Babbitt use the singer, taped vocal sounds, and electronic sounds in *Philomel* (NAWM 164)? What is each component like? How do they relate? And how do they work together to suggest the story and the feelings of Philomel?

45. How does this excerpt from *Philomel* correlate with Babbitt's views about music expressed in his article "Who Cares If You Listen?" (see question 34 above)?

46. How did Xenakis and Ligeti use traditional instruments to create novel sounds and textures in *Metastaseis* and *Atmosphères*?

Music to Study

NAWM 165: Krzysztof Penderecki, *Threnody: To the Victims of Hiroshima* (1960), tone poem for string orchestra CD 12|33

47. What musical elements does Penderecki highlight in his *Threnody: To the Victims of Hiroshima* (NAWM 165)? In what ways is his compositional treatment of those elements conventional, and in what ways is it unconventional?

48. Why are the elements you listed above in particularly powerful in conveying a threnody (song of lamentation)? How might your experience of this work change if Penderecki had kept the original title *8′ 37″*?

49. How is Penderecki's approach to the tone poem similar to or different from Strauss's approach in *Don Quixote* (excerpted in NAWM 133)?

The Avant-Garde (HWM 931–936, NAWM 166)

50. What are the differences between modernist music, experimentalist music, and avant-garde music?

Music to Study

NAWM 166: John Cage, *Music of Changes*: Book I (1951),   CD 12|40   CD 6|84
chance composition for piano

51. When Cage created *Music of Changes* (NAWM 166), what elements of the music did he compose in advance? What aspects of the composition were left to chance?

52. Describe the form of Music of Changes. How is it articulated? What marks off the sections? What do the three segments in Book I (marked by CD track numbers) have in common, and how do they differ?

53. What is the difference between chance music (like *Music of Changes*) and indeterminacy?

54. How does this excerpt from *Music of Changes* illustrate Cage's thinking about music in his lecture "Changes"? (See the excerpt in HWM, p. 934.)

55. Compare the sound, style, and experience of listening to Cage's *Music of Changes* (NAWM 166) with the sound, style, and experience of listening to Babbitt's *Philomel* (NAWM 164). How are they similar, and how are they different?

56. Compare Cage's ideas about music in his lecture "Changes" with Babbitt's "Who Cares If You Listen?" Do they share any common concerns about the current state of music? How do they differ in their concerns and in their solutions? How are these differences reflected in their music?

57. What is *performance art*? In what ways is it avant-garde? How does it relate to Cage's work?

Quotation and Collage (HWM 936–938)

58. Describe the use of quotation and collage techniques in one piece from the 1960s. How are these techniques in the twentieth century similar to or different from techniques of glossing and troping from the Middle Ages (see chapter 3) or the cantus firmus and imitation masses of the Renaissance (see chapters 8–10)?

Band and Wind Ensemble Music (HWM 938–940, NAWM 167)

59. Who are some of the primary patrons of band and wind ensemble music? How is this similar to or different from music for other ensembles, such as orchestras and operas?

60. What are the main differences between a marching band and a wind ensemble? What are the main differences between an orchestra and a wind ensemble? Who created the first wind ensemble? When and where was it created?

Music to Study

NAWM 167: Karel Husa, *Music for Prague 1968* (1968), concert band suite, first movement, Introduction and Fanfare, Adagio–Allegro ⸤CD 12|43⸥

61. In what measures and in what instruments do portions of the Czech chorale tune "You Who Are God's Warriors" appear in the first movement of Husa's *Music for Prague 1968* (NAWM 167)? How much of the tune is heard in these measures?

62. What effect does Husa create by waiting until the end of the last movement to present the chorale in its entirety? What extramusical idea does it portray? Why is it appropriate for this particular piece?

63. Compare the first movement of Husa's *Music for Prague 1968* with John Philip Sousa's *The Stars and Stripes Forever* (NAWM 135). Although these are both works for band, how do they differ in terms of their function? What kind of event is each typically performed for, and what mood or moods does each evoke?

Roll Over, Beethoven (HWM 940)

64. What has led to the emergence of repertoires of classics in pop music, musical, jazz, and film music?

65. What has been the reception of music in the classical tradition from the postwar period? What has been the impact of the new ideas and sounds that music pioneered?

TERMS TO KNOW

Terms Related to Popular Music and Jazz

pop music
charts
country music
rhythm-and-blues
rock and roll, rock

folk music
soul
salsa
bebop, bop
free jazz

Terms Related to Classical Music

total serialism
prepared piano
musique concrète
electronic music
chance

indeterminacy
performance art
concert band
wind ensemble

NAMES TO KNOW

Names Related to Popular Music and Jazz

Elvis Presley
The Beatles
Motown
Richard Rodgers
Leonard Bernstein

Charlie Parker
Dizzy Gillespie
Miles Davis
Ornette Coleman
John Coltrane

Names Related to Classical Music

Olivier Messiaen
Quatuor pour la fin du temps
Benjamin Britten
Peter Grimes
War Requiem
Samuel Barber
Alberto Ginastera
Michael Tippett
Milton Babbitt
Pierre Boulez
Luciano Berio
Elliott Carter
John Cage
Harry Partch

George Crumb
Tōru Takemitsu
Karlheinz Stockhausen
Philomel
Iannis Xenakis
Krzysztof Penderecki
Threnody: To the Victims of Hiroshima
György Ligeti
Music of Changes
Witold Lutosławski
Peter Maxwell Davies
George Rochberg
Karel Husa, *Music for Prague 1968*

REVIEW QUESTIONS

1. Add the composers, performers, and major works discussion in this chapter to the twentieth-century timeline you made for chapter 30.

2. Describe the effects that advancements in electronic technologies had on the activities of composition, performance, and listening, in both popular and classical traditions.

3. Describe the varieties of popular music that were marketed to the public in the 1950s and 1960s. How was each variety targeted at a particular audience? How did these different varieties relate to one another?

4. Trace the changing functions of jazz from World War I to about 1970. Are there genres in classical music that underwent similar transformations?

5. Contrast the music and artistic aims of Messiaen, Britten, Babbitt, and Cage. What was each after, and how does the music of each reflect his goals?

6. Trace developments in music notation in the twentieth century. What motivated composers to create new ways of writing music? How does this compare with new notations in the Middle Ages?

7. Write a piece of music using either chance operations or indeterminacy. What must be determined in advance in the approach you chose?

8. Quotation and collage are among the many significant compositional techniques after World War II. How is the way composers in the later twentieth century quoted or referred to existing pieces of music in their own new compositions similar to or different from the same activity in the nineteenth century? The eighteenth century? How about even earlier? When we know what is quoted, how does that change our experience of a piece of music?

9. In this chapter, you have learned about many diverse styles of music in the classical tradition. You have also learned of new ways of thinking about music. Why did composers begin to ask, "What is music?" and what conclusions did they draw? Where did they look for answers? What solutions did they arrive at? Write your own essay stating your personal philosophy of music. Refer to composers quoted in this chapter, and incorporate their thoughts into your own. State why you agree or disagree with what they had to say.

Chapter 35 | The End of the Millennium

CHAPTER OBJECTIVES

After you complete the reading, study of the music, and study questions for this chapter, you should be able to

1. summarize the impact of globalism on musical style in the later twentieth century;
2. explain some of the most important new musical trends at the end of the twentieth century, and name the most significant composers and characteristic works associated with those trends;
3. describe the impact of non-Western musics on music of the Western classical tradition;
4. describe the effects of technological developments on music in the later twentieth century; and
5. describe ways in which the culture and styles of popular music and of classical music affected each other.

CHAPTER OUTLINE

I. Introduction (HWM 941)

> In the last thirty years of the twentieth century and the beginning of the twenty-first, the Western musical tradition continued to diversify. This chapter will look at only a few issues and four musical trends.

II. A Global Culture (HWM 942–44)

> The late 1960s and 1970s brought a series of political and economic shocks to Western nations.

> 1. Detente and democracy
> In the 1970s, tensions began to ease between the U. S. and the Soviet Union, and the last dictatorships of Western Europe were replaced by democracies.

2. Collapse of European communism
   By 1990, the people of central and eastern Europe freed themselves from Soviet domination, and the Soviet Union dissolved the following year.

3. New conflicts
   After the end of the Cold War, new conflicts emerged, including regional tensions, civil wars, and terrorism.

4. Global economy
   By the 1990s, almost every country was part of the global economy.

5. Global links
   A new global culture emerged with the spread of technology and easy travel.

6. Global arts
   Global links fostered a global market for the world's diverse music and arts.

III. The Changing World of Music (HWM 944–50)

Crossing and blending musical traditions have become commonplace.

A. Broadening the Meaning of "Art Music"
   The idea of art music began in the tradition of concert music, but spread to other traditions.

1. Jazz repertory
   By the end of the millennium, jazz was widely accepted as art music with its own repertory of classics and historical performance ensembles.

2. Rock museums
   Museums were created to preserve the legacies of rock music and country music.

3. Musicals
   The musical became recognized as a tradition of classics. New musicals, such as those by Stephen Sondheim (b. 1930) and Andrew Lloyd Webber (b. 1948), often aspire to the level of art music more than entertainment.

4. Asian classical music
   Asian classical music has made western listeners aware that western classical music is one of many prestigious musical traditions.

B. New Technologies
   Since the 1970s, new *digital* technologies have altered the ways musicians work with music and listeners consume it.

1. Sampling
   One significant new technique is *sampling,* patching together digital segments of recorded sound.

2. Computer music
   Advances in computing offered new possibilities that composers explored, including computer-synthesized sounds and computer transformations of sound.

Music in Context: Digital Technologies

In the early 1970s and early 1980s, music joined the digital revolution, and musicians in both popular and classical traditions were using digital synthesizers. Some musicians combined live performers with synthesized or computer-generated music. Consumers have enjoyed a variety of increasingly efficient products for listening to music, from vinyl records to CDs to mp3 files to file-sharing Internet sites.

C. Mixed Media

Music in the late twentieth century has grown closer to other performance arts, as it increasingly has become part of *mixed media* artworks.

1. Stage shows and music videos

By the 1980s, elaborate stage shows and *music videos* combined pop music with costumes, staging, lighting, dancing, and sets.

2. Laurie Anderson

Laurie Anderson (b. 1947), a leading performance artist, combines a wide range of media, from literature to music to visual art, in her works.

3. Spectacle works

A new genre of musical theater emerged in the 1990s with works like *STOMP* (1991), in which the process of making music itself became a visual spectacle.

4. Film music

Although many films used existing music, there was a return to full-scale symphonic scores organized around leitmotives, as in the music by John Williams (b. 1932) for the six *Star Wars* movies (1977–2005).

D. Trends

The broadening concept of music as an art, new technologies, and mixed media are only three of many trends in recent music. Other trends resulted from pressures within traditions.

IV. Niches in Popular Music (HWM 950–52)

Popular music has splintered into niche markets and competing trends, each identified with particular social groups.

1. Disco

Disco was a style of dance music in the 1970s that catered primarily to African-Americans, Latinos, and gay men before spreading across the globe.

2. Punk, New Wave, alternative rock, and grunge

Punk, New Wave, alternative rock, and grunge became emblems for youth of a certain age, offending or being incomprehensible to most of their elders.

3. Rap

Rap began as part of African-American urban youth culture in the 1970s, and by the 1990s, styles adapted from it spread around the world.

4. Musical subcultures
Other types of music, such as women's music and Christian rock, foster collective feeling among particular groups.

V. Minimalism and Postminimalism (HWM 952–56, NAWM 168)

Minimalism is an approach in which materials are reduced to a minimum and procedures simplified. It began as an aesthetic but became a set of techniques, as composers of minimalist works absorbed a variety of influences to create what has been called the leading musical style of the late twentieth century.

1. Minimalism in art
Minimalist artworks focused on basic forms and materials and did not seek to express feelings.

2. Early minimalism in music
A parallel movement was nurtured among musicians such as La Monte Young (b. 1935) and Terry Riley (b. 1935).

A. From Avant-Garde to Widespread Appeal
Three other Americans brought minimalist procedures into art music intended for a broad audience.

1. Steve Reich
Steve Reich (b. 1936) developed a minimalist effect called phasing. He attracted a wide range of listeners, and by the 1980s applied minimalist techniques to works with significant emotional content.

2. Philip Glass
Philip Glass (b. 1937) writes music that emphasizes multilayered ostinatos, rapid pulse, constant repetition, simple melodies, consonance, and slowly changing harmonies, and his music has won a diverse following. He secured his reputation with a series of major works, including operas.

3. John Adams
John Adams (b. 1947) began his career writing minimalist works (like *Phrygian Gates,* 1977–78) and then blended minimalist techniques with elements from popular and classical music in works like his opera *Nixon in China* (1987).   **Music: NAWM 168**

VI. The New Accessibility (HWM 956–64, NAWM 169–171)

While many composers made a living teaching at universities or conservatories, obtaining repeat performances of their music was difficult. Some composers sought to attract wider interest by writing more accessible music.

A. Accessible Modernism
Some composers wrote accessible music in a modernist idiom.

1. Ellen Taaffe Zwilich
Ellen Taaffe Zwilich (b. 1939) joins continuous developing variation with older formal devices of recurrence and contrast.   **Music: NAWM 169**

B. Radical Simplification

Other composers combined a radical simplification of material and procedures with a return to diatonic music.

1. Arvo Pärt

Arvo Pärt (b. 1935) used simple materials influenced by Baroque and medieval traditions to create a highly individual style. The method he called "tintinnabuli" joins a simple diatonic melody with other voices that sound only notes of the tonic triad. **Music: NAWM 170**

C. Quotation and Polystylism

Another approach was *postmodernism,* in which all styles are equally available as musical material, to be employed as the composer sees fit.

1. Alfred Schnittke

Alfred Schnittke (1934–1998) used new Western trends during the 1960s and then turned to what he called *polystylism,* a combination of new and older styles created through quotation or stylistic allusion.

2. John Corigliano

John Corigliano (b. 1938) frequently juxtaposes styles to convey meanings.

3. Peter Schickele and P. D. Q. Bach

Peter Schickele (b. 1935), under the guise of P. D. Q. Bach, uses quotation and stylistic allusion for humorous effect.

D. Neo-Romanticism

Some composers adopted the tonal idiom or sounds and gestures of Romanticism, a trend known as *neo-Romanticism.*

1. Penderecki

Penderecki focused increasingly on neo-Romantic works in the mid-1970s and beyond.

2. Rochberg

Having turned from serialism to quotation in the 1960s, Rochberg moved to a mix of neo-Romanticism and early modernism in the 1970s.

3. David Del Tredici

David Del Tredici (b. 1937) embraced neo-Romanticism to create whimsical, immediately comprehensible music for setting texts from Lewis Carroll's *Alice's Adventures in Wonderland,* as in *Final Alice* (1975).

E. Extramusical Imagery and Meanings

Some composers invoked extramusical meanings and imagery, hoping that listeners would accept unusual sounds if their meanings were clear.

1. Sofia Gubaidulina

The works of *Sofia Gubaidulina* (b. 1931) often have a spiritual dimension. Her sonata *Rejoice!* expresses the transcendence from ordinary reality to a state of joy. **Music: NAWM 171**

2. John Tavener

The music of *John Tavener* (b. 1944) also has centered on spiritual concerns, including sacred choral music and instrumental works.

3. R. Murray Schafer
   R. Murray Schafer (b. 1933) traversed a wide variety of styles, but his most striking innovation is what he calls "environmental music."

4. Joan Tower
   Many works by *Joan Tower* (b. 1938) are based on images.

F. Direct Communication
   By the 1990s, most composers sought to maintain individuality yet write music that nonspecialist audiences could grasp.

VII. Interactions with Non-Western Musics (HWM 964–65, NAWM 172)

Many currents in Western music were inspired by the musics of Asia and Africa.

1. Classical composers
   Some composers, including Chinese-born *Bright Sheng* (b. 1955), drew directly on Asian musics, as illustrated in his solo cello suite *Seven Tunes Heard in China* (1999).   **Music: NAWM 172**

2. World Beat
   Pop artists in Europe and America incorporated World Beat, a term referring to African popular musics that reached international audiences, into their own music. These works go beyond nineteenth-century exoticism in the respect they show for the intrinsic value of the traditions on which they draw.

VIII. The New Millennium (HWM 965)

Music today is too diverse and trends change too quickly to know now what the music of the recent past will be remembered in the future. The variety of music available around the world leaves the future of new music wide open.

STUDY QUESTIONS

A Global Culture (HWM 942–44)

1. Describe the effects that globalism has had and continues to have on composition, performance, and listening.

The Changing World of Music (HWM 944–50)

2. In what ways have the concepts of "art music" and of a classical repertoire changed in the twentieth century? In what Western traditions are there now repertoires of classics?

3. How has digital technology changed concepts of music composition, performance, listening, and distribution?

4. How has music's relationship with the visual arts, dance, and drama changed over the course of the twentieth century? What kinds of mixed media works involving music have emerged since 1970?

Niches in Popular Music (HWM 950–52)

5. What are some new trends in popular music that developed since 1970? What is the relationship of each one to earlier popular styles? In what ways does each one relate to or reinforce the identity of its target audience?

Minimalism and Postminimalism (HWM 952–56, NAWM 168)

6. Describe the origins of and philosophy behind minimalism in art and music.

7. How did minimalism in music evolve from an avant-garde aesthetic to a widely used set of techniques? Briefly trace changes in the music of Reich and of Glass to show this development.

Music to Study

NAWM 168: John Adams, *Phrygian Gates* (1977–78), ⸢CD 12|50⸣
  for piano, excerpt

8. How does Adams use repetition in *Phrygian Gates* (NAWM 168)? How does he vary the material?

9. In Adams's terminology, what is a "gate"? Where do gates occur? What changes at each one? How do they relate to the work's title?

10. In what sense is this work minimalist? How does its style resemble minimalist art as seen in Figure 35.6 in HWM, p. 953?

11. In what sense is *Phrygian Gates* complex?

12. How can you follow this excerpt from *Phrygian Gates*? In your opinion, what should you listen for?

13. What does *Phrygian Gates* have in common with a piano piece by Beethoven (see NAWM 108) or by another nineteenth-century composer (see NAWM 116–120), and what is different?

The New Accessibility (HWM 956–64, NAWM 169–171)

14. Aside from minimalism, what other approaches did composers develop to reconnect with a wider audience? Give an example of each approach.

Music to Study

NAWM 169: Ellen Taaffe Zwilich, Symphony No. 1 (1982),   [CD 12|59]
    first movement

NAWM 170: Arvo Pärt, *Seven Magnificat Antiphons* (1988, rev. 1991),
    choral antiphons, excerpts

      170a: No. 1, *O Weisheit*   [CD 12|65]

      170b: No. 6, *O König aller Völker*   [CD 12|66]

15. What does the first movement of Zwilich's Symphony No. 1 (NAWM 169) have in common with other symphonic works in the classical tradition by composers such as Beethoven (NAWM 109) and Shostakovich (NAWM 154)?

16. Why is the form of this movement easy to hear? What does Zwilich's method of generating form in this movement have in common with the fourth movement of Brahms's Fourth Symphony (NAWM 132)?

17. What pitch sets does Zwilich use in this movement? How are these motives reinterpreted over the course of the movement? In what new contexts do they appear?

18. What is *tintinnabuli style,* and how does Pärt use it in his Magnificat Antiphons (NAWM 170)? What rules and procedures are held in common between *O Weisheit* (NAWM 170a) and *O König aller Völker* (NAWM 170b), and what rules or procedures change?

19. Compare the two choral antiphons by Pärt (NAWM 170) with the examples of early polyphony in NAWM 14. In what ways is Pärt's approach similar to those medieval methods of embellishing a given melody, and in what ways is it different? What harmonic intervals are most common in early polyphony? In Pärt's antiphons?

20. Compare Pärt's antiphons with Adams's *Phrygian Gates* (NAWM 168). What aspects of Pärt's antiphons are minimalist? Refer to specific measures to illustrate your points.

21. What are the differences between modernism and *postmodernism*?

22. Compare how Schnittke, Corigliano, and Schickele (in both personas) approach using multiple styles. How do their approaches resemble or differ from Mozart's use of diverse styles (see NAWM 105 and chapter 22, question 25)? Or Ives's (see NAWM 148 and chapter 31, question 44)?

23. What is the difference between Romanticism and *neo-Romanticism*? In your opinion, how is Rochberg's act of composing in a style like that of Beethoven different from Beethoven's act of composing in a similar style? What meanings do you think are conveyed?

24. What is Del Tredici's attitude toward communication with the audience, as summarized in his statement on p. 962 of HWM? How does this contrast with Babbitt's point of view (see chapter 34, questions 34 and 45)?

Music to Study

NAWM 171: Sofia Gubaidulina, *Rejoice!* Sonata for Violin and Violoncello (1981), fifth movement, *Listen to the still small voice within*

⟨ CD 12|67 ⟩

25. In Gubaidulina's *Rejoice!*, measures 1–33 introduce a basic sequence of ideas, which is then varied and added to over the course of the movement. Chart the form of the violin part, using the following code, using the prime sign (') for variants, and introducing new letters as needed for new material. Start each repetition of the basic sequence on a new line.

Motive	A	B	C	B'	C'	B"	D	E
Measure	1	5	10	13	16	20	25	29

Motive	A
Measure	33

Motive	A
Measure	

Motive	A
Measure	

26. How does Gubaidulina use repetition, variation, and contrast in this movement? How is this like traditional eighteenth- and nineteenth-century procedures, and how is it different?

27. How does Gubaidulina convey the spiritual lesson of this movement (*Listen to the still small voice*)?

28. Compare the excerpts from Shostakovich's Symphony No. 5 (NAWM 154) with this movement from Gubaidulina's *Rejoice!* Sonata. What was each trying to achieve in these works? What musical procedures or traditions did each find useful in achieving these aims? As a composer under the Soviet Union, how was her political situation similar to and different from his, and how does that influence how you experience this work?

Interactions with Non-Western Musics (HWM 964–65, NAWM 172)

Music to Study

NAWM 172: Bright Sheng, *Seven Tunes Heard in China*   [CD 12|75] [CD 6|87]
(1995), solo cello suite, No. 1: Seasons

29. What characteristics from the Western classical tradition and from Chinese musical traditions did Sheng blend in *Seven Tunes Heard in China*, No. 1: Seasons (NAWM 172)?

30. How is Sheng's blending of traits like Bartók's synthesis of eastern and western European musical styles in *Music for Strings, Percussion and Celesta* (NAWM 147)? How is Sheng's approach different?

The New Millenium (HWM 965)

31. In your opinion, what musical developments of the late twentieth century will have the biggest impact on music of the future? Why do you think they are so significant?

TERMS TO KNOW

digital
sampling
mixed media
music videos

minimalism
postmodernism
polystylism
neo-Romanticism

NAMES TO KNOW

Laurie Anderson
Steve Reich
Philip Glass
John Adams
Ellen Taaffe Zwilich
Arvo Pärt
Alfred Schnittke
John Corigliano

Peter Schickele
David Del Tredici
Sofia Gubaidulina
John Tavener
R. Murray Schafer
Joan Tower
Bright Sheng

REVIEW QUESTIONS

1. Add the composers, performers, and major works discussed in this chapter to the twentieth-century timeline you made for chapter 30.
2. Of all the changes described in the first half of this chapter—globalization; classical repertoires in jazz, musicals, and popular music; digital technologies; mixed media; niche markets in popular music—which do you think will be the most important in the long run? Why? Which of them, if any, have common sources or causes, and how do they affect one another?
3. Trace the evolution of minimalism and styles influenced by minimalism. How does it compare to other trends, such as serialism or the avant-garde? What do you think the appeal of minimalism was and is, to composers and audiences? Why did it become so successful?
4. Why did composers in the last decades of the twentieth century seek to widen their music's appeal? What earlier twentieth-century trends were they responding to? What strategies did they use, and which strategies do you think were most successful? In your opinion, were these composers right to try to widen their appeal? Why or why not?
5. Add to your essay from Review Question 5 in chapter 33. Who are some of the most significant women composers in the later twentieth century? What roles do women play in musical culture in the later twentieth century? Do you think this is still an important essay to write, or do you think that the question of women in music is no longer an issue? Explain your answer.
6. Of all the pieces covered in chapters 34 and 35 (NAWM 159–172), which one or two do you like the best? Which one or two do you like the least? Write an essay in which you explain what is especially good about the piece(s) you like and what is unappealing about the piece(s) you like less, as if you were writing a review or trying to persuade a friend about which CD to purchase. Explain what it is you find most valuable in music and how your judgments are based on those values.

7. Compose a minimalist piece. Choose any instrumentation you wish. After you have finished your composition, write an essay about your experience. What did you find particular easy or difficult about writing a composition in this style?
8. Write an essay describing how and why the role of the composer changed from the eighteenth century to the twentieth century.